John Fulton Blair

The Apostolic Gospel

With a critical reconstruction of the text

John Fulton Blair

The Apostolic Gospel
With a critical reconstruction of the text

ISBN/EAN: 9783337280116

Printed in Europe, USA, Canada, Australia, Japan

Cover: Foto ©Thomas Meinert / pixelio.de

More available books at **www.hansebooks.com**

THE
APOSTOLIC GOSPEL

WITH

A CRITICAL RECONSTRUCTION OF THE TEXT

BY

J. FULTON BLAIR, B.D.

LONDON
SMITH, ELDER, & CO., 15 WATERLOO PLACE
1896

PREFACE

The subject of the present volume has gradually become prominent in recent years through the labour of New Testament critics. The Apostolic Gospel is a primitive document which now exists only as one among other elements contained in the four canonical gospels, and especially in the first and the third. Systematic attempts have been made to restore this document to its original form by the method of comparative criticism. My work differs in several respects from the attempts which have hitherto been made. It is more conservative, inasmuch as it preserves and admits into the text a number of narratives and sayings which have been rejected by critics even like Weiss and Wendt, who are not negative in their tendency. It is also a departure from current opinion, inasmuch as it involves a new estimate of the gospels and a new conception of Christ's teaching and ministry. My argument is based entirely on textual evidence. In accordance with such evidence I have rearranged the sayings which are scattered through the gospels or gathered together into secondary formations; and the result is a series of discourses, each of which is authenticated by a clear connection of thought and by adaptation to the historical situation. The memoir thus gained is chronological. It agrees in outline with the fourth gospel; it enables us to distinguish the constituents of the second; it reveals the origin of the first and third; and it takes its place as the oral tradition of the apostles, with perhaps a few accretions, but now for the first time restored to its earliest written form.

My work is divided into three parts : 1. The Introduction ; 2. The Text of the Apostolic Gospel ; and 3. A Critical Reconstruction of that Text.

In the Introduction my aim is to indicate the advance which has already been made, the method by which the problem may be solved, the data available for this purpose, and the relation of the investigation to the larger questions concerning the origin of the gospels. The historical books of the New Testament, as Dr. Westcott has repeatedly stated, are distinguished by one common characteristic from the histories of modern times. They were written, not merely to give information regarding the great events of the past, but also, and more particularly, to present this information in such a way as to serve a practical purpose. This must always be remembered. It accounts for the differences of arrangement and interpretation which surprise the modern reader of the gospels, and is sufficient in itself to justify the critical method. When a critic ventures to express the opinion that historical sequence has not been habitually preserved, or that certain texts have been recorded by the evangelists in a secondary form and connection, he is sometimes regarded with suspicion ; but a little consideration will show that the opinion in question is perfectly compatible with a high conception of the Christian testimony and with reverence for the Christian faith.

In the text of the Apostolic Gospel the Revised Version of 1881 has been printed. The letters which introduce the subsections refer the reader to corresponding subsections in the reconstruction of the text. The italics in the text represent departures from the reading which is indicated in the margin by the book, chapter, and verse. Thus the reading in Luke iii. 16 (p. 24) is ' whose shoes I am not worthy to unloose.' The word ' bear ' which is in italics in the text has been taken from Matthew iii. 11.

The freedom which I have exercised in the third division of the book requires no justification. I have written, not as an apologist, nor as an advocate of naturalism, but simply as a critic of the documents; and my one aim has been to follow without deviation the path defined by the evidence.

I venture in conclusion to express the hope that, although the reader may not be able to agree with me in my view of the origin of the gospels, and although he may reserve his judgment in relation to many details until the verification is complete, he will find in the criticism of the discourses a fresh and suggestive contribution to one of the most important of subjects. If this hope should be happily fulfilled the labour of many silent years will be abundantly rewarded.

J. F. B.

GLASGOW 1895.

CONTENTS

	PAGE
INTRODUCTION	
THE TEXT	23
A CRITICAL RECONSTRUCTION OF THE TEXT	81

THE SECTIONS

SECT.
1.—THE PREACHING OF JOHN THE BAPTIST	23, 81
2.—THE BAPTISM OF JESUS	24, 82
3.—THE TEMPTATION IN THE WILDERNESS	24, 83
4.—THE CALL OF THE FOUR DISCIPLES	25, 86
5.—THE SERMON ON THE MOUNT	25, 88
6.—THE HEALING OF THE CENTURION'S SON	27, 101
7.—THE RAISING OF THE WIDOW'S SON	28, 103
8.—JOHN SENDS MESSENGERS	28, 105
9.—THE SAMARITAN VILLAGE	30, 108
10.—THE HEALING OF THE LEPERS	30, 111
11.—THE REJECTION IN NAZARETH	30, 113
12.—THE HEALING OF THE PALSY	31, 114
13.—THE MISSION OF THE TWELVE	32, 116
14.—THE RETURN OF THE TWELVE	33, 121
15.—THE HALF-HEARTED DISCIPLES	34, 128
16.—THE PARABLE OF THE SOWER	35, 130
17.—PARABLES IN THE DESERT PLACE	35, 133
18.—THE MIRACLE OF THE LOAVES	37, 138
19.—THE STILLING OF THE STORM ON THE SEA	38, 140
20.—THE DUMB DEMONIAC	38, 142
21.—A WOMAN'S BLESSING	39, 149
22.—THE LEAVEN OF THE PHARISEES	40, 150
23.—THE HEALING OF A BLIND MAN	40, 153
24.—THE CALL OF A PUBLICAN	40, 156

SECT.	PAGE
25.—The Doctrine of Fasting	42, 162
26.—The Breaking of the Sabbath in the Cornfields	43, 165
27.—The Sabbath Question in a Synagogue	43, 167
28.—The Purging of the Temple	44, 170
29.—A Challenge of Christ's Authority	44, 173
30.—The Tradition of the Elders	45, 178
31.—The Righteousness of the Pharisees	46, 182
32.—A Series of Catch-Questions	49, 191
33.—The Son of David	51, 198
34.—The Widow's Mites	51, 199
35.—The Temple made without Hands	52, 200
36.—A Prediction of Judgment	52, 202
37.—The Narrow Gate	52, 208
38.—The Morrow of Messiah and Afterwards	53, 213
39.—The Temple Tax	54, 215
40.—Martha and Mary	54, 216
41.—The Entrance into Jerusalem	54, 216
42.—The Story of a Penitent Woman	56, 222
43.—The Doctrine of Riches	57, 226
44.—The Pharisees and Dives allied and condemned	60, 247
45.—The Doctrine of Marriage	61, 250
46.—The Kingdom and the Child	62, 267
47.—The Doctrine of Prayer	63, 272
48.—The Coming of the Kingdom	66, 288
49.—The Last Supper	70, 319
50.—A Discourse on the Road to the Garden	72, 345
51.—The Agony and the Arrest in the Garden	74, 353
52.—The Court of the High Priest	75, 356
53.—The Meeting of the Council	75, 358
54.—The Court of Pilate	76, 359
55.—Barabbas and Jesus	76, 360
56.—The Crucifixion	76, 362
57.—The Burial	78, 370
58.—The Empty Tomb	78, 372

THE
APOSTOLIC GOSPEL

INTRODUCTION

In his 'Introduction to the Literature of the Old Testament' Professor Driver incidentally deprecates the common report that critics are in a state of internecine conflict with one another. This, he says, is misleading language. He distinguishes two areas of investigation, one in which the data are clear and critics are agreed, and another in which the data are complicated or ambiguous, and in which 'it is not more than natural that independent judges should differ;' and the first of these areas is a large one, the second is a 'margin of uncertainty.'[1] He writes as a critic of the Old Testament, and his 'Introduction' affords abundant evidence, which the public is beginning to recognise, that, instead of being the art of disturbing faith, criticism is the making of knowledge. But the language which is deprecated by Professor Driver when applied to Old Testament studies, seems at first sight not far from the truth when transferred to the field of the New Testament. The divergence of modern opinion on the subject of the gospels is extremely bewildering to the student. The whole field seems devoted to conflict. Since the publication in 1835 of Vatke's history of the religion of the Old Testament, the work of Hebrew scholars has resulted in practical unanimity; but the movement which was represented in the same year by Strauss has not been similarly advanced. The uncertainty is still so general and the prospect of a settlement so remote that speculative and dogmatic theologians, impatient for immediate results, have

[1] *Introduction*, p. xii.

invaded and claimed the debatable ground, some insisting that the problem of the documents is insoluble, and others, in the name of the churches, unfurling the banner of tradition. It is not surprising that the forces of philosophy and ecclesiasticism should thus take possession of the wavering field; for they have never been neutral, and the failure of the critics may not unreasonably be urged as a plea for such intervention. But the critics are after all not quite prepared to confess that they have utterly failed; they do not welcome the invaders; they have still some faith in their own method. Professor Huxley may not be an authority on the subject of the gospels, but at least he is interested in the subject, and knows what constitutes a problem. And he does not call to mind any problem of natural science, which has come under his notice, 'more difficult, or more curiously interesting, as a mere problem, than that of the origin of the synoptic gospels, and that of the historical value of the narratives which they contain.'[1] The students of a subject so complicated may surely be excused for trying the patience of the theologians. The longest way round is sometimes, as the proverb says, the shortest way home. Poverty of result is not necessarily a proof of final failure; and in any case the critics cannot accept a theory, either from philosophy or from the churches, if it is not verified by the facts with which they are concerned, without renouncing their science and resigning their function.

When compared with the admirable results which have been gained by Old Testament scholars, the critics of the gospels unquestionably present a poor record. Their achievement has hitherto been chiefly negative, in relation not merely to traditional opinions, but also to one another; and the common report which is deprecated by Dr. Driver has so far some semblance of truth. But, on the other hand, just as in the case of the Old Testament, two areas of investigation can be distinguished—one in which the data are clear and critics are agreed, and another in which the data are complicated or ambiguous, and in which 'it is not more than natural that independent judges should differ.' The second of these areas is a large one, and the first is comparatively

[1] *Essays on Controversial Questions*, p. 413.

small; but still the distinction can be made. Two well-attested conclusions represent and define the area of certainty. The first of these is the conclusion, recognised by the following critics, Wilke, Weisse, Ritschl, Holtzmann, Weizsäcker, Weiss, Volkmar, Wendt, that the second gospel, substantially as we have it at present, was in existence before the first and the third, and was used as a source of information by the later synoptic evangelists. The second is that in the gospels according to Matthew and Luke another source can be detected, which, whether oral or written, was esteemed as highly authoritative, and was combined with our second gospel and a few independent traditions to constitute the first and the third. These are well-established results. They form a nucleus for further investigation; and indicating as they do the lines on which criticism must proceed, they cannot be regarded as insignificant.

It will, of course, be impossible in an introductory chapter such as this to discuss the great subject of the gospels with the attention to details which it demands. The writer has a new solution of the problem which he wishes to indicate briefly. He does not profess to have reached finality, even in his own assurance; but having gone through all the ground, impelled by the single aim of reducing, by legitimate means, the large area of uncertainty which baffles the student and disturbs the religious world, he now submits the outline of an argument which will afterwards be more adequately discussed.

The source which, in combination with Mark, has been largely used by the first and third evangelists, is recognised by all the critics to be one of first-rate importance. For the sake of convenience, and without intending at present to suggest any theory of its origin, we may call it, after the example of Weiss, the apostolic source. The existence of this source, as an oral tradition or as a written gospel, in the days of Matthew and Luke, is established by the fact that the two later gospels contain parallel incidents and logia which have not been borrowed from Mark. In the disposition of this material, as well as in phraseology, they differ from one another, and each contains material peculiar to itself. These are facts which require to be explained; but if, as is now believed, Mark is a constituent of Matthew and Luke, the conclusion is equally certain that the additional incidents and logia, which are common to the later evangelists, represent a second source of information, on determining the nature and contents of which the progress of criticism will depend. The reconstruction of the apostolic source is indeed at the present day the first problem of gospel criticism. It is a problem which demands so much delicate perception, and the data are so exceedingly complicated, that theologians assume inevitable failure; and even the most undaunted critic, who believes in his method, and is predisposed to anticipate success, may well hesitate to venture for the prize. Attempts, however, have been made, and preliminary work has been done. Weiss, e.g., illustrious for keen analysis and also for lame conclusions, has classified the contents of the source, acknowledging that much of the classification can only be conjectural. With similar caution, but making a surer advance, Wendt has discussed the subject. These critics are fairly representative, and they agree in at least two results. In the first place, the source, as reconstructed by them, contains incidents and logia without chronological arrangement and without clear sequence of thought; and, secondly, it is not a full account of the ministry, but is simply a fragment of reminiscences, beginning at the preaching of the Baptist and ending before the Passion.

Now, obviously, whatever may be the value of a reconstruction which exhibits such features as these, it does not enable us, by unlocking the gospels, to find out the secret of their origin. Nothing can be done with such a source alone. It may or may not be one of the constituents of Mark; but this at least is evident, that it cannot be a key to the origin of Mark, and still less to the origin of the fourth gospel. Wendt argues, like Holtzmann, for the original independence of Mark. He believes that Mark is a composite gospel; but, among the elements of which it is composed, he does not include the apostolic source. Weiss, on the other hand, as strongly maintains that the apostolic source, combined with a recollection of the preaching of Peter, constitutes our second gospel. These opinions are, no doubt, widely divergent, but they meet in one general result; for Weiss reaches, like Wendt, as the ultimate of critical analysis, two main synoptic sources which are independent in relation to one another, and cannot be traced to a common original, and with these he accounts for the origin of Mark and the later synoptic gospels. The critics are here practically unanimous. They do not believe that the apostolic source, restored by comparative criticism, is the only fountain of history from which the gospels have proceeded. In Mark they find another source from which traditions flowed to form confluent streams. The hypothesis of a primitive gospel is therefore scarcely entertained unless by versatile journalists. To solve the synoptic problem the critics require rather two primitive gospels; and the Papias tradition, according to which the memoirs of Peter were written by Mark, and the logia in Hebrew by Matthew, seems to them to confirm the data at which they have arrived by analysis. Unfortunately, however, they are still 'at internecine conflict with one another' on the subject of the contents of the sources; and, without insisting too much on the *a priori* objection that the existence of two sources with contents so fixed, and yet so different, and in each case of so fragmentary a nature, is itself an improbability, the inference is reasonable, and indeed is almost inevitable, that the analysis which exhibits such divergent results is somehow seriously defective. Let us put the matter to the test.

The third gospel is acknowledged to be for the most part a combination of two sources. One of these is our gospel according to Mark, and the other is the unknown quantity which is designated apostolic. Our Mark is Luke's chief authority. He accepts Mark's order of events, and inserts his additional material in the framework provided by the earlier evangelist. Two digressions are clearly distinguishable—the first from ch. vi. 12 to ch. viii. 3; and the second, which is described by Dr. Westcott as 'the great episode,' from ch. ix. 51 to ch. xviii. 14. These digressions represent the apostolic source; and the question is, Are we able to reconstruct the original by distinguishing what is primary from what is either editorial or otherwise secondary in arrangement and expression and substance? With the gospel according to Luke alone, the undertaking would certainly be hopeless, for the ingenuity of the critic would be constantly baffled by the impossibility of verifying his results; but we possess other data for comparison—the parallel incidents and logia in Matthew, and the gospels according to Mark and John. Let me now ask the reader to exercise for a moment that gift of imagination which is so necessary for the scientific investigator and so helpful to the interested student. If Luke had in his hands, besides Mark, a gospel of high authority which he wished to combine with Mark; if this gospel consisted not merely of logia with a few selected events, but of all the facts which were known to the writer from the beginning of the ministry to the cross; if these facts were narrated in chronological order, and in many cases were parallel to Mark's facts; and finally, if, for reasons which are capable of definition, this gospel had been largely superseded by Mark, which was richer in incidents but contained much less of the teaching, so that Mark had become the standard of history before the third gospel was written, what would be the probable characteristics of the combination thus proposed and effected? It is conceivable, on the one hand, that the editor, with such documents before him, would supplement Mark's narratives seriatim by material derived from the other authority, and would gather into longer discourses the teaching which permitted such treatment. Or, on the other hand, he might, while not altogether neglecting this method, insert in Mark's framework, at appropriate places, accumulations of loose materal derived from the other source; and in such a case the following phenomena might be confidently predicted. First, the incidents taken from Mark, and already recorded in the history, would not be repeated by the editor, although contained in the other source, if such incidents were recognised as identical. Secondly, a few incidents in their different versions would not be recognised as clearly identical, and therefore duplication would arise. Thirdly, Mark being accepted and followed as the standard, the original arrangement of the other source would be entirely upset by combination; the bones would be removed from the body, and thus a new editorial arrangement, especially of the teaching, would be permitted, and indeed would be inevitable. So far scientific imagination. What now are the facts with which we have to deal in considering the problem before us? The first gospel, like the third, is admitted to be for the most part a combination of the apostolic source with Mark. And obviously the characteristics of the combination, in the case of the first gospel, agree precisely with the first of the imagined alternatives; for Matthew, as a fact, does extend Mark's discourses by logia drawn from his other authority, and instead of inserting the material, which could not be thus utilised, in the form of a loose digression, he adapts it seriatim to the narratives of Mark, preserving as far as possible the original historical situation. Luke's method, on the other hand, whatever the apostolic source may have been in outline and contents, whether fragmentary or complete, chronological or without articulation, is obviously in agreement with the second alternative; and not only so, but the agreement extends to the predicted phenomena which would be exhibited in the case supposed. The critics have failed to perceive this fact, but nevertheless it is a fact, and one of supreme importance. The arrangement in Luke's two digressions is, to a large extent, palpably artificial. No critic contends that the sequence is strictly historical. The story of the penitent woman e.g. (Luke vii. 36-50) is an unmistakable illustration of the statement that the Son of Man came eating and drinking, and was the Friend of sinners. The lawyer who asked a catch-question is introduced as one of the wise and understanding, from whom the truth of the kingdom had been hidden (Luke x. 25-37). Mary is one of the babes to whom the Father reveals Himself (Luke x. 38-42); and the teaching on the subject of prayer represents a characteristic of the childlike spirit (Luke xi. 1-13). The sequence in these cases is admirably adapted for the edification of the Christian community, but just for that reason it is not likely to be historical. Historical events do not as a rule follow one another with the aptness of illustrations in a popular sermon. Allowance must no doubt be made for exceptions; but the possibility that these cases are exceptional, if not excluded by the narratives themselves, is certainly not encouraged. The penitent was a woman 'in the city' (Luke vii. 37), but the city was not Nain: it was much more probably Jerusalem (Mark xiv. 3). The lawyer asked his question in Jerusalem (Mark xii. 28), and Bethany was the village of Martha and Mary; but according to the sequel in Luke, if after the return of the seventy Jesus paid a visit to Jerusalem, He returned immediately to Galilee (Luke xi. 14–26, cf. Matt. xii. 22–37; Mark iii. 22–30), and that is distinctly improbable. The greater probability unquestionably is that the narratives thus introduced by the evangelist belonged originally to a later period, and were set free to be taken from that period of the source by the rearrangement involved in combining it with Mark. Details need not be multiplied. The evidence is of two kinds. There are clear indications like those above mentioned of design on the part of the editor; and there are also cases of what may be called helpless articulation, that is, of a sequence which is neither historical nor useful for edification, but is rather purely verbal, and can only be satisfactorily explained by the desire of the editor to utilise the most of his material (Luke xii. 3, 58). Wendt makes the remark that the nature of the source seems to have been such as to permit unintentional dislocations, when its contents were reproduced from memory.[1] As far as the dislocations are concerned, he alludes to an obvious fact, which is admitted by the critics; but the evidence tends rather to the conclusion that the dislocations were distinctly intentional—that the editor had an aim, in accomplishing which he necessarily detached a large portion of his material from its context in the source, and that, with a view to edification, he rearranged this material according to the opportunities presented. In such a case the theory of recollection is insecure; the use of a document is more probable.

The question, however, remains, How is the source to be restored? If, in Luke's digressions, it is represented by loose material to some extent artificially arranged, and if in the first gospel its contents are dispersed, how are we to discover the original arrangement, and how are the whole contents to be

[1] *Die Lehre Jesu*, Erster Theil, S. 189.

INTRODUCTION 9

defined? Must not our method be purely conjectural? The difficulty of the undertaking must of course be acknowledged; but the author of this volume maintains that the problem is not insoluble. He believes in the sufficiency of the data and of the critical method; and he ventures to affirm that the critics have somehow here again overlooked a few facts of fundamental importance. First, there are many narratives, in Luke's digressions, which do not owe their position to the editorial motive of edifying the readers. They do not illustrate a statement or a theme introduced immediately before. They are rather themselves new starting points, which suggest new illustrations, and determine the rearrangement; and there is nothing to forbid the conjecture that they represent the original sequence. The following are the narratives in question: The Sermon on the Mount with its sequel as far as the discourse suggested by the messengers of John (Luke vi. 12-vii. 35), the mission and return of the seventy (Luke ix. 51-x. 24), the cure of the dumb demoniac with its sequel, the demand for a sign (Luke xi. 14-32), the warning against the leaven of the Pharisees (Luke xii. 1), the report concerning the Galileans whose blood Pilate mingled with their sacrifices (Luke xiii. 1-5), the discourse on the door and the warning against Herod the fox (Luke xiii. 22-33), the announcement of the duty of disciples (Luke xiv. 25-35), the doctrine of riches (Luke xvi. 1-15), the law of Moses and the doctrine of marriage (Luke xvi. 16-18), the kingdom in relation to the children (Luke xvii. 1, 2), the doctrine of forgiveness and service (Luke xvii. 3-10), the discourse on the coming of the kingdom (Luke xvii. 20-xviii. 8). In the meantime this list is provisional. The position of a few of the passages cited may be due to editorial motive, and other passages representing the original sequence may not be mentioned here. We cannot at present discuss details; but the list is approximately correct. We have gained, therefore, a fact and a conjecture.

Secondly, the belief is generally maintained by the critics that Luke has omitted some material which he found in the source; but the data which enable us to detect these omissions have not been fully perceived. Wendt, e.g., in his admirable study of the subject, distinguishes three groups of material. By comparative criticism of Matthew and Luke he reaches a series of incidents and logia which the source, as he argues, contained; but when he completes his analysis he has still a number of discourses and sayings, which remain unattached, in his hands, and with these he forms two smaller groups, consisting respectively of stray logia peculiar to Matthew and stray logia peculiar to Luke. It is obvious that a classification like Wendt's is virtually a confession of failure. He begins by acknowledging that the contents of the source can be restored. His aim is to attain this end; but at last he is reduced to the feeble expedient of forming two appendices. He lays a foundation, but he does not complete his work; and the consequence is that theologians behold, and begin to mock him, saying, This man began to build and was not able to finish. One fact has been fully recognised by Wendt, and indeed by all the critics. They perceive that the logia in Matthew enable us to detect a number of omissions in Luke. The mere fact that the first gospel contains fragments which are absent from the third is not, of course, a proof that their absence is due to intentional omission, for the sources might conceivably be different; but the evidence becomes quite convincing when the fragments in question complete the thought which is common to the context of the gospels, and when by a study of the variations we can give a reason for the omissions. Here, then, is a means of reconstruction which is successfully employed by the critics. They enlarge the contents of Luke's digressions by a comparative study of Matthew. But, although the fact has been somehow overlooked, we certainly possess additional data, which enable us to advance to much larger results; for by careful study of the variations, by textual evidence which he who runs may read, and by comparing the digressions with Mark, the omissions can be shown to be much more numerous than the critics are disposed to believe. The two later evangelists in following Mark differ sometimes both from Mark and from one another in language and details. These differences, as a rule, can be explained by the purpose, mode of thinking, and style peculiar to each evangelist. When a variation is not exceptional, but rather one of a class, editorial activity may be safely inferred, and in some cases without any need of assuming an external authority. There are differences, however, which cannot thus be reduced to rule as purely personal phenomena. They suggest the hypothesis of a second source, which contained the narratives in question, and which, whether oral or written, was collated with Mark by each of the later evangelists. Since a second source is admitted by all, the hypothesis simply is that the evangelists borrowed details from this source, by memory or otherwise, when reproducing Mark's narratives. In some cases this is a necessary hypothesis, and in others antecedently probable. We may therefore reasonably argue that the additional details, not taken from Mark, if they cannot be satisfactorily explained as purely editorial, and if no reason can be adduced in any particular case sufficient to forbid the inference drawn, authenticate the narratives containing such details as constituents of the apostolic source. Two classes of omissions may be thus recognised. The stray logia gathered together by Wendt and put into two appendices may be placed in their original context; and the following narratives, which are found in Mark, may be claimed as apostolic: The complaint on the subject of fasting (Mark ii. 18–22; Luke v. 33–39; Matt. ix. 14–17), the plucking of corn on the Sabbath (Mark ii. 23–28; Luke vi. 1–5; Matt. xii. 1–8), and the complaint about washing of hands (Mark vii. 1–23; Luke xi. 37–41; Matt. xv. 1–20). This list is not exhaustive; it is merely intended to illustrate a line of argument. Again, by textual evidence and comparison of the digressions with Mark, the number of omissions may be still further enlarged. After the woes pronounced against the Pharisees, the statement is made by Luke that 'when Jesus was come out from thence, the Scribes and the Pharisees began to press upon him vehemently, and to provoke him to speak of many things; laying wait for him, to catch something out of his mouth' (Luke xi. 53, 54), and this statement is not intelligible unless on the supposition that the provocation was exemplified in the source. The reader expects to find in the sequel a number of artful catch-questions, but the sequel in Luke is of quite a different nature; and the probability is that we have here editorial arrangement. What, then, are we bound to infer? That Luke has abbreviated an original, which is now for ever hopelessly lost? By no means; for Mark has preserved a series of catch-questions which admirably suit the occasion (Mark xii. 13-34), and one of these has already been put by Luke into an earlier context, thus breaking the original sequence (Luke x. 25-37, cf. Mark xii. 28-34). Moreover, a statement, which is similar to the one just quoted from Luke, is made in the fourth gospel immediately after the narrative of the purging of the Temple (John ii. 23-25), and Nicodemus resembles in some respects the lawyer who was one of Christ's questioners. If the evidence is not absolutely convincing, it must certainly be sufficiently conclusive to every critic accustomed to deal with probabilities and acquainted with the phenomena of the gospels; and the conclusion, as a clear probability, is that the catch-questions recorded by Mark were contained in the apostolic source, and were omitted by Luke, partly because one of them had been recorded already, partly because in his digression he did not wish to extend the subject, and partly because his purpose was to return to his standard, Mark, when the questions might be fully reproduced (Luke xx. 19-40).

Now, if the reader of this paper will review the argument, he will not fail to perceive that another fact of the utmost importance for defining the contents of the apostolic source is involved in those above mentioned. For, thirdly, the sequence distinguished as probably original, when considered along with the omissions, affords presumptive evidence that the source was chronological. The history proceeds from Galilee to Jerusalem, and again from Jerusalem to Galilee. The mountain discourse was delivered in Galilee; its sequel is also Galilean. The discourse addressed to the messengers of John, and afterwards to the assembled people, suggests a visit to Jerusalem, but this was again followed by a return to Galilee, for the cure of the dumb demoniac, the demand for a sign, and the warning against the leaven of the Pharisees are undoubtedly Galilean narratives. The report concerning the people whose blood Pilate mingled with their sacrifices presupposes a visit to Jerusalem. The warning

against Herod the fox demands a locality which was either
Peræa or Galilee, and thus suggests a return from Jerusalem
to the north. The announcement of the duty of disciples
follows in the fourth gospel the last entrance into Jerusalem
(John xii. 23-32); and, finally, the discourse on the coming of
the kingdom was delivered before the Last Supper (Mark xiii.
1-37; Matt. xxiv. 1-xxv. 46; Luke xxi. 5-36).

As an outline sketch of the ministry, the above certainly
possesses a great degree of probability; for, according to the
fourth gospel, the incidents and logia were gathered round the
feasts, and that is what one would expect. The omissions,
moreover, when placed in their original context—an achievement which is not insuperably difficult, if the data are taken
into account—fill up the slender outline, and the result which
is ultimately gained is a chronological gospel, the contents of
which are incidents and logia appropriate to the historical
situation. Nor is that all; our survey has not been completed.
The hypothesis of a primitive gospel, extending from the
Sermon on the Mount to the discourse on the coming of the
kingdom, is one which, if verified, would be a notable gain.
But the question might still be asked, Is such a gospel conceivable? Would an early evangelist, acquainted with the
facts by tradition or personal knowledge, be likely to compose
such a gospel, without an historical beginning and end? The
supposition is scarcely probable; but among the data to be
considered there is still another fact which delivers us from
the awkward conclusion. For, fourthly, we can argue both
backwards and forwards from the source as reconstructed.
In the introduction to the Sermon on the Mount the statement
is made that Jesus called His disciples, and chose from them
twelve to be prepared for a special mission (Luke vi. 13, cf.
Matt. v. 1), and an earlier period of the ministry is clearly
required to account for this band of disciples. In the narrative, again, concerning the messengers sent by John the
following facts are involved: that John had baptised in the
wilderness (Luke vii. 29), that he came eating no bread nor
drinking wine (ver. 33), that like a true prophet he was neither
a reed nor a courtier (vv. 24-28), that the Pharisees and the
lawyers rejected his message, while people of the disreputable

classes believed and were baptised (vv. 29, 30), that he had been cast into prison (Matt. xi. 2), and that, although he had made the acquaintance of Jesus, he had not recognised Him as Messiah (Luke vii. 19). If the source which contained these details, instead of being a fragment of reminiscences, was a chronological gospel, comprising such incidents and logia as the preceding argument has defined, an earlier account of the Baptist may be confidently inferred; for the details in question are incidental, and the readers are supposed to be already familiar with the historical facts. We are therefore warranted in concluding that the source did not begin at the Sermon on the Mount, but contained a preliminary narrative in which John was introduced as the forerunner of Jesus, and sufficient time was allowed for the formation of a band of disciples. Now, before the Sermon on the Mount in the gospel according to Matthew a short series of narratives is to be found of precisely the kind demanded (Matt. iii. 1-iv. 22); and as these contain details which have not been borrowed from Mark, and cannot be explained as purely editorial, they probably formed part of the apostolic source. It is not maintained that throughout this section Matthew has preserved, without loss or addition, the original form and substance; that is a matter to be determined by comparative criticism. But the narratives themselves, whatever the original in each case was, may be claimed as apostolic; and thus we can argue backwards from the Sermon on the Mount in Luke's digression to the preaching of John, the baptism of Jesus, the temptation in the wilderness, and the call of the four disciples.

The next question is, Are we able to argue forwards from the discourse on the coming of the kingdom to the Supper and the events of the Passion? The attention of the reader is invited to the following facts. First, in returning to Mark at the end of his long digression (Luke xviii. 14), the third evangelist continues as before to supplement Mark's narratives by material derived from another source. We cannot account otherwise for the story of Zacchæus (Luke xix. 1-10), the parable of the Pounds (xix. 11-27), the tears shed over Jerusalem (xix. 41-44), the discourse delivered at the Supper (xxii. 14-38), the details of the agony and arrest in the garden (xxii. 39-53), and the incident of the weeping women (xxiii. 27-31). These narratives were certainly not invented by Luke. They represent a source, and, unless good reason can be shown to the contrary, the probability is that the apostolic source already combined with Mark is the one which is here still followed. Secondly, when the digressions are carefully analysed and the original arrangement is restored, a few passages remain as loose material without an historical context, unless such a context can be found for them in the later period of the history. The following may be cited as examples: Luke xii. 49, 50, 2-9, 51-53, 11, 12. Thirdly, according to the testimony of the fourth gospel, a few sayings which agree almost verbally with these were addressed to the disciples after the Supper (John xv. 18-21; xvi. 2, 3, cf. Luke xii. 11, 51-53; John xiv. 15-17, 25, 26; xvi. 7-15, cf. Luke xii. 12; John xiv. 26; xvi. 13, cf. Luke xii. 2; John xvi. 33, cf. Luke xii. 4, 5). Fourthly, the discourse which, according to Luke, was addressed to the disciples at the Supper, while indisputably authentic, is obviously also incomplete (Luke xxii. 14-38). It lacks articulation and sequence of thought. It may no doubt be explained as a fragment of recollection, but the disciple who remembered so much of what happened on this memorable occasion would not be likely to forget details which would make the history more intelligible. We are rather forced to the conclusion that the evangelist, in combining his two sources, has already put into his long digression material taken from the history of the Supper, and that now, in following the order of Mark, he combines with Mark's brief narrative the apostolic material which remains to be utilised. The writer does not maintain that this argument is complete. He is not attempting at present to reconstruct the source. He is simply mentioning the data which have hitherto been overlooked by the critics; and the facts to which he invites attention are sufficient, if not to prove, at least to suggest the probability, that the apostolic source contained an account of the Passion. He will even go farther, and affirm, in accordance with the results of his own investigation, that the critic who proceeds to the work of reconstruction, and is faithful to the data observed, will be led from one narrative to another, by the evidence of the variations and the necessity of the history, until the Passion at last is complete, and he stands beside the empty tomb with a clear conception of the ministry, a new comprehension of the teaching, and a finer appreciation of that great Personality which has gained the homage of men.

A brief statement remains to be made regarding the general significance of the reconstruction suggested. Let us suppose that the data are sufficient, and that the source which was used by Matthew and Luke can really be restored with approximate completeness by a careful study of the gospels. How does this affect the large problem? Can the area of uncertainty be further reduced? Or, with doubtful gains of ingenuity, do we simply return to the starting point, and accept with docility the conclusion of the critics, that the first three evangelists derived the most of their material from two earlier sources, which are independent in relation to one another, and also in relation to the fourth gospel, and cannot be reduced to a common original? A discussion of the question is impossible within the limits of this paper, but the reader who has followed the argument has at least a right to expect from the author a plain statement of the results to which in investigating the subject he has himself been led. He does not believe that the two sources are really independent. On the contrary, he is prepared to prove—by arguing, of course, from probabilities—that the second gospel is a primitive harmony, and not a recollection of the preaching of Peter. He believes that the apostolic source, which existed at first as an oral tradition, was committed to writing, at different places by different men, to meet the requirements of the Christian society, and that Mark is a combination of the versions. He is also prepared to prove that the fourth gospel is a primitive commentary, or, in other words, an elaborated version of the apostolic source, with the incidents adapted to the evangelist's purpose, and the logia partly reproduced and partly displaced by reflections which the original suggested. He does not accept the common assumption that the synoptic problem is altogether distinct from the Johannine. He maintains that the two coalesce, and that in solving the one the critic will solve also the other. He believes, in short, that the four gospels are simultaneous equations, that the unknown quantity is the apostolic source, and that the value of x can be discovered.

In relation to the statement just made, two kindred subjects demand a few words. The question may be asked, What becomes of the miracles when the documents are subjected to the severely critical analysis which has been indicated above ? The apostolic source, the earliest which criticism can discover, contained beyond question narratives involving miracle. These cannot be eliminated by comparative criticism; reduced in number they still remain, and no exercise of ingenuity can get rid of them. But if, as the present writer maintains, the apostolic source existed at first as an oral tradition, and was committed to writing at different places by different men, the hypothesis that the miracles were oral accretions is certainly not excluded. An upholder of the mythical theory may fairly enough argue that legendary narratives might find their way into the tradition before it was committed to writing; and the critic whose one aim is historical truth within the limits of his province must frankly admit that the mythical theory is made competent by evidence derived from the gospels. For, in the first place, our gospels contain duplicate miracles which can be identified by analysis. And, secondly, in the apostolic source, as reconstructed by criticism, there is no indication that Jesus was conscious of possessing miraculous power; on the contrary, His sayings unequivocally rebuke the demand made by the Jews for signs, and His teaching on the subject of the heavenly kingdom involves a view of the future which is scarcely compatible with the supposition that the miracles in our gospels are historical. And, thirdly, the follower of Strauss may contend, with some degree of probability, that the miracles of healing, which constitute, with perhaps only two exceptions, the traditions in question, were suggested by the logia of the source; for Jesus and His disciples were undoubtedly accustomed to practise the healing art, restoring demoniacs, and anointing the sick with oil (Mark vi. 13), and among the logia of the source there are two remarkable passages which together might influence Christian belief, and determine both the number of the miracles and even their constituent details. When John sent messengers from his prison to verify the report that Messiah had come, Jesus quoted in reply an ancient prophecy which announced that in the days of the restoration the eyes of the blind would be opened, the ears of the deaf would be unstopped, the lame man would leap as an hart, the tongue of the dumb would sing, and the poor would have good tidings preached to them (Luke vii. 18-23; Matt. xi. 2-6); and again, in the synagogue of Nazareth, after quoting a similar prophecy, He directly applied it to Himself (Luke iv. 16-30). That Jesus did not find in these prophecies a recital of the miracles which, according to our gospels, He wrought, but rather, as originally intended, an announcement in figurative language of the blessings involved in the kingdom of God, is proved in each case by the sequel; for the occasion of stumbling to which He referred in addressing the messengers of John was just the absence of miracles (Luke vii. 23), and the people of Nazareth, who expected a literal fulfilment, rejected His message because they did not witness even a work of healing (Luke iv. 23). They had heard a report of certain cures which had been accomplished at Capernaum, but these were not necessarily miracles. We do not know anything about them. This, however, we know—and the fact is well worthy of notice—that the miracles which cannot be eliminated by purely comparative criticism represent just such traditions as might be suggested by the logia—the healing of the blind, deaf, lame, and dumb, the deliverance of the captives and the bruised, and mercy shown to those who were not of the Prophet's own country (Luke iv. 25-27). If, again, as we have reason to believe, the apostolic source contained no account of the manifestations after the resurrection from the dead, the reader, like the critic, must frankly admit the competence of the mythical theory.

The second subject to be considered is the relation of our argument to the ecclesiastical traditions preserved on the origin of the gospels. The weightiest of these is undoubtedly the one quoted by Eusebius, and traced back to Papias, who lived in the first half of the second century. This tradition has generally been regarded as a satisfactory refutation of the hypothesis of a primitive gospel, for according to Papias there were two early sources. Matthew wrote the logia in Hebrew, and each one interpreted them as he was able. And 'Mark, having become the interpreter of Peter, wrote down accurately all his reminiscences, without, however, recording in order what was either said or done by Christ. For neither did he hear the Lord nor did he follow Him, but afterwards attended Peter, who adapted his instructions to the needs of his hearers, but had no design of giving a connected account of the Lord's oracles.' Now certainly the tradition in question is not to be lightly set aside in favour of internal evidence; for, whatever the historical truth may be, Papias was acquainted with two sources, and he represents the belief of the Christian society in the midst of which he lived, or at least the belief of an earlier witness who is described as John the elder. He may have been to some extent mistaken, but no one can reasonably doubt that facts underlie his opinion. The Papias tradition may be analysed into three constituents. First, the earliest source was 'The Logia,' supposed to have been written in Hebrew by Matthew. That this source was the earliest is not indeed distinctly stated ; but since the second source mentioned by Papias was believed to be unchronological, the first was probably the standard of judgment. Secondly, there were different interpretations of the logia, made by each as he was able. Thirdly, Papias was acquainted with a later source, which did not preserve the logia sequence. He describes it as unchronological, and believes that its author was Mark. The relation of these statements to the opinions expressed in the foregoing pages must be perfectly evident to the reader. Instead of refuting, they confirm the hypothesis of a primitive gospel. For the apostolic source, as far as we know, may be the document described as 'The Logia ;' and the different interpretations to which Papias alludes, although this is not essential to our argument, may be the versions which were written independently. And, finally, the description of the source compiled by Mark agrees perfectly with our second gospel, which is not, however, as Papias believed, a recollection of the preaching of Peter, but simply a combination of the versions which interpreted the primitive gospel.

THE APOSTOLIC GOSPEL

§ 1.—*The Preaching of John the Baptist*

Mk. i. 1   **a.**¹—The beginning of the gospel of Jesus Christ. Even
2   as it is written in Isaiah the prophet, The voice of one crying
3   in the wilderness, Make ye ready the way of the Lord, make
his paths straight.
4   **b.**—John came, who baptised in the wilderness and preached
6   the baptism of repentance unto remission of sins. And he
was clothed with camel's hair, and had a leathern girdle about
5   his loins and did eat locusts and wild honey. And there went
out unto him all the country of Judæa and all they of Jeru-
Matt. iii. 7   salem. And he preached, saying, Ye offspring of vipers, who
8   warned you to flee from the wrath to come? Bring forth
9   therefore fruit worthy of repentance; and think not to say
within yourselves, We have Abraham to our father; for I say
unto you, that God is able of these stones to raise up children
10   unto Abraham. And even now is the axe laid unto the root
of the trees: every tree therefore that bringeth not forth good
fruit is hewn down, and cast into the fire.
Lu. iii. 10   **c.**—And the multitudes asked him, saying, What then must
11   we do? And he answered and said unto them, He that hath
two coats, let him impart to him that hath none; and he that
12   hath food, let him do likewise. And there came also publicans
to be baptised, and they said unto him, Master, what must
13   we do? And he said unto them, Extort no more than that
14   which is appointed you. And soldiers also asked him, saying,
And we, what must we do? And he said unto them, Do
violence to no man, neither exact anything wrongfully; and
be content with your wages.
15   **d.**—And as the people were in expectation, and all men
reasoned in their hearts concerning John, whether haply he
16   were the Christ, John answered, saying unto them all, I indeed

¹ The letters which introduce the subdivisions are intended for reference to the discussion of the text (see p. 81).

baptise you with water, but there cometh he that is mightier than I, whose shoes I am not worthy *to bear*; he shall baptise
17 you with the Holy Spirit and with fire; whose fan is in his hand, throughly to cleanse his threshing floor, and to gather the wheat into his garner; but the chaff he will burn up with unquenchable fire.

§ 2.—*The Baptism of Jesus*

Mk. i. 9   And it came to pass in those days that Jesus came from Nazareth of Galilee and was baptised of John in the Jordan.
10 And straightway coming up out of the water, he saw the heavens rent asunder and the Spirit as a dove descending
11 upon him; and a voice came out of the heavens, Thou art my beloved Son, in thee I am well pleased.

§ 3.—*The Temptation in the Wilderness*

12   a.—And straightway the Spirit driveth him forth into the
13 wilderness, and he was in the wilderness forty days, tempted of Satan, *and he did eat nothing in those days.*
Matt. iv. 3   b.—And the tempter came and said unto him, If thou art the Son of God, command *this stone* that it become bread.
4 But he answered and said, It is written, Man shall not live by bread alone.
5   c.—Then the devil taketh him into *Jerusalem*, and he set
6 him upon the pinnacle of the temple, and saith unto him, If thou art the Son of God, cast thyself down; for it is written, He shall give his angels charge concerning thee; and on their hands they shall bear thee up, lest haply thou
7 dash thy foot against a stone. Jesus said unto him, Again it is written, Thou shalt not tempt the Lord thy God.
8   d.—Again, the devil taketh him unto an exceeding high mountain, and sheweth him all the kingdoms of the world
9 and the glory of them. And he said unto him, All these things will I give thee, if thou wilt fall down and worship
10 me. Then saith Jesus unto him, Get thee hence, Satan: for it is written, Thou shalt worship the Lord thy God, and him
11 only shalt thou serve. Then the devil leaveth him, and behold, angels came and ministered unto him.

e.—Now when he heard that John was delivered up, he ¹³withdrew into Galilee, and leaving Nazareth he came and dwelt in Capernaum, which is by the sea, in the borders of ¹⁷Zebulun and Naphtali. From that time began Jesus to preach and to say, Repent ye; for *the kingdom of God* is at hand.

§ 4.—*The Call of the Four Disciples*

Mk. i. 16 And passing along by the sea of Galilee, he saw Simon and Andrew the brother of Simon casting a net in the sea: ¹⁷for they were fishers. And Jesus said unto them, Come ye after me, and I will make you to become fishers of men. ¹⁸And straightway they left the nets, and followed him. And ¹⁹going on a little further, he saw James the son of Zebedee, and John his brother, who also were in the boat mending the ²⁰nets. And straightway he called them; and they left their father Zebedee in the boat with the hired servants, and went after him.

§ 5.—*The Sermon on the Mount*

Lu. vi. 12 **a.**—And it came to pass in these days, that he went out into the mountain to pray; and he continued all night in ¹³prayer to God. And when it was day, he called his disciples; and he chose from them twelve (whom also he named ¹⁴apostles): Simon (whom he also named Peter), and Andrew his brother, and James and John (*and them he surnamed Boanerges, which is, sons of thunder*), and Philip and Bar-¹⁵tholomew, and Matthew and Thomas, and James the son of ¹⁶Alphæus, and Simon which was called the Zealot, and Judas the son of James, and Judas Iscariot (which also betrayed him).

²⁰ **b.**—And he lifted up his eyes on his disciples, and said, Blessed are ye poor: for yours is the kingdom of God. ²¹Blessed are ye that hunger now: for ye shall be filled. Blessed are ye that weep now: for ye shall laugh. Blessed ²²are ye, when men shall hate you, and when they shall separate you from their company, and reproach you, and cast ²³out your name as evil, for the Son of Man's sake. Rejoice in that day, and leap for joy: for behold, your reward is great in

heaven: for in the same manner did their fathers unto the
24 prophets. But woe unto you that are rich! for ye have
25 received your consolation. Woe unto you, ye that are full
now! for ye shall hunger. Woe unto you, ye that laugh now!
26 for ye shall mourn and weep. Woe unto you, when all men
shall speak well of you! for in the same manner did their
fathers to the false prophets.

Matt. v. 38   c.—Ye have heard that it was said, An eye for an eye,
39 and a tooth for a tooth; but I say unto you, Resist not him
that is evil, but whosoever smiteth thee on thy right cheek,
40 turn to him the other also. And if any man would go to law
with thee, and take away thy coat, let him have thy cloke
41 also. And whosoever shall compel thee to go one mile, go
42 with him twain. Give to him that asketh thee, and from
him that would borrow of thee turn not thou away.

43   d.—Ye have heard that it was said, Thou shalt love thy
44 neighbour and hate thine enemy; but I say unto you, Love
your enemies; *do good to them that hate you, bless them that
45 curse you,* pray for them that *despitefully use* you; that ye
may be sons of your Father which is in heaven; for he
maketh his sun to rise on the evil and the good, and sendeth
46 rain on the just and the unjust. For if ye love them that
love you, what reward have ye? do not even the publicans
47 the same? And if ye salute your brethren only, what do ye
more than others? do not even the Gentiles the same? And
Lu. vi. 34 if ye lend to them of whom ye hope to receive, what *reward*
35 have ye? Even sinners lend to sinners, to receive again as
much. Be ye merciful, even as your Father is merciful.

Matt. vii. 1   e.—Judge not, that ye be not judged; for with what
2 judgment ye judge, ye shall be judged; and with what
3 measure ye mete, it shall be measured unto you. And why
beholdest thou the mote that is in thy brother's eye, but
4 considerest not the beam that is in thine own eye? Or how
wilt thou say to thy brother, Let me cast out the mote out of
5 thine eye? And lo! the beam is in thine own eye. Thou
hypocrite, cast out first the beam out of thine own eye, and
then shalt thou see clearly to cast out the mote out of thy
12 brother's eye. All things, therefore, whatsoever ye would
that men should do unto you, even so do ye also unto them.

15 f.—Beware of false prophets which come to you in sheep's
16 clothing, but inwardly are ravening wolves. By their fruits
ye shall know them. Do men gather grapes of thorns, or
17 figs of thistles? Even so every good tree bringeth forth
18 good fruit; but the corrupt tree bringeth forth evil fruit. A
good tree cannot bring forth evil fruit, neither can a corrupt
20 tree bring forth good fruit. Therefore by their fruits shall ye
Lu. vi. 45 know them. The good man out of the good treasure of his
heart bringeth forth that which is good, and the evil man out
of the evil treasure bringeth forth that which is evil; for out
of the abundance of the heart his mouth speaketh.
Matt. vii. 21 g.—Not every one that saith unto me, Lord, Lord, shall
enter into the kingdom of God; but he that doeth the will of
24 my Father which is in heaven. Every one, therefore, which
heareth these words of mine, and doeth them, shall be
likened unto a wise man, which built his house upon the
25 rock; and the rain descended and the floods came, and the
winds blew, and beat upon that house; and it fell not; for it
26 was founded upon the rock. And every one that heareth
these words of mine, and doeth them not, shall be likened
unto a foolish man, which built his house upon the sand;
27 and the rain descended, and the floods came, and the winds
blew, and smote upon that house; and it fell; and great was
the fall thereof.

§ 6.—*The Healing of the Centurion's Son*

Lu. vii. 1 After he had ended all his sayings, he entered into
2 Capernaum. And a certain centurion's *son* was sick and at
3 the point of death. And when he heard concerning Jesus,
he sent unto him elders of the Jews, asking him that he
4 would come and save his *son*. And they, when they came to
Jesus, besought him earnestly, saying, He is worthy that
5 thou shouldest do this for him: for he loveth our nation, and
6 himself built us our synagogue. And Jesus went with them.
And when he was now not far from the house, the centurion
sent friends to him, saying unto him, Lord, trouble not
thyself; for I am not worthy that thou shouldest come under
7 my roof: wherefore neither thought I myself worthy to

come unto thee; but say the word, and my *son* shall be
8 healed. For I also am a man set under authority, having
under myself soldiers: and I say to this one, Go, and he
goeth; and to another, Come, and he cometh; and to my
9 servant, Do this, and he doeth it. And when Jesus heard
these things, he marvelled at him, and turned and said unto
the multitude that followed him, I say unto you, I have not
10 found so great faith, no, not in Israel. And they that were
sent, returning to the house, found the *son* whole.

§ 7.—*The Raising of the Widow's Son*

11 And it came to pass soon afterwards, that he went to a
city called Nain; and his disciples went with him and a great
12 multitude. Now when he drew near to the gate of the city,
behold, there was carried out one that was dead, the only
son of his mother, and she was a widow: and much people of
13 the city was with her. And when the Lord saw her, he had
14 compassion on her, and said unto her, Weep not. And he
came nigh and touched the bier: and the bearers stood still.
15 And he said, Young man, I say unto thee, Arise. And he
that was dead sat up, and began to speak. And he gave him
16 to his mother. And fear took hold on them all; and they
glorified God, saying, A great prophet is arisen among us;
17 and, God hath visited his people. And this report went forth
concerning him in the whole of Judæa, and all the region
round about.

§ 8.—*John sends Messengers*

18 a.—And the disciples of John told him of all these things.
19 And John calling unto him two of his disciples sent them to
the Lord, saying, Art thou he that cometh, or look we for
20 another? And when the men were come unto him, they
said, John the Baptist hath sent us unto thee, saying, Art
22 thou he that cometh, or look we for another? And he
answered and said unto them, Go your way, and tell John
the things which ye *do hear and see*; the blind receive their
sight and the lame walk, (the lepers are cleansed and) the
deaf hear, (and the dead are raised up), and the poor have

JOHN SENDS MESSENGERS

23 good tidings preached to them. And blessed is he whosoever shall find none occasion of stumbling in me.

24 b.—And when the messengers of John were departed, he began to say unto the multitudes concerning John, What went ye out into the wilderness to behold? A reed shaken
25 with the wind? But what went ye out to see? A man clothed in soft raiment? Behold, they which are gorgeously
26 apparelled, and live delicately, are in kings' courts. But what went ye out to see? A prophet? Yea, I say unto you,
27 and much more than a prophet. This is he of whom it is written, Behold, I send my messenger before thy face, who
28 shall prepare thy way before thee. *Verily* I say unto you, Among them that are born of women there is none greater than John; yet he that is but little in the kingdom of God is greater than he.

Matt. xxi. 28
c.—But what think ye? A man had two sons: and he came to the first and said, Son, go work to-day in the vine-
29 yard. And he answered and said, I will not: but afterward
30 he repented himself and went. And he came to the second and said likewise. And he answered and said, I go, sir, and
31 went not. Whether of the twain did the will of his father? They say, The first. Jesus saith unto them, Verily I say unto you, that the publicans and the harlots go into the
32 kingdom of God before you. For John came unto you in the

Lu. vii. 30 way of righteousness and ye rejected for yourselves the
29 counsel of God, being not baptised of him: but the publicans and the harlots justified God, being baptised with the baptism of John.

31 d.—Whereunto then shall I liken the men of this genera-
32 tion, and to what are they like? They are like unto children that sit in the market place, and call one to another; which say, We piped unto you, and ye did not dance; we wailed,
33 and ye did not *mourn*. For John the Baptist is come eating no bread nor drinking wine; and ye say, He hath a devil.
34 The Son of Man is come eating and drinking; and ye say, Behold, a gluttonous man, and a winebibber, a friend of
35 publicans and sinners! And wisdom is justified of all her children.

§ 9.—*The Samaritan Village*

ix. 52 And he entered into a village of the Samaritans, and they
53 did not receive him. And when his disciples James and John
54 saw this, they said, Lord, wilt thou that we bid fire to come
55 down from heaven and consume them? But he turned and
rebuked them.

§ 10.—*The Healing of the Lepers*

xvii. 12 And as he entered into a certain village, there met him ten
men that were lepers, which stood afar off: and they lifted up
13 their voices, saying, Jesus, Master, have mercy on us. And
14 when he saw them, he said unto them, Go and show yourselves
unto the priests. And it came to pass, as they went, they
15 were cleansed. And one of them, when he saw that he was
16 healed, turned back, with a loud voice glorifying God; and he
fell upon his face at his feet, giving him thanks: and he was
17 a Samaritan. And Jesus answering said, Were not the ten
18 cleansed? but where are the nine? Were there none found
19 that returned to give glory to God, save this stranger? And
he said unto him, Arise, and go thy way: thy faith hath made
thee whole.

§ 11.—*The Rejection in Nazareth*

iv. 16 a.—And he came to Nazareth, where he had been brought
up; and he entered, as his custom was, into the synagogue
17 on the Sabbath day, and stood up to read. And there was
delivered unto him the book of the prophet Isaiah. And he
opened the book, and found the place where it was written,
18 The Spirit of the Lord is upon me, because he anointed me
to preach good tidings to the poor: he hath sent me to proclaim release to the captives, and recovering of sight to the
19 blind, to set at liberty them that are bruised, to proclaim the
20 acceptable year of the Lord. And he closed the book, and
gave it back to the attendant, and sat down; and the eyes of
21 all in the synagogue were fastened on him. And he began
to say unto them, To-day hath this scripture been fulfilled in
your ears.

THE REJECTION IN NAZARETH

Mk. i. 22 **b.**—And they were astonished at his teaching, for he taught them as having authority, and not as the scribes. And
vi. 3 they said, Is not this the carpenter, the son of Mary and brother of James and Joses and Judas and Simon? And are not his sisters here with us?

Lu. iv. 23 **c.**—And he said unto them, Doubtless ye will say unto me this parable, Physician, heal thyself: whatsoever we have heard done at Capernaum, do also here in thine own country.
25 But *verily* I say unto you, There were many widows in Israel in the days of Elijah, when the heaven was shut up three years and six months, when there came a great famine over
26 all the land; and unto none of them was Elijah sent, but only to Zarephath, in the land of Sidon, unto a woman that was a
27 widow. And there were many lepers in Israel in the time of Elisha the prophet; and none of them was cleansed, but only
24 Naaman the Syrian. No prophet is acceptable in his own country.
28 **d.**—And they were all filled with wrath in the synagogue,
29 as they heard these things; and they rose up, and cast him forth out of the city, and led him unto the brow of the hill whereon their city was built, that they might throw him down
30 headlong. But he passing through the midst of them went
viii. 1 his way. And it came to pass soon afterwards, that he went about through cities and villages, preaching and bringing the good tidings of the kingdom of God, and with him the twelve
2 and certain women which had been healed of evil spirits and infirmities, Mary that was called Magdalene, from whom seven
3 devils had gone out, and Joanna the wife of Chuza Herod's steward, and Susanna, and many others, which ministered unto them of their substance.

§ 12.—*The Healing of the Palsy*

xiii. 10 And he was teaching in one of the synagogues on the
11 Sabbath day. And, behold, a woman which had a spirit of infirmity eighteen years; and she was bowed together, and
12 could in no wise lift herself up. And when Jesus saw her, he called her, and said to her, Woman, thou art loosed from thine
13 infirmity. And he laid his hands upon her; and immediately

14 she was made straight, and glorified God. And the ruler of the synagogue, being moved with indignation because Jesus had healed on the sabbath, answered and said to the multitude, There are six days in which men ought to work; in them therefore come and be healed, and not on the day of the Sab-
15 bath. But the Lord answered him, and said, Ye hypocrites, doth not each one of you on the Sabbath loose his ox or his
16 ass from the stall, and lead him away to watering? And ought not this woman, being a daughter of Abraham, whom Satan had bound, lo, these eighteen years, to have been loosed
17 from this bond on the day of the Sabbath? And as he said these things, all his adversaries were put to shame; and all the multitude rejoiced for all the glorious things that were done by him.

§ 13.—*The Mission of the Twelve*

Mk. vi. 7. a.—And he called unto him the twelve, and began to send them forth by two and two, and he gave them authority
Lu. x. 2 over the unclean spirits. And he said unto them, The harvest is plenteous, but the labourers are few: pray ye therefore the Lord of the harvest that he send forth labourers into his
3 harvest. Go your ways: behold, I send you forth as lambs in
Matt. vii. 6 the midst of wolves. Give not that which is holy unto the dogs, neither cast your pearls before the swine, lest haply they trample them under their feet, and turn and rend you.

Lu. x. 4 b.—Carry no purse, no wallet, no shoes: and salute no
5 man on the way. And into whatsoever house ye shall enter,
6 first say, Peace be to this house. And if a son of peace be there, your peace shall rest upon him; but if not, it shall
7 turn to you again. And in that same house remain, eating and drinking such things as they give: go not from house to house.

8 c.—And into whatsoever city ye enter, and they receive you, eat such things as are set before you: *for the labourer is*
9 *worthy of his food*: and heal the sick that are therein, and say unto them, The kingdom of God is come nigh unto you.
Matt. x. 8 Freely ye received, freely give. But into whatsoever city ye
Lu. x. 10 shall enter, and they receive you not, go out into the streets
11 thereof and say, Even the dust from your city that cleaveth

THE MISSION OF THE TWELVE   33

to our feet, we do wipe off against you: howbeit know this,
12 that the kingdom of God is come nigh. *Verily* I say unto
you, It shall be more tolerable in that day for Sodom, than
16 for that city. He that heareth you heareth me; and he
that rejecteth you rejecteth me; and he that rejecteth me
rejecteth him that sent me.

Mk. vi. 12   d.—And they went out and preached that men should
13 repent. And they cast out many devils, and anointed with
oil many that were sick and healed them.

§ 14.—*The Return of the Twelve*

Lu. x. 17   a.—And the *twelve* returned with joy, saying, Lord, even
18 the devils are subject unto us in thy name. And he said
unto them, I beheld Satan fallen as lightning from heaven.
19 Behold, I have given you authority to tread upon serpents
and scorpions, and over all the power of the enemy: and no-
20 thing shall in any wise hurt you. Howbeit in this rejoice not,
that the spirits are subject unto you; but rejoice that your
Matt. xi. names are written in heaven. (Then began he to upbraid
20 the cities wherein most of his mighty works were done,
Lu. x. 13 because they repented not.) Woe unto thee, Chorazin! woe
unto thee, Bethsaida! for if the mighty works had been done
in Tyre and Sidon which were done in you, they would have
14 repented long ago, sitting in sackcloth and ashes. Howbeit
it shall be more tolerable for Tyre and Sidon in the judgment
15 than for you. And thou, Capernaum, shalt thou be exalted
Matt. xi. unto heaven? thou shalt be brought down unto Hades; for
23 if the mighty works had been done in Sodom which were done
24 in thee, it would have remained until this day. Howbeit I
say unto you, that it shall be more tolerable for the land of
Sodom in the judgment, than for thee.

Mk. viii.   b.—And Jesus went forth and his disciples into the villages
27 of Cæsarea Philippi: and in the way he asked his disciples,
28 saying unto them, Who do men say that I am? And they
told him, saying, John the Baptist: and others, Elijah; but
29 others, One of the prophets. And he asked them, But who
say ye that I am? Peter answereth and saith unto him,
Thou art the Christ.

D

Lu. x. 21 **c.**—In that same hour *Jesus answered and said*, I thank thee, O Father, Lord of heaven and earth, that thou didst hide these things from the wise and understanding, and didst reveal them unto babes: yea, Father; for so it was well 22 pleasing in thy sight. All things have been delivered unto me of my Father: and no one knoweth who the Son is, save the Father; and who the Father is, save the Son, and he to Matt. xi. whomsoever the Son willeth to reveal him. Come unto me, 28 all ye that labour and are heavy laden, and I will give you 29 rest. Take my yoke upon you, and learn of me; for I am meek and lowly in heart: and ye shall find rest unto your 30 souls. For my yoke is easy, and my burden is light.

Lu. x. 23 **d.**—And turning to the disciples, he said, Blessed are the 24 eyes which see the things that ye see: for I say unto you, that many prophets and *righteous men* desired to see the things which ye see, and saw them not; and to hear the things which ye hear, and heard them not.

Mk. ix. 11 **e.**—And they asked him, saying, The Scribes say that 12 Elijah must first come. And he said unto them, Elijah 13 indeed cometh first, and restoreth all things; but I say unto you, that Elijah is come, and they have also done unto him whatsoever they listed, even as it is written of him.

§ 15.—*The half-hearted Disciples*

iii. 7 **a.**—And Jesus with his disciples withdrew to the sea: and a great multitude from Galilee followed: and from Judæa, 8 and from Jerusalem, and from Idumæa, and beyond Jordan, and about Tyre and Sidon, a great multitude, hearing what 9 great things he did, came unto him. And he spake to his disciples, that a little boat should wait on him because of the 10 crowd, lest they should throng him: for he had healed many; insomuch that as many as had plagues pressed upon him that they might touch him.

Matt. viii. **b.**—And there came a certain Scribe and said unto him, 19 Master, I will follow thee whithersoever thou goest. And 20 Jesus saith unto him, The foxes have holes, and the birds of the heaven have nests; but the Son of Man hath not where to 21 lay his head. And another of the disciples said unto him,

	22	Lord, suffer me first to go and bury my father. But Jesus saith unto him, Follow me; and leave the dead to bury their
Lu. ix. 61		own dead. And another also said, I will follow thee, Lord; but first suffer me to bid farewell to them that are at my
	62	house. But Jesus saith unto him, No man, having put his hand to the plough, and looking back, is fit for the kingdom of God.

§ 16.—*The Parable of the Sower*

Mk. v. 2, 3. And he said unto them in his teaching, Hearken: Behold, 4 the sower went forth to sow; and it came to pass, as he sowed, some seed fell by the wayside, and the birds came and 5 devoured it. And other fell on the rocky ground, where it had not much earth; and straightway it sprang up, because 6 it had no deepness of earth: and when the sun was risen, it was scorched; and because it had no root, it withered away. 7 And other fell among the thorns, and the thorns grew up, and 8 choked it, and it yielded no fruit. And others fell into the good ground, and yielded fruit, growing up and increasing; and brought forth, thirty-fold, and sixty-fold, and a hundred-9 fold. And he said, Who hath ears to hear, let him hear.

§ 17.—*Parables in the Desert Place*

vi. 31   a.—And he saith unto the disciples, Come ye yourselves apart into a desert place, and rest a while. For there were many coming and going, and they had no leisure so much as 32 to eat. And they went away in the boat to a desert place apart.

John vi. 3   b.—And Jesus went up into the mountain, and there he sat with his disciples.

Matt. xiii. 10
Mk. iv. 11   c.—And they said unto him, Why speakest thou unto them in parables? And he answered and said, Unto you is given the mystery of the kingdom of God: but unto them 12 that are without, all things are done in parables: that seeing they may see, and not perceive; and hearing they may hear, and not understand; lest haply they should turn again, and 13 it should be forgiven them. And he saith unto them, Know ye not this parable? (and how shall ye know all the

14 parables?) The sower soweth the word. And these are they
15 by the wayside, where the word is sown; and when they
have heard, straightway cometh Satan, and taketh away the
16 word which hath been sown in them. And these in like
manner are they that are sown upon the rocky places, who,
when they have heard the word, straightway receive it with
17 joy; and they have no root in themselves, but endure for a
while; then, when tribulation or persecution ariseth because
18 of the word, straightway they stumble. And others are they
that are sown among the thorns; and these are they that
19 have heard the word, and the cares of the world, and the
deceitfulness of riches, and the lusts of other things entering
20 in, choke the word, and it becometh unfruitful. And those
are they that were sown upon the good ground: such as hear
the word, and accept it, and bear fruit, thirty-fold, and sixty-fold, and a hundred-fold.

26 d.—And he said, So is the kingdom of God, as if a man
27 should cast seed upon the earth; and should sleep and rise
night and day, and the seed should spring up and grow, he
28 knoweth not how. The earth beareth fruit of herself; first
29 the blade, then the ear, then the full corn in the ear. But
when the fruit is ripe, straightway he putteth forth the sickle,
because the harvest is come.

30 And he said, How shall we liken the kingdom of God? or
Lu. xiii. in what parable shall we set it forth? It is like unto a grain
19 of mustard seed, which a man took and cast into his own
garden; and it grew, and became a tree; and the birds of the
heaven lodged in the branches thereof.

20 And again he said, Whereunto shall I liken the kingdom
21 of God? It is like unto leaven, which a woman took and hid
in three measures of meal, till it was all leavened.

Matt. xiii. e.—The kingdom of God is like unto a treasure hidden in
44 the field; which a man found, and hid; and in his joy he goeth
and selleth all that he hath, and buyeth that field.

45 Again, the kingdom of God is like unto a man that is a
46 merchant seeking goodly pearls: and having found one pearl
of great price, he went and sold all that he had, and bought it.

47 Again, the kingdom of God is like unto a net, that was
48 cast into the sea, and gathered of every kind: which, when

it was filled, they drew up on the beach; and they sat down and gathered the good into vessels, but the bad they cast away.

24 Again, the kingdom of God is like unto a man that sowed
25 good seed in his field: but while men slept, his enemy came
26 and sowed tares also among the wheat, and went away. But when the blade sprang up, and brought forth fruit, then
27 appeared the tares also. And the servants of the householder came and said unto him, Sir, didst thou not sow good seed in
28 thy field? Whence then hath it tares? And he said unto them, An enemy hath done this. And the servants say unto him,
29 Wilt thou then that we go and gather them up? But he saith, Nay; lest haply while ye gather up the tares, ye root
30 up the wheat with them. Let both grow together until the harvest: and in the time of the harvest I will say to the reapers, Gather up first the tares, and bind them in bundles to burn them: but gather the wheat into my barn.

§ 18.—*The Miracle of the Loaves*

Mk. vi. 34 a.—And he came forth and saw a great multitude, and he had compassion on them, because they were as sheep not having a shepherd.

35 b.—And when the day was now far spent, his disciples came unto him, and said, The place is desert, and the day is
36 now far spent: send them away, that they may go into the country and villages round about, and buy themselves some-
37 what to eat. But he answered and said unto them, Give ye them to eat. And they say unto him, Shall we go and buy two hundred pennyworth of bread, and give them to eat?
38 And he saith unto them, How many loaves have ye? Go and see. And when they knew, they say, Five, and two fishes.

39 c.—And he commanded them that all should sit down by
40 companies upon *the ground*. And they sat down in ranks, by
41 hundreds, and by fifties. And he took the five loaves and the two fishes, and looking up to heaven, he blessed, and brake the loaves; and he gave to the disciples to set before them; and
42 the two fishes divided he among them all And they did all

43 eat, and were filled. And they took up broken pieces, twelve
44 basketfuls, and also of the fishes. And they that ate the
loaves were five thousand men.
45 d.—And straightway he constrained his disciples to enter
into the boat, and to go before him unto the other side to
Bethsaida, while he himself sendeth the multitude away.
46 And after he had taken leave of them, he departed into the
mountain to pray.

§ 19.—*The Stilling of the Storm on the Sea*

47 a.—And when even was come, the boat was in the midst
48 of the sea, and he alone on the land. And seeing them distressed in rowing, for the wind was contrary unto them, about
the fourth watch of the night he cometh unto them, walking
49 on the sea; and he would have passed by them: but they,
when they saw him walking on the sea, supposed that it was
50 an apparition, and cried out: for they all saw him, and were
troubled. But he straightway spake with them, and saith
51 unto them, Be of good cheer: it is I; be not afraid. And he
went up unto them into the boat, and the wind ceased: (and
52 they were sore amazed in themselves; for they understood not
concerning the loaves, but their heart was hardened).
53 b.—And when they had crossed over, they came to the
54 land unto Gennesaret, and moored to the shore. And when
they were come out of the boat, straightway the people knew
55 him, and ran round about that whole region, and began to carry
about on their beds those that were sick, where they heard he
56 was. (And wheresoever he entered, into villages, or into cities,
or into the country, they laid the sick in the market-places,
and besought him that they might touch if it were but the
border of his garment: and as many as touched him were
made whole.)

§ 20.—*The Dumb Demoniac*

Lu. xi. 14 a.—And *there was brought to him a dumb man possessed
with a devil.* And it came to pass when the devil was gone
out, the dumb man spake; and the multitudes marvelled.
Mk. iii. 22 b.—But *the Pharisees* said, He hath Beelzebub, and, By the

THE DUMB DEMONIAC

23 prince of the devils casteth he out the devils. And he, *knowing their thoughts,* said unto them, How can Satan cast out
24 Satan? And if a kingdom be divided against itself, that king-
25 dom cannot stand. And if a house be divided against itself, that
26 house will not be able to stand. And if Satan hath risen up against himself, and is divided, he cannot stand, but hath an

Lu. xi. 19 end. And if I by Beelzebub cast out devils, by whom do your sons cast them out? Therefore shall they be your judges.
20 But if I by *the Spirit of God* cast out devils, then is the king-

Matt. xii. dom of God come upon you. Or how can one enter into the
29 house of the strong man and spoil his goods, except he first
30 bind the strong man? and then he will spoil his house. He that is not with me is against me, and he that gathereth not
31 with me scattereth. Therefore I say unto you, Every sin and blasphemy shall be forgiven unto men; but the blasphemy
32 against the Spirit shall not be forgiven. And whosoever shall speak a word against the Son of Man, it shall be forgiven him; but whosoever shall speak against the Holy Spirit, it shall not be forgiven him, neither in this world, nor in that which is to come.

Mk. ix. 38   c.—John said unto him, Master, we saw one casting out devils in thy name; and we forbade him, because he followed
39 not us. But Jesus said, Forbid him not: for there is no man which shall do a mighty work in my name, and be able quickly
40 to speak evil of me. For he that is not against us is for us.

Lu. xi. 24   d.—The unclean spirit, when he is gone out of the man, passeth through waterless places, seeking rest; and finding none, he saith, I will turn back unto my house whence I came
25 out. And when he is come, he findeth it swept and garnished.
26 Then goeth he, and taketh to him seven other spirits more evil than himself; and they enter in and dwell there: and the last state of that man becometh worse than the first.

§ 21.—*A Woman's Blessing*

27 And it came to pass, as he said these things, a certain woman out of the multitude lifted up her voice, and said unto him, Blessed is the womb that bare thee, and the breasts
28 which thou didst suck. But he said, Yea rather, blessed are they that hear the word of God and keep it.

§ 22.—*The Leaven of the Pharisees*

Matt. xii.
38 a.—Then certain of the Scribes and Pharisees answered
39 him, saying, Master, we would see a sign from thee. But he
answered and said unto them, An evil and adulterous generation seeketh after a sign ; and there shall no sign be given to
41 it but the sign of Jonah. The men of Nineveh shall stand up
in the judgment with this generation, and shall condemn it :
for they repented at the preaching of Jonah ; and behold, a
42 greater than Jonah is here. The queen of the south shall rise
up in the judgment with this generation, and shall condemn
it : for she came from the ends of the earth to hear the wisdom
of Solomon ; and behold, a greater than Solomon is here.
Lu. xii. 1   b.—*And he said* unto his disciples, Beware ye of the leaven
of the Pharisees.

§ 23.—*The Healing of a Blind Man*

Mk. viii.
22   And they bring to him a blind man, and beseech him to
23 touch him. And he took hold of the blind man by the hand,
and brought him out of the village ; and when he had spit on
his eyes, and laid his hands upon him, he asked him, Seest
24 thou aught ? And he looked up, and said, I see men ; for I
25 behold them as trees, walking. Then again he laid his hands
upon his eyes ; and he looked stedfastly, and was restored,
and saw all things clearly.

§ 24.—*The Call of a Publican*

Lu. xix. 1   a.—And he entered and was passing through Jericho.
And behold, a man called by name Zacchæus ; and he was a
3 chief publican, and he was rich. And he sought to see Jesus
who he was ; and could not for the crowd, because he was
4 little of stature. And he ran on before, and climbed up into
a sycomore tree to see him : for he was to pass that way.
5 And when Jesus came to the place, he looked up, and said
unto him, Zacchæus, make haste, and come down ; for to-day
6 I must abide at thy house. And he made haste, and came
7 down, and received him joyfully. And when *the Pharisees*

saw it, they all murmured, saying, He is gone in to lodge wit
8 a man that is a sinner. And Zacchæus stood, and said unto
the Lord, Behold, Lord, the half of my goods I give to the
poor; and if I have wrongfully exacted aught of any man, I
9 restore four-fold. And Jesus said unto him, To-day is salvation
come to this house, forasmuch as he also is a son of Abraham.
10 For the Son of Man came to seek and to save that which was
lost.

xv. 3   b.—And he spake unto them this parable, saying, What
4 man of you, having a hundred sheep, and having lost one of
them, doth not leave the ninety and nine in the wilderness,
5 and go after that which is lost, until he find it? And when
6 he hath found it, he layeth it on his shoulders, rejoicing. And
when he cometh home he calleth together his friends and his
neighbours, saying unto them, Rejoice with me, for I have
7 found my sheep which was lost. I say unto you, that even
so there shall be joy in heaven over one sinner that repenteth,
more than over ninety and nine righteous persons, which need
no repentance.

8   c.—Or what woman having ten pieces of silver, if she lose
one piece, doth not light a lamp, and sweep the house, and
9 seek diligently until she find it? And when she hath found
it, she calleth together her friends and neighbours, saying,
Rejoice with me, for I have found the piece which I had lost.
10 Even so, I say unto you, there is joy in the presence of the
angels of God over one sinner that repenteth.

11   d.—And he said, A certain man had two sons: and the
12 younger of them said to his father, Father, give me the portion of thy substance that falleth to me. And he divided
13 unto them his living. And not many days after the
younger son gathered all together, and took his journey
into a far country; and there he wasted his substance
14 with riotous living. And when he had spent all, there
arose a mighty famine in that country; and he began to
15 be in want. And he went and joined himself to one of
the citizens of that country; and he sent him into his
16 fields to feed swine. And he would fain have been filled
with the husks that the swine did eat: and no man gave unto
17 him. But when he came to himself he said, How many hired

servants of my father's have bread enough and to spare, and
18 I perish here with hunger! I will arise and go to my father,
and will say unto him, Father, I have sinned against heaven,
19 and in thy sight: I am no more worthy to be called thy son:
20 make me as one of thy hired servants. And he arose, and
came to his father. But while he was yet afar off, his father
saw him, and was moved with compassion, and ran, and fell
21 on his neck, and kissed him. And the son said unto him,
Father, I have sinned against heaven, and in thy sight: I am
22 no more worthy to be called thy son. But the father said to
his servants, Bring forth quickly the best robe, and put it on
23 him; and put a ring on his hand, and shoes on his feet: and
bring the fatted calf, and kill it, and let us eat, and make
24 merry: for this my son was dead, and is alive again; he was
25 lost, and is found. And they began to be merry. Now his
elder son was in the field: and as he came and drew nigh to
26 the house, he heard music and dancing. And he called to him
one of the servants, and inquired what these things might be.
27 And he said unto him, Thy brother is come; and thy father
hath killed the fatted calf, because he hath received him safe
28 and sound. But he was angry, and would not go in: and his
29 father came out, and intreated him. But he answered and
said to his father, Lo, these many years do I serve thee, and
I never transgressed a commandment of thine: and yet thou
never gavest me a kid, that I might make merry with my
30 friends: but when this thy son came, which hath devoured
thy living with harlots, thou killedst for him the fatted calf.
31 And he said unto him, Son, thou art ever with me, and all
32 that is mine is thine. But it was meet to make merry and be
glad: for this thy brother was dead, and is alive again; and
was lost, and is found.

§ 25.—*The Doctrine of Fasting*

Mk. ii. 18 a.—And John's disciples and the Pharisees were fasting:
and they come and say unto him, Why do John's disciples
and the disciples of the Pharisees fast, but thy disciples fast
19 not? And Jesus said unto them, Can the sons of the bridechamber fast, while the bridegroom is with them? As long

THE DOCTRINE OF FASTING 43

as they have the bridegroom with them, they cannot fast.
20 But the days will come, when the bridegroom shall be taken
21 away from them, and then will they fast in that day. No
man seweth a piece of undressed cloth on an old garment:
else that which should fill it up taketh from it, the new from
22 the old, and a worse rent is made. And no man putteth new
wine into old wine-skins: else the wine will burst the skins,
and the wine perisheth, and the skins: but they put new
wine into fresh wine-skins.

Lu. v. 39   b.—And no man having drunk old wine desireth new: for
he saith, The old is good.

Matt. xiii. 52   c.—Therefore every Scribe who hath been made a disciple
to the kingdom of God is like unto a man that is a householder, which bringeth forth out of his treasure things new
and old.

§ 26.—*The Breaking of the Sabbath in the Cornfields*

Mk. ii. 23   a.—And it came to pass, that he was going on the sabbath
day through the cornfields; and his disciples began, as they
24 went, to pluck the ears of corn. And the Pharisees said unto
him, Behold, why do they on the sabbath day that which is
25 not lawful? And he said unto them, Did ye never read
what David did, when he had need, and was an hungred, he,
26 and they that were with him? How he entered into the
house of God, when Abiathar was high priest, and did eat the
shewbread, which it is not lawful to eat save for the priests,
and gave also to them that were with him?

Matt. xii. 5   b.—Or have ye not read in the law, how that on the
sabbath day the priests in the temple profane the sabbath,
and are guiltless?

ix. 13   c.—Go ye, and learn what this meaneth, I desire mercy
and not sacrifice.

Mk. ii. 27   d.—And he said unto them, The sabbath was made for
man, and not man for the sabbath.

§ 27.—*The Sabbath Question in a Synagogue*

Lu. xiv. 1   And it came to pass, when he went into *the synagogue* on
2 a sabbath, that they were watching him. And behold, there

3 was before him a certain man which had the dropsy. And
5 they asked him, saying, Is it lawful to heal on the sabbath,
or not? And he said unto them, Which of you shall have
an ass or an ox fallen into a well, and will not straightway
6 draw him up on a sabbath day? And they could not answer
again unto these things.

§ 28.—*The Purging of the Temple*

Mk. xi. 1 And they come to Jerusalem: and he entered into the temple, and began to cast out them that sold and them that bought in the temple, and overthrew the tables of the money-
17 changers, and the seats of them that sold the doves. And he said unto them, Is it not written, My house shall be called a house of prayer for all the nations? but ye have made it a den of robbers.

§ 29.—*A Challenge of Christ's Authority*

27 a.—And as he was walking in the temple, there come to
28 him the chief priests, and the Scribes and the elders; and they said unto him, By what authority doest thou these things? Or who gave thee this authority to do these things?
29 And Jesus said unto them, I will ask of you one question, and answer me, and I will tell you by what authority I do these
30 things. The baptism of John, was it from heaven, or from
31 men? Answer me. And they reasoned with themselves, saying, If we shall say, From heaven; he will say, Why then
32 did ye not believe him? But should we say, From men— they feared the people: for all verily held John to be a
33 prophet. And they answered Jesus and say, We know not. And Jesus saith unto them, Neither tell I you by what authority I do these things.

Matt. xvi. 1   b.—And they asked him to shew them a sign from heaven.
Lu. xii. 54 And he said, When ye see a cloud rising in the west, straight-way ye say, There cometh a shower; and so it cometh to pass.
55 And when ye see a south wind blowing, ye say, There will be
56 a scorching heat; and it cometh to pass. Ye hypocrites, ye know how to interpret the face of the earth and the heaven;

but how is it that ye know not how to interpret this time?
57 And why even of yourselves judge ye not what is right?

Mk. xii. 1   c.—A man planted a vineyard, and set a hedge about it, and digged a pit for the winepress, and built a tower, and let it out to husbandmen, and went into another country *for a*
2 *long time*. And at the season he sent to the husbandmen a servant, that he might receive from the husbandmen of the
3 fruits of the vineyard. And they took him, and beat him,
4 and sent him away empty. And again he sent unto them another servant; and him they wounded in the head, and
5 handled shamefully. And he sent another, and him they killed: and many others; beating some, and killing some.
6 He had yet one, a beloved son: he sent him last unto them,
7 saying, They will reverence my son. But those husbandmen said among themselves, This is the heir; come, let us kill
8 him, and the inheritance shall be ours. And they took him, and killed him, and cast him forth out of the vineyard.
9 What therefore will the lord of the vineyard do? he will come and destroy the husbandmen, and will give the vineyard unto
10 others. Have ye not read even this scripture: The stone which the builders rejected, the same was made the head of

Lu. xx. 18 the corner? Every one that falleth on that stone shall be broken to pieces; but on whomsoever it shall fall, it will scatter him as dust.

Mk. xii. 12   d.—And they sought to lay hold on him; and they feared the multitude; for they perceived that he spake the parable against them: and they left him, and went away.

§ 30.—*The Tradition of the Elders*

Matt. xv. 1   a.—Then there came to him Pharisees and Scribes, saying,
2 Why do thy disciples transgress the tradition of the elders?
3 for they wash not their hands when they eat bread. And he answered and said unto them, Why do ye also transgress the
4 commandment of God because of your tradition? For God said, Honour thy father and thy mother: and, He that
5 speaketh evil of father or mother, let him die the death. But ye say, Whosoever shall say to his father or his mother, That wherewith thou mightest have been profited by me is given to

6 God; he shall not honour his father. And ye have made void
7 the word of God because of your tradition. Ye hypocrites,
8 well did Isaiah prophesy of you, saying, This people honoureth
9 me with their lips; but their heart is far from me. But in
vain do they worship me, teaching as their doctrines the precepts of men.

10 b.—And he called to him the multitude, and said unto
11 them, Hear, and understand: not that which entereth into
the mouth defileth the man; but that which proceedeth out
of the mouth, this defileth the man.

12 c.—Then came the disciples, and said unto him, Knowest
thou that the Pharisees were offended, when they heard this
13 saying? But he answered and said, Every plant which my
14 heavenly Father planted not, shall be rooted up. Let them
alone: they are blind guides. And if the blind guide the
15 blind, both shall fall into a pit. And Peter answered and
16 said unto him, Declare unto us the parable. And he said,
17 Are ye also even yet without understanding? Perceive ye not,
that whatsoever goeth into the mouth passeth into the belly,
18 and is cast out into the draught? But the things which proceed out of the mouth come forth out of the heart; and they
19 defile the man. For out of the heart come forth evil thoughts,
murders, adulteries, fornications, thefts, false witness, railings:
20 these are the things which defile the man: but to eat with
unwashen hands defileth not the man.

§ 31.—*The Righteousness of the Pharisees*

xxiii. 1 a.—Then spake Jesus to his disciples, saying, The Scribes
2
3 and the Pharisees sit on Moses' seat: all things therefore
whatsoever they bid you, these do and observe: but do not
4 ye after their works; for they say, and do not. Yea, they
bind heavy burdens and grievous to be borne, and lay them
on men's shoulders; but they themselves will not move them
5 with their finger. But all their works they do to be seen of
men: for they make broad their phylacteries, and enlarge the
6 borders of their garments, and love the chief place at feasts,
7 and the chief seats in the synagogues, and the salutations in
8 the market-places, and to be called of men, Rabbi. But be

not ye called Rabbi: for one is your teacher, and all ye are
9 brethren. And call no man your father on the earth: for one
10 is your Father, which is in heaven. Neither be ye called
masters: for one is your master, even the Christ.

v. 14   b.—Ye are the light of the world. A city set on a hill
15 cannot be hid. Neither do men light a lamp, and put it under
the bushel, but on the stand; and it shineth unto all that are
16 in the house. Even so let your light shine before men, that
they may see your good works, and glorify your Father which
is in heaven.

vi. 1   c.—Take heed that ye do not your righteousness before
men, to be seen of them: else ye have no reward with your
2 Father which is in heaven. When therefore thou doest alms,
sound not a trumpet before thee, as the hypocrites do in the
synagogues and in the streets, that they may have glory of
men. Verily I say unto you, They have received their reward.
3 But when thou doest alms, let not thy left hand know what
4 thy right hand doeth: that thine alms may be in secret: and
5 thy Father which seeth in secret shall recompense thee. And
when ye pray, ye shall not be as the hypocrites: for they love
to stand and pray in the synagogues and in the corners of the
streets, that they may be seen of men. Verily I say unto you,
6 They have received their reward. But thou, when thou prayest,
enter into thine inner chamber, and having shut thy door,
pray to thy Father which is in secret, and thy Father which
16 seeth in secret shall recompense thee. Moreover when ye fast,
be not, as the hypocrites, of a sad countenance: for they disfigure their faces, that they may be seen of men to fast.
17 Verily I say unto you, They have received their reward. But
thou, when thou fastest, anoint thy head, and wash thy face;
18 that thou be not seen of men to fast, but of thy Father which
is in secret: and thy Father, which seeth in secret, shall
recompense thee.

xiv. 8   d.—When thou art bidden of any man to a marriage feast,
sit not down in the chief seat; lest haply a more honourable
9 man than thou be bidden of him, and he that bade thee and
him shall come and say to thee, Give this man place; and
then thou shalt begin with shame to take the lowest place.
10 But when thou art bidden, go and sit down in the lowest place;

that when he that hath bidden thee cometh, he may say to thee, Friend, go up higher; then shalt thou have glory in the
11 presence of all that sit at meat with thee. For every one that exalteth himself shall be humbled; and he that humbleth
12 himself shall be exalted. When thou makest a dinner or a supper, call not thy friends, nor thy brethren, nor thy kinsmen, nor rich neighbours; lest haply they also bid thee again, and
13 a recompense be made thee. But when thou makest a feast, bid the poor, the maimed, the lame, the blind: and thou shalt be blessed; because they have not wherewith to recompense
14 thee; for thou shalt be recompensed in the resurrection of the just.

Matt.xxiii. e.—But woe unto you, Scribes and Pharisees, hypocrites!
13 because ye shut the kingdom of God against men: for ye enter not in yourselves, neither suffer ye them that are entering in
15 to enter: Woe unto you, Scribes and Pharisees, hypocrites! for ye compass sea and land to make one proselyte; and when he is become so, ye make him two-fold more a son of Gehenna
16 than yourselves. Woe unto you, ye blind guides, which say, Whosoever shall swear by the temple, it is nothing: but whosoever shall swear by the gold of the temple, he is a debtor.
17 Ye fools and blind: for whether is greater, the gold, or the
18 temple that hath sanctified the gold? And, Whosoever shall swear by the altar, it is nothing; but whosoever shall swear
19 by the gift that is upon it, he is a debtor. Ye blind: for whether is greater, the gift, or the altar that sanctifieth the
20 gift? He therefore that sweareth by the altar, sweareth by
21 it, and by all things thereon. And he that sweareth by the temple, sweareth by it, and by him that dwelleth therein.
22 And he that sweareth by the heaven, sweareth by the throne of God, and by him that sitteth thereon.

v. 33 Ye have heard that it was said to them of old time, Thou shalt not forswear thyself, but shalt perform unto the Lord
34 thine oaths: but I say unto you, Swear not at all; neither by
35 the heaven, for it is the throne of God; nor by the earth, for it is the footstool of his feet; nor by Jerusalem, for it is the
36 city of the great King. Neither shalt thou swear by thy head,
37 for thou canst not make one hair white or black. But let your speech be, Yea, yea; Nay, nay; and whatsoever is more

xxiii. 2 than these is of the Evil One. Woe unto you, Scribes and Pharisees, hypocrites! for ye tithe mint and anise and cummin, and have left undone the weightier matters of the law, judgment, and mercy, and faith: but these ye ought to have done,
24 and not to have left the other undone. Ye blind guides, which
25 strain out the gnat, and swallow the camel. Woe unto you, Scribes and Pharisees, hypocrites! for ye cleanse the outside of the cup and of the platter, but within they are full from
26 extortion and excess. Thou blind Pharisee, cleanse first the inside of the cup and of the platter, that the outside thereof
27 may become clean also. Woe unto you, Scribes and Pharisees, hypocrites! for ye are like unto whited sepulchres, which outwardly appear beautiful, but inwardly are full of dead men's
28 bones, and of all uncleanness. Even so ye outwardly appear righteous unto men, but inwardly ye are full of hypocrisy and
29 iniquity. Woe unto you, Scribes and Pharisees, hypocrites!
30 for ye build the sepulchres of the prophets, and say, If we had been in the days of our fathers, we should not have been
31 partakers with them in the blood of the prophets. Wherefore ye witness to yourselves, that ye are sons of them that slew
32 the prophets. Fill ye up then the measure of your fathers.
33 Ye serpents, ye offspring of vipers, how shall ye escape the
Lu. xi. 49 judgment of Gehenna? Therefore also said the wisdom of God, I will send unto them prophets, and *wise men, and*
50 *Scribes*; and some of them they shall kill and persecute; that the blood of all the prophets, which was shed *on the earth*,
51 may be required of this generation; from the blood of Abel *the righteous* unto the blood of Zachariah, who perished between the altar and the sanctuary: yea, I say unto you, it shall be required of this generation.

§ 32.—*A Series of Catch-Questions*

53 *a.*—And (when he was come out from thence) the Scribes and the Pharisees began to press upon him vehe-
54 mently, and to provoke him to speak of many things; laying wait for him, to catch something out of his mouth.

Mk. xii. 13 *b.*—And they send unto him certain of the Pharisees and of
14 the Herodians. And when they were come, they say unto him,

Master, we know that thou art true, and carest not for any one; for thou regardest not the person of men, but of a truth teachest the way of God: Is it lawful to give tribute unto Cæsar, or not? Shall we give, or shall we not give? 15 But he, knowing their hypocrisy, said unto them, Why tempt ye me? bring me a penny, that I may see it. And 16 they brought it. And he saith unto them, Whose is this image and superscription? And they said unto him, 17 Cæsar's. And Jesus said unto them, Render unto Cæsar the things that are Cæsar's, and unto God the things that are God's. And they marvelled greatly at him.

18   c.—And there come unto him Sadducees, which say that 19 there is no resurrection; and they asked him, saying, Master, Moses wrote unto us, If a man's brother die, and leave a wife behind him, and leave no child, that his brother should take his wife, and raise up seed unto his brother. 20 There were seven brethren: and the first took a wife, and 21 .dying left no seed; and the second took her, and died, 22 leaving no seed behind him; and the third likewise: and the 23 seven left no seed. Last of all the woman also died. In the resurrection whose wife shall she be of them? for the seven 24 had her to wife. Jesus said unto them, Is it not for this cause that ye err, that ye know not the scriptures, nor the 25 power of God? For when they shall rise from the dead, they neither marry, nor are given in marriage; but are as 26 angels in heaven. But as touching the dead, that they are raised; have ye not read in the book of Moses, in the place concerning the bush, how God spake unto him, saying, I am the God of Abraham, and the God of Isaac, and the God of 27 Jacob? He is not the God of the dead, but of the living: ye do greatly err.

25   d.—And behold, a certain lawyer stood up and tempted him, saying, Master, what shall I do to inherit eternal life? 26 And he said unto him, What is written in the law? how 27 readest thou? And he answering said, Thou shalt love the Lord thy God with all thy heart, and with all thy soul, and with all thy strength, and with all thy mind; and thy neigh- 28 bour as thyself. And he said unto him, Thou hast answered 29 right: this do, and thou shalt live. But he, desiring to

justify himself, said unto Jesus, And who is my neighbour?
30 Jesus made answer and said, A certain man was going down from Jerusalem to Jericho; and he fell among robbers, which both stripped him and beat him, and departed, leaving him
31 half dead. And by chance a certain priest was going down that way: and when he saw him, he passed by on the other
32 side. And in like manner a Levite also, when he came to the
33 place, and saw him, passed by on the other side. But a certain Samaritan, as he journeyed, came where he was: and
34 when he saw him, he was moved with compassion, and came to him, and bound up his wounds, pouring on them oil and wine; and he set him on his own beast, and brought him to
35 an inn, and took care of him. And on the morrow he took out two pence, and gave them to the host, and said, Take care of him; and whatsoever thou spendest more, I, when I
36 come back again, will repay thee. Which of these three, thinkest thou, proved neighbour unto him that fell among
37 the robbers? And he said, He that shewed mercy on him. And Jesus said unto him, Go, and do thou likewise.

§ 33.—*The Son of David*

Mk. xii. 35 And Jesus answered and said, as he taught in the temple, How say the Scribes that the Christ is the Son of
36 David? David himself said in the Holy Spirit, The Lord said unto my Lord, Sit thou on my right hand, till I make
37 thine enemies the footstool of thy feet. David himself calleth him Lord, and whence is he his son? And the common people heard him gladly.

§ 34.—*The Widow's Mites*

41 And he sat down over against the treasury, and beheld how the multitude cast money into the treasury; and many
42 that were rich cast in much. And there came a poor widow,
43 and she cast in two mites, which make a farthing. And he called unto him his disciples, and said unto them, Verily I say unto you, This poor widow cast in more than all they
44 which are casting into the treasury: for they all did cast in of their superfluity; but she of her want did cast in all that she had, even all her living.

§ 35.—*The Temple made without Hands*

xiii. 1   And as he went forth out of the temple, one of his disciples saith unto him, Master, behold, what manner of
2   stones and what manner of buildings! And Jesus said unto him, *Destroy this temple, that is made with hands; and in three days I will build another, made without hands.*

§ 36.—*A Prediction of Judgment*

Lu. xiii. 1   Now there were some present at that very season which told him of the Galileans, whose blood Pilate had mingled
2   with their sacrifices. And he answered and said unto them, Think ye that these Galileans were sinners above all the
3   Galileans, because they have suffered these things? I tell you, Nay; but, except ye repent, ye shall all in like manner
4   perish. Or those eighteen, upon whom the tower in Siloam fell, and killed them, think ye that they were offenders above
5   all the men that dwell in Jerusalem? I tell you, Nay; but, except ye repent, ye shall all likewise perish.

§ 37.—*The Narrow Gate*

23   a.—And one said unto him, Lord, are they few that be
Matt. vii. saved? And he said unto them, *Strive to enter in* by the
13   narrow gate: for wide is the gate, and broad is the way, that leadeth to destruction, and many be they that enter in thereby.
14   For narrow is the gate, and straitened the way, that leadeth unto life, and few be they that find it.

xiv. 6   b.—A certain man made a great supper; and he bade many:
17   and he sent forth his servant at supper time to say to them
18   that were bidden, Come; for all things are now ready. And they all with one consent began to make excuse. The first said unto him, I have bought a field, and I must needs go out
19   and see it: I pray thee have me excused. And another said, I have bought five yoke of oxen, and I go to prove them: I
20   pray thee have me excused. And another said, I have married
21   a wife, and therefore I cannot come. And the servant came, and told his lord these things. Then the master of the house

being angry said to his servant, Go out quickly into the streets and lanes of the city, and bring in hither the poor and maimed
22 and blind and lame. And the servant said, Lord, what thou
23 didst command is done, and yet there is room. And the lord said unto the servant, Go out into the highways and hedges, and constrain them to come in, that my house may be filled.
24 For I say unto you, That none of those men which were bidden shall taste of my supper.

xiii. 25   c.—When once the master of the house is risen up, and hath shut to the door, and ye begin to stand without, and to knock at the door, saying, Lord, open to us; and he shall
26 answer and say to you, I know you not whence ye are: then shall ye begin to say, We did eat and drink in thy presence,
27 and thou didst teach in our streets; and he shall say, I tell you, I know not whence ye are; depart from me, all ye workers
28 of iniquity. There shall be the weeping and gnashing of teeth, when ye shall see Abraham, and Isaac, and Jacob, and all the prophets, in the kingdom of God, and yourselves cast forth
29 without. And they shall come from the east and west, and from the north and south, and shall sit down in the kingdom
30 of God. And, behold, there are last which shall be first, and there are first which shall be last.

Matt. xxii. 2
11   d.—A certain king made a marriage feast for his son. And when the king came in to behold the guests, he saw there a
12 man which had not on a wedding garment: and he saith unto him, Friend, how camest thou in hither not having a wedding
13 garment? And he was speechless. Then the king said to the servants, Bind him hand and foot, and cast him out into the outer darkness; there shall be the weeping and gnashing of
14 teeth. For many are called, but few chosen.

§ 38.—*The Morrow of Messiah and Afterwards*

John x. 40   a.—And he went away again beyond Jordan into the place where John was at the first baptising; and there he abode.

Lu. xiii. 31   b.—And there came certain Pharisees, saying to him, Get
32 thee out, and go hence: for Herod would fain kill thee. And he said unto them, Go and say to that fox, Behold, I cast out devils and perform cures to-day and to-morrow, and the third

33 day I am perfected. Howbeit I must go on my way to-day and to-morrow and the day following: for it cannot be that a prophet perish out of Jerusalem.

§ 39.—The Temple Tax

Matt. xvii. 24 And when they were come to Capernaum, they that received the half-shekel came to Peter, and said, Doth not your master 25 pay the half-shekel? He saith, Yea. And when he came into the house, Jesus spake first to him, saying, What thinkest thou, Simon? the kings of the earth, from whom do they receive toll or tribute? from their sons or from strangers? 26 And when he said, From strangers, Jesus said unto him, 27 Therefore the sons are free. But, lest we cause them to stumble, (go thou to the sea, and cast a hook, and take up the fish that first cometh up; and when thou hast opened his mouth, thou shalt find a shekel: that take, and give unto them for me and thee).

§ 40.—Martha and Mary

Lu. x. 38 Now as they went on their way, he entered into a certain village: and a certain woman named Martha received him into 39 her house. And she had a sister called Mary, which also sat 40 at the Lord's feet, and heard his word. But Martha was cumbered about much serving; and she came up to him, and said, Lord, dost thou not care that my sister did leave me to 41 serve alone? bid her therefore that she help me. But the Lord answered and said unto her, Martha, Martha, thou art 42 anxious and troubled about many things: but one thing is needful: for Mary hath chosen the good part, which shall not be taken away from her.

§ 41.—The Entrance into Jerusalem

Lu. x. 37 a.—And as he was now drawing nigh *to Jerusalem*, even at the descent of the Mount of Olives, the disciples began to rejoice and praise God with a loud voice for all the mighty 38 works which they had seen; saying, Peace in heaven, and 39 glory in the highest. And some of the Pharisees from the

Matt. xxi. multitude said unto him, Hearest thou what these are saying?
¹⁶ And *he answered and said*, Yea: did ye never read, Out of the
Lu. xix. 40 mouth of babes and sucklings thou hast perfected praise? I tell you, that, if these shall hold their peace, the stones will cry out.

41 b.—And when he drew nigh, he saw the city and wept
42 over it, saying, If thou hadst known in this day, even thou, the things which belong unto peace! but now they are hid
xiii. 34 from thine eyes. O Jerusalem, Jerusalem, which killeth the prophets, and stoneth them that are sent unto her! how often would I have gathered thy children together, even as a hen gathereth her *chickens* under her wings, and ye would not!
35 Behold, your house is left unto you: and I say unto you, Ye shall not see me *henceforth*, until ye shall say, Blessed is he that cometh in the name of the Lord.

xiv. 25 c.—And he turned, and said, If any man cometh unto me,
26 and hateth not his own father, and mother, and wife, and children, and brethren, and sisters, yea, and his own life also,
27 he cannot be my disciple. Whosoever doth not bear his own
28 cross, and come after me, cannot be my disciple. For which of you, desiring to build a tower, doth not first sit down and count the cost, whether he have wherewith to complete it?
29 Lest haply, when he hath laid a foundation, and is not able to
30 finish, all that behold begin to mock him, saying, This man
31 began to build, and was not able to finish. Or what king, as he goeth to encounter another king in war, will not sit down first, and take counsel whether he is able with ten thousand to meet him that cometh against him with twenty thousand?
32 Or else, while the other is yet a great way off, he sendeth an
33 ambassage, and asketh conditions of peace. So therefore, whosoever he be of you that renounceth not all that he hath,
Matt. v. 13 he cannot be my disciple. Ye are the salt of the earth: but if the salt have lost its savour, wherewith shall it be salted? it is thenceforth good for nothing, but to be cast out and
Lu. xiv. 35 trodden under foot of men. He that hath ears to hear, let him hear.

§ 42.—*The Story of a Penitent Woman*

vii. 36 And he entered into the house of *Simon the leper*, and sat
37 down to meat. And behold, a woman which was in the city, a sinner; and when she knew that he was sitting at meat in *Simon's* house, she brought an alabaster cruse of ointment,
38 and standing behind at his feet, weeping, she began to wet his feet with her tears, and wiped them with the hair of her head, and kissed his feet, and anointed them with the ointment.
Mk. xiv. 4 But there were some that had indignation among themselves, saying, To what purpose hath this waste of the ointment been
5 made? For this ointment might have been sold for above three hundred pence, and given to the poor. And they
6 murmured against her. But Jesus said, Let her alone; why
7 trouble ye her? She hath wrought a good work on me. For ye have the poor always with you, and whensoever ye will ye
8 can do them good: but me ye have not always. She hath done what she could: she hath anointed my body aforehand
Lu. vii. 40 for the burying. And Jesus said unto *Simon*, Simon, I have
41 somewhat to say unto thee. And he saith, Master, say on. A certain lender had two debtors: the one owed five hundred
42 pence, and the other fifty. When they had not wherewith to pay, he forgave them both. Which of them therefore will
43 love him most? Simon answered and said, He, I suppose, to whom he forgave the most. And he said unto him, Thou
44 hast rightly judged. And turning to the woman, he said unto Simon, Seest thou this woman? I entered into thy house, thou gavest me no water for my feet: but she hath wetted my feet with her tears, and wiped them with her hair.
45 Thou gavest me no kiss: but she, since the time I came in,
46 hath not ceased to kiss my feet. My head with oil thou didst not anoint: but she hath anointed my feet with ointment.
47 Wherefore I say unto thee, Her sins, which are many, are forgiven; for she loved much: but to whom little is forgiven,
48 the same loveth little. And he said unto her, Thy sins are
50 forgiven: thy faith hath saved thee; go in peace.

§ 43.—*The Doctrine of Riches*

xii. 13   **a.**—And one out of the multitude said unto him, Master,
14 bid my brother divide the inheritance with me. But he said unto him, Man, who made me a judge or a divider over you?
15 And he said unto them, Take heed, and keep yourselves from all covetousness: for a man's life consisteth not in the abundance
16 of the things which he possesseth. And he spake a parable unto them, saying, The ground of a certain rich man brought forth plentifully: and he reasoned within himself, saying,
17 What shall I do, because I have not where to bestow my
18 fruits? And he said, This will I do: I will pull down my barns, and build greater; and there will I bestow all my corn
19 and my goods. And I will say to my soul, Soul, thou hast much goods laid up for many years; take thine ease, eat,
20 drink, be merry. But God said unto him, Thou foolish one, this night is thy soul required of thee; and the things which
21 thou hast prepared, whose shall they be? So is he that layeth up treasure for himself, and is not rich toward God.

xvi. 1   **b.**—There was a certain rich man, which had a steward; and the same was accused unto him that he was wasting his
2 goods. And he called him, and said unto him, What is this that I hear of thee? render the account of thy stewardship;
3 for thou canst be no longer steward. And the steward said within himself, What shall I do, seeing that my lord taketh away the stewardship from me? I have not strength to dig;
4 to beg I am ashamed. I am resolved what to do, that, when I am put out of the stewardship, they may receive me into
5 their houses. And calling to him each one of his lord's debtors, he said to the first, How much owest thou unto my lord?
6 And he said, A hundred measures of oil. And he said unto
7 him, Take thy bond, and sit down quickly and write fifty. Then said he to another, And how much owest thou? And he said, A hundred measures of wheat. He saith unto him, Take
8 thy bond, and write fourscore. And his lord commended the unrighteous steward because he had done wisely: for the sons of this world are for their own generation wiser than the
9 sons of the light. And I say unto you, Make to yourselves friends by means of the mammon of unrighteousness; that,

when it shall fail, they may receive you into the eternal taber-
10 nacles. He that is faithful in a very little is faithful also in
much : and he that is unrighteous in a very little is un-
11 righteous also in much. If therefore ye have not been faithful
in the unrighteous mammon, who will commit to your trust the
12 true riches ? And if ye have not been faithful in that which
is another's, who will give you that which is your own ?

Mk. x. 23   c.—And Jesus looked round about, and saith unto his
disciples, How hardly shall they that have riches enter into
25 the kingdom of God! It is easier for a camel to go through
a needle's eye, than for a rich man to enter into the kingdom
26 of God. And they were astonished exceedingly, saying unto
27 him, Then who can be saved ? Jesus looking upon them
saith, With men it is impossible, but not with God : for all
28 things are possible with God. Peter began to say unto him,
Lo, we have left *our own*, and have followed thee ; *what then*
29 *shall we have* ? Jesus said, Verily I say unto you, There is no
man that hath left house, or brethren, or sisters, or mother,
30 or father, or children, or lands, for my sake, but he shall
Matt. xx. 1 receive a hundred-fold, *and shall inherit* eternal life. The
kingdom of God is like unto a man that is a householder,
which went out early in the morning to hire labourers into
2 his vineyard. And when he had agreed with the labourers
3 for a penny a day, he sent them into his vineyard. And he
went out about the third hour, and saw others standing in the
4 marketplace idle ; and to them he said, Go ye also into the
vineyard, and whatsoever is right I will give you. And they
5 went their way. Again he went out about the sixth and the
6 ninth hour, and did likewise. And about the eleventh hour
he went out, and found others standing; and he saith unto
7 them, Why stand ye here all the day idle ? They say unto
him, Because no man hath hired us. He saith unto them,
8 Go ye also into the vineyard. And when even was come, the
lord of the vineyard saith unto his steward, Call the labourers,
and pay them their hire, beginning from the last unto the
9 first. And when they came that were hired about the
10 eleventh hour, they received every man a penny. And when
the first came, they supposed that they would receive more ;
11 and they likewise received every man a penny. And when

THE DOCTRINE OF RICHES

they received it, they murmured against the householder,
12 saying, These last have spent but one hour, and thou hast made them equal unto us, which have borne the burden of the
13 day and the scorching heat. But he answered and said to one of them, Friend, I do thee no wrong: didst not thou
14 agree with me for a penny? Take up that which is thine, and go thy way; it is my will to give unto this last, even as
15 unto thee. Is it not lawful for me to do what I will with mine own? or is thine eye evil, because I am good?

Lu. xi. 34   d.—The lamp of thy body is thine eye: when thine eye is single, thy whole body also is full of light; but when it is
35 evil, thy body also is full of darkness. Look therefore
36 whether the light that is in thee be not darkness. If therefore thy whole body be full of light, having no part dark, it shall be wholly full of light, as when the lamp with its

xii. 33 bright shining doth give thee light. Sell that ye have, and give alms; make for yourselves purses which wax not old, a treasure in the heavens that faileth not, where no thief
34 draweth near, neither moth destroyeth. For where your

xvi. 13 treasure is, there will your heart be also. No *man* can serve two masters: for either he will hate the one, and love the other; or else he will hold to one, and despise the other. Ye cannot serve God and mammon.

Matt.vi.25   e.—Therefore I say unto you, Be not anxious for your life, what ye shall eat, or what ye shall drink; nor yet for your body, what ye shall put on. Is not the life more than the
26 food, and the body than the raiment? Behold *the ravens*, that they sow not, neither do they reap, nor gather into barns; and your heavenly Father feedeth them. Are not ye of much
27 more value than *the birds of the heaven*? And which of you
28 by being anxious can add one cubit unto his stature? And why are ye anxious concerning raiment? Consider the lilies of the field, how they grow; they toil not, neither do they
29 spin: yet I say unto you, That even Solomon in all his glory
30 was not arrayed like one of these. But if God doth so clothe the grass of the field, which to-day is, and to-morrow is cast into the oven, shall he not much more clothe you, O ye of
31 little faith? Be not therefore anxious, saying, What shall we eat? or, What shall we drink? or, Wherewithal shall we be

32 clothed? For after all these things do the Gentiles seek; but your heavenly Father knoweth that ye have need of all these
Lu. xii. 31 things. Howbeit seek ye his kingdom, and these things shall
Matt. vi. 34 be added unto you. Be not therefore anxious for the morrow: for the morrow will be anxious for itself. Sufficient unto the day is the evil thereof.

§ 44.—*The Pharisees and Dives allied and condemned*

Lu. xvi. 14 And the Pharisees, who were lovers of money, heard all
15 these things; and they scoffed at him. And he said unto them, Ye are they that justify yourselves in the sight of men; but God knoweth your hearts; for that which is exalted
xviii. 10 among men is an abomination in the sight of God. Two men went up into the temple to pray; the one a Pharisee,
11 and the other a publican. The Pharisee stood and prayed thus with himself, God, I thank thee, that I am not as the rest of men, extortioners, unjust, adulterers, or even as this
12 publican. I fast twice in the week; I give tithes of all that I
13 get. But the publican, standing afar off, would not lift up so much as his eyes unto heaven, but smote his breast, saying,
14 God, be merciful to me a sinner. I say unto you, This man went down to his house justified rather than the other: for every one that exalteth himself shall be humbled; but he that
xvi. 19 humbleth himself shall be exalted. Now there was a certain rich man, and he was clothed in purple and fine linen, faring
20 sumptuously every day: and a certain beggar named Lazarus
21 was laid at his gate, full of sores, and desiring to be fed with the crumbs that fell from the rich man's table; yea, even the
22 dogs came and licked his sores. And it came to pass, that the beggar died, and that he was carried away by the angels into Abraham's bosom: and the rich man also died, and was
23 buried. And in Hades he lifted up his eyes, being in torments,
24 and seeth Abraham afar off, and Lazarus in his bosom. And he cried and said, Father Abraham, have mercy on me, and send Lazarus that he may dip the tip of his finger in water,
25 and cool my tongue; for I am in anguish in this flame. But Abraham said, Son, remember that thou in thy lifetime receivedst thy good things, and Lazarus in like manner evil things: but now here he is comforted, and thou art in

THE PHARISEES AND DIVES ALLIED AND CONDEMNED

26 anguish. And beside all this, between us and you there is a great gulf fixed, that they which would pass from hence to you may not be able, and that none may cross over from
27 thence to us. And he said, I pray thee, therefore, father,
28 that thou wouldest send him to my father's house; for I have five brethren; that he may testify unto them, lest they also
29 come into this place of torment. But Abraham saith, They
30 have Moses and the prophets; let them hear them. And he said, Nay, father Abraham; but if one go to them from the
31 dead, they will repent. And he said unto him, If they hear not Moses and the prophets, neither will they be persuaded, if one rise from the dead.

§ 45.—*The Doctrine of Marriage*

Mk. x. 2   a.—And there came unto him Pharisees, and asked him, Is it lawful for a man to put away his wife? tempting him.
3 And he answered and said unto them, What did Moses
4 command you? And they said, Moses suffered to write a
5 bill of divorcement, and to put her away. But Jesus said unto them, For your hardness of heart he wrote you this
6 commandment. But from the beginning of the creation,
7 Male and female made he them. For this cause shall a man leave his father and mother, and shall cleave to his wife;
8 and the twain shall become one flesh: so that they are no
9 more twain, but one flesh. What therefore God hath joined
10 together, let not man put asunder. And in the house the disciples asked him again of this matter. And he saith
Lu. xvi. 18 unto them, Every one that putteth away his wife, and marrieth another, committeth adultery: and he that marrieth one that is put away from a husband committeth adultery.
Matt. xix. 10   b.—The disciples say unto him, If the case of the man
11 is so with his wife, it is not expedient to marry. But he said unto them, All men cannot receive this saying, but they to
12 whom it is given. For there are eunuchs, which were so born from their mother's womb: and there are eunuchs, which were made eunuchs by men: and there are eunuchs, which made themselves eunuchs for the kingdom of God's
v. 27 sake. He that is able to receive it, let him receive it. Ye

have heard that it was said, Thou shalt not commit adultery:
28 but I say unto you, that every one that looketh on a woman
to lust after her hath committed adultery with her already in
29 his heart. And if thy right eye causeth thee to stumble,
pluck it out, and cast it from thee: for it is profitable for
thee that one of thy members should perish, and not thy
30 whole body be cast into Gehenna. And if thy right hand
causeth thee to stumble, cut it off, and cast it from thee: for
it is profitable for thee that one of thy members should
Mk. ix. 49 perish, and not thy whole body go into Gehenna. For every
one shall be salted with fire.

Lu. xvi. 16   c.—The law and the prophets were until John: from that
time *the kingdom of God suffereth violence, and men of violence
take it by force.*

Matt. v. 17   d.—*But* think not that I came to destroy the law or the
18 prophets: I came not to destroy, but to fulfil. For verily I
say unto you, Till heaven and earth pass away, one jot or one
tittle shall in no wise pass away from the law, till all things
19 be accomplished. Whosoever therefore shall break one of
these least commandments, and shall teach men so, shall be
called least in the kingdom of God: but whosoever shall do
and teach them, he shall be called great in the kingdom of
20 God. For I say unto you, that except your righteousness
shall exceed the righteousness of the Scribes and Pharisees,
ye shall in no wise enter into the kingdom of God.

§ 46.—*The Kingdom and the Child*

Mk. x. 13   a.—And they brought unto him little children, that he
14 should touch them: and the disciples rebuked them. But
when Jesus saw it, he was moved with indignation, and said
unto them, Suffer the little children to come unto me; forbid
15 them not: for of such is the kingdom of God. Verily I say
unto you, Whosoever shall not receive the kingdom of God
16 as a little child, he shall in no wise enter therein. And he
took them in his arms, and blessed them, laying his hands
upon them.

Matt. xviii.   b.—*And he said unto his disciples,* See that ye despise
10 not one of these little ones; for I say unto you, that in

THE KINGDOM AND THE CHILD

heaven their angels do always behold the face of my Father
J. xvii. 1 which is in heaven. *Woe unto the world because of occasions
of stumbling! for it must needs be that the occasions come*; but
2 woe unto him through whom they come! It were well for
him if a *great* millstone were hanged about his neck, and he
were *sunk in the depth of* the sea, rather than that he should
cause one of these little ones to stumble.
att. x. 41   c.—He that receiveth a prophet in the name of a prophet
shall receive a prophet's reward; and he that receiveth a
righteous man in the name of a righteous man shall receive a
42 righteous man's reward. And whosoever shall give to drink
unto one of these little ones a cup of cold water only, in the
name of a disciple, verily I say unto you, He shall in no wise
lose his reward.

§ 47.—*The Doctrine of Prayer*

Lu. xi. 1   a.—And it came to pass, as he was praying in a certain
place, that when he ceased, one of his disciples said unto him,
Lord, teach us to pray, even as John also taught his disciples.
att. vi. 7 *And he said unto them,* When ye pray, use not vain repetitions,
as the Gentiles do; for they think that they shall be heard
8 for their much speaking. Be not therefore like unto them:
for your Father knoweth what things ye have need of, before
Lu. xi. 2 ye ask him. After this manner therefore pray ye: Father,
3 Hallowed be thy name. Thy kingdom come. Give us *this
4 day* our daily bread. And forgive us *our debts, as we also have
forgiven our debtors.* And bring us not into temptation.
xvii. 3   b.—Take heed to yourselves: if thy brother sin, rebuke
4 him; and if he repent, forgive him. And if he sin against
thee seven times in the day, and seven times turn again to
Matt. vi. thee, saying, I repent; thou shalt forgive him. For if ye
14 forgive men their trespasses, your heavenly Father will also
15 forgive you. But if ye forgive not men their trespasses,
v. 23 neither will your Father forgive your trespasses. If therefore
thou art offering thy gift at the altar, and there rememberest
24 that thy brother hath aught against thee, leave there thy gift
before the altar, and go thy way, first be reconciled to thy
.u. xii. 58 brother, and then come and offer thy gift. *And* as thou art
going with thine adversary before the magistrate, on the way

give diligence to be quit of him; lest haply he hale thee unto the judge, and the judge shall deliver thee to the officer, and 59 the officer shall cast thee into prison. I say unto thee, Thou shalt by no means come out thence, till thou have paid the very last mite. Ye have heard that it was said to them of old 21 time, Thou shalt not kill; and whosoever shall kill shall be in 22 danger of the judgment: but I say unto you, that every one who is angry with his brother shall be in danger of the judgment; and whosoever shall say to his brother, Raca, shall be in danger of the council; and whosoever shall say, Thou fool, 36 shall be in danger of the Gehenna of fire. And I say unto you, that every idle word that men shall speak, they shall give 37 account thereof in the day of judgment. For by thy words thou shalt be justified, and by thy words thou shalt be condemned.

Matt. v. 21, 22

xii. 36, 37

xviii. 21
c.—Then came Peter, and said to him, Lord, how oft shall my brother sin against me, and I forgive him? until seven 22 times? Jesus saith unto him, I say not unto thee, Until 23 seven times; but, Until seventy times seven. Therefore is the kingdom of God likened unto a certain king, which would 24 make a reckoning with his servants. And when he had begun to reckon, one was brought unto him, which owed him ten 25 thousand talents. But forasmuch as he had not wherewith to pay, his lord commanded him to be sold, and his wife, and 26 children, and all that he had, and payment to be made. The servant therefore fell down and worshipped him, saying, Lord, 27 have patience with me, and I will pay thee all. And the lord of that servant, being moved with compassion, released him, 28 and forgave him the debt. But that servant went out, and found one of his fellow-servants, which owed him a hundred pence: and he laid hold on him, and took him by the throat, 29 saying, Pay what thou owest. So his fellow-servant fell down and besought him, saying, Have patience with me, and I will 30 pay thee. And he would not; but went and cast him into 31 prison, till he should pay that which was due. So when his fellow-servants saw what was done, they were exceeding sorry, 32 and came and told unto their lord all that was done. Then his lord called him unto him, and saith to him, Thou wicked servant, I forgave thee all that debt, because thou besoughtest

33 me: shouldest not thou also have had mercy on thy fellow-
34 servant, even as I had mercy on thee? And his lord was wroth, and delivered him to the tormentors, till he should pay
35 all that was due. So shall also my heavenly Father do unto you, if ye forgive not every one his brother from your hearts.

Lu. xiii. 6 A certain man had a fig tree planted in his vineyard; and he
7 came seeking fruit thereon, and found none. And he said unto the vine-dresser, Behold, these three years I come seeking fruit on this fig tree, and find none: cut it down;
8 why doth it also cumber the ground? And he answering saith unto him, Lord, let it alone this year also, till I shall
9 dig about it, and dung it: and if it bear fruit thenceforth, well; but if not, thou shalt cut it down.

xi. 5 d.—And he said unto them, Which of you shall have a friend, and shall go unto him at midnight, and say to him,
6 Friend, lend me three loaves; for a friend of mine is come to me from a journey, and I have nothing to set before him;
7 and he from within shall answer and say, Trouble me not: the door is now shut, and my children are with me in bed; I
8 cannot rise and give thee? I say unto you, Though he will not rise and give him, because he is his friend, yet because of his importunity he will arise and give him as many as he
9 needeth. And I say unto you, Ask, and it shall be given you; seek, and ye shall find; knock, and it shall be opened unto
10 you. For every one that asketh receiveth; and he that seeketh

Matt. vii. findeth; and to him that knocketh it shall be opened. Or
9 what man is there of you, who, if his son shall ask him for a
10 loaf, will give him a stone; or if he shall ask for a fish, will
11 give him a serpent? If ye then, being evil, know how to give good gifts unto your children, how much more shall your Father which is in heaven give good things to them that ask him?

Lu. xvii. 5 e.—And the apostles said unto the Lord, Increase our
6 faith. And the Lord said, If ye have faith as a grain of mustard seed, ye would say unto this sycamine tree, Be thou rooted up, and be thou planted in the sea; and it would have
7 obeyed you. But who is there of you, having a servant plowing or keeping sheep, that will say unto him, when he is come in from the field, Come straightway and sit down to meat;

F

8 and will not rather say unto him, Make ready wherewith I may sup, and gird thyself, and serve me, till I have eaten
9 and drunken; and afterward thou shalt eat and drink? Doth he thank the servant because he did the things that were
10 commanded? Even so ye also, when ye shall have done all the things that are commanded you, say, We are unprofitable servants; we have done that which it was our duty to do.

§ 48.—*The Coming of the Kingdom*

20 a.—And being asked by the Pharisees, when the kingdom of God cometh, he answered them and said, The kingdom of
21 God cometh not with observation: neither shall they say, Lo, here! or, There! for lo, the kingdom of God is in the midst of you.

22 b.—And he said unto the disciples, The days will come, when ye shall desire to see one of the days of the Son of Man, and

Matt. xxiv. ye shall not see it. If therefore they shall say unto you,
26 Behold, he is in the wilderness; go not forth: Behold, he is
27 in the inner chambers, believe it not. For as the lightning cometh forth from the east, and is seen even unto the west;

Mk. xiii. so shall *the Son of Man be in his day.* But of that day or that
32 hour knoweth no one, not even the angels in heaven, neither

Lu. xvii. the Son, but the Father. And as it came to pass in the days
26 of Noah, even so shall it be also in the days of the Son of Man.
27 They ate, they drank, they married, they were given in marriage, until the day that Noah entered into the ark, and
28 the flood came, and destroyed them all. Likewise even as it came to pass in the days of Lot; they ate, they drank, they
29 bought, they sold, they planted, they builded; but in the day that Lot went out from Sodom it rained fire and brimstone
30 from heaven, and destroyed them all: after the same manner
31 shall it be in the day that the Son of Man is revealed. In that day, he which shall be on the housetop, and his goods in the house, let him not go down to take them away: and let
32 him that is in the field likewise not return back. Remember

Mk. viii. Lot's wife. For what doth it profit a man, to gain the whole
36
37 world, and forfeit his life? For what should a man give in

Lu. xvii. exchange for his life? Whosoever shall seek to gain his life
33

shall lose it; but whosoever shall lose his life shall preserve
34 it. I say unto you, In that night there shall be two men on
one bed; the one shall be taken, and the other shall be left.
35 There shall be two women grinding together; the one shall
37 be taken, and the other shall be left. And they answering
say unto him, Where, Lord? And he said unto them, Where
the *carcase* is, thither will the eagles also be gathered together.

xii. 32   c.—Fear not, little flock; for it is your Father's good
xxi. 34 pleasure to give you the kingdom. But take heed to yourselves,
lest haply your hearts be overcharged with surfeiting, and
drunkenness, and cares of this life, and that day come on you
35 suddenly as a snare: for so shall it come upon all them that
36 dwell on the face of all the earth. But watch ye at every
season, making supplication, that ye may prevail to escape
all these things that shall come to pass, and to stand before
the Son of Man.

xviii. 2   There was in a city a judge, which feared not God, and
3 regarded not man: and there was a widow in that city; and
she came oft unto him, saying, Avenge me of mine adversary.
4 And he would not for a while: but afterward he said within
5 himself, Though I fear not God, nor regard man; yet because
this widow troubleth me, I will avenge her, lest she wear me
6 out by her continual coming. And the Lord said, Hear what
7 the unrighteous judge saith. And shall not God avenge his
elect, which cry to him day and night, and he is long-suffering
8 over them? I say unto you, that he will avenge them speedily.
Howbeit when the Son of Man cometh, shall he find faith on
Matt. xxv. the earth? Then shall the kingdom of God be likened unto
1 ten virgins, which took their lamps, and went forth to meet
2 the bridegroom. And five of them were foolish, and five were
3 wise. For the foolish, when they took their lamps, took no
4 oil with them: but the wise took oil in their vessels with their
5 lamps. Now while the bridegroom tarried, they all slumbered
6 and slept. But at midnight there is a cry, Behold, the bride-
7 groom! Come ye forth to meet him. Then all those virgins
8 arose, and trimmed their lamps. And the foolish said unto
the wise, Give us of your oil; for our lamps are going out.
9 But the wise answered, saying, Peradventure there will not be
enough for us and you: go ye rather to them that sell, and

10 buy for yourselves. And while they went away to buy, the bridegroom came; and they that were ready went in with him
11 to the marriage feast: and the door was shut. Afterward come
12 also the other virgins, saying, Lord, Lord, open to us. But he answered and said, Verily I say unto you, I know you not.

Mk. xiii. 13 Watch therefore, for ye know not the day nor the hour. It
34 is as when a man, sojourning in another country, having left his house, and given authority to his servants, to each one his
35 work, commanded also the porter to watch. Watch therefore: for ye know not when the lord of the house cometh, whether at even, or at midnight, or at cock-crowing, or in the morning;

Lu. xii. 36 37 lest coming suddenly he find you sleeping. Blessed are those servants, whom the Lord when he cometh shall find watching: verily I say unto you, that he shall gird himself, and make
38 them sit down to meat, and shall come and serve them. And if he shall come in the second watch, and if in the third, and
39 find them so, blessed are those servants. But know this, that if the master of the house had known in what hour the thief was coming, he would have watched, and not have left his
40 house to be broken through. Be ye also ready: for in an hour that ye think not the Son of Man cometh.

41 d.—And Peter said, Lord, speakest thou this parable unto
42 us, or even unto all? And the Lord said, Who then is the faithful and wise steward, whom his lord shall set over his household, to give them their portion of food in due season?
43 Blessed is that servant, whom his lord when he cometh shall
44 find so doing. *Verily* I say unto you, that he will set him
45 over all that he hath. But if that servant shall say in his heart, My lord delayeth his coming; and shall begin to beat the men-servants and the maid-servants, and to eat and drink,
46 and to be drunken; the lord of that servant shall come in a day when he expecteth not, and in an hour when he knoweth not, and shall cut him asunder, and appoint his portion with
47 the unfaithful. And that servant, which knew his lord's will, and made not ready, nor did according to his will, shall be
48 beaten with many stripes; but he that knew not, and did things worthy of stripes, shall be beaten with few stripes. And to whomsoever much is given, of him shall much be required: and to whom they commit much, of him will they ask the more.

THE COMING OF THE KINGDOM 69

xix. 12 A certain nobleman went into a far country, to receive for
Matt. xxv. himself a kingdom, and to return. And he called his own
14
15 servants, and delivered unto them his goods. And unto one
he gave five talents, to another two, to another one; to each
Lu. xix. 13 according to his several ability. And he said unto them,
Trade ye herewith till I come; *and he went on his journey.*
14 But his citizens hated him, and sent an ambassage after him,
15 saying, We will not that this man reign over us. And it came
to pass, when he was come back again, having received the
kingdom, that he commanded these servants, unto whom he
had given the money, to be called to him, that he might know
16 what they had gained by trading. And the first came before
him, saying, Lord, *thou deliveredst unto me five talents:* lo, I
17 *have gained other five talents.* And he said unto him, Well
done, thou good servant: because thou wast found faithful in
18 a very little, have thou authority over *five* cities. And the
second came, saying, Lord, *thou deliveredst unto me two talents:*
19 *lo, I have gained other two talents.* And he said unto him also,
20 Be thou also over *two* cities. And the other came, saying,
Lord, behold here is thy *talent,* which I kept laid up in a
21 napkin: for I feared thee, because thou art an austere man:
thou takest up that thou layedst not down, and reapest that
22 thou didst not sow. He saith unto him, Out of thine own
mouth will I judge thee, thou wicked servant. Thou knewest
that I am an austere man, taking up that I laid not down,
23 and reaping that I did not sow; then wherefore gavest thou
not my money into the bank, and I at my coming should have
24 required it with interest? And he said unto them that stood
by, Take away from him the *talent,* and give it unto him that
25 hath the ten *talents.* And they said unto him, Lord, he hath
26 ten *talents.* I say unto you, That unto every one that hath
shall be given; but from him that hath not, even that which
27 he hath shall be taken away from him. Howbeit these mine
enemies, which would not that I should reign over them, bring
Matt. xxv. hither, and slay them before me.
31 But when the Son of Man shall come in his glory, and all
32 the angels with him, then shall he sit on the throne of his glory:
and before him shall be gathered all the nations: and he shall
separate them one from another, as the shepherd separateth the

33 sheep from the goats: and he shall set the sheep on his right
34 hand, but the goats on the left. Then shall the King say unto them on his right hand, Come, ye blessed of my Father, inherit the kingdom prepared for you from the foundation of the world:
35 for I was an hungred, and ye gave me meat: I was thirsty, and ye gave me drink: I was a stranger, and ye took me in;
36 naked, and ye clothed me: I was sick, and ye visited me: I
37 was in prison, and ye came unto me. Then shall the righteous answer him, saying, Lord, when saw we thee an hungred, and
38 fed thee? or athirst, and gave thee drink? And when saw we thee a stranger, and took thee in? or naked, and clothed
39 thee? And when saw we thee sick, or in prison, and came
40 unto thee? And the King shall answer and say unto them, Verily I say unto you, Inasmuch as ye did it unto one of these
41 my brethren, even these least, ye did it unto me. Then shall he say also unto them on the left hand, Depart from me, ye cursed, into the eternal fire which is prepared for the devil
42 and his angels: for I was an hungred, and ye gave me no
43 meat: I was thirsty, and ye gave me no drink: I was a stranger, and ye took me not in; naked, and ye clothed me
44 not; sick, and in prison, and ye visited me not. Then shall they also answer, saying, Lord, when saw we thee an hungred, or athirst, or a stranger, or naked, or sick, or in prison, and
45 did not minister unto thee? Then shall he answer them, saying, Verily I say unto you, Inasmuch as ye did it not unto
46 one of these least, ye did it not unto me. And these shall go away into eternal punishment: but the righteous into eternal life.

§ 49.—*The Last Supper*

Mk. xiv. 1   a.—Now after two days was the feast of the passover and the unleavened bread: and the chief priests and the Scribes sought how they might take him with subtilty, and kill him:
2 for they said, Not during the feast, lest haply there shall be
10 a tumult of the people. And Judas Iscariot, he that was one of the twelve, went away unto the chief priests, that he might
11 deliver him unto them. And they, when they heard it, were glad, and promised to give him money. And he sought how he might conveniently deliver him unto them.
17   b.—And when it was evening he cometh with the twelve.

Lu. xxii.
15 and he said unto them, With desire I have desired to eat
16 this passover with you before I suffer: for I say unto you, I will not eat it, until it be fulfilled in the kingdom of God.
17 And he received a cup, and when he had given thanks, he
18 said, Take this, and divide it among yourselves: for I say unto you, I will not drink from henceforth of the fruit of the
xii. 49 vine, until the kingdom of God shall come. I came to cast fire upon the earth; and how I wish it were already kindled!
50 But I have a baptism to be baptised with; and how am I
xxii. 19 straitened till it be accomplished! And he took bread, and when he had given thanks, he brake it, and gave to them, saying, This is my body which is given for you: this do in
20 remembrance of me. And the cup in like manner after supper, saying, This cup is the new covenant in my blood,
Matt. xvi.
19 even that which is poured out for you. I *give unto you* the
18 keys of the kingdom of God, and the gates of Hades shall
xviii. 18 not prevail against *you*. Verily I say unto you, What things soever ye shall bind on earth shall be bound in heaven: and what things soever ye shall loose on earth shall be loosed in
19 heaven. Again I say unto you, that if two of you shall agree on earth as touching anything that they shall ask, it shall be
20 done for them of my Father which is in heaven. For where two or three are gathered together in my name, there am I in the midst of them.

Mk. x. 35   c.—And there come near unto him James and John, the sons of Zebedee, saying unto him, Master, we would that thou shouldest do for us whatsoever we shall ask of thee.
36 And he said unto them, What would ye that I should do for
37 you? And they said unto him, Grant unto us that we may sit, one on thy right hand, and one on thy left hand, in thy
38 glory. But Jesus said unto them, Ye know not what ye ask. Are ye able to drink the cup that I drink? or to be baptised
39 with the baptism that I am baptised with? And they said unto him, We are able. And Jesus said unto them, The cup that I drink ye shall drink; and with the baptism that I am
40 baptised withal shall ye be baptised: but to sit on my right hand or on my left hand is not mine to give: but it is for
41 them for whom it hath been prepared. And when the ten heard it, they began to be moved with indignation concerning

42 James and John. And Jesus called them to him, and saith unto them, Ye know that they which are accounted to rule over the Gentiles lord it over them; and *they that have authority over them are called Benefactors*. But ye shall not be so: but he that is the greater among you, let him become as the younger; and he that is chief, as he that doth serve. 27 For whether is greater, he that sitteth at meat, or he that serveth? is not he that sitteth at meat? But I am in the midst of you as he that serveth. The disciple is not above 25 his master, nor the servant above his lord: *but the disciple when he is perfected shall be* as his master, and the servant as his lord. If they have called the master of the house Beelzebub, how much more shall they call them of his household! 26 Fear them not therefore: for there is nothing covered, that shall not be revealed; and hid, that shall not be known. 27 What I tell you in the darkness, speak ye in the light: and what ye hear in the ear, proclaim upon the housetops. And I say unto you my friends, Be not afraid of them which kill the body, and after that have no more that they can do. 5 But I will warn you whom ye shall fear: Fear him, which after he hath killed hath power to cast into Gehenna; yea, I say unto you, Fear him. Are not two sparrows sold for a farthing? and not one of them shall fall on the ground 30 without your Father: but the very hairs of your head are 31 all numbered. Fear not: ye are of more value than many 32 sparrows. *And I say unto you*, Every one who shall confess me before men, him will I also confess before my Father 33 which is in heaven. But whosoever shall deny me before men, him will I also deny before my Father which is in 28 heaven. But ye are they which have continued with me 29 in my temptations; and I appoint unto you, even as my 30 Father appointed unto me a kingdom, that ye may eat and drink at my table in my kingdom; and ye shall sit on thrones judging the twelve tribes of Israel.

§ 50.—*A Discourse on the Road to the Garden*

39 a.—And he came out, and went, as his custom was, unto the Mount of Olives; and the disciples also followed him.

A DISCOURSE ON THE ROAD TO THE GARDEN 73

Mk. xiv. 27 And Jesus saith unto them, All ye shall be offended: for it is written, I will smite the shepherd, and the sheep shall be
28 scattered abroad. Howbeit, after I am raised up, I will go
29 before you into Galilee. But Peter said unto him, Although all shall be offended, yet will not I. And Jesus saith unto
Lu. xxii. him, Simon, Simon, behold, Satan asked to have you, that
31
32 he might sift you as wheat: but I made supplication for thee, that thy faith fail not: and do thou, when once thou hast
33 turned again, stablish thy brethren. And he said unto him, Lord, with thee I am ready to go both to prison and to death.
34 And he said, I tell thee, Peter, the cock shall not crow this day, until thou shalt thrice deny that thou knowest me.
35 b.—And he said unto them, When I sent you forth without purse, and wallet, and shoes, lacked ye anything?
36 And they said, Nothing. And he said unto them, But now, he that hath a purse, let him take it, and likewise a wallet: and he that hath none, let him sell his cloke, and buy a
37 sword. For I say unto you, that this which is written must be fulfilled in me, And he was reckoned with transgressors: for
38 that which concerneth me hath fulfilment. And they said, Lord, behold, here are two swords. And he said unto them,
xii. 51 It is enough. Think ye that I am come *to send* peace *on* the
52 earth? I tell you, Nay; but rather *a sword*: for there shall be from henceforth five in one house divided, three against
53 two, and two against three. They shall be divided, father against son, and son against father; mother against daughter, and daughter against her mother; mother in law against her daughter in law, and daughter in law against her mother in
Matt. x. 16 law. Be ye therefore wise as serpents, and harmless as
17 doves. But beware of men: for they will deliver you up to
18 councils, and in their synagogues they will scourge you; yea and before governors and kings shall ye be brought for my
19 sake, for a testimony to them and to the Gentiles. But when they deliver you up, be not anxious how or what ye shall speak: for it shall be given you in that hour what ye shall
20 speak. For it is not ye that speak, but the Spirit of your
21 Father that speaketh in you. And brother shall deliver up brother to death, and the father his child: and children shall rise up against parents, and cause them to be put to death.

22 And ye shall be hated of all men for my name's sake: but he
23 that endureth to the end, the same shall be saved. But when they persecute you in this city, flee into the next: for verily I say unto you, Ye shall not have gone through the cities of Israel, till the Son of Man be come.

§ 51.—*The Agony and the Arrest in the Garden*

Lu. xxii.
40 a.—And when he was at the place, he said unto them,
41 Pray that ye enter not into temptation. And he was parted from them about a stone's cast; and he kneeled down and
42 prayed, saying, Father, if thou be willing, remove this cup
43 from me: nevertheless not my will, but thine, be done. (And there appeared unto him an angel from heaven, strengthening
44 him.) And being in an agony he prayed more earnestly: and his sweat became as it were great drops of blood falling down
45 upon the ground. And when he rose up from his prayer, he came unto the disciples, and found them sleeping for sorrow,
46 and said unto them, Why sleep ye? rise and pray, that ye enter not into temptation.

47 b.—While he yet spake, behold, a multitude, and he that was called Judas, one of the twelve, went before them; and he
48 drew near unto Jesus to kiss him. But Jesus said unto him,
49 Judas, betrayest thou the Son of Man with a kiss? And when they that were about him saw what would follow, they said, Lord,
50 shall we smite with the sword? And a certain one of them smote the servant of the high priest, and struck off his right
Matt. xxvi. ear. Then saith Jesus unto him, Put up again thy sword
52 into its place: for all they that take the sword shall perish
53 with the sword. Or thinkest thou that I cannot beseech my Father, and he shall even now send me more than twelve
54 legions of angels? How then should the scriptures be ful-
Lu. xxii. filled, that thus it must be? And Jesus said unto the chief
52 priests, and captains of the temple, and elders, which were come against him, Are ye come out, as against a robber, with
53 swords and staves? When I was daily with you in the temple, ye stretched not forth your hands against me: but this is your hour, and the power of darkness.

§ 52.—*The Court of the High Priest*

54 And they seized him, and led him away, and brought him into the high priest's house. But Peter followed afar off.
55 And when they had kindled a fire in the midst of the court, and had sat down together, Peter sat in the midst of them.
56 And a certain maid seeing him as he sat in the light of the fire, and looking stedfastly upon him, said, This man also was
57 with him. But he denied, saying, Woman, I know him not.
60 And immediately, while he yet spake, the cock crew. And the
61 Lord turned, and looked upon Peter. And Peter remembered the word of the Lord, how that he said unto him, Before the
62 cock crow this day, thou shalt deny me thrice. And he went out, and wept bitterly.

§ 53.—*The Meeting of the Council*

66 And as soon as it was day, the assembly of the elders of the people was gathered together, both chief priests and
Mk. xiv. Scribes; and they sought witness against Jesus to put him
55
56 to death, and found it not. For many bare false witness
57 against him, and their witness agreed not together. And there stood up certain, and bare false witness against him,
58 saying, We heard him say, I will destroy this temple that is made with hands, and in three days I will build another
59 made without hands. And not even so did their witness
60 agree together. And the high priest stood up in the midst, and asked Jesus, saying, Answerest thou nothing? what is it
61 which these witness against thee? But he held his peace, and answered nothing. Again the high priest asked him, and saith unto him, Art thou the Christ, the Son of the
62 Blessed? And Jesus said, *If I tell you, ye will not believe: and if I ask, ye will not answer.* But ye shall see the Son of Man sitting at the right hand of power, and coming
63 with the clouds of heaven. And the high priest rent his clothes, and saith, What further need have we of witnesses?
64 Ye have heard the blasphemy: what think ye? And they
65 all condemned him to be worthy of death. And some began to spit on him, and to cover his face, and to buffet

him, and to say unto him, Prophesy: *who is he that struck thee?* And the officers received him with blows of their hands.

§ 54.—*The Court of Pilate*

Lu. xxiii.
1 And the whole company of them rose up, and brought him
2 before Pilate. And they began to accuse him, saying, We found this man perverting our nation, and forbidding to give tribute to Cæsar, and saying that he himself is Christ, a king.
3 And Pilate asked him, saying, Art thou the King of the Jews?
Mk. xv. 4 And he answered him and said, Thou sayest. And Pilate again asked him, saying, Answerest thou nothing? behold
5 how many things they accuse thee of. But Jesus no more answered anything; insomuch that Pilate marvelled.

§ 55.—*Barabbas and Jesus*

6 Now at the feast he used to release unto them one
7 prisoner, whom they asked of him. And there was one called Barabbas, lying bound with them that had made insurrection, men who in the insurrection had committed
8 murder. And the multitude went up and began to ask him
9 to do as he was wont to do unto them. And Pilate answered
10 them, saying, Will ye that I release unto you the King of the Jews? (For he perceived that for envy the chief priests had
11 delivered him up.) But the chief priests stirred up the multitude, that he should rather release Barabbas unto them.
12 And Pilate again answered and said unto them, What then shall I do unto him whom ye call the King of the Jews?
13 And they cried out again, Crucify him. And Pilate said
14 unto them, Why, what evil hath he done? But they cried
15 out exceedingly, Crucify him. And Pilate, wishing to content the multitude, released unto them Barabbas, and delivered Jesus, when he had scourged him, to be crucified.

§ 56.—*The Crucifixion*

16 And the soldiers led him away within the court, which is
17 the Prætorium; and they call together the whole band. And they clothe him with purple, and plaiting a crown of thorns,

18 they put it on him, *and a reed in his right hand*; and they
19 began to salute him, Hail, King of the Jews! And they smote his head with *the* reed, and did spit upon him, and
20 bowing their knees worshipped him. And when they had mocked him, they took off from him the purple, and put on him his garments. And they lead him out to crucify him.

Lu. xxiii. 26 And they laid hold upon one Simon of Cyrene, coming from the country, and laid on him the cross, to bear it after Jesus.
27 And there followed him a great multitude of the people, and
28 of women who bewailed and lamented him. But Jesus turning unto them said, Daughters of Jerusalem, weep not
29 for me, but weep for yourselves, and for your children. For behold, the days are coming, in which they shall say, Blessed are the barren, and the wombs that never bare, and the
30 breasts that never gave suck. Then shall they begin to say to the mountains, Fall on us; and to the hills, Cover us.
31 For if they do these things in the green tree, what shall be

Mk. xv. 22 done in the dry? And they bring him unto the place Golgotha, which is, being interpreted, The Place of a Skull.
23 And they offered him wine mingled with myrrh: but he
24 received it not. And they crucify him, and part his garments among them, casting lots upon them, what each
26 should take. And the superscription of his accusation was
27 written over, The King of the Jews. And with him they crucify two robbers; one on his right hand, and one on his
29 left. And they that passed by railed on him, wagging their heads, and saying, Ha! thou that destroyest the temple, and
30 buildest it in three days, save thyself, and come down from
31 the cross. In like manner also the chief priests mocking him among themselves with the Scribes said, He saved
32 others; himself he cannot save. Let the Christ, the King of Israel, now come down from the cross, that we may see and believe. And they that were crucified with him reproached
34 him. And Jesus cried with a loud voice, Eloi, Eloi, lama sabachthani? which is, being interpreted, My God, my God,
35 why hast thou forsaken me? And some of them that stood
36 by, when they heard it, said, Behold, he calleth Elijah. And one ran, and filling a sponge full of vinegar, put it on a reed, and gave him to drink, saying, Let be; let us see

37 whether Elijah cometh to take him down. And Jesus
40 uttered a loud voice, and gave up the ghost. And there were
also women beholding from afar: among whom were Mary
Magdalene, and *Joanna*, and Mary the mother of James;
41 who, when he was in Galilee, followed him, and ministered
unto him; and many other women which came up with him
unto Jerusalem.

§ 57.—*The Burial*

Lu. xxiii.
50   And behold, a man named Joseph, who was a councillor,
51 a good man and a righteous (he had not consented to their
counsel and deed), a man of Arimathæa, who was looking
52 for the kingdom of God: this man went to Pilate, and asked
53 for the body of Jesus. And he took it down, and wrapped it
in a linen cloth, and laid him in a tomb that was hewn in
54 stone, where never man had yet lain. And it was the day of
55 the Preparation, and the Sabbath drew on. And the women,
which had come with him out of Galilee, followed after, and
56 beheld the tomb, and how his body was laid. And they
returned, and prepared spices and ointments.

§ 58.—*The Empty Tomb*

56   And on the sabbath they rested according to the com-
xxiv. 1 mandment. But on the first day of the week, at early dawn,
they came unto the tomb, bringing the spices which they had
2 prepared. And they found the stone rolled away from the
3 tomb. And they entered in, and found not the body. And
Mk. xvi. 8 they went out and fled from the tomb; for trembling and
astonishment had come upon them; (and they said nothing
Lu. xxiv. 9 to any one; for they were afraid). And they told all these
11 things to the eleven, and to all the rest. And these words
appeared in their sight as idle talk; and they disbelieved
12 them. But Peter arose, and ran unto the tomb; and stooping and looking in, he seeth the linen cloths by themselves;
and he departed to his home, wondering at that which was
come to pass.

A CRITICAL RECONSTRUCTION
OF THE TEXT

§ 1.—*The Preaching of John the Baptist*

In the first part of 'Die Lehre Jesu' Wendt maintains that Mark was not acquainted with the apostolic source, and that Matthew and Luke, possessing an independent knowledge of this source, reproduced it from memory in following the second gospel as their standard. In attempting to restore the apostolic original he accordingly omits the material which was borrowed by the later evangelists from Mark, and begins without any historical introduction at the preaching of John the Baptist (Matt. iii. 7-12). He admits that his result is fragmentary; but the history, he says, has been lost. The large questions involved must be reserved for discussion elsewhere; but cumulative evidence will be found in this volume to disprove Wendt's assumption; and since the source, whether oral or written, admittedly contained an account of the details recorded by Mark (cf. Luke vii. 24-35), we may place the Baptist's preaching in its historical setting.

a.[1]—A few ancient authorities omit the description of Jesus as the Son of God (Mark i. 1). If Mark began his gospel with such a confession of faith, the words are probably editorial. An ancient copyist corrected ver. 2 by substituting 'the prophets' for 'Isaiah' (R.V. margin). We follow his example and omit the quotation from Malachi, which can only be explained as an interpolation suggested by Luke vii. 27.

b.—Mark states that the people who went out to John from Judæa and Jerusalem were baptised by him, confessing their sins. According to the third gospel, on the other hand, the people were addressed as 'the offspring of vipers,' and were not accepted as penitents (Luke iii. 7). As this agrees with

[1] The letters are intended for reference to the text as printed in this volume.

a later passage in the source (Luke vii. 24–30), we conclude that Mark's reading is secondary. In the first gospel Mark's statement is reproduced, and the preaching is addressed to the Pharisees and Sadducees (Matt. iii. 7). The two sources are here obviously combined.

c.—This section is peculiar to Luke and is rejected by Wendt. We consider it to be primary for three reasons: (1) The context is admitted to be a faithful reproduction of the apostolic source. (2) The teaching is precisely what one would expect from the Baptist. (3) The Ebionitic tendency which critics have detected in the author of the third gospel is probably in most cases imaginary. Luke certainly has much sympathy for the poor and the outcasts of society, but the question is whether this sympathy was not expressed in the source. The sequel will show that Matthew systematically omits the teaching which tends towards Ebionism, whereas Luke preserves the original.

d.—The Baptist's proclamation of the kingdom of God would excite the curiosity of the people, and they would ask, no doubt with incredulity, if he professed to be Messiah. We therefore adopt into the text the introductory statement which makes the preaching intelligible. The reading, 'whose shoes I am not worthy to bear,' is peculiar to Matthew, and can scarcely be explained as editorial. The baptism with fire is attested by the agreement of Matthew and Luke.

§ 2.—*The Baptism of Jesus*

The priority of Mark's version is established by clear critical evidence. (1) In the gospel according to Matthew, Jesus is recognised by the Baptist as Messiah. His baptism is explained as a fulfilment of righteousness, and the voice which came out of the heavens is represented as addressed to the spectators; but according to the testimony of the apostolic source, Jesus had not been recognised as Messiah (Luke vii. 19, cf. Mark i. 7), and the subsequent conduct of the Baptist is simply inexplicable, unless we assume with Mark that the voice was heard only by Jesus. (2) Luke's version, which closely agrees with Mark's, exhibits two variations. Luke adds that Jesus was praying, and that the Spirit descended 'in a bodily form.' The first of these additions may be adequately explained as an editorial inference intended for the edification of the readers; and the second, which makes the vision objective, is, like the voice in the first gospel, incompatible with the mission of John's messengers. We therefore conclude that Mark has preserved the original. The question, however, still remains, Was this narrative contained in the apostolic source? If the additional details which are given by Matthew and Luke represent a later belief, the second gospel was their only authority, and how can we argue from the presence of this narrative in the second gospel to its presence in the apostolic source? We can do so without any difficulty; for the earlier section on the preaching of the Baptist, which was admittedly contained in the source, demands as its sequel some association of the Baptist with Jesus, and the narrative of the Temptations, which can be shown to be apostolic, presupposes the Baptism.

§ 3.—*The Temptation in the Wilderness*

Mark's version of the Temptation in the Wilderness, as Weiss truly says, is 'scarcely intelligible' unless as an abridgment of a more detailed account. Since the second evangelist undoubtedly had no knowledge of our first and third gospels, the authority, he adds, which contained this account can only have been the apostolic source, lying at the foundation of these two gospels.[1] Other explanations are conceivable, but the one thus stated by Weiss is by far the most reasonable and convincing. For, in the first place, we may affirm without hesitation that if the temptation narrative presupposes the baptism of Jesus, the voice from heaven at the baptism equally demands as its sequel an account of specific temptations such as those recorded by Matthew and Luke. Mark's meagre version is a link without the pendant, an outline from which the contents have disappeared. And, secondly, on the supposition that Mark was acquainted with the larger narrative the meagreness of his version can be explained. It is not an

[1] *Introduction to the New Testament*, vol. ii. p. 248.

exceptional phenomenon. No allusion is made in the second gospel to the messengers who were sent by the Baptist with the question, 'Art thou he that cometh, or look we for another?' (Luke vii. 19). Wendt would probably account for this silence by his theory that Mark was not acquainted with the apostolic source; but whether Mark was acquainted with the apostolic source or not, no one can seriously maintain, with any degree of probability, that he had never heard of the incident. Why, then, has it been omitted? Not because he systematically omits the logia, for he records the sayings of Jesus when it suits his purpose to do so. The only satisfactory explanation is that he did not wish to put into his history anything which might convey the idea that the mission of Jesus was questionable; and precisely for this reason he omits the specific temptations.

a.—According to Matthew and Luke the proposals were made by the tempter at the end of the forty days; but this is probably a misconception. The later evangelists are combining the apostolic source with Mark, and they adopt the simplest method. They add at the end of Mark's statement the details which Mark has omitted.

b.—Since the temptation was purely personal, and not, as an ingenious writer has suggested, a proposal to provide bread for the people,[1] 'this stone' is probably the correct reading. The second clause of the quotation from Deut. viii. 3 may be an editorial enlargement. It is peculiar to Matthew. The later replies are curt and peremptory.

c.—The mountain-temptation has been placed second by Luke, probably to avoid the awkward transition from the wilderness to the Temple, and again from the Temple to a mountain, perhaps also to make the text, 'Thou shalt not tempt the Lord thy God,' the climax of the narrative. 'The holy city' is a secondary expression (cf. Matt. xxvii. 53).

d.—Luke here is distinctly secondary. An antithesis is no doubt involved between the kingdom of God and the kingdoms of the world. The sovereignty of the devil over the

[1] W. W. Peyton, *The Expositor*, 1889.

kingdoms of the world is recognised even in Matthew's version ; the ministry begins with a trial of strength. But Luke's version is too explanatory. It betrays, like the later addition, 'for a season' the interpreter or preacher who writes for the edification of the public. The ministry of angels has been omitted by Luke because it seems to him to be incompatible with the repudiation of angelic protection.

e.—A brief historical statement is added by all the evangelists. The change of residence, which is mentioned by Matthew alone, is authenticated by the fact that the home of Jesus had hitherto been in Nazareth (Mark i. 9 ; Luke ii. 4, 39, 51), and that henceforth his centre is Capernaum. The allusion in the first gospel to the fulfilment of prophecy (Matt. iv. 15, 16) is one of a series of such notes. It is certainly an editorial enlargement. The account of the early preaching has probably been preserved in its original form by Matthew. Mark's phrase, 'Believe in the gospel,' is an ecclesiastical paraphrase of the primary text. Luke omits the text altogether. He simply says that 'Jesus taught in their synagogues, being glorified of all' (Luke iv. 15); but he adds another text and a few notes of a sermon (Luke iv. 16-30). An editorial purpose is evident in this addition. He wishes to place as near the beginning of the ministry as possible an example of the preaching of Jesus and of the reception which He gained from the people. That the narrative of the rejection in Nazareth has been removed from its original context by Luke is proved quite conclusively by the fact that this narrative presupposes a residence and ministry in Capernaum (Luke iv. 23). The question whether 'the kingdom of heaven' or 'the kingdom of God' is the original expression has been much discussed by the critics. The prevalent opinion is in favour of 'the kingdom of God.' I am not at all sure that this opinion is justified by the evidence, but the subject need not at present be discussed. 'The kingdom of God' will be substituted in this volume for Matthew's 'kingdom of heaven,;' but in every text, without a single exception, the kingdom of God means the kingdom of heaven. According to Schurer and Wendt, Matthew's phrase is simply an illustration of the Jewish custom of using some circumlocution for the name of

God.[1] This may or may not be true; but in any case the kingdom of God as proclaimed by Jesus is a kingdom which has not merely its perfect realisation in heaven, but is not and never will be realised on the earth. It is always an anticipation, and never an accomplished fact, and its coming is identified with the second coming of Messiah to be the Judge of men and to take His disciples to their reward. 'In my Father's house are many mansions: if it were not so, I would have told you; for I go to prepare a place for you. And if I go and prepare a place for you, I come again and will receive you unto myself; that where I am, there ye may be also' (John xiv. 2, 3). This text though Johannine is a faithful translation of the teaching contained in the apostolic source.

§ 4.—*The Call of the Four Disciples*

An interesting study is presented by the narrative now before us. Matthew's version agrees verbally with Mark's. Luke's version, on the other hand, if not altogether, is largely independent (Luke v. 1–11); and since as a rule in such cases he follows the apostolic source, there is reason to believe *a priori* that he does so on this occasion. But the critics are of quite a different opinion. Wendt omits the narrative entirely; he excludes even the version of Mark from his reconstruction of the apostolic source. Weiss, again, who maintains that Luke derives his material, not from two sources, but from three, concludes that the call of the disciples is a narrative taken from the third, with features of Mark's version interwoven.[2] That the apostolic source contained at least a similar narrative is exceedingly probable, and is not disputed by Wendt; and since two versions have been preserved we may fairly place one of them in our reconstruction, reserving the whole subject of the origin of the second gospel. But the question is, Which one? What are the features of Luke's version which distinguish it from the narratives of the apostolic source, or make its authenticity doubtful?

(1) The context is indisputably secondary. The rejection

[1] *The Teaching of Jesus* (Wendt), vol. i. p. 371.
[2] *Introduction to the New Testament*, vol. ii. p. 296.

in Nazareth has already been substituted by Luke for Mark's version of the call of the four (Luke iv. 16-30). The apostolic source contained, as we have seen, a brief statement of the removal from Nazareth to Capernaum (Matt. iv. 13). Luke therefore passes immediately from the rejection in Nazareth to the Capernaum incidents in the second gospel (Luke iv. 31-44). At the first available opportunity he returns to record the incident omitted. His editing can be followed quite clearly, and the inference is involved that Mark's context is original—a conclusion which is confirmed by the allusion to Simon in Luke iv. 38, for this allusion implies that Simon had already been called; in other words, that the context in which Luke places the call is distinctly editorial. (2) The introductory details resemble so closely the account given by Mark of a later incident which also happened at the Sea of Galilee, that their originality may be fairly suspected (Luke v. 1-3, cf. Mark iv. 1). (3) In the fourth gospel appendix a miraculous draught of fishes is recorded, which is parallel to the miracle in the narrative now before us (John xxi. 6). If the appendix was written by a later editor and not by the author of the fourth gospel, as there is reason to believe, and if Luke's version of the call is an account of the same event as the call recorded by Mark—which is critically indisputable—the miracle in question represents a floating tradition, the details of which were uncertain, and its claim to be regarded as an integral element of the narrative in the apostolic source is correspondingly diminished. The conjecture indeed is perfectly legitimate that the tradition arose from the parable of the Draw Net (Matt. xiii. 47, 48). In this connection another fact should be noted. The fishes, according to Luke, were forsaken (Luke v. 11). Was the miracle, then, intended to be simply didactic? In such a case we are very near the explanation suggested by J. Estlin Carpenter, who believes that the narrative is an allegory, which embodies ecclesiastical reflection on the subject of the mission to the Gentiles.[1] (4) Peter's exclamation, 'Depart from me, for I am a sinful man, O Lord' (Luke v. 8), is open to the serious objection that it is scarcely in accordance with the

[1] *The First Three Gospels*, pp. 206-208.

elementary faith of the disciples. (5) The narrative contains no sayings such as those which authenticate Luke's account of the rejection in Nazareth as a genuine apostolic tradition. For these reasons we must conclude that Luke's version of the call is secondary, and that the theory of a third source, as far as this narrative is concerned, is altogether unnecessary.

§ 5.—*The Sermon on the Mount*

The Sermon on the Mount is the *pons asinorum* of the gospels. Here the difficulty begins, and success or failure is determined. Two preliminary questions demand consideration. (1) In the first gospel the Sermon immediately follows the call of the four disciples : in the third it is placed somewhat later. Have we any means of determining which of the evangelists has preserved the original connection ? At first sight the evidence appears to be in favour of Luke ; for the second gospel is the standard of each evangelist, and Matthew places the Sermon in an historical situation which breaks the sequence of Mark (Mark i. 21), whereas in the third gospel it follows the healing of the man with the withered hand—a position in which Mark seems to have found it (Mark iii. 7-19, cf. Luke vi. 12-18 ; Matt. iv. 23-v. 1). If Mark really had the Sermon before him when he recorded the names of the twelve (Mark iii. 13-19), and if his sequence is reliable, the inference is inevitable that Matthew has broken the original order for the sake of an editorial purpose. But the student who examines the subject more closely will arrive, I think, at a different conclusion. It is perfectly conceivable, and not antecedently improbable, that Matthew, for the sake of affording near the beginning of his gospel a comprehensive view of the teaching of Jesus, should have thus transferred the Sermon from a later to an earlier position ; but the fact must not be overlooked that from the preaching of the Baptist to the Sermon on the Mount he is indebted for at least some of his material to the apostolic source. The preaching of the Baptist and the narrative of the temptations have not, as we have seen, been taken from Mark ; and although the baptism of Jesus and the call of the disciples, as far as internal evi-

THE SERMON ON THE MOUNT

dence permits us to judge, may be narratives borrowed from the second gospel, they may quite as well be from the other source. The question therefore arises, Have we any reason to suppose that Mark has rearranged the original? If a theory can be repeated into truth, the second is the chronological gospel; but if facts possess any weight, the balance mocks the theologians. At present we must confine our attention to the limited subject before us. Have we any reason to believe that Mark in this particular section of the history confirms the Papias tradition by lack of chronological sequence? According to the apostolic source Jesus left Nazareth after the imprisonment of the Baptist, and dwelt in Capernaum by the sea. Mark does not record this statement, but he alludes incidentally to the fact that before the baptism Jesus had lived in Nazareth (Mark i. 9), and after the call of the four he relates a few incidents which happened in Capernaum (Mark i. 21-39). The section which follows in his history is without articulation of place or time (Mark i. 39-iii. 6). The transition from one narrative to another is in every case indefinite (Mark i. 40; ii. 1, 13, 18, 23; iii. 1)—a fact which is worthy of notice since the earlier transitions are precise (Mark i. 12, 14, 21, 29, 32, 35). A link of thought-connection is, however, quite apparent; for the narratives of which the section is composed illustrate, without exception, the relation of Jesus to the law and to its official representatives. Now thought-connection like this between historical incidents which are not otherwise consecutive may be confidently recognised as editorial; and the internal evidence, as we shall see, forbids the supposition that these incidents happened at the beginning of the ministry (Mark ii. 15, 20; iii. 6). The Sermon on the Mount, if represented by the names of the twelve (Mark iii. 13-19), might accordingly be originally situated before the section in question, that is, before Mark i. 40; and from this situation to the earlier one, in which the Sermon is placed by Matthew, there is only another step which is justified by the step already taken, and is indeed made necessary by the context (Mark i. 38, 39). We may therefore provisionally conclude, reserving the second gospel for discussion in detail, that Mark's order is not chronological; that Luke, who follows Mark in placing the mountain-discourse after the healing of the man with the withered hand, adopts a secondary sequence; and that Matthew has preserved the original historical situation. (2) The next question is, What was the subject of the Sermon? If the first gospel is primary in contents as well as in connection, this question may be answered at once; for Matthew's version consists chiefly of an elaborate comparison between the old law and the new, and the subject may be stated generally as 'The Righteousness of the Kingdom of God.' But a right connection is not a guarantee of the contents: the two questions must be kept distinct. Matthew, again, may in many cases exhibit the primary text, and yet the contents of Luke's version may be a nearer approximation to the contents of the Sermon in the source. We are not at present concerned with details of expression, but simply with the constituent teaching. What, then, is the comparative value of the versions? If the Cambridge 'Companion to the Bible' may be taken to represent the opinion which prevails among English scholars, they accept Matthew's version as the standard. The statement is confidently made by the author of the section on the gospel history, that analysis exhibits 'the orderly arrangement of a set discourse, which refutes the theory that the Sermon is a collection by St. Matthew of words of the Lord spoken at different times.'[1] The scholars of England have frequently been reproached for lack of critical discrimination, and unfortunately the indictment is so far true that, with few exceptions, in the case at least of the New Testament they have not cultivated critical study. The opinion e.g. which has been adopted by the Cambridge University Press is one which at the present day a critic might excusably ignore. I do not maintain, and no critic will maintain, that the Sermon on the Mount in Matthew's version is altogether a mere collection of sayings; but the orderly arrangement to which this writer refers, instead of refuting the theory that the sayings in Matthew's version have been detached in some cases from their original context, is rather so distinctly artificial as to refute the Cambridge opinion. The discourse is full of surprises. The connection

[1] *The Cambridge Companion to the Bible*, p. 185.

is occasionally by no means obvious (Matt. vii. 6, 7, 12, 15). A few passages are repeated by the evangelist in a later context (Matt. v. 31, 32, cf. xix. 9; vii. 17, 18, cf. xii. 33). One of the Baptist's sayings has been put into the mouth of Jesus (Matt. iii. 10, cf. vii. 19). Many of the allusions are incomprehensible at the beginning of the ministry (e.g. Matt. v. 17, 20; vi. 1; vii. 6). Luke's version is altogether unintelligible if Matthew has added nothing to the original; for the omissions in the third gospel do not consist merely 'of passages bearing on the Jewish law and therefore less applicable to Gentile readers.'[1] On the contrary, Luke omits passages which can only be related to the Jewish law by a process of exegetical imagination (Matt. v. 5, 8, 9, 14, 23, 24; vii. 6), and adopts other passages the relation of which to the Jewish law is unmistakable (Matt. v. 38-48, cf. Luke vi. 27-36), and introduces several sayings at a later time in such a way as to prove that they were not originally in the Sermon on the Mount (Matt. v. 13, cf. Luke xiv. 34, 35; Matt. v. 15, cf. Luke xi. 33; Matt. v. 18, cf. Luke xvi. 17; Matt. v. 25, 26, cf. Luke xii. 58, 59; Matt. v. 32, cf. Luke xvi. 18; Matt. vi. 9-13, cf. Luke xi. 1-4; Matt. vi. 22, 23, cf. Luke xi. 34-36; Matt. vi. 24, cf. Luke xvi. 13; Matt. vi. 25-33, cf. Luke xii. 22-31; Matt. vii. 7-11, cf. Luke xi. 9-13; Matt. vii. 13, 14, cf. Luke xiii. 24; Matt. vii. 22, 23, cf. Luke xiii. 25-27). And, finally, the supposition that the Sermon in Matthew's version is to some extent a collection of sayings, if refuted by the Cambridge Press, possesses the singular merit of being generally accepted by the critics. Weiss and Wendt, who seldom agree with one another, and differ here as usual in details, represent the general opinion when they maintain that Matthew's version is an enlargement and Luke's an abridgment of the original.

In his reconstruction of the source Wendt omits from Matthew's version the following passages: Matt. v. 13-16, 25, 26, 29[b], 30; vi. 7-15, 19-34; vii. 6-11, 13, 14, 20, 22, 23.[2] When these passages are eliminated and placed in their proper context (Wendt places some of them in an appendix,

---

[1] *The Cambridge Companion to the Bible*, p. 185.
[2] *Die Lehre Jesu*, Erster Theil, S. 52-70.

as logia gone astray), the subject of the Sermon still remains 'the Righteousness of the Kingdom of God.' On this point Wendt is emphatic and clear, and indeed he has few opponents. He seems, however, to be aware of a somewhat serious difficulty; for incidentally he betrays the consciousness that the Sermon, as reconstructed by him, is not adapted to its environment. 'It is possible,' he says, 'that the author of the logia (or apostolic) source placed the Sermon at the beginning on account of the significance of its contents.'[1]

Let us look at this confession for a little. A discourse on the subject of Righteousness, containing an elaborate comparison between the old law and the new, is supposed to have been delivered by Jesus soon after the call of the four disciples. No event can be found to suggest the discourse, for the call of the twelve is insufficient. The disciples could not be prepared for such an elaborate instruction. Their faith was immature: they scarcely believed that their Master was the Christ. They had not been called for the immediate purpose of proclaiming the gospel to their countrymen. They could not have formed any idea, which required to be elaborately corrected, regarding Christ's relation to the law (Matt. v. 17). They had not yet been confronted by the antagonism of the official representatives of Judaism: the conflicts with the Pharisees were later. The whole supposition is beset with improbabilities, and the possibility suggested by Wendt is prudent in the circumstances. But surely there is another possibility, which is that Wendt is mistaken, that the reconstruction which sets free a few sayings to be ultimately imprisoned in an appendix confines a large number of sayings in a Sermon to which they are foreign. In other words, the contents of Luke's version may represent with approximate fidelity the original contents of the Sermon. In venturing to maintain this opinion we leave the good company of the critics, but analysis will justify the departure; and this at least is certain, that Luke's version is historically intelligible. The Sermon was directly suggested by the imprisonment of the Baptist and by the call of the twelve. Its subject is, 'The true Prophet.' The false prophet may be judged by his popu-

[1] *Die Lehre Jesu*, Erster Theil, S. 190.

larity. All men speak well of him because he flatters their prejudices. The true prophet, on the other hand, is a man who has never been popular. He is like John the Baptist. The people may flock to hear him, but they flock as quickly away. They do not accept his message. They do not respect his person. His credentials are not signs and wonders, but rather the truth which he speaks and the correspondent truth which he lives. He is not a reed nor a courtier. He is poor and hungry and sad, reproached and hated and persecuted. He resists not him that is evil. He believes in God, who is good. He manifests the love of God. He is merciful, as the Father is merciful. He does unto others as he would that others should do to him, and he does this without reciprocity; for what the others do to him is what he would do to no man. Hold yourselves away from the false prophets—so Jesus says to His disciples—do not be like unto them. They may wear the skin of a sheep, but inwardly they are ravening wolves. Be attentive to that which is within; for out of the abundance of the heart the mouth speaketh. Dig deep, and lay a foundation—not on the sand of popular opinion, but on the rock of the truth of God ; and so, when the rain descends, and the rivers break into flood, and the winds blow wild and beat down high things in the day of the wrath of God, your house will be able to stand.

The Sermon in Luke's version is homogeneous, and fits into the historical situation.

a.—We omit for three reasons the statement regarding the great number of people who followed Jesus to hear Him and to be healed of their diseases. (1) No words or works have yet been recorded to account for the presence of these people. (2) The Sermon, according to the explicit testimony of both Matthew and Luke, was addressed to the twelve (Luke vi. 20; Matt. v. 1, 2), and the teaching presupposes that the hearers had been recently called to undertake a prophetic mission (Luke vi. 23–26; Matt. vii. 15). (3) The statement in question is parallel to one in the second gospel which is, as will be shown, of a composite nature—a combination of two statements originally distinct, one of them preceding the Sermon in the source, and the other preceding the parable of the Sower (Mark iii. 7-19). We conclude that Matthew and Luke have combined the two statements like Mark, and that the people were assembled on the later occasion. At the end of the Sermon, Matthew adds a few words which he takes from another connection in Mark (Matt. vii. 28, 29, cf. Mark i. 22), and his method is similar at the beginning. Expanding the Sermon, he also enlarges the audience. He thinks that so important a manifesto could not be addressed merely to the disciples. For this reason, as well as for editorial convenience, he carries forward the names of the twelve to the narrative of their subsequent mission (Matt. x. 1-5). That they were really called earlier is proved by Matt. x. 1.

b.—Two facts of a general nature become apparent at once to the reader who compares the two versions of the Beatitudes. The first is that in Matthew's version they are better fitted than in Luke's for the edification of believers, and the second is that the woes are peculiar to Luke's version. Three inferences are possible: (1) that Matthew has preserved the original text, (2) that Luke's version represents the original in which the woes were included, (3) that although Luke on the whole has preserved the original, the woes are a later addition. The fact that the Beatitudes in the first gospel are better fitted than those in Luke for the edification of believers, while not in itself conclusive, tends certainly to favour the supposition that the text of Luke is primary; and the evidence becomes quite convincing if Luke's text can be shown to be required by the historical situation, and if Matthew's variations can be accounted for in each particular case. Now obviously the Beatitudes in the first gospel are singularly free from any connection with the history. There is nothing whatever to prepare for them. They are not retrospective but anticipatory. Luke's text, on the other hand, is as clearly conditioned by the occasion, for the twelve had just been called to be prepared for a special mission, and four at least of their number had become poor for the sake of the kingdom. Again, the Baptist, who was a true prophet and an illustrious example for the prophets, had been recently imprisoned by Herod. The Baptist had been hungry and poor. Like the ancient prophets, he had been hated and reproached, and his name had been cast out as evil; but his reward would be great in heaven. It is perfectly obvious that the allusion to the false prophets, contained even in the version of Matthew, could not be addressed to the people from Galilee, and Decapolis, and Jerusalem, and Judæa, and from beyond Jordan; for these people were not prophets and never would be, and the words are unintelligible unless we take for granted that the persons addressed had been called by Jesus to undertake a prophetic mission. They were the spiritual descendants, the later representatives of the prophets; and since history repeats itself, and had been repeated in the case of John the Baptist, they could not expect to escape persecution unless by being unfaithful to their calling. The history demands Luke's version. The facts above mentioned enable us indeed to go farther and affirm that the woes which are really inseparable from the text are also most appropriate to the occasion; for the rich are not denounced because they are rich nor the popular because they are popular, but the prophet who, unlike the Baptist, is rich and successful and happy, is declared to be a false prophet (cf. Matt. vii. 15). The statement has frequently been made that Ebionism underlies Luke's text. If this statement means that, according to Luke's version of the Beatitudes, the poor, just because they are poor, are the heirs of the kingdom of God, it is simply a blunder—excusable, perhaps, but nevertheless a blunder; for the persons addressed were poor prophets, and the aim of Jesus was to comfort and instruct His disciples, who had given up such wealth as they had for the sake of their higher calling, and who might be in danger of concluding that they had made a mistake. The suspicion that Luke's text is Ebionitic has induced many scholars to decide in favour of Matthew; but the truth rather is that Matthew has altered the original, not merely for the sake of edification, but also, and more specifically, to avoid the erroneous inferences which Luke's text might conceivably suggest. He does this systematically, as we shall see farther on. The poor become thus the poor in spirit. The hungry become those who hunger and thirst after righteousness. The hated and unpopular and despised become those who are persecuted for righteousness' sake. The woes are omitted altogether; and the original number of clauses is made up by the addition of other four Beatitudes derived from the Sermon which follows. The blessedness of the meek, the merciful, the pure in heart, the peacemakers, has been inferred from the teaching which must now be examined in detail.

c.—Of the section Matt. v. 13-37, which we have omitted from the text, Wendt omits vv. 13-16, 25, 26, 29^b, 30. He does this not only because the passages in question are doubtfully adapted to Matthew's context, but also because another context demands them. For precisely the same reasons we omit the whole of the section. The declaration on the subject of the relation of the kingdom to the law and the prophets, with which Wendt begins the Sermon after the introductory Beatitudes (vv. 17-20), is no more connected with the Beatitudes than the earlier verses rejected by him (vv. 13-16). If the subject of the Sermon was righteousness, and especially the new righteousness in relation to the old, the warning, 'Think not that I came to destroy the law or the prophets,' forms undoubtedly a suitable beginning; but the subject of the Sermon can only be determined by criticism, and since the whole section can be placed in a more suitable context, and indeed in a context which demands each different member, Wendt's method requires us to look for another beginning. For the sake of avoiding repetition, the passages omitted will not be discussed at present, but the reader may depend upon finding them when the proper time comes. We have now simply to notice the connection between the introductory Beatitudes and the beginning of the Sermon in Luke's version. The disciples have been taught as sons of the prophets to expect persecution like the Baptist. How are they to endure persecution? The question immediately arises; and the answer delivered immediately is, 'Resist not him that is evil.' The details of expression in Luke's version demand the most careful attention. He puts out of sight the antithesis between the old law and the new. The word 'but,' however, with which the section begins (Luke vi. 27), shows clearly that he had it before him. He begins with the precept, 'Love your enemies;' but that this is a secondary beginning is proved: (1) by the verse which immediately follows (ver. 29);

(2) by the repetition of the precept in ver. 35; (3) by the general incoherence of the section, which shows that the original order has been somehow disturbed; (4) by the fact that a reason can be given for the omission of the precept, 'Resist not him that is evil.' The reason is to be found in the history of the Church; for the statement has frequently been made, from the earliest times to these days in which Tolstoi has appeared, that Jesus taught the doctrine of non-resistance. Luke wishes to avoid this inference, and therefore he omits the saying. The inference, however, as generally maintained, is certainly illegitimate; for, in the first place, the persons addressed were the future apostles, who had renounced the ordinary duties of life for the sake of their special calling, and the urgency of whose mission detached them from the social obligation to defend the right and redress the wrong; and secondly, the teaching of Jesus is determined throughout by the speedy coming of the heavenly kingdom. He does not anticipate a long historical development. On the contrary, He proclaims unequivocally that the great Day of Judgment will soon overwhelm evildoers, who need not therefore be resisted. Do not waste time in attending to such matters as personal dignity—so He says virtually to His disciples—do not even take into account the evil involved in the temporary triumph of the wrong-doer. Your mission is urgent, and the authority which I give you is for building up: it is not for casting down. The kingdom of God is at hand, and when the kingdom comes, the word which is written will be fulfilled, 'Vengeance is mine: I will repay, saith the Lord.'

The coat ($\chi\iota\tau\acute{\omega}\nu$) might be claimed by a creditor, but the cloke ($\iota\mu\acute{a}\tau\iota o\nu$) was protected by law: it could not be legally alienated. Matthew's text is therefore clearly the original. The meaning is, Abandon every legal right rather than go to law. Do not allow yourselves to be protected. Surrender your property voluntarily. The words 'Ask them not again' (Luke vi. 30) prove that the case is one of borrowing as in Matthew, and not as in Luke of theft or compulsion.

d.—The question, 'If ye love them that love you, what thank have ye?' (Luke vi. 32) clearly presupposes the general precept, 'Love your enemies.' Luke omits this precept because he has already placed it at the beginning of the section (ver. 27). He now substitutes the golden rule (ver. 31). The antithesis between the old law and the new, if presupposed by the word 'but' at the beginning, must certainly have introduced this later section. We reach, therefore, the text of Matthew. The following variations in Luke's version should be noted. He substitutes the word 'thank' for 'reward' ($\chi\acute{a}\rho\iota s$ for $\mu\iota\sigma\theta\acute{o}s$), to avoid the least appearance of legalism (ver. 32). He substitutes 'sinners' for 'publicans,' and again 'sinners' for 'the Gentiles,' to avoid occasions of stumbling (vv. 32, 33). He exercises himself always like Paul to have a conscience void of offence. Again, he substitutes 'sons of the Most High' for 'sons of your Father,' converting an ethical condition into a title of dignity (ver. 35). Afterwards he uses the word 'Father,' which was therefore undoubtedly in the original (ver. 36). He also changes 'He maketh his sun to rise on the evil and the good, and sendeth rain on the just and the unjust,' into 'He is kind toward the unthankful and the evil,' distinguishing thus, but perhaps not intentionally, the God of grace from the God of nature (ver. 35). All these variations are secondary. Matthew, on the other hand, has probably omitted Luke vi. 34, which is required to complete the parallelism (cf. Matt. v. 42). The whole section concludes with a precept which is rendered by Luke thus : 'Be ye merciful, even as your Father is merciful' (ver. 36), whereas Matthew's text is, 'Ye therefore shall be perfect, as your heavenly Father is perfect' (Matt. v. 48). We prefer Luke's text for two reasons : (1) because 'merciful' ($o\iota\kappa\tau\acute{\iota}\rho\mu o\nu\epsilon s$) is a more definite word than 'perfect' ($\tau\acute{\epsilon}\lambda\epsilon\iota o\iota$), and agrees better with the teaching in the discourse ; (2) because Matthew, having already converted Luke's text into one of the introductory Beatitudes, has now a special reason for enlarging the significance of the original. The precept in the first gospel stands at the end of a division, and constitutes an appropriate climax.

e.—The connection so far is clear, and the discourse in Luke's version, when the secondary variations are corrected, agrees perfectly with the historical situation ; but the sequel is a little more obscure. The section Matt. vi. 1–34 is entirely absent from Luke's version. Has Matthew enlarged, or has Luke abridged, the original? Wendt omits from this section vv. 7–15, 19–34, because these verses are doubtfully connected in the Sermon, and are demanded by other contexts. For precisely these reasons we omit the whole of the section. We come, therefore, again to Luke's sequel, and the question arises, What is the thought-connection? The disciples have been taught to love their enemies. In a later passage they are instructed to hate their friends (Luke xiv. 26). To love their enemies and hate their friends—clearly a paradoxical combination! The love is defined by the hatred. The meaning is, on the one hand, that there are higher interests than those of friendship, and, on the other hand, that the motions of mere private resentment, proceeding, as they do, from inordinate love of oneself, must be repressed and guarded against. The measure of a man's love for himself must be the measure of his love for an enemy. 'Thou shalt love thy neighbour as thyself.' But, obviously, if truth and goodness occupy the first place in our affections, if we love God with all our heart and soul and strength and mind, our disposition and conduct towards an enemy will be largely determined by what manner of man he is. If his enmity is not merely a personal matter between him and us, but if he is also, and manifestly, the enemy of truth and goodness, we can scarcely even love him as ourselves. Yes, but then how difficult it is to judge correctly the motives of men, and to form a true estimate of their life! Judgment is immutable, and must be; for truth is different from error, and goodness is different from sin, and the perfection of the heavenly Father consists both in justice and love. But who art thou, O man, that thou shouldest judge thy neighbour? Evil and error exist in thee, and yet thou lovest thyself. Why beholdest thou the mote that is in thy brother's eye, but considerest not the beam that is in thine own eye? Thou hypocrite, cast out first the beam out of thine own eye, and then shalt thou see clearly to cast out the mote out of thy brother's eye. Such was the teaching of Jesus. Reflection reveals a clear thought-connection. We may even confidently affirm that the precept, 'Love your enemies,' demands as its sequel the section which follows in Luke's version. The text has, however, unquestionably been preserved more faithfully by Matthew. The addition in Luke vi. 37, 38 is probably not original. The first clause of ver. 38 is not quite compatible with the second. According to the first clause a greater, according to the second an equal, measure will be returned; and the whole Sermon clearly presupposes that the disciples must expect suffering and persecution instead of reciprocity in kindness. The recompense promised is from God, not from man (cf. vv. 20-23). The parable of the blind guides has, according to Weiss, been preserved by Luke in its original connection (ver. 39);[1] but the context in the first gospel is much more appropriate (Matt. xv. 14), and we may provisionally conclude that Luke has placed this fragment in the Sermon on the Mount to prepare for the parable of the Mote and the Beam. Luke vi. 40 must also be pronounced an interpolation: the true context will afterwards appear. We conclude the section with the golden rule for three reasons: (1) because the situation proposed is the most appropriate; (2) because Luke has already substituted this saying for the precept, 'Love your enemies' (ver. 31); (3) because in Matthew's version it really occupies the position proposed, ch. vii. 6-11 being one of Matthew's interpolations.

f.—This section begins impossibly in the third gospel, ' For there is no good tree that bringeth forth corrupt fruit; nor again a corrupt tree that bringeth forth good fruit' (ver. 43). We therefore turn to Matthew's version. The original context of Matt. vii. 6-11, 13, 14 will afterwards be discovered. Omitting these verses, we reach the warning against false prophets (ver. 15). Now obviously this warning is appropriate in the Sermon on the Mount, being simply a return to the beginning. It confirms, indeed, the result of our analysis; for it makes the teaching rounded, and enables us to detect interpolations. The Sermon is essentially a contrast between the wolfish spirit of the false prophet and the merciful spirit of the true; and the additional teaching in Matthew's version is foreign to the subject. The warning against false prophets does not mean, Beware of the teaching of such prophets. The meaning rather is that the disciples of Jesus, being prophets themselves, must

[1] *Introduction to the New Testament*, vol. ii. p. 293.

make and keep themselves true. The Master therefore concludes His discourse by stating in figurative language two laws of the spirit of life, 'A good tree cannot bring forth evil fruit, neither can a corrupt tree bring forth good fruit.' You live what you inly are, and cannot live what you are not. What is in a man will come out, and you cannot get out what is not in. This is the law of moral uniformity. But man is not a thistle or a thorn that he should not be able to bear good fruit. He is a soil, and the gospel is a seed. He is a builder, who can choose his foundation, and build on the sand or on the rock, for time or for eternity, for the world or for the kingdom of God; and a day is coming which will test man's work, whether it be good or evil. This is the law of responsibility. We omit Matt. vii. 19 because this verse has been borrowed from the preaching of the Baptist (Matt. iii. 10), and because it does not lead to the conclusion, 'Therefore by their fruits ye shall know them' (Matt. vii. 20). Luke vi. 45 is probably here in its original context as an application or interpretation of the preceding instruction. Matthew records this saying after the casting out of an unclean spirit (Matt. xii. 35).

g.—The Sermon concludes in each version with the parable of the Builders. Matt. vii. 22, 23 has been detached from another context, as we shall afterwards see. Luke vi. 46 is obviously secondary: (1) because the disciples at this early period were not accustomed to say, 'Lord, Lord,' without obeying their Master; (2) because the text in the third gospel is an abstract from Matthew's more appropriate version (Matt. vii. 21).

§ 6.—*The Healing of the Centurion's Son*

That Luke has preserved the sequence of the source in recording this miracle immediately after the Sermon on the Mount can scarcely be doubted. Matthew's narrative of the leper, like the version already recorded by Luke, has been taken from the second gospel (Mark i. 40–45; Matt. viii. 1-4; Luke v. 12–16); and the centurion story follows. The two witnesses therefore agree. The healing of the nobleman's son is generally considered to be another version of the same incident (John iv. 46–54), and Wendt in his reconstruction of the apostolic source from the narratives of Matthew and

Luke substitutes the word 'son' for 'servant.' In the third gospel the man is a bondservant, δοῦλος (Luke vii. 2, 3, 10), whereas the word used by Matthew is παῖς (Matt. viii. 6, 8, 13), and is distinguished from δοῦλος (Matt. viii. 9). Now παῖς may mean a servant; but since Matthew has made the distinction, and the word in the fourth gospel is 'son,' and Luke uses the word παῖς as well as δοῦλος (Luke vii. 7), we must conclude with Wendt that the latter word is secondary. In his analysis of the details Wendt is, however, unreliable. He combines the two versions in such a way as to mutilate the narrative of Luke. His reconstruction consists of the following passages:[1] Matt. viii. 5, 6; Luke vii. 4, 5; Matt. viii. 7-10, 13. He thus inserts in the midst of Matthew's narrative two verses borrowed from Luke; and these, instead of being words spoken by the messengers who were sent by the centurion (Luke vii. 4), are supposed to have been spoken by the spectators when the centurion himself went to Jesus. But this is an arbitrary supposition. It is not permitted by Luke's version, the language of which is explicit, and indeed it is rendered distinctly improbable by the sequel in Wendt's reconstruction; for he omits two verses from Matthew's account (Matt. viii. 11, 12), and he does not perceive that the addition of these verses by Matthew from a later context necessarily involves the exclusion of the messengers from the narrative. The two verses added by Matthew are certainly not here in their original context. But Matthew introduces these verses, and they demand the exclusion of the messengers; for these messengers were elders of the Jews who earnestly interceded for the Gentile (Luke vii. 3), and according to Matthew's addition the sons of the kingdom—in other words, such men as these elders—would be cast forth into outer darkness. The one passage is incompatible with the other, but Matthew's addition is editorial; we must therefore conclude that the messengers were in the original—a conclusion which is confirmed by the fourth gospel (John iv. 51). The reader should also notice that the frequently alleged Ebionism of the source or of Luke himself is contradicted by the narrative before us; for the centurion

---

[1] *Die Lehre Jesu*, Erster Theil, S. 70-72.

was a rich man, and yet he was a good man, one who out of the good treasure of his heart produced good things.

§ 7.—*The Raising of the Widow's Son*

The critics seem generally reluctant to admit that this narrative was contained in the apostolic source. Weiss e.g. expresses the opinion that Luke has taken the narrative from his third source,[1] an authority which probably never existed outside of the critic's imagination. The hypothesis is quite unnecessary. 'The incident seems to owe its place,' according to J. Estlin Carpenter, 'to the evangelist's desire to prepare the way for the statement in ver. 22, "the dead are raised up;" and the language of its sequel, ver. 16, implies that it has been modelled on prophetic example.'[2] With the influence of prophetic example we are not at present concerned, as the question is: Can we trace the narrative to the source, or must we, on the other hand, regard it as a purely editorial interpolation? Mr. Carpenter seems to favour the second alternative. Wendt, again, who is always interesting and frequently acute, rejects the incident entirely, with the remark that we do not know from what source Luke derived it.[3] He urges two objections against the supposition that it was contained in the apostolic source. In the first place, he points out the publicity of the miracle, and the different character of the miracles in Mark (Mark i. 43; v. 37-43; vii. 33, 36; viii. 23, 26); and since Mark, as he thinks, has undoubtedly preserved the original tradition in the shrinking of Jesus from publicity, he argues that Luke's narrative is secondary. And, secondly, he accounts for the interpolation, like J. Estlin Carpenter, by the evangelist's desire to illustrate the saying, 'Go your way, and tell John the things which ye do hear and see: the blind receive their sight, and the lame walk, the lepers are cleansed, and the deaf hear, and the dead are raised up, and the poor have good tidings preached to them' (Matt. xi. 4, 5; Luke vii. 22). Luke, he points out, has prefixed to this saying

---
[1] *Introduction to the New Testament*, vol. ii. p. 297.
[2] *The First Three Gospels*, p. 197.
[3] *Die Lehre Jesu*, Erster Theil, S. 73.

the editorial statement, 'In that hour he cured many of diseases and plagues and evil spirits; and on many that were blind he bestowed sight' (Luke vii. 21); and since the evangelist could not insert in the same context the narrative of the raising of the widow's son, an illustration which came somehow to his hands, Wendt argues ingeniously that the miracle has been carried back one step. To this plausible argument there are serious objections. The critic has allowed himself to be deceived. We need not press the objection that the miracles in the second gospel are not invariably represented as having been wrought in private, or that Jesus, according to Mark, did not invariably require that no report should be spread (Mark v. 19). But the assumption that Mark, in making prominent this feature of the miracles, has preserved the apostolic tradition, must not be too readily granted. In relation to the first and third gospels the second is certainly primary, but the conclusion does not follow that Mark is an independent and reliable authority. The absence of publicity in the second gospel is not in itself an argument against publicity in the apostolic source; for the two sources may surely exhibit different characteristics, and the presence of this element in the apostolic source may quite as well be an argument against the apostolicity of Mark. The question is one of fact, and if Wendt's contention is to be admitted, it must be for a different reason. We therefore pass to his second objection. He believes that the historical statement in Luke vii. 21 is an editorial inference drawn from the reply of Jesus to the messengers sent by John. The absence of this statement from Matthew's report, as well as the improbability that many suffering from blindness and diseases and plagues and evil spirits should be so conveniently assembled, is in favour of Wendt's opinion; and, since Luke has interpolated the statement, why should not the narrative of the raising of the dead be also an editorial interpolation? To this we may reply that there is surely an important difference between the statement and the narrative in question. The statement may be purely editorial, but the narrative is not likely to have been invented by Luke. It presupposes a source. Wendt does not assert the contrary, and as long as he does not tell us from what source the narrative has been derived we are justified in assuming that the authority which Luke has been following since the Sermon on the Mount is here again reproduced. But the narrative has, perhaps, been removed by Luke from another context in the source. Have we any reason to believe that the original sequence has been preserved? If the statement, 'The dead are raised up' (Luke vii. 22), might suggest the interpolation of the narrative, the narrative might quite as well, on the other hand, suggest the later statement; and, indeed, the second is the more probable hypothesis. For the reply of Jesus to the messengers sent by John was evidently an allusion to an ancient prophecy (Isa. xxxv. 5, 6; lxi. 1), and in this prophecy there is no mention whatever of the raising of the dead. I do not maintain that the statement in question was not in the apostolic source when first it was committed to writing, but I venture to suggest as a probability that in the original tradition the prophecy was quoted, and that the early Christians adapted it to its situation in the traditional gospel. In such a case the narrative of the raising of the dead has been preserved by Luke in its original context. Again, a journey in the direction of Nain at this particular time is required by the progress of the history. Matthew omits both the journey and the miracle; he keeps us still in Capernaum (Matt. viii. 14). But Matthew is combining the apostolic source with Mark, and the incidents which follow in his history have been chiefly taken from the second gospel. Luke, on the other hand, who has laid Mark aside in the meantime, takes us from Capernaum to Nain, and then he introduces the messengers from John; and the sequel presupposes a visit to Jerusalem. This statement will be verified when we reach the later narratives.

§ 8.—*John sends Messengers*

a.—John the Baptist had been imprisoned by Herod in Machærus, a fortress east of the Dead Sea. He heard a report, not of the particular miracles before mentioned, as Luke says for the sake of connection, but rather quite generally of the works of Jesus (Matt. xi. 2), and he sent messengers

106   A CRITICAL RECONSTRUCTION OF THE TEXT

to verify the news. He had not already recognised and proclaimed that Jesus was the Christ. Wendt, following Scholten, suggests that the word δύο in Luke's version is a secondary reading for διά (Matt. xi. 2) ;[1] but διά may quite as well be a secondary reading for δύο, and the Johannine tradition that the Baptist sent two of his disciples to Jesus confirms the number in the third gospel (John i. 35). Luke vii. 21 is an editorial inference. That Jesus did not intend this text to be a recital of miracles but rather of the spiritual blessings which Messiah would bring is proved: (1) by the fact that the messengers who were instructed to tell John what they heard and saw did not see all the miracles mentioned; (2) by the similar text quoted in Nazareth and followed by an announcement which was rejected on account of the absence of miracles (Luke iv. 16–30); (3) by the last words addressed to the messengers, 'Blessed is he whosoever shall find none occasion of stumbling in me' (Luke vii. 23). The disciples of John could find no occasion of stumbling in Jesus if He gave sight to the blind and raised the dead before them. The possibility of stumbling consisted in the absence of such works. We therefore conclude that Jesus in quoting the prophecy preserved its original significance, that this prophecy was first interpreted literally (Matthew), and that Luke supplied what seemed to be necessary by reporting its literal and immediate fulfilment.

b.—According to Wendt, the quotation from Malachi (Matt. xi. 10; Luke vii. 27) was not in the original tradition, but was interpolated by Matthew and borrowed from Matthew by Luke.[2] We admit the quotation for three reasons: (1) because textually it is appropriate and unobjectionable; (2) because the assumption that Luke was acquainted with the first gospel is supported by no adequate evidence; (3) because the quotation is undoubtedly an interpolation in the second gospel (Mark i. 2), and was probably inserted there by an editor or copyist who found it in the later context. Wendt argues that Matt. xi. 14 is unintelligible if the quotation in ver. 10 is retained, and therefore he rejects the quotation; but

---

[1] *Die Lehre Jesu*, Erster Theil, S. 73.   [2] *Ibid.* S. 74.

the truth is, as will afterwards be seen, that the whole fragment Matt. xi. 12–14 has been detached from a later context like the enlargements of the Sermon on the Mount.

c.—Adopting Wendt's admirable suggestion, we insert here the parable of the Two Sons (Matt. xxi. 28–32). He gives three reasons for the transference : (1) the correspondence of Luke vii. 29, 30 with the conclusion of the parable (Matt. xxi. 32) ; (2) the adaptation of the parable to the situation in the passage before us ; (3) the desire of the evangelists to bring the narrative into harmony with the second gospel. Mark states that people from Judæa and all they of Jerusalem went out to the wilderness, and were baptised by John, confessing their sins (Mark i. 5). In the apostolic source, on the other hand, according to the testimony of Jesus Himself, the people were simply influenced by curiosity (Matt. xi. 7–9) and the Pharisees did not repent (Matt. xxi. 31, 32). Matthew avoids the apparent contradiction by carrying forward the whole parable. Luke preserves a remnant, but revises the original language. He turns 'the publicans and the harlots' into 'all the people and the publicans' (Luke vii. 29). These reasons are sufficiently convincing. The narrative in each gospel is unquestionably so abrupt as to favour the theory of omission ; and the parable of the Two Sons, which is appropriate to the situation and represented by the fragment in the third gospel, has been placed by Matthew in a secondary context, as we shall afterwards see. The explanation which Wendt gives of the omission is perfectly satisfactory in itself; but the fact should not be overlooked that in the parable the teaching of the Baptist is represented as sufficient, if believed and acted upon, to bring a man into the kingdom—a representation which might well be omitted entirely by Luke because not conducive to edification, and one which, being verbally at variance with Matt. xi. 11, might be provisionally omitted by Matthew.

d.—The pronoun of the second person in Luke's version is certainly original. Matthew puts the fact out of sight that the Pharisees were addressed by Jesus. Luke preserves the direct application, and thus justifies the inference that the pronoun of the second person was also in the earlier passage instead of 'the Pharisees and the lawyers' (Luke vii. 30). The last verse is rendered differently in each gospel. In the first the reading is, 'Wisdom is justified by her works' (Matt. xi. 19); in the third, 'Wisdom is justified of all her children' (Luke vii. 35). The word 'all' is sufficient in itself to guarantee the reading of Luke; for the meaning is that men may differ from one another like Jesus and John, and yet each may be Wisdom's son. Avoiding the large tribute paid to John and applying the text to the hearers of the discourse, Matthew misses its significance. If Luke's version is primary our conclusion that the parable of the Two Sons was originally a member of this context is confirmed; for according to the parable the teaching of John was sufficient to bring a man into the kingdom, and the designation of John as a son of Wisdom like Jesus Himself involves the sufficiency of his teaching.

§ 9.—*The Samaritan Village*

We have now reached a point of departure in our criticism. Assuming that the apostolic source was an unchronological collection of logia, the critics have also taken for granted that the narratives which follow, in the third gospel, the address suggested by the messengers of John represent the original sequence. A little reflection will show that the inference is unreliable; for in the first place, as far as we have gone, the source does seem to be chronological, and secondly, the arrangement of the sequel in the third gospel has been determined by an editorial purpose. Details will be examined when we reach the original context of each fragment. In the meantime we simply notice the fact that the narrative of the anointing (Luke vii. 36-50) illustrates the saying, 'The Son of Man is come eating and drinking, a friend of publicans and sinners' (Luke vii. 34). If the apostolic source was chronological and Luke accepted Mark as his standard, we can readily understand that a number of the apostolic narratives would be set free for rearrangement, and that Luke would dispose of them for the edification of his readers. We may therefore provisionally conclude that the story of the penitent woman has been transferred from a later period. The section which follows has been reproduced from the second gospel

(Luke viii. 4–ix. 50). The second of Luke's digressions, described by Dr. Westcott as 'the great episode,' begins at the Samaritan village (Luke ix. 51–56). The position of this incident might conceivably be explained as editorial, for the narrative bears an obvious relation to the preceding one taken from Mark (Luke ix. 49, 50); but since Luke here returns to the apostolic source, the supposition that he begins at a definite historical point, from which he intends to move onwards, is certainly much more probable than the alternative that an incident has been selected from a later context in the interior. An instructive coincidence must now be observed. According to the second gospel which Luke has just left, Jesus is going up to Jerusalem; and the Samaritan incident presupposes a journey either from or towards the city. In passing through the village of the Samaritans, Jesus was either travelling from Galilee to Jerusalem or from Jerusalem to Galilee. The alternative at first sight does not seem to be permitted, for the journey in the second gospel is definite. Jesus was going to Jerusalem to be present at the feast of the Passover; and Luke marks the transition from one source to the other by distinctly declaring that He stedfastly set His face to go to Jerusalem (Luke ix. 51). But surely the fact is strange and significant that after the journey to Jerusalem we find ourselves immediately in Galilee. The sections which follow the Samaritan narrative give an account of Galilean incidents. The half-hearted disciples made their proposals at the sea (Luke ix. 57–62; Matt. viii. 18–22). The whole-hearted disciples were sent out from Galilee, and returned to their Master in Galilee (Luke x. 1–24; Matt. x. 1–42; Mark vi. 7–30). If the position of the narrative of the anointing is due to editorial arrangement, the situation of the section which follows the return of the missionaries is as clearly editorial (Luke x. 25–xi. 13). We thus reach the story of the demoniac and its sequel, the demand for a sign; and these are Galilean incidents (Luke xi. 14–32; Matt. xii. 22–50; Mark iii. 22–35). At present we need not go farther. Proceeding from the second gospel we anticipate a journey to Jerusalem, and Luke confirms the expectation in his transition to the apostolic source;

but suddenly, and without any preparation for the turn of events, we find ourselves back again in Galilee. Three explanations are conceivable. The first is that the section of the apostolic source into which we have now entered is destitute of chronological sequence. This theory, however, is excluded by the sequence of the earlier period as well as by the incidents themselves; for the evidence afforded by the earlier period is distinctly in favour of chronological order, and the incidents above mentioned are historically consecutive. The second explanation is that although Jesus started from Galilee to be present in Jerusalem at the feast of the Passover, He returned to Galilee without completing the journey. This theory, however, is utterly improbable; for in the first place Mark knows nothing about such a change of purpose, and secondly the beginning of 'the great episode' is identified by Matthew with the earlier period in the second gospel (Matt. ix. 32–x. 42; xi. 20–30; xii. 32–45), and thirdly the episode itself is thus altogether unintelligible. It is not one episode but many, a very medley of episodes. The sequence baffles the observer, and a harmony of the gospels is impossible. The third explanation is much more satisfactory, and is indeed the only one which possesses any degree of probability. Luke is combining two sources, he is following Mark as his standard, and his difficulty is to make a complete combination. He cannot attain this end without losing the chronological connection; for the second is a peculiar gospel which differs very much from the apostolic source, although the latter, instead of being a fragmentary collection of logia, is a consecutive account of the ministry. The journey in the apostolic source is really from Jerusalem to Galilee, and Luke combines his authorities (1) by prefixing the statement adopted from Mark that Jesus is going to Jerusalem; (2) by making the Samaritan village a meeting-place of the sources; (3) by arranging in the best manner possible, with a view to edification and without altogether obscuring the original chronological order, the material of the apostolic source which could not otherwise be adapted to the outline provided by Mark; (4) by repeating at intervals the preliminary statement (Luke xiii. 22;

xiv. 25; xvii. 11); and finally by returning to the second gospel (Luke xviii. 15). The sequel in this volume will verify the explanation proposed, and we need not anticipate the argument. Before proceeding onwards we must take a single step backwards. The journey through Nain has already been alleged to be demanded by the progress of the history, and this has been mentioned as a reason for accepting the conclusion that Luke in recording the miracle is reproducing the sequence of the source. Now clearly, if the Samaritan village was reached when Jesus and His disciples were travelling to Galilee, a visit to Jerusalem is presupposed. Nain would be visited in the course of the earlier journey. The messengers from John would arrive when Jesus was in Jerusalem, or at least in the neighbourhood of the city. The history becomes thus intelligible; and the suggestion is confirmed by the fact that, according to the testimony of the fourth gospel, Jesus paid a visit to Jerusalem after the healing of the nobleman's son (John v. 1).

The incident of the Samaritan village is authenticated as a narrative contained in the source by the names of the two disciples, James and John (Luke ix. 54). When Luke is writing freely his order is invariably John and James (Luke viii. 51; ix. 28). The messengers have been introduced by Luke to make the journey a royal progress (Luke ix. 51). This detail is incompatible with the second gospel, and is made meaningless by the apostolic source, in which the journey was from Jerusalem to Galilee.

§ 10.—*The Healing of the Lepers*

After the Samaritan incident the statement is made that Jesus went with His disciples to another village (Luke ix. 56). An incident clearly happened in this village, for the statement is otherwise inexplicable; but the paragraph which follows is not an account of what happened there. The men came to Jesus as He went in the way (Luke ix. 57), but the way did not lie between Jerusalem and Galilee (Matt. viii. 18–22). How, then, is the sequel to be discovered? According to the heading in Luke xvii. 11, when Jesus was passing to Jerusalem through Samaria, He entered into a certain village, and ten men that were lepers met Him. Here obviously we have just such an incident as is needed. The one narrative fits into the other. In the second case, however, Jesus was going to Jerusalem; and in the first case He was going to Galilee. This seems to be a serious objection. How can the difficulty be avoided? In following Mark as his standard, Luke reproduces before the narrative of the lepers Mark's account of the journey. If the narrative has really been transferred to the later context, the necessity of reproducing Mark's account is perfectly evident; for soon afterwards we are taken to Jerusalem (Luke xix. 29), and the history is then borrowed from Mark. The preliminary statement is therefore not an insuperable difficulty. It is simply an editorial heading in which Luke has preserved the locality indicated in the source. If a reason is demanded for the transference, we can give, not one reason, but two. (1) The ten lepers, or at least the nine, were sent by Jesus to Jerusalem; and since, according to the narrative, they were expected back to give thanks for their cure, a journey to Jerusalem might well be considered by Luke to be necessary. But after the first Samaritan incident he records a long series of events many of which happened in Galilee, and this in itself would suggest that the story of the lepers should be transferred from the beginning to the end of the digression. (2) The connection at the end of the digression is unmistakably editorial. The teaching on faith and service was not, as we shall see, delivered on the road to Jerusalem (Luke xvii. 5–10); and the narrative of the lepers serves to illustrate the teaching, for the ten men had faith, but the Samaritan alone avoided the reproach of unprofitable service. He did more than the things which were commanded; he returned to give glory to God. Editorial activity is obvious, and thus two narratives which were put asunder by the evangelist are joined together by criticism. We are not at present concerned with the questions whether Luke's narrative is another version of the same event as the one recorded in the second gospel (Mark i. 40–45), and whether if the two are identical Luke's version is primary or Mark's. We are simply reconstructing the apostolic source.

§ 11.—*The Rejection in Nazareth*

In returning from Jerusalem to the north, Jesus would pass through Nazareth. Luke has certainly placed the story of the rejection near the beginning of his gospel to illustrate Christ's preaching and the reception which He gained from the people; for Luke iv. 23 presupposes some ministry in Capernaum, and the connection is purely editorial. Wendt carries the narrative into one of his appendices, thus taking for granted that the original connection has been hopelessly lost; but Wendt has overlooked two important facts. The first is that, although Luke has introduced the narrative prematurely, it could not be in the source much later; for the people in Nazareth were so badly prepared for the teaching of Jesus that they asked with astonishment, 'Is not this Joseph's son?' (Luke iv. 22), and the prophecy which was read in the synagogue was quoted in the reply to the messengers of John (Luke iv. 18; vii. 22). The second fact is that Mark also reports a visit paid by Jesus to His own country and His rejection there, and that he places this narrative before the mission of the twelve (Mark vi. 1-6), i.e. in precisely the position which is suggested by the return from Jerusalem to the north. We are not therefore reduced to mere conjecture in our reconstruction of the source.

a.—Wendt finds in the editorial context a confirmation of his theory that Luke was acquainted with the first gospel. He argues that the early situation which Luke gives to the narrative was suggested by Matt. iv. 12; but the truth is that the first evangelist in ch. iv. 12 is reproducing the apostolic source, which was one of the sources of Luke. The theory is therefore unnecessary.

b.—The three passages Mark i. 22; vi. 2, 3; Luke iv. 22, exhibit a significant parallelism. Our use of the first must no doubt seem arbitrary to the reader; but the question is one merely of words, and we need not attempt a justification which would involve a discussion of the second gospel. The large subject must meanwhile be reserved. The allusion to mighty works in Mark vi. 2 is clearly secondary; it is probably a

I

reminiscence of Luke iv. 23 as well as a review of the miracles. The people of Nazareth rejected Jesus because He did not even heal anybody (Luke iv. 23-30). The first clause of Mark vi. 5 is therefore a reproduction of the original; the second is editorial. Luke iv. 22 is probably an abbreviation of the original. 'The words of grace' is unquestionably a secondary expression.

c.—We transpose the saying, 'No prophet is acceptable in his own country' (Luke iv. 24), to the end of the section. Wendt omits the proverb altogether. He believes that it has been borrowed from Mark, like the wonder of the people (Luke iv. 22). The truth rather is that Mark's version is secondary; for the point is, not that Jesus has received honour elsewhere, but simply that like the prophets He receives no honour in His own country. The additional words in the second gospel, 'Among his own kin and in his own house,' were probably suggested by the names of Christ's mother and brethren and sisters (Mark vi. 3, 4, cf. John iv. 44).

d.—Mark states that after the rejection in Nazareth, Jesus went round about the villages teaching (Mark vi. 6). We enlarge this statement by substituting a similar paragraph contained in the apostolic source, and placed by Luke in the same relative position, not after the narrative of the rejection —a sequence forbidden by the context in Mark, since Jesus went to Capernaum (Mark i. 21; Luke iv. 31)—but before the parable of the Sower (Luke viii. 1-3).

§ 12.—*The Healing of the Palsy*

The tour through the cities and villages which is mentioned by Mark (Mark vi. 6), and of which there was also a record in the apostolic source (Luke viii. 1-3), would not be likely to be included in the tradition, unless followed by a definite incident which happened in the course of the journey. The departure of the twelve on their mission (Mark vi. 7-13) is clearly not a suitable incident, since the journey was made by Jesus with His disciples (Luke viii. 1-3); and the parable of the Sower, which was delivered at the sea to a very great multitude (Mark iv. 1; Luke viii. 4), could not be a reminiscence of the journey, since Jesus with His disciples, instead of passing through the cities and villages of Galilee, went afterwards across the sea into the country of the Gadarenes (Mark v. 1 ; Luke viii. 26). What, then, was the incident in the source? The incident adopted is certainly free for our purpose. Dr. Westcott admits that its position in Luke's digression has been determined by editorial motive. He classifies the whole section Luke xiii. 10-xiv. 24 under the heading 'Lessons of Progress,' and he believes that the daughter of Abraham represents the Church, which after being set free grows both outwardly and inwardly (Luke xiii. 18-21).[1] That the arrangement is due to the evangelist's aim of ministering to the edification of his readers can scarcely be doubted by any student of the gospels. The woman may not be intended to represent the Church; but the ruler of the synagogue and the other adversaries of Jesus undoubtedly resemble unfruitful fig trees which are spared instead of being cut down, and the daughter of Abraham, on the other hand, notwithstanding her long physical infirmity, is not considered to be a sinner (Luke xiii. 1-5). The connection with the earlier context is, therefore, quite as clear as with the later; and this connection is editorial, for events do not happen with a view to the edification of believers. So far the argument is unassailable, but how can we advance to the conclusion suggested? I beg the reader to notice (1) that the narrative is followed in the third gospel by the parables of the Mustard Seed and Leaven (Luke xiii. 18-21), which according to the testimony of Matthew were delivered at the Sea of Galilee (Matt. xiii. 31-33, cf. Mark iv. 30-32) ; (2) that Luke's account of the tour through the cities and villages is followed by the parable of the Sower (Luke viii. 1-3) ; (3) that Mark, in the section which has already been recognised as a collection of incidents made to serve a purpose, introduces a narrative of the healing of the palsy after the story of the leper and before a visit to the seaside (Mark ii. 1-12) ; (4) that in the fourth gospel Christ's visit to Jerusalem is followed by a similar narrative (John v. 1-18), and that this again is followed by a journey to the sea (John vi. 1). The objection

[1] *Introduction to the Study of the Gospels*, p . 393-395.

116 A CRITICAL RECONSTRUCTION OF THE TEXT

may be urged that the narratives though similar are different. Undoubtedly they are different in several details, but as certainly they resemble one another; and the question is whether the variations are not such as can be shown from the case of other narratives to be perfectly compatible with original identity. We do not at present discuss this question, as too much space would be required. We argue from the general similarity of construction and situation, and the conclusion is a clear probability that the narrative of the woman in the third gospel was originally in the situation adopted; for we also are advancing to the sea, and the parables will soon demand our attention.

Wendt believes that there was no miracle in the source. He omits the second clause of vv. 12, 13, and 17; and so, according to him, the original statement was that when Jesus saw the woman He laid His hands upon her, and that the ruler immediately made his complaint. The conjecture is scarcely probable. We are not at present concerned with the primitive tradition, but simply with the written source; and the probability is that Luke has simply reproduced his original.

§ 13.—*The Mission of the Twelve*

Luke has already reproduced Mark's report of the charge to the twelve (Luke ix. 1-6, cf. Mark vi. 7-13), but the much longer account contained in the apostolic source seems to him to justify repetition. The two incidents are certainly identical. The number seventy represents the nations of the world, and Luke has perhaps followed a tradition according to which the charge was a preparation for the Gentile mission; but in such a case the tradition could not originate until the second gospel had been written, and was available for comparison with the apostolic source. That the number of the disciples in the source was twelve is proved beyond dispute by the allusion to Luke x. 4 in Luke xxii. 35, and by the fact that the number is twelve in Matthew's version, which represents the apostolic source with editorial additions like those in the Sermon on the Mount (Matt. x. 1-42). The only question is, When was the charge delivered and when were the twelve sent out? According to the testimony of Mark, the

incident happened at some time between the visit of Jesus to
Nazareth and the miracle of the loaves. In the first gospel
the context is less clear; for Matthew is combining his sources
in such a way that we cannot at present derive any evidence
from his method. We therefore pass to Luke. The miracle
of the loaves is not recorded in the digression, and so we have
no direct evidence that it was contained in the apostolic source.
As far as we have gone a suitable situation has certainly not
been discovered. But the earlier narratives already discussed
have enabled us to conclude that Jesus passed through Nazareth in returning from Jerusalem to the north, that He went
with His disciples on a tour through the cities and villages,
and that at some time in the course of this journey the
daughter of Abraham was healed. We thus reach the charge
to the twelve. We have no reason to believe that the situation of this narrative is editorial. The story of the half-
hearted disciples has been prefixed by Luke to prepare the
way for the charge which follows (Luke ix. 57-62). The
situation of this story is certainly editorial, for Matthew's version enables us to perceive that Luke's variations have been
determined by his desire to adapt the narrative to the apostolic charge; but the situation of the charge cannot thus
be explained. We must, therefore, conclude that the sequence
of the source has been followed—a conclusion which is confirmed by the second gospel. The reader should also notice
that the saying, 'I send you forth as lambs in the midst of
wolves' (Luke x. 3), is made historically intelligible by the
conduct of the ruler of the synagogue in the case of the
daughter of Abraham.

a.—The introductory statement in the third gospel is
excluded by the textual evidence (Luke x. 1). J. Estlin
Carpenter suggests that the allusion here is to the activity of
the exalted Christ.[1] The meaning, however, seems rather to
be that the seventy were sent out as Jesus went up to Jerusalem to prepare the way before Him (cf. Luke ix. 52). But
such a mission is out of the question. It is incompatible with
the second gospel and is foreign to the apostolic source. We
must therefore substitute Mark's introduction to the charge.

[1] *The First Three Gospels*, p. 331.

The statement in the first gospel, that Jesus had compassion for the multitudes because they were distressed and scattered as sheep not having a shepherd (Matt. ix. 36), is obviously out of place, for the twelve were not sent to be the shepherds of these people, and they were themselves described as lambs. Mark has preserved the original context (Mark vi. 34).

Matthew's introduction to the charge raises an interesting question. The introduction is, 'Go not into any way of the Gentiles, and enter not into any city of the Samaritans, but go rather to the lost sheep of the house of Israel' (Matt. x. 5). Wendt admits this into the text, and certainly we must acknowledge that after the success of the Gentile mission such a saying would not be likely to appear as a secondary variation; but on the other hand the description of the disciples as lambs in the midst of wolves seems awkward in relation to the mission to lost sheep. The first evangelist is conscious of the awkward combination; for he carries forward the description of the disciples, partly on this account and partly to serve as an introduction to the editorial sequel (vv. 17–23). Again, it is scarcely credible that the disciples were limited in their mission to the house of Israel and specially forbidden to go in the way of the Gentiles; for, according to the apostolic source, the Gentiles participated in Christ's ministry. What, then, are we to make of Matthew's introduction? The question is a delicate and difficult one. I venture, however, to make a suggestion. In Matthew's version of the Sermon on the Mount a saying occurs which was not originally in the Sermon, and for which a context must be found—' Give not that which is holy unto the dogs, neither cast your pearls before the swine, lest haply they trample them under their feet, and turn again and rend you' (Matt. vii. 6). This saying was originally situated near the beginning of the charge to the twelve. On account of the strangeness of the saying, Luke omits it altogether. Matthew, on the other hand, preserves the original in the Sermon on the Mount; and now in the charge to the twelve, partly because the original has already been introduced, and partly to state clearly what he believes to be the meaning, he substitutes an explanatory equivalent. He identifies the Gentiles with the dogs, and the Samaritans with the swine. This suggestion avoids the difficulties. For Matthew is not introducing a fragment which is purely editorial; he is simply giving an interpretation, a mistaken interpretation, no doubt, but still one which would occur to a Jewish Christian. And, on the other hand, the limitation of the mission is avoided; for the dogs were not the Gentiles, and the swine were not the Samaritans. The expression 'lost sheep of the house of Israel' occurs again in Matt. xv. 24 as a variation from Mark. In this latei case the expression is unquestionably editorial; and we may reasonably infer, taking the first case into account, that it is one of the evangelist's favourite phrases.

b.—Matthew has combined this paragraph with the next. The result is confusion and the loss of several details. Dr. Abbott is disposed to believe that Luke's text contains corruptions. He specially refers to the precept, 'Salute no man on the way.' 'This precept,' he says, 'is well fitted for Gehazi in haste, but not fitted for disciples of Jesus going forth to carry a gospel of conciliation through Galilee.'[1] Dr. Abbott has entirely misconceived the nature of the apostolic mission. The disciples were not sent forth to carry a gospel of conciliation which they might preach at their leisure. On the contrary, they were required to be, like Gehazi, or rather like Jonah, in haste; for their message was similar to the Baptist's (Luke x. 10–12). The whole charge implies urgency, and the mission was soon completed. The additional sayings in the first gospel, as we shall afterwards see, have been detached from their original context. Luke, therefore, has preserved the original with approximate fidelity. The variations are chiefly due to the fact that Matthew, in introducing the additional sayings, set free by his combination of the apostolic source with Mark, has lost the historical significance of the charge. The urgency of the mission requires that no man should be saluted on the road; for such salutations might lead to delay, and would indicate looseness of purpose. And as clearly the precept in the first gospel to seek out those who were worthy in the cities or villages entered is excluded by

[1] *The Common Tradition of the Synoptic Gospels*, p. xxxviii.

the nature of the case (Matt. x. 11). Luke's text, 'For the labourer is worthy of his hire,' has probably, as Wendt suggests, been transposed from ver. 8 to ver. 7. In ver. 7 the meaning is that the missionary must accept without question the food which is set before him. In ver. 8 the right of the labourer to his food is the thought required by the connection. The word 'hire' is probably secondary (cf. 1 Tim. v. 18).

c.—Luke has perhaps omitted the text, ' Freely ye received, freely give,' on account of the secondary word 'hire.' In the first gospel the woes pronounced on the cities of Chorazin, Bethsaida, and Capernaum precede the discourse which was delivered when the twelve returned (Matt. xi. 20-24) ; in the third they form part of the earlier charge (Luke x. 13-15). According to Wendt the context in the first gospel is editorial, and Luke has preserved the original situation.[1] We accept Matthew's context for two reasons. (1) The woes fall away from Luke's context when the thought is closely examined. The connection is merely verbal. Jesus contemplated the possibility that certain cities might reject the message of His disciples ; but this was merely a possibility and not an accomplished event. When the twelve returned from their mission they reported some measure of success ; for they came with joy and said,'Lord, even the devils are subject unto us in thy name' (Luke x. 17). But the wise and understanding had rejected their message, and the people had been chiefly influenced by curiosity. In the later context the woes are intelligible : in the earlier they are out of place. (2) The words with which Luke concludes the charge are unmistakably primary (ver. 16). Matthew has adapted these words to an additional saying derived from a later connection (Matt. x. 40). But if the woes were pronounced on the cities when the charge was delivered to the twelve, Luke's conclusion is belated and inconsequent. Ver. 16 continues the thought expressed in ver. 12, but bears no inner relation to the intervening passage, which is therefore clearly an interpolation.

[1] *Die Lehre Jesu,* Erster Theil, S. 89, 90.

§ 14.—*The Return of the Twelve*

The charge to the twelve was immediately followed in the source by their return. Jesus might continue His ministry in their absence, and other disciples might be with Him, but we possess no record of the interval (Mark vi. 30; Luke x. 17).

a.—The report given by the twelve of their success in casting out devils has been entirely omitted by Matthew. He is making a new combination of the teaching, and therefore he suppresses details which would indicate the original context. For the same reason the heading with which he introduces the woes may be partly editorial (Matt. xi. 20). The cities were upbraided by Jesus not merely because they witnessed His mighty works without being moved to repentance, but also, and more specifically, because they did not repent in response to the preaching of the twelve. Luke has adapted the woes to their editorial context. He omits Matt. xi. 23^b, 24 on account of Luke x. 12. The allusion to Sodom in each passage would suggest the combination.

b–d. Wendt tries to show that there is a close and sufficient thought-connection between Luke x. 17–20 and verses 21–24. He explains 'these things' (ver. 21) as 'the power over all enemies and the preservation from all evils granted even here upon earth to the disciples whose names are inscribed in heaven;'[1] and according to him 'Jesus does not conceive of that power conferred on Him by God as an ability to ward off, in a miraculous and external way, the earthly trials and evils, but as the ability to overcome these earthly troubles through humble submission.'[2] This exegesis is ingenious, but scarcely convincing. It is open to the following objections. (1) The saying in ver. 19 does not in itself bear the meaning attached to it. Jesus says to the twelve, 'Nothing shall in any wise hurt you.' According to Wendt this means, 'You will be able by humble submission to overcome all earthly evils;' but surely the idea of submission is entirely foreign to the text. The preservation from evil is defined by the authority to tread upon serpents and scorpions, and over all the power of the

---

[1] *The Teaching of Jesus*, vol. i. p. 230. [2] *Ibid.* p. 231.

enemy. It does not therefore consist in submission, but rather in the victory of aggressive endeavour. Two statements are made by Jesus. The first is that the disciples may be assured of the victory in their conflict with the power of the enemy; and the second is that the only joy which endures has its source in the heavenly kingdom. (2) The supposition that 'all things have been delivered unto Jesus' in the sense that He is able 'to overcome all earthly troubles through humble submission' reduces the significance of the teaching; for ver. 22 is a statement of His Messianic consciousness, and the meaning rather is that just because He is Messiah, with power and authority from the Father, the power of the enemy has already been virtually overcome (ver. 18). He has already received the dominion, and the issue of the conflict is certain. (3) If the things for which Jesus thanked the Father consist in the assurance that nothing can harm those whose blessedness lies beyond the reach of earthly change, these things might be hidden from the wise and understanding, but, on the other hand, they were equally hidden from the babes, for the disciples themselves, as the history testifies, did not possess the assurance that submission is spiritual victory. They believed that earthly success was essential to the mission of their Master, and consequently also to their own; and there is not the slightest indication in the context that they manifested a spirit of submission and faith for which Jesus might thank the Father. Wendt tries to read between the lines. Taking for granted, in the first place, that the teaching at the beginning contains a meaning which it does not contain, he then proceeds to assume that this supposed meaning was not only perceived by the disciples, but was even adopted as the expression of their faith. He assumes that the narrative is elliptical, and so far he is certainly not mistaken. We require to read between the lines, for the thought-connection is not clear. But, since the saying which follows undoubtedly constitutes the earliest expression by Jesus of His Messianic consciousness, one would rather expect to find between the lines an acknowledgment of Him as Messiah. For this He might well thank the Father, and this certainly, if revealed to the babes, would be hidden from the wise and understanding.

The transition from ver. 20 to ver. 21 is not made by Wendt without mediation. He puts in a stepping-stone furnished by his own imagination, and the end is, after all, that we do not get over to the meaning of the subsequent saying. The stepping-stone which I venture to propose has at least the merit of being serviceable; it takes us right over to the other side. But is the mediation legitimate? You suppose that after the return of the twelve they declared their conviction that Jesus was the Christ, and that this confession on their part was followed by the thanksgiving to the Father. And that is conceivable enough. It makes the teaching intelligible. But you borrow a passage from the second gospel which belongs to a different context; and thus you join together, by an exercise of critical imagination, what Scripture has kept asunder. So the reader may exclaim with indignant incredulity. Imagination is sometimes useful to the critic, but it must be scientific imagination, disciplined, and subject to reason. Conjectural emendations are only justified by the plea of necessity, and textual evidence may be fairly demanded for the combination here proposed. How, then, is the suggestion to be maintained? I submit the following facts. (1) On the supposition that the confession of Peter was situated in the apostolic source before the thanksgiving to the Father, Luke's omission of the narrative is intelligible, for the confession of Peter has already been reproduced from the second gospel (Luke ix. 18–20). (2) The sayings in the second gospel which follow the confession have been detached from their original context. This will be shown farther on. (3) The opinions of the people regarding Jesus, which are mentioned before the confession (Mark viii. 28), are quoted also after the charge to the twelve in a passage which is largely editorial (Mark vi. 14, 15). (4) The first evangelist has reproduced the confession from Mark, but he adds a few sayings which are peculiar to himself. The famous text concerning the building of the Church and the power of the keys (Matt. xvi. 18, 19) will be discussed when we reach its original context. In the meantime we have simply to observe that Peter is represented as one of the babes who perceive things hidden from the wise and understanding. 'Blessed art thou, Simon Barjonah: for flesh and blood hath not revealed it unto thee, but my Father which is in heaven' (ver. 17). These words coincide with Luke x. 21, and thus confirm the probability that the thanksgiving was preceded by the confession. (5) The fourth gospel equivalent for the confession of Peter occurs after the account of a discourse delivered in the synagogue of Capernaum, and in this account there are details which recall the rejection in Nazareth (John vi. 42, 60, 61). But the rejection in Nazareth was situated in the apostolic source almost immediately before the mission and return of the twelve. The situation of the confession in the fourth gospel is therefore more in accordance with our argument than with the situation in Mark. Again, the context in the fourth gospel contains several passages which coincide with the sayings addressed to the twelve after they gave in their report. The thanksgiving with its sequel is represented by the following texts. 'This is the work of God, that ye believe on him whom he hath sent' (John vi. 29). 'For him the Father, even God, hath sealed' (ver. 27). 'I came down from heaven, not to do mine own will, but the will of him that sent me' (ver. 38). 'Every one that hath heard from the Father and hath learned cometh unto me. Not that any man hath seen the Father, save he which is from God, he hath seen the Father' (vv. 45, 46). 'No man can come unto me except it be given unto him of the Father' (ver. 65). 'Ye have seen me, and yet believe not. All that which the Father giveth me shall come unto me; and him that cometh to me I will in no wise cast out' (vv. 36, 37). These texts are simply paraphrases in the Johannine style of the teaching which was delivered after the return of the twelve; and in the last of the series the allusion to the unbelief of the cities is combined not merely with the thanksgiving, but also with the gracious invitation, 'Come unto me, all ye that labour and are heavy laden, and I will give you rest' (Matt. xi. 28-30). The second and fourth gospels cannot at present be analysed in detail, and accordingly the argument is incomplete; but the evidence above mentioned is sufficient to justify the provisional conclusion that the thanksgiving was preceded by the confession of Peter.

We now pass to the gracious invitation. The authenticity of this remarkable passage has been much disputed by the critics. Two reasons have been urged against the supposition that the words were spoken by Jesus. In the first place, Luke has omitted them, a fact which demands explanation. Wendt accepts the invitation, and indeed makes it the key to the whole passage, thus opening a meaning which is foreign to the text; but he leaves Luke's omission unexplained.[1] Professor Bruce suggests that 'Luke found in his source, probably written on the margin, as illustrative examples, the three incidents recorded in ch. x. 25-42; xi. 1-13,' and introduced these as a substitute;[2] but this is a futile conjecture which no student of the documents can entertain. The more sensible method would be to give first the text and then the illustrative examples. The story of the penitent woman is an illustration of the text, 'The Son of Man is come eating and drinking . . . a friend of publicans and sinners' (Luke vii. 34), but Luke has added the illustration to the text, and this is his habitual practice. The supposition that the incidents were noted on the margin of the source is fanciful and altogether unnecessary. Luke is combining two sources, and has, by adopting one of them as his standard, the material of the other for rearrangement. He is not a mechanical writer who derives all his suggestions from without: he possesses literary capacity which enables him to make original combinations. And finally, if the incidents cited illustrate the invitation, they illustrate more clearly the thanksgiving which Luke has retained; for the lawyer is one of the wise and understanding, Mary is one of the babes, and prayer is the language of children. Other scholars have failed to account for Luke's omission of the text, and all suggestions are to be welcomed; but Professor Bruce has scarcely succeeded. In view of such conjectures, a fact may not be unworthy of notice. Luke has preserved the sequel. He proceeds to report that Jesus turning to His disciples said privately, 'Blessed are the eyes which see the things that ye see: for I say unto you that many prophets and kings desired to see the things which ye

---

[1] *Die Lehre Jesu*, Erster Theil, S. 92.   [2] *The Kingdom of God*, p. 35.

see, and saw them not; and to hear the things which ye hear, and heard them not' (Luke x. 23, 24). These words have been transferred by Matthew to the parable of the Sower, a manifestly secondary context (Matt. xiii. 16, 17). The situation in the third gospel is correct. Now what is the meaning of the statement that Jesus spoke 'privately' to His disciples? Are we to understand that the preceding sayings were delivered in public? The supposition is scarcely credible; for in the first place the twelve had been led away by their Master to the villages of Cæsarea Philippi, and secondly there is nothing whatever in the context to indicate that strangers had assembled to hear Him. The twelve handed in a private report. Jesus asked them what people said of Him; and His reply to Peter's confession was certainly not intended for the ears of a general audience. But the gracious invitation remains to be taken into account. Did Jesus address this invitation to a promiscuous crowd from the villages of Cæsarea Philippi? The inference would occur to an editor, and the word 'privately' thus becomes intelligible. And in such a case we are able not merely to decide that the invitation was contained in Luke's source, but even to explain the omission; for the text thus interpreted presupposes the presence of people who had not yet found rest by bearing Christ's burden and yoke, and according to the testimony of Mark, already reproduced by Luke, the disciples were charged to tell no man what they had learned (Mark viii. 30; Luke ix. 21). But the inference, although suggested by the original, is certainly unreliable. We need not assume the presence of any crowd. On the contrary, we are bound to conclude that the invitation was merely an apostrophe which expressed in emotional language, and with the directness of Hebrew speech, the thoughts suggested by Peter's confession. I say we are bound to accept this conclusion, for otherwise a second and fatal objection may be urged against the authenticity of the text. The self-exposition involved in the invitation is not parallel to the earlier statement, 'All things have been delivered unto me of my Father; and no one knoweth who the Son is, save the Father; and who the Father is, save the Son, and he to whomsoever the Son willeth to reveal him'

(Luke x. 22). In the earlier passage Jesus simply expresses His Messianic consciousness, and He represents it as similar in kind to the consciousness of the babes. In the invitation, on the other hand, He expounds His moral virtues. As Messiah, Jesus could be, and was, meek and lowly in heart; but in publicly proclaiming His meekness and lowliness He ceased to be meek and lowly. The psychological difficulty is insuperable if we assume that the proclamation was public; and this, when combined with the textual evidence, weighs down the balance against Matthew. But if the gracious invitation was not addressed to an audience, if it was simply an apostrophe delivered in the presence of the twelve, involving no public claim, inviting no public inspection of virtues concealed in the heart, the difficulty entirely disappears. The text is too remarkable to be the utterance of anyone but Jesus. Its authenticity is guaranteed by Luke's word 'privately' and by the Johannine paraphrase (John vi. 37). The first objection betrays imperfect observation; the second involves a misapprehension. The gracious invitation is even demanded by the thought in the context; for if Jesus concluded by saying, 'No one knoweth who the Father is save the Son, and he to whomsoever the Son willeth to reveal him,' the inference is permitted, and indeed is almost unavoidable, that in certain cases, and without respect to individual capacity, the Son is unwilling to reveal the Father. But such an inference would certainly be mistaken; and the thought is corrected by the impassioned supplementary call, 'Come unto me, all ye that labour and are heavy laden, and I will give you rest.'

A few additional details should be noticed. (1) The charge reported by Mark to tell no man of Messiah (Mark viii. 30) was probably suggested to the evangelist by the text, 'I thank thee, O Father, Lord of heaven and earth, that thou didst hide these things from the wise and understanding, and didst reveal them unto babes: yea, Father; for so it was well pleasing in thy sight' (Luke x. 21). (2) Matthew substitutes 'the Son' for 'who the Son is,' thus obscuring the text by enlarging its significance for the sake of edification (Matt. xi. 27). (3) Matthew has preserved a primary expression in his rendering of Luke x. 23, 24. He places these verses after the parable of the Sower, and adapts them to the editorial context; but the reading, 'many prophets and righteous men,' is less likely to be a secondary variation than ' many prophets and kings ' (Matt. xiii. 16, 17).

e.—The allusion to the prophets and righteous men has reminded the disciples of the opinion maintained by the Scribes that Elijah must come before Christ. The addition which we have borrowed from the second gospel appropriately completes the whole section. The following reasons may be given for its transference. (1) In the second gospel the fragment is an interpolation. The second clause of ver. 12 interrupts the thought which is expressed immediately before and resumed in ver. 13; and the connection between ver. 9 and ver. 11 is by no means clear. The whole passage is incoherent. (2) The interpolation is introduced soon after the confession of Peter, and thus the situation proposed agrees approximately with Mark's. (3) After the charge to the twelve, Mark quotes the opinions of the people regarding Jesus, and then he proceeds to explain that John had been slain by Herod (Mark vi. 14-29). The explanation is certainly editorial, but was probably suggested by the source. If the later interpolation (Mark ix. 11, 12ᵃ, 13) formed part of the section which reported the mission and return of the twelve, Mark's account of John's death is intelligible. (4) In the first gospel the saying which identifies John with Elijah is also an interpolation which Matthew has introduced soon after the charge to the twelve (Matt. xi. 14). These little details are significant. The student who is acquainted with the phenomena of the gospels will be able to appreciate their value.

§ 15.—*The half-hearted Disciples*

Jesus returns with His disciples from the villages of Cæsarea Philippi to the Sea of Galilee. He has now been recognised as Messiah, and His own self-consciousness is clearer than before. His teaching becomes more peremptory. The mission of the twelve in Chorazin, Bethsaida, and Capernaum, notwithstanding the subjection of the devils, has been apparently a failure. The people will not repent; they are moved by

THE HALF-HEARTED DISCIPLES

curiosity, but not by genuine faith. The wise and understanding are unsympathetic; they are not open to the revelation of the Father. At the Sea of Galilee a great crowd gathers together. Three men are detached from the crowd, and introduced as representatives of the rest. They hear, and perhaps understand, but they do not obey the call; they have no Christian history. Jesus speaks to the people at the sea. His discourse is the parable of the Sower, a summary of His mission as a preacher, of the purpose which He has in view, and of the reception which is given to His message. The parable has probably been suggested by the three half-hearted disciples. The twelve do not understand the new method of teaching. They ask an explanation; and they find to their great astonishment that the hope of a popular recognition has now been abandoned by their Master, and that He is making a new departure. The significance of this may not yet be fully apparent to Himself, and is certainly not perceived by them, but the history shows whither it tends.

We transfer the narrative of the half-hearted disciples from its position in the third gospel to the sequel of the apostolic mission for three reasons. (1) Luke has adapted the original to make it serve as an introduction to the charge. (2) Matthew enables us to determine with confidence the original situation of the narrative. He states, that 'when Jesus saw great multitudes about him, he gave commandment to depart to the other side' (Matt. viii. 18). The incident in question immediately follows (vv. 19-22), and could not happen on the other side; for the fact is afterwards mentioned that the boat had not been entered (ver. 23). We find therefore that Jesus is at the sea, that there is a great assembly of people, and that a boat is in readiness to be used. (3) After the healing of the palsied man, Mark states in his editorial section, the contents of which have been gathered together in consecutive order, but without the incidents which originally intervened (Mark i. 40-iii. 6), that Jesus went to the seaside; and, in the narrative which follows, the peremptory call 'Follow me' is addressed to a publican, as in the case of the half-hearted disciples (Mark ii. 13-17). I make the suggestion, which analysis of the second gospel will con-

K

firm, that Mark found in his source the story of the half-hearted disciples, and passed on to a similar but later narrative which served his purpose better.

a.—The first words in Luke's version, 'As they went in the way,' have clearly been suggested by the secondary situation (Luke ix. 57, cf. ver. 51). Mark's historical statement agrees with the description which Matthew gives of the circumstances (Matt. viii. 18), and precedes the parable of the Sower (Mark iv. 1). The intervening passage (Mark iii. 13-35) is an interpolation made necessary or expedient by the evangelist's combination of his sources. The Sermon on the Mount is represented by vv. 13-19; the incidents reported in vv. 20-35 have been transferred from a later section, as will be afterwards shown; and in vv. 11, 12, Mark anticipates the contents of the source.

b.—Luke's reading here is 'a certain man' (Luke ix. 57). The more definite word is primary. The reply of Jesus presupposes that the man was a Scribe, one who on account of his respectable profession would shrink from a vagrant life. The address 'Master' is thus also authenticated. In introducing the case of the second man, Luke has departed from the original (Luke ix. 59). He assumes that the man had been called by Jesus to publish abroad the kingdom of God (ver. 60), and therefore he puts the call at the beginning. This is an editorial inference suggested by the charge to the whole-hearted disciples. The third case would not be likely to be invented by Luke. It is very much a duplication of the second. The second man wished to be excused as long as his father lived, and the third to bid farewell to his friends at home; but just for this reason the third case would be readily omitted. Matthew adapts Christ's teaching to the supposed requirements of secular life.

§ 16.—*The Parable of the Sower*

The section which follows in the third gospel the first expression by Jesus of His Messianic consciousness has already been recognised as editorial (Luke x. 25-xi. 13). The narratives will appear later in their original context; meanwhile we pass to the sequel. The next incident reported by Luke is the casting out of an unclean spirit (Luke xi. 14–26). This incident is recorded by Matthew soon after the return of the twelve (Matt. xii. 22–37), and is presupposed by the passage in the second gospel which occupies a similar situation (Mark iii. 22–30). But obviously, if our reconstruction is correct, the casting out of the unclean spirit is a little premature; for Jesus and His disciples are still at the sea, and a boat is in readiness to receive them. They intend to cross to the other side. How, then, is the order of the source to be restored? I venture to make the suggestion that Luke has omitted a section, the constituents of which he has already borrowed from Mark. This section contained the parables, the miracle of the loaves, and the stilling of the storm on the sea. Let us put the matter to the test. Luke has already reproduced the parable of the Sower from the second gospel, and has therefore a reason for not recording it again (Luke viii. 4–18). But the question arises, How are we to argue from one parable to the others, and how can we be sure that these parables were contained in the apostolic source after the account of the half-hearted disciples? When Matthew reports the parable of the Sower he is following Mark as his standard, and enlarging Mark's narrative by additional material derived from his other source (ch. xiii.). We may therefore confidently infer that the apostolic source contained the parables which Mark has for some reason omitted; but since Matthew occasionally inserts fragments in his history for the sake of edification, without regard to their historical situation, the presence of these additional parables in the first gospel does not guarantee that they were originally delivered after the parable of the Sower. Here, however, the third gospel is helpful to the student; for two of these parables are recorded by Luke after the healing of the palsy (Luke xiii. 18–21), i.e. in a position which is relatively the same as Matthew's, if our context is correct for the parable of the Sower. Luke obviously could not repeat after the case of the palsy the charge to the twelve and their return, and the narrative of the half-hearted disciples, all of which he has already reported. If, then, the parable of the Sower was contained in the source after the narrative of the half-hearted disciples, the other parables were associated with it, and the subject is accordingly simplified. Now Mark, in the historical statement already examined and adopted (Mark iii. 7-10), reports that, when the people were assembled at the sea, Jesus 'spake to his disciples that a little boat should wait on him because of the crowd' (ver. 9) ; and the second gospel contains no other allusion to this boat until we are told that Jesus entered into the boat and sat in the sea and delivered the parable of the Sower (Mark iv. 1). The intervening section is an editorial interpolation, recognisable as such by the evidences of combination which it presents, and by the incoherence of the history (Mark iii. 13-35). We must therefore conclude that the parable of the Sower was addressed to the people at the sea soon after Christ's arrival, and that the other parables were afterwards delivered in a manner to be determined in the sequel. Again, the miracle of the loaves and the stilling of the storm on the sea are associated together in all the gospels (with the exception of the third, in which the stilling of the storm is omitted because a duplicate has already been recorded, Luke ix. 10-17 ; viii. 22-25). The one miracle is inseparable from the other. The only question is, Were these narratives contained in the apostolic source, and did they follow the teaching by parables ? After the parable of the Sower, Mark reports the stilling of a storm (Mark iv. 35-41, cf. Luke viii. 22-25), and after the return of the twelve he reports both the miracle of the loaves and its sequel (Mark vi. 30-52). The two storm-narratives differ in details, and since each is recorded by Mark the incidents may be supposed to be different; but the return of the twelve, as we have seen, was followed in the source by the parable of the Sower, and thus the two narratives coalesce. Matthew records the second soon after the parable of the Sower (Matt. xiv. 22-33). Luke evidently identifies it with the first, since he omits the second altogether. John records only one storm-narrative, and he places it in his history after the miracle of the loaves, which is preceded by the healing of the palsy (John vi. 16-21). We therefore conclude, following the example of Luke, that the two incidents were originally identical ; and the inference is involved that the miracle of the loaves and the stilling of the storm on the sea were reported in the source after the parabolic teaching.

Matthew and Luke have each borrowed the parable of the Sower from Mark. Their variations are purely editorial. Matthew substitutes 'on that day' for 'again,' omits 'growing up and increasing,' and places the largest increase first. Luke omits the degrees of increase (Luke viii. 8). He makes no allowance for poor capacity.

§ 17.—*Parables in the Desert Place*

a.—We have concluded that the parables were delivered before the miracle of the loaves. Mark vi. 31, 32 is therefore available for comparison with Mark iv. 10–35. We have also learned from the first gospel that, when Jesus entered into the boat, He intended to cross to the other side (Matt. viii. 18, cf. Mark iii. 9). Now, after the parable of the Sower we are told by Mark that, when Jesus was alone, the twelve asked an explanation of the teaching (Mark iv. 10); and He could not be alone with the twelve until they were crossing the sea, or had reached the other side. Presumably they would be occupied with the boat and with their own reflections until the land was reached. Between the parable of the Sower and its sequel, a voyage is accordingly presupposed. An account of this is given in Mark vi. 31, 32.

b.—The place to which Jesus went with His disciples is made definite in the fourth gospel. Here the transition from the mountain to the multitude is abrupt. The people followed Jesus (John vi. 2), but, since He went in a boat, He would arrive before them, and would therefore be in the mountain alone with the twelve. Between ver. 3 and ver. 4 we must read the parables and the conversation which He had with His disciples. The introduction of this narrative would not serve the purpose of the fourth evangelist.

c.—Matthew is combining the apostolic source with Mark, and has preserved a few primary details. The reply of Jesus shows that the twelve did not merely ask of Him the parable (Mark iv. 10, 13), but rather wished to know why He used such a method of teaching. The reply presents a difficulty. Did Jesus mean, as the fragments in Mark iv. 21-25 appear to suggest, that the parable was intended to give light? Or did He really adopt the new method of teaching to baffle the idle curiosity of the people, and to separate from among them those who had ears to hear? Since a teacher uses illustrations to make his meaning plain, the first of these alternatives is antecedently probable; but the context cannot be explained unless by accepting the second (cf. Luke x. 22). Matthew is secondary in ch. xiii. 11, and again in vv. 14, 15. He identifies the mysteries with the parables, whereas Jesus described the kingdom as a mystery, a truth long hidden and at last revealed. The prophecy has been quoted as usual by Matthew; in the original it was merely suggested. There are two interpolations in Matthew's version. The first is ver. 12, reproduced from Mark iv. 25. This saying will afterwards be found in its original context. The second (vv. 16, 17) originally followed the thanksgiving and gracious invitation (Luke x. 23, 24). Luke changes ' lest haply they should turn again and it should be forgiven them ' into an ecclesiastical equivalent, ' that they may not believe and be saved ' (Luke viii. 12). The following variations are to be noted in the explanation of the parable. (1) Matthew substitutes ' the word of the kingdom ' for ' the word,' ' the evil one ' for ' Satan,' and ' understand ' for ' accept.' He omits ' the lusts of other things.' (2) Luke substitutes ' temptation ' for ' tribulation or persecution,' ' with patience ' for the different degrees of increase, and ' that which he thinketh he hath ' for ' even that which he hath.' These variations are secondary. Matthew has already inserted the fragments Mark iv. 21-24 in an earlier context (Matt. v. 15; x. 26; vii. 2). Mark's question, ' How shall ye know all the parables? ' (ver. 13) may be an editorial anticipation of the parables which follow. Wendt believes that the parable of the Lamp (Mark iv. 21) was originally the complement of the parable of the Sower;[1] but the truth is that the whole paragraph (vv. 21-25) consists of fragments detached from their original situations and introduced here to supplement the parable of the Sower. The

[1] *The Teaching of Jesus*, vol. i. p. 126.

half-hearted disciples illustrate the different kinds of unproductive soil. They probably suggested the parable. The Scribe represents the stony ground. The third man has thorns in the spirit. The second may represent the wayside or an aggravated case of the thorns.

d.—The parable of the Seed which sprang up and grew without intervention of the sower is peculiar to the second gospel, and is rejected by Weiss. He believes it to be a remould of the parable of the Tares (Matt. xiii. 24-30).[1] The conjecture must be dismissed for the following reasons. (1) The parable of the Tares rather presupposes the parable of the Seed, which conveys quite a different idea, and would not be likely to be invented by the evangelist. (2) Mark's parable is an appropriate sequel to that of the Sower, and an introduction not less appropriate to the rest of the parables. Jesus here defines the work of the preacher who sows the seed but does not help it to grow, and He represents the growth as an inevitable process which passes through definite stages before the fruit is ripe. (3) A sufficient reason can be given for the omission of the parable by Matthew and Luke. In the Epistle of James an allusion is, perhaps, made to the parable of the Sower, 'Receive with meekness the implanted word, which is able to save your souls' (James i. 21), and in such a case the author of this epistle enables us to perceive that the parable which follows in the second gospel was liable to be misinterpreted, for he adds, 'Be ye doers of the word, and not hearers only, deluding your own selves' (ver. 22). Mark's parable seems to favour quietism or even antinomianism, and might therefore be omitted by the later evangelists to avoid an occasion of stumbling. We adopt Luke's version of the parable of the Mustard Seed for two reasons. (1) Because the sowing of the seed in a man's own garden limits the application of the parable to the individual life, and gives the man something to do. He cannot help the seed to grow, but at least, like the preacher, he is a sower. (2) Because the com-

---

[1] *Introduction to the New Testament*, vol. ii. p. 223. J. Estlin Carpenter on the other hand, expresses the opinion that 'the parable of the Wheat an the Tares is a secondary formation out of the beautiful parable of the Husbandman and the Seed.'—*The First Three Gospels*, pp. 73, 74.

parative expansiveness of the seed is probably a secondary detail borrowed from Luke xvii. 6. The point is not that the seed is less than all seeds, but rather that, possessing in itself the principle of growth, it expands to a measure of development which could not be anticipated from the germ. This brings us to the parable of the Leaven. The hearer of the word or the man who sows the seed in his own garden is certainly sympathetic. The word is implanted or innate; it is not foreign to himself, but is rather in a sense his own— that for which he has a natural affinity. But nevertheless the seed comes from without, and has therefore a large sphere of activity within. The whole man must be influenced by the word until he becomes a new man, reorganised by the kingdom of God. The seed is hid in the soil, but soon it becomes manifest in the shoot. The leaven is hid in three measures of meal, but the whole is ultimately leavened. The second parable shows that the application of the first must be limited to individual experience. The figure represents individualism, and the idea that the number of the elect is a definite quantity, three measures of meal to be leavened, is foreign to the mind of Jesus.

e.—The parables of the Treasure and the Pearl, preserved by Matthew alone, convey supplementary ideas. The kingdom of God is man's best, worth all a man has and more. It is sometimes an unexpected discovery, but the discovery is usually made when a man is seeking something of the kind. One finds the best without looking for it. Another seeks and finds; he visits the markets for pearls. These parables were probably omitted by Mark and Luke on account of the purchase which is involved. Buying, like boasting, is excluded by grace. The parables of the Draw Net and the Tares were certainly delivered as a pair. They supplement one another. The first teaches that all sorts of men, being hearers of the word, may profess to repent and believe, that the good can be distinguished from the bad, and that soon—very soon—the bad will be excluded from the kingdom. The second conveys the supplementary thought that the kingdom is intended only for the good, that badness may be traced to the enemy, and that life is not meant for summary judgment. Life is for fruit bearing, not for the gathering of roots; for construction, not for destruction; for growth, and not for burning. Immediate judgment would not be expedient, but the harvest is a day of judgment. These parables might be omitted by Mark and Luke because they seem to forbid church discipline. The truth is, as we shall afterwards see more clearly, that Jesus did not contemplate the formation of a church. He did not anticipate a long historical development. He believed what He said when He taught that the final harvest was near. The parable of the Householder, with which Matthew concludes the series, is evidently a convenient editorial conclusion, but as evidently is foreign to the subject. The original context will be afterwards discovered. I venture to make the suggestion that the parable of the Tares was originally the last of the series, that Matthew has substituted this for Mark's parable of the Seed which sprang up and grew without intervention of the sower, and that now at the end of the series he borrows a parable from a later context to take the place of the parable of the Tares. In arrangement as well as in constituent details Matthew's narrative is largely editorial. Adopting the second gospel as his standard, he omits the voyage across the sea, and he adds an interpretation of the last two parables (Matt. xiii. 49, 50, 34–43). We reject the exegesis for the following reasons. (1) The whole account of Christ's movements from Matt. xiii. 1 to ver. 43 is an editorial reproduction of the second gospel. Mark states that Jesus went first into a boat, that when He was alone the disciples came asking an explanation, that the later parables were addressed to the people, and that afterwards in private all things were expounded to the twelve. Matthew adopts this order of events, but enlarges Mark iv. 33, 34). He infers that 'privately' means 'in the house' (ver. 36). He quotes a prophecy which he says was fulfilled (ver. 35); and then, before passing to the parables which Mark has omitted, he interprets the parable of the Tares. The statement in the second gospel that afterwards Jesus expounded all things to the disciples may seem to warrant the inference that Mark was acquainted with the interpretation of the Tares; but the inference is scarcely legitimate, for the statement in question is simply an editorial repetition. Mark's order of events in this section has certainly been determined by editorial motive. He wishes to bring the parables together, and to connect the first with its interpretation. The parables of the Mustard Seed, and of the Seed which sprang up and grew without intervention of the sower, were not addressed to the people; they presuppose that the hearers were disciples. Mark simply returns in ver. 34 to the statement already made in ver. 10, and the interpretation to which the word 'expounded' refers is the interpretation of the parable of the Sower. We therefore conclude that the interpretation of the Tares is a secondary enlargement, suggested by the statement in the second gospel that all things were privately expounded to the twelve. (2) This enlargement presupposes the Gentile mission. The field is the world (ver. 38), and the statement in ver. 41 is probably, as Weiss suggests, a polemic against Gentile libertinism. The word translated iniquity is ἀνομία. (3) In attaching a meaning to every little detail, the interpretations in question remind us more of the triumphant disciple than of the Teacher who delivered the parables. They illustrate the allegorical method which was prevalent in the early Church.

§ 18.—*The Miracle of the Loaves*

a.—The introduction in the second gospel is elliptical: ver. 31 did not originally follow ver. 30, and ver. 34 did not originally follow vv. 32, 33. Several narratives have been omitted, because Mark has already introduced them. In ver. 34 the statement is made that Jesus 'came forth and saw a great multitude.' This obviously requires explanation. If the people 'ran together on foot from all the cities' and outwent Christ's company, the statement can only mean that He came out of the boat; but in such a case the great multitude would be seen before He came out of the boat. The truth is that Mark's narrative is elliptical, and that Jesus came forth from the mountain, into which He had gone with His disciples (John vi. 3). Mark has already recorded a few of the parables which were delivered at the mountain; and now, for the sake of bringing the people together without any loss of time, he interpolates ver. 33, the phraseology of which has been borrowed from the source in ver. 54. The statement in ver. 34 that 'he began to teach them many things' is probably an allusion to the parables. Luke says that 'he spake to them of the kingdom of God' (Luke ix. 11). Jesus had compassion on the people, not because they needed teaching, nor, as Matthew infers, because some of them were sick (Matt. xiv. 14), but because they had nothing to eat and some had come from far (Mark viii. 3).

b.—The fact is here worthy of notice that the five loaves and two fishes (Mark vi. 38), like the seven loaves in the duplicate narrative (Mark viii. 5), agree numerically with the seven parables delivered to the disciples at the mountain.

c.—'The green grass' is probably an editorial embellishment. In the duplicate the word is 'ground' (Mark viii. 6). The narrative here exhibits a curious resemblance to the account of the Last Supper. Jesus blesses and breaks the loaves, and gives to the disciples to set before the people, who are seated in ranks, by hundreds and by fifties; and the provision is small—five barley loaves and two fishes. What are these among so many? In the fourth gospel the narrative has obviously an allegorical significance; for Jesus is the Prophet like unto Moses (John vi. 14), and the bread which He gives is His flesh, the true bread which came down from heaven (ver. 51). We have certainly good reason to believe that the Johannine account contains later ideas, put into the original narrative for the sake of the edification of believers. The only question is, Was the original narrative formed under the influence of these later ideas? J. Estlin Carpenter, following Dr. Pfleiderer, is disposed to reply in the affirmative;[1] but the desire to find 'for the religious and social customs of a later day a point of contact with the life of Christ,' would scarcely be sufficient in itself to constitute the original tradition. It might suggest the interpretation, but an original to be interpreted is presupposed. Whatever the origin of the narrative may have been, we have no reason to doubt that it was contained in the written source, and was reproduced by Mark with insignificant variations. The question regarding the original tradition is one with which we are not at present concerned.

[1] *The First Three Gospels*, pp. 210, 211.

140   A CRITICAL RECONSTRUCTION OF THE TEXT

d.—The place to which the disciples went is differently named in the different versions—Bethsaida (Mark vi. 45), the parts of Dalmanutha (Mark viii. 10), the borders of Magadan (Matt. xv. 39). We know little or nothing of these places, but evidently the voyage was from the eastern to the western side of the sea.

§ 19.—*The Stilling of the Storm on the Sea*

a.—The definite statement of time, 'When even was come,' agrees with the parallel account in Mark iv. 35. The conclusion of Mark's narrative may be editorial (Mark vi. 51^b, 52). John knows nothing about the amazement of the disciples, and the supposition that they were amazed at the miracle on the sea, because they did not understand the miracle of the loaves, i.e. did not understand that He who multiplied the loaves could also walk on the sea, is somewhat incoherent. Matthew's version is based upon Mark's, but contains additional details, which are secondary. (1) He interpolates a story about Peter which seems to have been a vague floating tradition, since the author of the fourth gospel appendix records a parallel incident in his account of the manifestations of Jesus (Matt. xiv. 28-31, cf. John xxi. 7). (2) He substitutes for Mark's last words a conclusion which represents what he himself would have said and done if placed in the situation of the twelve (ver. 33). If an allegorical element can be detected in the Johannine narrative of the loaves, it is equally apparent in the account of the sea miracle which follows; for when the disciples were willing to receive Jesus into the boat, straightway the boat was at the land whither they were going (John vi. 21). This is a new version of the miracle, and can only be accounted for on the supposition that the ideas of a later time have been allegorically wrought into the text. Jesus has distributed the loaves which represent His flesh, the bread broken for men; and now He comes to the disciples when a great storm has arisen and there is nothing but a boat between them and despair. He comes walking on the sea, and they are afraid. They have doubts regarding the apparition; but they hear the voice of their Master, and receive Him into the boat, and straightway they reach the land. The narrative is an allegory of the resurrection. The belief in the resurrection was the making of the church. Dr. Abbott suggests that the calming of the storm and the casting out of the unclean spirit originated in a common tradition—the muzzling of a pneuma or ruach;[1] and J. Estlin Carpenter believes that the sea-miracle arose out of 'some such utterance of trust' as Ps. cvii. 28-30.[2] More plausible conjectures might be made, but at present we are simply reconstructing the source; and that the narrative contained in the source was substantially in agreement with Mark's account we have no reason to doubt.

b.—The historical statement with which the narrative concludes is probably to some extent editorial (vv. 53-56). Matthew omits the allusion in ver. 56 to a tour through villages and cities and the country (Matt. xiv. 34-36). He is using the second gospel as his source, and has no doubt omitted ver. 56 to preserve the continuity of the history; but the author of the fourth gospel is not following Mark as his standard, and he possesses no knowledge of this tour. Mark also has reached the end of a section, for the narratives which follow do not represent the historical sequel. We may, therefore, fairly argue that ver. 56 is an editorial enlargement, which simply indicates that Mark is passing from one source to another. The parallel passage in the fourth gospel betrays editorial perplexity (John vi. 22-25). The evangelist knows nothing about the dismissal of the people (cf. Mark vi. 45). They are standing next day on the eastern side of the sea: they seem to have been standing there during the night. Jesus and His disciples cross the sea in one boat, but after they return to the western side a boat is somehow left (ver. 22). The people see only one boat (ver. 22); but immediately afterwards the statement is made parenthetically that boats came from Tiberias after Jesus had given thanks for the bread (ver. 23). All this is exceedingly doubtful, and the difficulty raises an important question. There is no direct literary dependence between the fourth gospel and the second. The evidence which some critics have adduced in favour of such dependence

---

[1] *The Kernel and the Husk*, p. 220.
[2] *The First Three Gospels*, p. 202.

is insignificant and worthless; it simply proves similarity of source. We possess, then, two independent versions of an incident which happened at the Sea of Galilee; and these versions account differently for the transference of the people from the eastern to the western side. One of them betrays editorial perplexity. How could this perplexity arise? Two answers may be given to the question. The first is that the original tradition was not explicit—a supposition which is scarcely probable. The second is that the tradition had accumulated in such a way, before being committed to writing, that editorial conjectures were necessary to avoid the difficulties which arose. This favours the mythical theory.

§ 20.—*The Dumb Demoniac*

We have seen that the account of the half-hearted disciples was followed in the source by the parable of the Sower, the parables delivered in the desert place, the miracle of the loaves and the stilling of the storm on the sea, that Luke to avoid repetition has omitted these narratives from his digression, and that he has substituted other four paragraphs which will afterwards be found in their original context (Luke x. 25–xi. 13). The next incident in the digression is the casting out of an unclean spirit; and the question arises, Have we any evidence that this narrative originally followed the stilling of the storm on the sea? In the fourth gospel the incident is not recorded, but John has a purpose which determines his choice of material. Matthew places the incident in a context borrowed from Mark. He is following Mark as his standard, and enlarging Mark's narrative by material drawn from the apostolic source. Matt. xii. 1–14 is a reproduction of Mark ii. 23–iii. 6. Matt. xii. 15–21 has been substituted for Mark iii. 7–12, because the statement about the multitude has already been prefixed to the Sermon on the Mount. Mark iii. 13–21 has been omitted because the names of the twelve have already been mentioned (Matt. x. 2–4), and the teaching in Mark iii. 22–30 has been enlarged from the apostolic source (Matt. xii. 23–37). No direct evidence can therefore be derived from the first gospel; but the fact is worthy of notice that the whole of the section thus taken from Mark has been introduced by Matthew after the return of the twelve from their mission (Matt. xi. 25-30). We now come to the testimony of the second gospel. The whole section Mark iii. 13-35 is an editorial interpolation which represents within itself historical sequence, but not in relation to the context, for the parable of the Sower originally followed the statement in Mark iii. 7-10. Now this interpolated section is very curious and significant. Jesus goes up into the mountain (ver. 13), which is presumably on the other side of the sea (ver. 9). When He comes down from the mountain with His disciples, the people are gathered together again: they cannot so much as eat bread (ver. 20); and the Scribes accuse Jesus of being in league with Beelzebub (ver. 22). The sequence here agrees evidently with that of our reconstruction. After addressing to the people at the sea the parable of the Sower, Jesus crossed with His disciples to the mountain. When He came down from the mountain He fed the people with five loaves and two fishes (the statement in Mark iii. 20 is repeated before the miracle of the loaves, Mark vi. 31). He crossed the sea to the western side, and cast out an unclean spirit. The agreement is too close to be merely a coincidence; and if Mark here preserves historical sequence, as we have every reason to believe, the inference is involved that the miracle of the loaves and the stilling of the storm were followed by the demoniac incident. But the question may be asked, What about the names of the twelve and the allusion in ver. 20 to a house? Mark has omitted the Sermon on the Mount, with which the names of the twelve were associated in the source (Luke vi. 13-16). The Sermon was originally situated after the call of the four (Mark i. 20), but Mark for editorial reasons passes to a series of Capernaum incidents (vv. 21-39), and then he introduces a section to illustrate Christ's relation to the law and to its official representatives (Mark i. 40-iii. 6). The interpolated section to which we are now devoting our attention affords obviously an opportunity to record the names of the twelve—the earliest opportunity possible, since the Sermon on the Mount has been omitted. The names therefore present no difficulty.

The allusion to the house is, however, undoubtedly mysterious. In the desert the house would be out of place; and immediately after the statement is made that Jesus went into a house, we find that He is not in a house, but rather among the people, and that His friends go out to lay hold on Him (vv. 20, 21). What is the meaning of this? The narrative is unmistakably elliptical; and the only satisfactory explanation is that the house is either purely editorial, like the similar statement in Matt. xiii. 36, or an abstract from the narrative which followed in Mark's source the Sermon on the Mount (cf. Luke vii. 1–10), and that the passage beginning with the words, 'And the multitude cometh together again' (ver. 20), and ending at ver. 35, has been taken from the later visit to the mountain. When the second gospel is analysed in detail additional evidence will be discovered; for the stilling of the storm in Mark iv. 35–41 has the casting out of an unclean spirit for its sequel (Mark v. 1–20), and the conflict with the Pharisees in Mark vii. 1–23 is an interpolated fragment which Mark has substituted for the conflict already recorded in ch. iii. 22–30. But the argument is already sufficient to establish the probability that the four narratives omitted by Luke in his digression were followed in the apostolic source by the demoniac incident.

a.—For Luke's abrupt statement that Jesus 'was casting out a devil which was dumb,' we substitute Matthew's introduction (cf. Mark vi. 55). According to Matthew the man was both dumb and blind, but the blindness is a secondary detail [1] (Matt. xii. 22). Matthew gives expression to the amazement of the people (ver. 23).

b.—The word 'Pharisees' in Matthew's version certainly represents the original. Mark's equivalent is 'Scribes,' and he infers that they came from Jerusalem (Mark iii. 22). Luke avoids, as usual, occasions of stumbling. He is by nature conciliatory. He makes the original indefinite—'some of them said' (Luke xi. 15). According to Mark's version Jesus Himself was described as a demoniac (ver. 22)—a detail which authenticates itself, and the omission of which by the later evangelists is perfectly intelligible (cf. Matt. x. 25).

[1] See 'The Healing of a Blind Man,' § 23.

Luke xi. 16 is probably an editorial anticipation of a later narrative (ver. 29). The reply of Jesus to the Pharisees consists of five distinct and consecutive thoughts. (1) He shows the incoherence and absurdity of the charge. (2) He applies the *tu quoque* argument. 'By whom,' He asks, 'do your sons cast them out?' (3) He explains his own precedure, and indicates the truth which is involved. He casts out devils by the Spirit of God, and therefore the kingdom is at hand. (4) He states for what end He has come—to dispossess the devil. (5) He rebukes and warns the Pharisees. They hinder the consummation and oppose the work of God. To speak against the Son of Man is a pardonable sin, but he who blasphemes the Spirit shuts himself out of the kingdom. Wendt's analysis of this passage is singularly perverse and ineffectual. Assuming the existence in early times of two independent sources, one of them a large constituent of Mark, and the other the apostolic source, he attempts to reconstruct the apostolic source by excluding from the first and third gospels every detail which Mark has also recorded. He thus admits only the second and third members of the thought-sequence noted above. But the assumption that Mark had no knowledge of the apostolic source is a mistake which makes criticism futile; and Wendt's reconstruction of the passage before us is open to the following objections. (1) He overlooks the fact that the sequence which is constituted by retaining the passages rejected by him is perfectly clear and intelligible, and that the omission of different details by the evangelists can without any difficulty be accounted for. Luke carries forward the definition of the unpardonable sin to what seems to him a more suitable context (Luke xii. 10). For the sake of distinguishing the work of Jesus from the exorcism which was common among the Jews, Mark avoids the admission that the sons of the Pharisees cast out devils; and he omits the saying, 'He that is not with me is against me,' because these words verbally contradict a more gracious saying which he intends to record (Mark ix. 40). (2) The sequence in Wendt's reconstruction is much less clear and intelligible than the sequence which he rejects on account of his private assumption; for he

L

admits the severe and peremptory saying, 'He that is not with me is against me, and he that gathereth not with me scattereth'—a saying which demands in the antecedent teaching a similar severity and not such a fragment of mildness as Wendt selects for the apostolic source. (3) He admits a few verses which Matthew in accordance with his editorial method has taken from another context. The original situation of Matt. xii. 33-35 has already been found in the Sermon on the Mount, and we are approaching a narrative which will claim vv. 36, 37. (4) He accepts Matthew's context for the passage on the return of the unclean spirit, and is again mistaken (Matt. xii. 43-45, cf. Luke xi. 24-26).

A few notes should be added on the variations before we proceed to the sequel. The words, 'knowing their thoughts,' are found in the versions of Matthew and Luke. There is no sufficient evidence that Luke was acquainted with the first gospel. We must therefore conclude that these words were contained in the source. Luke xi. 21, 22 betrays editorial expansion. The allusion to the armour is superfluous. Matthew's version contains the reading, 'If I by the Spirit of God cast out devils' (Matt. xii. 28). Luke substitutes 'by the finger of God' (Luke xi. 20). Wendt prefers Luke's reading. We adopt Matthew's for two reasons. (1) The Spirit of God is mentioned again in the sequel (Matt. xii. 31, 32). (2) Jesus certainly did not intend to convey the idea that His work was an evidence of miraculous power in Him; for the sons of the Pharisees cast out devils, and yet they were opposed to the kingdom. Luke makes the miracle prominent according to his custom; but the narrative shows that what Jesus made prominent was the moral power which He manifested. Mark avoids the explicit statement that a word against the Son of Man would be forgiven (Mark iii. 28-30). The acknowledgment does not seem to him to be conducive to edification.

c, d.—Luke adds to the rebuke of the Pharisees a mysterious saying on the subject of the unclean spirit's return (Luke xi. 24-26). The connection of this passage with the context is so obscure, that Wendt adopts Matthew's situation (Matt. xii. 43-45). He expounds the text as follows:

'While the Jews of His time rocked themselves in security with the thought that the great divine judgment upon the people of Israel belonged to the past, and that further judgments of God could only touch the heathen people who were hostile to Israel, Jesus refers to the example of the demon of sickness, which, after it has gone out of the man but finds again a predisposition in him, returns to him with sevenfold power, so that the last state of the man is worse than the first; so would it be with that evil generation: the judicial punishment from which they supposed they had become for ever free, would break in again with intensified force, because in their sinfulness they provoked the return of judgment.'[1] The explanation here given seems at first sight fairly satisfactory. When interpreted thus, the context in the first gospel is undoubtedly elliptical; but Luke's context is more than elliptical, for the reader who can pass from ver. 23 to ver. 24 is a brave and accomplished mountaineer. Reflection, however, is unfavourable to Wendt's exegesis. He does not overcome the difficulties. The figure, in the first place, is strange and unexpected. The Pharisees who demanded a sign from heaven were perhaps the men who had witnessed the expulsion of the unclean spirit, and so they might catch the meaning of the figure; but one would rather expect a figure so strange to be directly connected in the source with teaching of a similar nature. The case, again, which Jesus supposes is that of a single man, and the man is described in such a way as to forbid the application to that generation. The generation is an evil generation, but the man is not an evil man. He is simply in a dangerous condition of vacancy. His qualities are negative, not positive. His first state is bad and his last state is worse; but the intermediate stage, which, according to the interpretation, represents the generation, is simply one of emptiness. Wendt identifies the unclean spirit with the judgment of God, but that is surely an incredible meaning. God's judgments are wrought in righteousness. The whole exegesis is strained and fanciful, and must be definitely set aside. Whatever the truth may be, Wendt has failed to perceive it. Since the context in the first gospel is

[1] *The Teaching of Jesus*, vol. ii. p. 361.

unsuitable, we cannot do better than return to Luke's. The chasm between ver. 23 and ver. 24 is unmistakable, but the reason may be that a fragment has been omitted by Luke because already inserted in his history. The abruptness of the gospel transitions is usually to be explained in this way. How, then, are we to find the lost bridge? The second gospel, instead of being chronological throughout, is really artificially arranged, and is a combination of sources. The facts which our investigation has required us to notice, tend certainly to such a conclusion. Now Mark in ch. ix. 38-40 records an episode which is well worthy of careful study. The connection is editorial; for, in the first place, the transition from ver. 40 to ver. 41 is awkward and almost impossible, and secondly Matthew has preserved a parallel passage which shows beyond dispute that ver. 41 originally followed a saying like ver. 37, and that Mark has wrongly transferred the application of ver. 41 from 'the little ones' to the disciples of Jesus (Matt. x. 41, 42). The teaching will be examined in detail when we reach the proper context; meanwhile we may reasonably infer that the episode in the second gospel is an interpolation. We now proceed to another fact. Luke begins his second digression immediately after the interpolation. He follows Mark from the parable of the Sower to the exclamation of John (Luke viii. 4-ix. 50), and then he passes to the apostolic source. Why has he chosen this point of departure? Perhaps for no particular reason; but probably because he recognises in the episode interpolated by Mark an incident contained in the apostolic source. For the sake of combining his sources he identifies the journeys which were really in different directions, and when he reaches the incident borrowed from Mark, he omits it to avoid repetition. The result is a chasm in the demoniac narrative. In conclusion we have simply to observe that the bridge is composed of good material, and leads to the other side. John hears the stern rebuke addressed by Jesus to the Pharisees. The words, 'He that is not with me is against me, and he that gathereth not with me scattereth,' remind him of an event which has happened in his own experience; and perhaps to receive more light on the subject, perhaps expecting commendation, he relates the incident to his Master. Jesus tells him that he has made a mistake. The casting out of unclean spirits is not in any case to be forbidden. It cannot indicate hostility, but is rather, as far as it goes, a work well pleasing to God. It does not, however, go far enough; for the unclean spirit may return with seven other spirits more evil than himself. Emptiness is a dangerous condition. A house requires an inhabitant. The unclean spirit is only effectually expelled when dispossessed by the Spirit of God. Reconstructed thus the whole passage becomes luminous and intelligible.

§ 21.—*A Woman's Blessing*

The sequence here is not in any degree doubtful. Luke's pendant to the teaching on the subject of the unclean spirit coincides with Mark iii. 31-35. The identity of the two incidents is unmistakable. The only question is, Which version represents the original? In favour of Mark's version the following facts may be mentioned. (1) Mark iii. 21 demands as its sequel an incident like Mark's. If ver. 21 is primary, the incident which follows can scarcely be secondary. (2) Matthew's version agrees with Mark's, and in the context he is indebted to the apostolic source (Matt. xii. 46-50). (3) The fourth evangelist testifies that the brethren of Jesus did not believe on Him (John vii. 5). (4) Editorial motive cannot be attributed to Luke, since he reproduces Mark's version (Luke viii. 19-21), and quotes afterwards a saying which is more severe and paradoxical (Luke xiv. 26); but the evangelist who committed Luke's source to writing might conceivably modify the original. On the other hand, we may argue (1) that Mark iii. 21 is simply an editorial anticipation of the sequel in vv. 31-35; (2) that the adoption of Mark's version by Matthew is due to editorial preference; (3) that the statement in the fourth gospel is either an independent fact or an inference drawn from the rejection in Nazareth (Mark vi. 3); (4) that the evangelist who committed Luke's source to writing would not be likely to modify the original and afterwards to record the harsher saying (Luke xiv. 26); (5) that a motive may be much more confidently attributed to Mark or to the circle in which Mark's version originated, for the Christians in early times were often cut off from the comfort and strength of earthly relationships, and a narrative such as Mark's would thus be conducive to edification. On the whole, the evidence is in favour of Luke's version, which possesses also the advantage in simplicity and appropriateness to the situation. The woman's exclamation authenticates itself as a feminine utterance; and the blessedness of keeping God's word is a contrast to the danger of the man in the parable, who had no word of God to keep, but only an empty house.

§ 22.—*The Leaven of the Pharisees*

The agreement of Matthew and Luke in divergence from Mark is sufficient to prove that the next incident in the source was the demand for a sign (Matt. xii. 38–42; Luke xi. 29–32). The connection is perfectly clear. The Pharisees have been rebuked for their foolish accusation. The mistake of John has been corrected. The woman has been taught wherein blessedness consists, and now the Pharisees demand some external proof that Jesus speaks the words of God. In the second gospel we find an account of this incident after the feeding of the four thousand (Mark viii. 11, 12). The stilling of the storm on the sea, and the demoniac narrative, with its pendant, have already been recorded by Mark, and therefore cannot be repeated. They are recognised by the evangelist, who has here taken up another source, whereas the miracle of the loaves appears on account of the variations to be different from the duplicate already introduced. Mark's sources are certainly parallel. The incidents are identical.

a.—Matthew's version is to some extent secondary. (1) The description of Jonah as 'the prophet' is superfluous (ver. 39) (2) The account given of the sign of Jonah is manifestly an editorial interpolation (ver. 40), for the context proves that the sign to which Jesus referred was not a miracle, but simply the moral phenomenon of a prophet with a message from God. Luke's version also contains secondary details. (1) The demand for a sign has already been anticipated, and is therefore not repeated (Luke xi. 16). (2) The identification of those who

asked the sign with the Scribes and Pharisees is avoided (ver. 16).
(3) Ver. 30 is an editorial explanation which weakens instead of
elucidating the text. (4) The order of the teaching has been
inverted on account of the explanation introduced. The last
reference was certainly, as in Matthew's version, to the Queen
of the South. Mark's narrative is fragmentary, and of less
value than the others. The questioning in ver. 11 is probably
an allusion to the demoniac incident; and the statement in
ver. 12 that Jesus sighed deeply in His spirit is scarcely compatible with the severe straightforwardness of the teaching.

b.—The public teaching was suggested by the incidents of
the ministry, and was frequently followed by instruction privately addressed to the twelve. This seems to have been the
method of Jesus. He accordingly said to the twelve after the
demand for a sign, ' Beware ye of the leaven of the Pharisees,'
i.e. beware of the perverse influence of those who demand
external proof of a message which is its own evidence. A
number of objections will no doubt here occur to the reader.
(1) Luke places the warning in a later context, and we pass
over the intervening material (Luke xi. 33-54). Does this
not seem to be arbitrary? The material in question is an
editorial accumulation. The fragments will soon be examined
and restored to their original situation. In the meantime we
simply observe the fact that the connection is clearly artificial.
The Pharisees have been rebuked for their lack of discernment,
and the sayings in vv. 33-36 bear undoubtedly some sort of
relation to the subject; but as certainly they contain much
which is altogether inexplicable on the supposition that they
were addressed to these Pharisees. The reply to the Pharisees
is complete in itself, and would only be weakened by enlargement. Again, the incident which follows illustrates their moral
perversity, but just for this reason is probably editorial in its
situation (vv. 37-41). The specific subject is different; and one
of the Pharisees who had been so sternly rebuked would surely
not straightway invite the Prophet to dine with him. And,
finally, we can scarcely conceive the possibility that in this
house there was an assembly of Pharisees and lawyers who
were terribly and elaborately denounced by a guest invited to
dinner (vv. 42-52). The supposition that the sequence is

historical can only be maintained by interpreters who are prepossessed by a theory. (2) The combination suggested may be described as a mere private conjecture, unsupported by textual authority, and if not contradicted by the testimony of Luke, at least incompatible with one of Mark's narratives which will presumably be claimed as a parallel (Mark viii. 13-21). The parallelism presumably will not be denied; and in view of the evidence already discovered for the composite nature of the second gospel, the historical identity of the warnings can scarcely be rationally disputed. The question is, Can any reliance be placed on the agreement of Mark's account with the narrative in the apostolic source? If this question is answered in the affirmative, the original connection of the warning with the rebuke of the demand for a sign will still be open for discussion, but the circumstances under which the warning was delivered will be different from those which we suppose. Mark states that Jesus left the Pharisees and went into a boat with His disciples to cross to the other side, that the warning was delivered in the boat, and that the disciples, who had only one loaf, indulged in exegetical speculation. Now this is antecedently improbable; for, according to a statement just made, Jesus had recently returned from the eastern side of the sea (Mark viii. 10). We are, therefore, to suppose that He crossed from the west to the east, and returned from the east to the west, and after rebuking the Pharisees went again from the west to the east. The movements are exceedingly erratic. Mark's purpose evidently is to bring Jesus from the east to the west that the demand for a sign may be recorded, and afterwards to transfer Him to the east that the journey to the villages of Cæsarea Philippi may be begun intelligibly (Mark viii. 27). But if, as we have found reason to believe, the journey to Cæsarea Philippi was made at an earlier time, two facts are clearly involved. The first is that Mark at ch. viii. 27 takes up another source, and the second is that the later voyage from west to east is an editorial inference suggested by the combination of the sources. The argument from Mark at this particular point to the contents of the apostolic source is extremely unreliable. We must, therefore, conclude that the combination proposed is not forbidden by the second gospel. And, instead of being forbidden by the testimony of Luke, it is rather in agreement with Luke's narrative; for the circumstances mentioned in Luke xii. 1, though described with editorial liberty, are just those required by the rebuke of the demand for a sign (cf. Luke xi. 14). (3) A third objection, however, may be urged. The historical sequence may be granted, but the interpretation of the warning may still be disputed. What did Jesus mean when He said to the twelve, 'Beware ye of the leaven of the Pharisees'? Mark leaves the question unanswered; but the later evangelists are explicit. He meant, according to Matthew, 'the teaching of the Pharisees and Sadducees' (Matt. xvi. 12); according to Luke, 'hypocrisy' (Luke xii. 1). Luke's interpretation confirms our conclusion that the warning was originally situated after the rebuke of the Pharisees; for obviously, since the saying conveys such a meaning to him, he could not connect it with the rebuke. He could only transfer it to another position and seek illustrative teaching. The interpretation which he gives is perfectly intelligible, for, according to the woes which Luke has just quoted, the great sin of the Pharisees was hypocrisy (Luke xi. 42-52). But, instead of defining the saying in relation to these woes, we must look for its meaning in the original context; and when we consult the history, two facts become self-evident: (1) that the interpretation of Matthew is approximately correct; (2) that Matthew, through following Mark as his standard, has missed the precise significance, which is, as has been stated, that the twelve should guard against the insidious and dangerous tendency to demand, in proof of the words of God, a supernatural wonder. The disciples of Jesus have unfortunately forgotten their Master's lesson. They still need to purge out the leaven of the Pharisees.

§ 23.—*The Healing of a Blind Man*

The gospels agree in reporting the cure of a blind man. In the first we have two blind men (Matt. ix. 27-31), in the second we have the man of Bethsaida (Mark viii. 22-26), in the fourth we have the man of Jerusalem (John ix. 1-41), and in the three synoptic gospels we have the man of Jericho (Mark x. 46-52; Matt. xx. 29-34; Luke xviii. 35-43). The evidence in favour of the last appears to be much the largest; but the versions are not independent, since Matthew and Luke follow Mark as their standard. At present a comparative criticism of the narratives will not be necessary for our purpose. A few remarks, however, must be made.

(1) The situation of such a narrative in the apostolic source can be determined with approximate accuracy. Mark states that Jesus went to Bethsaida, and there cured a blind man after the demand for a sign. Bethsaida Julias scarcely agrees with the description of the place as a village (Mark viii. 26), and Mark on account of his combination of sources is on the road to Cæsarea Philippi. The definition of the locality may therefore be questioned; but the narrative itself is probably in its original position. We have no reason to believe the contrary. The Bethsaida miracle is peculiar to Mark. When Matthew and Luke are following Mark, they avoid this particular incident, Matthew by simple omission, and Luke by the omission of a series of narratives. We need not at present investigate motives. The fact to be noticed is that although we have no direct evidence that the apostolic source contained an account of the Bethsaida miracle, the fragments which follow the rebuke of the Pharisees may be fairly claimed as an evidence that a similar narrative was found by Luke in this particular position. These fragments have been detached from their original context (Luke xi. 33-36). They bear some sort of relation to the rebuke of the Pharisees, and have therefore been added by the evangelist; but other sayings might conceivably have been selected by Luke to illustrate and enlarge the theme, and the question may be asked, Why has he chosen these particular sayings, which are concerned with the subject of light? I venture to suggest that the source contained after the rebuke an account of the cure of a blind man, and that Luke has omitted this narrative, partly because the substituted sayings illustrate the antecedent teaching, and partly because he intends to reproduce from Mark the cure of the man of Jericho (Luke xviii. 35-43). Two facts may be mentioned in favour of the suggestion. (a) When Matthew records the

casting out of the unclean spirit and the subsequent demand for a sign, he is following Mark as his standard, and enlarging Mark's narrative by material drawn from the apostolic source. Now Matthew does not record the case of the blind man, but according to him the demoniac was both dumb and blind (Matt. xii. 22). That the blindness is here an editorial addition is evident from the statement in ver. 22 that 'the dumb man' spake and saw; and if the apostolic source contained after the rebuke an account of the cure of a blind man the combination of infirmities is intelligible. (*b*) In ch. ix. 32-34 Matthew records a duplicate demoniac narrative, which is certainly another account of the incident reported in ch. xii. 22-24. This duplicate is preceded by an account of the healing of two blind men (Matt. ix. 27-31). The juxtaposition of the narratives in the source thus receives additional confirmation. But the sequence is inverted by Matthew, and this requires to be explained. Dr. Westcott suggests a good reason for the change when he shows, in his analysis of the first gospel, that the whole section from ver. 18 to ver. 34 is a presentation of the results of the testimony of signs. Faith is first confirmed (vv. 20-22), then raised (vv. 23-26), then attested (vv. 27-31), and finally unbelief is hardened (vv. 32-34).[1] The sequence is thus acknowledged to be editorial, and the probability is that in Matthew's source the demoniac narrative preceded the cure of the blind men.

(2) We adopt the narrative which Mark has preserved in ch. viii. 22-26 on account of its greater simplicity and the details which authenticate an early tradition (vv. 23-25). The fragments in Luke xi. 33-36 would be more likely to be suggested by Mark's version than by the parallel narrative in the first gospel.

(3) The cure of the blind, like the other miracles of a similar nature—the healing of the deaf and lame and dumb—was probably regarded, when the tradition was first committed to writing, as a fulfilment of the prophecy in Isaiah xxxv. 5, 6. The reply of Jesus to the messengers of John, the text chosen in the synagogue of Nazareth, and the statement in Matt. xv. 29-31 confirm the probability. The God of Israel means the God of the ancient prophecies and of their fulfilment in Jesus.

[1] *Introduction to the Study of the Gospels*, pp. 386-389.

§ 24.—*The Call of a Publican*

A brief review of the history may here be expedient as an introduction to the subsequent argument. Before He delivered the Sermon on the Mount, Jesus had paid a visit to Jerusalem, probably to be present at the feast of the Passover. He had then been baptised at the fords of the Jordan. He returned to Galilee, and after the imprisonment of the Baptist He began to proclaim that the kingdom of God was at hand. Disciples were attracted by His preaching. He chose from among them twelve, that they might be with Him and that He might send them forth to preach. He taught them by the example of John the nature and characteristics of the prophet. Soon afterwards He went with them to Jerusalem; the attraction was again probably the feast of the Passover. This visit was made memorable by the question which John asked through his messengers, and by the reply which they carried back to the prison. Jesus returned to Capernaum through Samaria and Nazareth. He was rejected by the people in Nazareth. He sent out the twelve on their mission. They returned and reported success as exorcists, but failure as the prophets of the kingdom. The wise and understanding were indifferent. The people would not repent; they would not believe that the Day of Judgment was threatening them. A journey was made to the villages of Cæsarea Philippi. On the way Peter made his confession. The babes had perceived the truth which the Father had hidden from others. Jesus was content to be recognised by the babes; it was His Father's will. He returned with His disciples to the Sea of Galilee. A new departure was now made. He abandoned the hope of a popular recognition, and withdrew into the circle of His disciples. When the people were expecting something marvellous and exciting, He delivered the parable of the Sower. He crossed to the other side of the sea, and there in the solitude of the mountain He instructed His disciples concerning the mystery of the kingdom. He returned with them to the neighbourhood of Capernaum. He cast out an unclean spirit, and rebuked the Pharisees severely for their foolish accusation and demand for a sign. He warned His disciples against the insidious evil, which they had probably themselves to some extent manifested, of requiring miraculous wonders to guarantee the revelation of the Father. These are, in historical order, the principal events which we have found in the primitive source.

An interval of at least a few months has elapsed since the last visit paid to Jerusalem; and the reader should not be surprised to find that another is about to be recorded. In the fourth gospel we are told that before the last Passover, Jesus went up to the feast of Tabernacles (John vii. 2, 10), and according to the testimony of the evangelist this journey was made soon after the incidents at the sea. If the fourth gospel is in any degree reliable as a history of the ministry of Jesus, we have some reason to expect that the journey to the feast of Tabernacles should be at least indicated by the sequel in Luke's digression. Apparently, however, there is not the slightest evidence which can be construed, by any exercise of ingenuity, in favour of the antecedent probability; for the sequel in Luke's digression is a heterogeneous collection of logia, artificially combined, and therefore free for rearrangement, but without historical setting. The reconstruction of the source does not seem to be feasible. If the evangelist can be appropriately described as a painter, according to the ancient tradition, on account of the pictorial art displayed in some of his narratives, he may be compared with equal propriety to a gardener on account of his arrangement of the logia. His two digressions are beds of transplanted flowers, arranged with some degree of skill, and fragrant in their beauty; but as no observer can argue from the appearance of a flower to the soil in which at first it grew, so also the desire of the critic to find for the logia their original context appears to be utterly hopeless. The difficulty of the undertaking upon which we have entered is sufficiently attested by the fact that the critics of the gospels, who are inferior to no scholars in acuteness, have acquiesced in failure. Their reconstruction is helpless. They do not accept Luke's order, but they cannot suggest a better; and the source becomes under their hands a mere accumulation of stones, or at best

158   A CRITICAL RECONSTRUCTION OF THE TEXT

an ancient flower garden. The question before us is, Have the critics overlooked any data by which the source used by Luke may be shown to be in agreement with the historical outline of the fourth gospel? I venture to reply in the affirmative. (1) The fragments which Luke has gathered together and arranged for edification are, for the most part, Jerusalem logia. They presuppose a residence in Jerusalem. To avoid overcrowding the argument I refer the reader to the rest of this volume. The details will be minutely examined, and the statement will then be verified. (2) The digression ends at ch. xviii. 14. From ch. xviii. 15 to the end of the gospel Luke follows Mark as his standard. He accepts Mark's order of events, and reproduces with characteristic variations the narratives of the earlier writer; but he also inserts in Mark's outline a number of narratives, some of them peculiar to himself, and others contained in the first gospel. The story of Zacchæus belongs to the first of these groups (Luke xix. 1–10). The narrative is peculiar to Luke, and the incident is reported to have happened in Jericho, when Jesus was on the road to Jerusalem. Now surely we have here a significant fact. Weiss says with characteristic perverseness that the story of Zacchæus has been taken by Luke from his third source.[1] When Weiss furnishes more convincing reasons than those he has given for the existence of this source, the statement will be worthy of consideration; in the meantime it is perfectly gratuitous. Wendt, on the other hand, relegates Zacchæus to an appendix. He suggests indeed that the narrative was originally a pendant to the story of the penitent woman (Luke vii. 36–50), and finds the connecting link in Matt. xxi. 31 [b];[2] but appreciating the fact that the connection is merely a conjecture, without sufficient evidence in its favour, he consigns the pendant, with fine impartiality, to the logia which have somehow gone astray, thus virtually acknowledging his failure as a critic. He believes that the story of Zacchæus has been taken by Luke from the apostolic source, and this must certainly be taken for granted in the absence of a more probable supposition; but surely the *credo*

[1] *Introduction to the New Testament*, vol. ii. p. 296.
[2] *Die Lehre Jesu*, Erster Theil, S. 169.

involves consequences which Wendt has failed to perceive. According to the fourth gospel, Jesus went from the sea to the feast of Tabernacles. The logia which follow the sea-incidents in the digression presuppose a residence in Jerusalem. Luke himself, in following Mark as his standard, shows that according to the apostolic source Jesus had an interview with Zacchæus, as He passed through Jericho on the road to Jerusalem. What further evidence do we require? We must choose between three possibilities—that the definition of the place is editorial, that the journey to Jerusalem presupposed by the narrative of Zacchæus was later than the journey to the feast of Tabernacles, or finally that it was this journey. But we have no reason whatever to suppose that the definition of the place is editorial, and the later journey, which was certainly made, was of a nature which scarcely permits such incidents, as we shall afterwards see; and thus the conclusion is gained that the call of Zacchæus has been carried forward by Luke on account of his combination of the two sources. (3) Two curious and suggestive coincidences present themselves now for consideration. One is that Luke has placed the call of Zacchæus immediately after the cure of a blind man (Luke xviii. 35-43, cf. Mark x. 46-52). The omission of the similar narrative, which according to our argument he found in his source after the rebuke of the Pharisees, is thus made more intelligible. He preserves the original connection of the incidents, but prefers Mark's version of the miracle. The other coincidence is that Mark records in his editorial section an account of a publican named Levi, who was called by Jesus at some time after a visit to the sea (Mark ii. 13-17). The correspondence is well worthy of notice. Levi, like Zacchæus, was a wealthy man. Jesus went to the house both of Levi and of Zacchæus. On each occasion there was murmuring because He went to lodge with a sinner; and in each case Jesus justified Himself for seeking and saving the lost. The following objections may be urged against the identification of the incidents. (*a*) In the first case the man was Levi; in the second his name was Zacchæus. According to the first evangelist, however, the name of the first man was Matthew (Matt. ix. 9); and if the publican in early tradition could have two names, he might just as well have three. (*b*) In the first case the man was at the seaside; in the second he was a citizen of Jericho. The inference, however, that Levi's place of toll was at the seaside, is scarcely justified by the narrative; for Mark makes two independent statements—that Jesus went to the sea and taught the multitudes there, and that afterwards ' as He passed by ' He saw Levi sitting at the toll booth. Mark's narrative is clearly elliptical. The incidents in this section illustrate a theme, and have therefore been brought together (Mark i. 40–iii. 6). The statement that Jesus taught by the seaside is scarcely intelligible, unless Mark found in his source some account of the seaside teaching. We accordingly infer that the original has been greatly abbreviated to serve an editorial purpose, and that the testimony of Mark does not exclude Luke's precise definition of the place. (*c*) Although the two narratives agree in outline, they differ in a few details. To Levi, who was sitting at the place of toll, Jesus said, 'Follow me;' to Zacchæus, who had climbed up a tree, He said, 'Make haste and come down, for to-day I must abide at thy house.' And Levi made simply a feast; Zacchæus made also a good resolution. The resolution, however, if known to Mark might be omitted for the sake of avoiding the inference that salvation consists in the giving of one's goods to the poor; and the words 'Follow me' may be legitimately explained as an abbreviation of the original call, suggested by the story of the half-hearted disciples—a narrative which Mark would find in his source associated with the teaching at the seaside. On the whole we must conclude that the two incidents are historically identical, and that Luke's version represents with greater fidelity the apostolic tradition, and thus our argument is confirmed for the context of the publican narrative.

a.—Wendt finds a difficulty in ver. 7 which reminds him too much of the publican Levi. He makes the suggestion that ver. 7 is an interpolation derived from Luke v. 30 and Luke xv. 2. The truth is that Zacchæus was Levi and Matthew. Luke systematically avoids the identification of the murmurers with the Pharisees. We may therefore take for granted that

Mark has preserved an original detail in ch. ii. 16. Luke's reading is, 'they all murmured.'

b.—The heading in Luke xv. 1, 2 suggests much critical reflection. It is clearly elliptical, for ver. 2 contains something which is not explained by ver. 1. The approach of the publicans and sinners to hear the teaching of Jesus could not provoke the murmur, 'This man receiveth sinners and eateth with them.' A house and a dinner or a supper are undoubtedly presupposed. Now Luke in his digressions records two narratives which satisfy the requirements of the case. One is the story of Zacchæus (Luke xix. 1-10), and the other is the story of the penitent woman (Luke vii. 36-50). In the first of these narratives the murmur is quoted; and in the second, after a text in which Jesus is described as 'a friend of publicans and sinners' (ver. 34), the Pharisee wisely reflects that, since the woman is a sinner, Jesus cannot be a prophet. The story of Zacchæus belongs, as we have seen, to an earlier period, and is therefore not available. The story of the penitent woman, on the other hand, is still in our hands for readjustment. The heading may be explained as follows. (1) After the teaching reported in Luke xiv. 25-35, Luke finds in his source the story of the penitent woman. He has already introduced this narrative, and accordingly avoids repetition. (2) The heading is an editorial abstract, a combination of literary reminiscences, introduced to make the parables intelligible. (3) The parables did not originally follow the story of the penitent woman, but the similar story of Zacchæus. Luke abstracts the parables from the story of Zacchæus, which he has not yet recorded, and cannot record here on account of his combination of sources; and he places the parables with an editorial heading in the position which was originally occupied by the story of the penitent woman. At first sight this criticism may seem to be arbitrary; but, on the contrary, the readjustment is necessary. For, in the first place, the parables are inappropriate as a justification of Christ's conduct in relation to the woman. In the story of the woman another parable is recorded which is fully adequate to the situation. Again, the last words of Jesus to the murmurers, 'The Son of Man came to seek and to save that which was lost,' constitute a verbal link which binds the parables of the Lost to the publican narrative; and, finally, Zacchæus is much more appropriately represented as a lost sheep, a lost piece of silver, and a prodigal son, than the woman who was redeemed by her love. According to Wendt, Matthew has certainly preserved the original context of the first parable [1] (Matt. xviii. 12–14). I reply that the certainty is by no means obvious. On the contrary, the application to the little ones in ver. 14 is an evidence that Matthew's context is secondary; for the sheep is one of a hundred that are in danger of going astray, and the little ones do not wander among the mountains. 'Of such is the kingdom of God.' In reproducing the story of Levi from Mark, Luke defines the call addressed to the sinners as a call to repentance (Luke v. 32). The addition was probably suggested by the parables of the Lost which appeared in the original context.

c.—Wendt suggests that 'In the presence of the angels of God' is editorial, and that the original was 'In the presence of God.' [2] He finds an allegorising tendency in the evangelist, and a desire to avoid the inference that God is like man, and has neighbours. This is superfine criticism.

d.—The elder brother may certainly be identified with the Pharisees who murmured over the restoration of Zacchæus. The Pharisees are not God's witnesses. They do not reveal the Father. The best on earth is a poor representation of the best in the heavenly kingdom.

§ 25.—*The Doctrine of Fasting*

The identification of Zacchæus with Levi involves an important consequence, which is helpful for the further reconstruction of the source. If the publican was a citizen of Jericho, the incidents which follow in the second gospel happened either in Jerusalem or while Jesus was in the neighbourhood of Jericho. Although Mark has little regard for historical sequence in his work as a whole, he selects his narratives in the order of the source, omitting such material as does not serve his purpose or has been already introduced. In the

[1] *Die ehre Jesu*, Erster Theil, S. 140.   [2] *Ibid.* S. 141.

editorial section e.g. with which we are at present concerned, the sequence so far is strictly historical, although a few narratives have been omitted; and we may reasonably argue that the same method has determined the sequel. But when Jesus and His disciples walked on the Sabbath through the cornfields they could obviously not be in Jerusalem (Mark ii. 23–28). The conclusion seems therefore to be warranted that Mark here records a series of incidents which happened in Jericho and its neighbourhood. Have we any direct evidence that these narratives were contained in the apostolic source? I submit the following facts, which will be verified in detail. (1) The teaching on the subject of fasting is authenticated by two fragments, one preserved by Luke (Luke v. 39), and the other by Matthew (Matt. xiii. 52). (2) The variations in Matthew's account of the breaking of the Sabbath in the cornfields show that he has another version before him or in his memory (Matt. xii. 5, 7); and since his second source is the one which we designate apostolic, the narrative was probably contained in this source. (3) A narrative which is parallel to the healing of the man with the withered hand (Mark iii. 1–6) is recorded by Luke among the logia of the second digression (Luke xiv. 2–6). The differences in detail do not exclude the historical identity of the incidents; and this identity is confirmed by the first evangelist and by the situation of Luke's version, as we shall see. These facts are sufficient to establish the affirmative.

a.—In ch. v. 33, Luke seems to take for granted that the teaching on fasting was delivered in Levi's house. The inference, however, is editorial. The allusion to John's disciples confirms our argument that the incident happened at Jericho, for the fords of the Jordan were near. In the earlier narrative the allusion to the many disciples who followed Jesus (Mark ii. 15) proves conclusively that the incident did not happen at the beginning of the ministry; and similarly the departure of the bridegroom in the teaching on fasting presupposes a later time (ver. 20). The parable of patching in Luke's version is to some extent editorial (Luke v. 36). The idea is much better conveyed by Mark.

b.—Wendt is puzzled by this fragment. He does not

know what to make of it. He places it in one of his appendices with the remark that Luke may have taken it either from another part of the source or from an independent tradition.[1] J. Estlin Carpenter, with his customary negative freedom, describes the fragment as 'a tender little apology (made by the evangelist) for those who could not at once accept the full consequences of larger principles.'[2] I decline to follow these writers. The fragment in question is neither an editorial addition, nor a saying derived from another part of the source, nor the deposit of a different tradition. It stands here in its original context, and is precisely what one would expect to find; for Jesus has described the ancient system as an old garment or wine-skin, and that is only a partial truth which requires to be supplemented. An old garment, like an old wine-skin, especially one as old as the law, is apt to be in a ruinous condition; but the law is old wine which is good, and after the drinking of which no man desireth new. The law must not be discarded like a garment or a wine-skin, which has served its purpose and is no longer of any use. It is treasure, and as such must be preserved. 'Every scribe who hath been made a disciple unto the kingdom of God is like unto a man that is a householder, which bringeth forth out of his treasure,' not merely what is new, but things both 'new and old.' These sayings have been omitted by Mark because they do not suit his purpose, which is, to give a representation of the antagonism of the Pharisees to Jesus.

c.—The parable of the Householder is demanded, as we have seen, by the context. It supplements Mark's narrative and the fragment preserved by Luke, and certainly is free for transposition. Matthew has introduced this parable as a suitable conclusion to the series in ch. xiii.; but his context is unquestionably secondary. The concluding parable bears no inner relation to the series; and the allusion to the Scribe who is a householder, which is inexplicable in Matthew's context, is appropriate in the address to the Pharisees. It recognises the fact, which is also conveyed by the teaching as

[1] *Die Lehre Jesu*, Erster Theil, S. 167, 168.
[2] *The First Three Gospels*, p. 327.

a whole, that a Scribe, notwithstanding his adhesion to the law, may be a disciple to the kingdom of God. A similar combination of two half truths to make a complete and rounded whole will be found in the later teaching. Luke has omitted the parable of the Householder because he writes for the edification of Gentile readers.

§ 26.—*The Breaking of the Sabbath in the Cornfields*

a.—Matthew adds the editorial inference 'they were an hungred' (Matt. xii. 1), and omits 'when Abiathar was high priest,' an unnecessary piece of information. Luke adds 'rubbing them in their hands' to indicate more clearly the desecration (Luke vi. 1).

b.—This question is an illustration of the method of Jesus, and must be regarded as primary. It supplements and completes the truth already suggested. Jesus has referred to the example of David, and at the end He states that the shewbread was reserved for the priests. Now He completes the reply by showing that even the priests are not careful to observe the Sabbath according to the traditions of the Pharisees. In the Temple they profane the Sabbath, and are guiltless. Mark has no desire to make a collection of the logia. His aim is to combine the incidents, and therefore he rejects one of the illustrations. The other seems to him to be sufficient. Luke reproduces Mark's narrative, its defects as well as its merits.

c.—The allusion to Hosea vi. 6 occurs twice in the first gospel, in the account of Levi's feast (Matt. ix. 13), and again in the passage before us (Matt. xii. 7). In the first context it is clearly an interpolation, for the subject of sacrifice is entirely foreign to the narrative. After the allusion to the priests who profane the Sabbath and are guiltless, the allusion is certainly appropriate. If the Sabbath may be broken for the sake of sacrifice, much more for mercy's sake. This is the argument of Jesus. He quotes the authority of a prophet to men who believe in the law and the prophets, and recognise no higher authority. The saying authenticates itself. Matthew, however, has exercised his right of revision. Ver. 6 is clearly an interpolation modelled after ch. xii. 41, 42. It is incompatible with the original saying in Mark ii. 27. The word 'guiltless' in ver. 7 may fairly be adduced as an evidence that ver. 5, which also contains the word, is here in its proper context; but the repetition is awkward and unnecessary. The more original form of the text has been preserved in Matt. ix. 13.

d.—Mark alone has preserved the saying, ' The sabbath was made for man, and not man for the sabbath.' This saying is certainly primary. No text to be found in the gospels can with greater confidence be attributed to Jesus. It is exquisitely true and appropriate. Man was not made for the law, but the law for man. The Pharisees had lost sight of this truth, and yet according to the law in which they trusted God desires mercy rather than sacrifice. The final statement which is added by Mark and substituted by Matthew and Luke for the great word Mark has retained is surely an editorial conclusion (Mark ii. 28; Matt. xii. 8; Luke vi. 5). We can only receive it on the authority of Mark, since Matthew and Luke simply follow the second evangelist; and the internal evidence is decidedly against the addition. Jesus has been meeting the Pharisees on their own ground. He could not otherwise convince them or effectually defend His disciples. He has quoted the authority of the law and the practice of both ancient and modern times. He has declared that the Sabbath is an institution of God's mercy, designed for the well-being of man; and the conclusion introduces a new order of ideas. The saying that ' the Son of Man is lord of the Sabbath ' might edify Christian believers, but could not convince the Pharisees, who did not recognise Christ's authority. It is even an illegitimate deduction; for the logical conclusion would be that the Sabbath was made for the Son of Man, and the lordship of the Son of Man over the Sabbath is not by any means involved. Mark's reasoning is distinctly irregular. His conclusion is too large for the premises; and the probability is that the Christian faith which impelled the first evangelist to interpolate the statement, ' A greater than the temple is here,' is disguised in the logic of the second gospel.

§ 27.—*The Sabbath Question in a Synagogue*

We do not require to prove that this narrative was contained in the apostolic source. Its presence in Luke's second digression is a sufficient attestation of the fact. The question simply is, Can we determine the original context? Have we any reason to believe that the healing of the man in the synagogue followed the incident in the cornfields and preceded the visit to Jerusalem? (1) The context in Luke's digression is to some extent editorial, as Dr. Westcott has observed. The section Luke xiii. 10–xiv. 24 has been classified by the well-known English scholar under the heading 'Lessons of Progress.' This section begins with the incident of the woman who represents, as he thinks, the Church (Luke xiii. 10–17). The deliverance of the Church is first allegorically depicted, and then its growth both outward and inward (vv. 18–21), and then the duty of individual effort (vv. 22–30), and finally the assurance of the believer in working (vv. 31–35). Dr. Westcott's classification, however questionable in details, recognises at least the self-evident fact that the connection is largely editorial. In our discussion of the apostolic source we have already gained the conclusion that the parables of the Mustard Seed and Leaven (vv. 18–21) followed, though not immediately, the healing of the woman in the synagogue (vv. 10–17). We may now provisionally assume, following the example of Dr. Westcott, that the fragments inserted after the parables (vv. 22–35) have been detached from their original context. But the situation of the incident in Luke xiv. 1–6 can scarcely be explained as editorial. Dr. Westcott classifies this incident under the heading of 'Formalism defeated;' but the deliverance and growth of the Church, and the duty and assurance of individual effort, could scarcely suggest to Luke that his subject in the sequel should be the formalists. The connection here is remote and fanciful, and we must rather infer that the original sequence has again become prominent. The defeat of the formalists followed, at some distance no doubt, but still in historical order, the parables of the Mustard Seed and

Leaven. This is the more reasonable inference. Now the reader will observe that the sequence detected agrees with that of our reconstruction; for the intervening incidents have already been recorded by Luke and cannot here be repeated, and the incident in the synagogue has been recorded because the variations from Mark's version already reproduced (Luke vi. 6-11) prevent the evangelist from recognising the historical identity of the incidents. (2) Notwithstanding the differences in detail, the two incidents may be recognised as identical. In each case the day was a Sabbath, the Pharisees were watching Jesus, He asked them if it was lawful to heal on the Sabbath or not, they held their peace, and the man was healed. The differences can in some cases be explained, and in others present no difficulty. Luke says e.g. that the incident happened in the house of a ruler of the Pharisees; but that in itself is scarcely probable, for the synagogue and the Sabbath are almost correlative, and the fragments in the editorial sequel afford a sufficient reason for the conversion of the synagogue into the house (vv. 7-14). The synagogues were not dining-halls. The incident has been adapted to the teaching. In Mark's version the man had a withered hand, in Luke's he was suffering from the dropsy; but the difference of the disease is not an insuperable difficulty, for the miracles exhibit many such differences which are quite compatible with original identity. And, finally, Matthew deliberately identifies the incidents. In reproducing the version of Mark he inserts details which agree with the version of Luke, and have certainly been derived from the apostolic source (Matt. xii. 9-14). We cannot surely be mistaken in following so good an example. (3) The narrative of the healing of the man with the withered hand, like the others from the call of Levi onwards, betrays by internal evidence that Mark has transferred it from a later period of the history. The statement in ver. 6 that 'the Pharisees went out and straightway with the Herodians took counsel against Jesus how they might destroy him' is premature at the beginning of the ministry, and is verbally linked to a later statement in Mark xii. 13. We may confidently conclude with Wendt that this link represents an original connection; and in such a case the healing of the man with the withered hand occupied a position in the source which agrees with the position of Luke's miracle. From the agreement of position to the identification of the incidents there is surely no room for debate. (4) A few coincidences remain to be observed. (*a*) The fragments which follow Luke's version were delivered, as we shall see, to the disciples when Jesus criticised for their instruction the teaching and the practice of the Pharisees. Now Luke has already in his digression quoted a few passages from the criticism of the Pharisees (Luke xi. 42-52), and immediately after he states that the Pharisees began to press upon Jesus and to provoke Him to speak of many things, laying wait for Him to catch something out of His mouth (vv. 53, 54). The catch-questions undoubtedly followed in the source; and the conclusion of Mark's version of the miracle (Mark iii. 6) is a link, as we have seen, which binds the healing of the man with the withered hand to the catch-questions of the Pharisees and Herodians (Mark xii. 13). (*b*) The catch-questions recorded by Mark form part of a series of incidents which include the purging of the Temple and go back to the healing of a blind man (Mark x. 46-52). Here obviously is another coincidence; for the Jericho incidents have already been recorded by Mark, and these were preceded, according to our reconstruction, by the healing of a man who was blind. (*c*) The purging of the Temple in the fourth gospel has been placed near the beginning of the history for an editorial purpose; and the account of the marriage at Cana which is given before the purging of the Temple reminds us very curiously of the teaching on the subject of fasting. These are merely mentioned as coincidences; but they possess a value of their own, and they lend some additional interest to an argument which is otherwise complete.

Matthew's version is a compound of the apostolic source with Mark. The beginning and the end of the narrative agree almost verbally with Mark's account (Matt. xii. 9, 13, 14). The intermediate verses represent the apostolic source; and, as Wendt very pertinently shows, the miracle is probably an inference.[1] The Pharisees asked, 'Is it lawful to heal on the sabbath?' And Jesus replied in the affirmative. The

[1] *Die Lehre Jesu*, Erster Theil, S. 138.

narrative would be preserved on account of the reply. A miracle would be sure to be inferred, and this would involve the transference of the question from the Pharisees to Jesus. Matthew's version, when distinguished from the details derived from Mark, is not at all likely to be secondary. Following the example of Wendt, we therefore bring Luke into agreement with Matthew. Wendt has failed to perceive that the introduction in ver. 1 has been adapted by Luke to the fragments recorded in the sequel (vv. 7-14).

§ 28.—*The Purging of the Temple*

Wendt argues from Mark iii. 6, which is verbally linked to Mark xii. 13, that the sections ch. ii. 1–iii. 6 and ch. xii. 13–37 were originally consecutive in a narrative which according to him was the veritable preaching of Peter. In this conclusion the fine gold of critical necessity is combined with Heidelberg alloy. The identification of Mark's source with the preaching of Peter is simply a private conjecture; and the inference that Mark xii. 13 originally followed Mark iii. 6 without intervention is scarcely justified by the facts. An original connection may be taken for granted, but we need not infer an immediate connection. On the contrary, a few facts, overlooked by Wendt, point to the intervention of incidents which Mark has himself recorded. (1) The provocation received in the synagogue is scarcely sufficient in itself to account for the resolution at which the Pharisees and Herodians arrived. Jesus had certainly manifested a disregard for the traditions of the Pharisees. He had shown Himself to be opposed to the patching of the old garment of legalism with a piece of undressed cloth. He had rebuked and almost ridiculed the representatives of orthodox piety. But this in itself, outside of Jerusalem (for we have no reason to believe that the neighbourhood of Jericho had been left when Jesus went into the synagogue), would scarcely be likely to excite so great a feeling of animosity that counsel would be taken to destroy Him. The Herodians moreover were not at all implicated in the questions which had hitherto been raised, and Mark's narrative contains nothing to account for the coalition. We must, therefore, surely conclude that the statement made by Mark in ch. iii. 6 is an editorial anticipation of the original sequel, and that the questioning did not immediately follow in the source. (2) The two fragments which Luke records after the discussion of the Sabbath question (Luke xiv. 7-14) have been taken, as we shall see, from a discourse on the Pharisees; and the denunciation of the Pharisees in Luke xi. 42-52 is also a fragment of this discourse; but the fragment of denunciation is followed by a statement which demands for its sequel the catch-questions (Luke xi. 53, 54), and a narrative is recorded immediately before which makes the discourse intelligible, providing an historical suggestion (Luke xi. 37-41). We accordingly conclude that, between the discussion in the synagogue and the questions by which Jesus was provoked, the incident concerning the traditions of the elders, and the subsequent discourse on the Pharisees, were originally situated. (3) The fourth gospel contains a brief statement which is parallel to Luke's relic of the questions. John states that when Jesus was among the people in Jerusalem, 'He did not trust himself unto them, for that he knew all men, and because he needed not that anyone should bear witness concerning man; for he himself knew what was in man' (John ii. 23-25). And immediately after this statement we have an account of the interview with Nicodemus. Now Nicodemus wonderfully resembles the Scribe who was one of Christ's questioners (Luke x. 25-37; Mark xii. 28-34); and the statement just quoted implies that the evangelist is acquainted with an attempt to entangle Jesus in a snare—an attempt which was somehow frustrated. And, finally, the section in which this statement is made is indebted for its position in the fourth gospel to an editorial motive; for the aim of the evangelist is to illustrate the nature of Christ's ministry. Messiah makes good better, turning water into wine. He purges the temple of Judaism. In Him is life, and the life is the light of men. The context is not to be depended upon. The internal evidence is in favour of the identification of Luke's statement with that of the fourth evangelist. We may fairly claim this as a probability, reserving the discussion of the fourth gospel. But the purging of the Temple and the challenge of Christ's authority precede the relic of the questioning (John ii. 13-22). And so we are entitled to make an advance in our argument; for if in the source the catch-questions were preceded by the discourse on the Pharisees—a sequence which is permitted, if not favoured, by the obvious abbreviation of an original in John ii. 23—this discourse was preceded in turn, according to the testimony of the fourth gospel, by the purging of the Temple and the challenge of Christ's authority. (4) The evidence gained separately from Luke and John is completed and combined by the testimony of Mark, who records, before the catch-questions, that Jesus went up to Jerusalem, that He entered into the Temple and cast out the merchants and the money changers, and that the Pharisees questioned His authority (Mark xi. 15-xii. 12). We reach, therefore, at last a series of narratives which group themselves in the following order : the raising of the Sabbath question in the synagogue, the purging of the Temple in Jerusalem, the challenge of Christ's authority, the discourse on the traditions of the elders, the discourse on the Pharisees, and the questions by which Jesus was provoked. Here obviously the Herodians might appear on the scene. Their coalition with the Pharisees ceases to be surprising; and the animosity which induced them to take counsel together for the summary removal of the Innovator becomes historically intelligible. The narratives of the series must of course be examined seriatim. They have simply been introduced to the reader at present as a series possessing good claim to be designated apostolic.

Mark's version of the purging of the Temple has been followed by Matthew and Luke. Luke greatly abridges the original; he is writing for Gentiles after the destruction of Jerusalem. Matthew has more reverence for the ancient system. He speaks of 'the temple of God' (ch. xxi. 12). He omits the statement that Jesus would not suffer any man to carry a vessel through the Temple (Mark xi. 16). He is not disposed to believe this; and the statement is so questionable, depending on the authority of Mark alone, that we follow the example of Matthew. Like Luke he omits 'for all the nations' (Mark xi. 17). This is a detail which would be likely to be omitted after the destruction of Jerusalem, but we are not therefore warranted in concluding that the second gospel was written earlier. Matthew adds two details which are peculiar to himself. One is the healing of a number of blind and lame people, who came to Jesus in the Temple (ver. 14), and the other is the crying of the children (vv. 15, 16). These incidents will be afterwards considered, when we reach the original context of the saying which constitutes their historical kernel. John's narrative is distinctly secondary in the following details. (1) He avoids the description of the Temple as 'a den of robbers.' The language seems to him to be improper: he substitutes 'a house of merchandise' (John ii. 16), a milder expression, which was evidently suggested by the allusion to the merchants and the money changers. (2) He converts the quotation into a direct statement, in which the Temple is described as 'my Father's house.' (3) He interpolates a text which the disciples remembered (ver. 17). If the disciples remembered this text at the time, it would not be likely to be omitted by Mark. In Mark's version, finally (ver. 18), is an editorial anticipation of the sequel, like Mark iii. 6. It points forward to Mark xii. 12.

§ 29.—*A Challenge of Christ's Authority*

The challenge of Christ's authority is guaranteed as a member of the series, not only by its presence in the second and fourth gospels after the purging of the Temple, but also and more directly by a fragment which Luke has preserved (Luke xii. 54–57). Wendt adds Luke xii. 54–59 to Luke xiii. 1–9, thus forming one continuous narrative.[1] The combination is open to the following objections. (1) Luke's order is unwarrantably inverted. The arrangement is certainly editorial; but if Luke xii. 54–59 originally followed Luke xiii. 1–9, what reason could Luke have for disturbing the original? He makes a free use of his material, but he does not rearrange it for the mere sake of exercise. The incident reported in Luke xiii. 1–5 constitutes a much better beginning for the

---

[1] *Die Lehre Jesu*, Erster Theil, S. 125–127.

section than Luke xii. 54–59. The inversion is distinctly a mistake. (2) The parable of the Fig Tree belongs properly, as we shall afterwards see, to a later context. (3) The connection of Luke xii. 58, 59 with the preceding verses is so remote as to be perfectly unintelligible. A demand has been made for a sign. Jesus reproaches the wonder-seekers for their inability to interpret the time (vv. 54–56) and for their lack of moral perception (ver. 57). Then, according to the sequel, he supposes the case of a man who is taking his adversary before a magistrate (ver. 58). The subject here is obviously the duty of forgiveness as in Matt. v. 23–26, and therefore the connection is editorial. The original context of vv. 58, 59 will be afterwards pointed out. In the meantime we may confidently conclude that the address to the wonder-seekers is independent (vv. 54–57); and the question is, When did the incident happen? The parallel passage in Matt. xvi. 1–4 is evidently an interpolation put into the outline of Mark (Mark viii. 11–13). The context in the second gospel has already been subjected to critical analysis, and no room has been found for the additional sayings; and moreover, according to the R.V. margin, the interpolated words 'are omitted by some of the most ancient and other important authorities.' No evidence is to be had from the first gospel. How, then, are we to determine the original context of the later demand for a sign? After the purging of the Temple, the fourth evangelist states that the Jews came to Jesus and said, 'What sign shewest thou unto us, seeing that thou doest these things?' (John ii. 18). The more pointed challenge recorded by Mark has been omitted by John, and the reply of Jesus cannot be identified with the passage at present under discussion; but these facts can be adequately explained, for the more pointed challenge, like the passage in question, is not suitable for the evangelist's purpose, and in such a case he either omits the original or substitutes a passage more congenial to his theme. This is his invariable practice. The evidence thus gained for the original context of the later demand for a sign is no doubt merely suggestive, and scarcely warrants the conclusion that the teaching which Luke has preserved in ch. xii. 54–57 was delivered after the purging of the Temple; but other two facts remain to be noticed.

(1) According to the testimony of Mark, Jesus began to speak in parables to the chief priests and Scribes and elders. Mark does not, however, record parables, but only the parable of the Vineyard (Mark xii. 1–12). Matthew adds other parables (Matt. xxi. 28–32; xxii. 1–14); but the parable of the Two Sons belongs, as we have seen, to an earlier context, and the parable of the Marriage Feast will afterwards be found in a later one. We cannot therefore legitimately infer that Mark found these parables in his source associated with the parable of the Vineyard. The plural must be otherwise explained. But the fragment on the signs of the weather, which might certainly be described as parabolic (cf. Luke xiv. 7), fulfils the requirements of the case; and since Mark has already recorded a similar incident, he might intelligibly omit the later demand. (2) The question, 'Why even of yourselves judge ye not what is right?' is clearly not the original conclusion of a narrative. Wendt takes for granted that the verses which follow in the digression constitute the original sequel; but that, as we have seen, is a mistake. A sequel, however, must be found, for the question cannot be final. Now the parable of the Vineyard is just such a sequel as one would expect. It answers the question; and when the two are combined and viewed in relation to the historical situation, the whole narrative gains in lucidity. The purging of the Temple has excited the anger of the chief priests and rulers. They do not approve of a Prophet who takes the law out of their hands. They ask Him to produce His authority. He evades the demand by a counter-question, to which, for private reasons, they dare not reply. Then they take for granted that He claims to be a prophet who has received a commission from God; and they ask Him to exhibit His credentials, in other words to show them a sign from heaven. He does not evade this demand. He replies with prophetic power and fire. They can read the signs of the weather, but are blind to the signs of the times. They cannot even distinguish right from wrong. 'Why even of yourselves judge ye not what is right?' The purging of the Temple is a clear case of right, for God's purpose is that His house should be called a house of prayer for all the nations. Why, then, are the rulers so blind? Why do they thus oppose

the moral preparation which is necessary for the coming of the kingdom of God? The parable of the Vineyard answers the question. They do not much desire that God's kingdom should come. They desire rather to make a kingdom for themselves. Their fathers were the keepers of the vineyard, and they killed the Master's servants. The last of God's messengers, the heir of the vineyard, Messiah Himself, has now come; and the rulers are conspiring against Him. He may be cast out and killed. Will the rulers then be successful? Will they attain their end? Nay, surely; the purpose of God will not be defeated. Messiah will receive His inheritance. His death will be His perfecting. The rejected Stone will become the head of the corner. The vineyard will be taken from the husbandmen, and they, with all God's enemies, will be broken to pieces or scattered as dust. If the question is asked why Luke has preserved merely the fragment, the answer is plain, in conclusion, that he is taking the teaching from its setting in the apostolic source for the sake of ultimately returning to Mark and reproducing Mark's narrative.

a.—Matthew states that Jesus was teaching in the Temple (Matt. xxi. 23), and Luke that He was preaching the gospel (Luke xx. 1). These are editorial inferences. Luke explains that the rulers were afraid of being stoned (ver. 6).

b.—The fragment in Luke xii. 54–57 was not addressed to the multitudes. The internal evidence proves clearly that Luke's heading has been carried forward from ch. xii. 1, for 'the hypocrites' (ver. 56) could not be the people. The people were never addressed thus, but only the Pharisees and priests. Wendt retains the word 'hypocrites' in his reconstruction, thus virtually refuting himself. The demand for a sign is presupposed. We prefer Luke's version to Matthew's (1) because the interpolation in the first gospel is of doubtful authenticity; (2) because the signs in Luke's version agree with the historical situation. In the month Ethanim, when the feast of Tabernacles was observed, people would be anxious about the weather, since ploughing and sowing then began; and Ethanim was a month of both heat and showers. The difference in Matthew's version was

A CHALLENGE OF CHRIST'S AUTHORITY

perhaps suggested by the different situation—before the feast of the Passover.

c.—The statement in the second gospel that Jesus began to speak in parables is an editorial heading, suggested by the omission of the last paragraph. The versions of Luke and Matthew are in some respects secondary. Matthew substitutes 'servants' for 'a servant' (vv. 34-36). He abbreviates the original (vv. 35, 36). He omits the word 'beloved.' He infers that the reply to Christ's question was made by the chief priests and elders and Scribes (ver. 41). He puts his own feeling into the reply. The husbandmen are 'miserable' men, and will be 'miserably' destroyed, and the others will render the fruits in their season (ver. 41). Luke substitutes the word 'parable' for 'parables,' thus making what seems to be a necessary correction (Luke xx. 9). He says that the parable was addressed to the people. He abbreviates the original (ver. 9). He interpolates the statement that when the alienation of the vineyard was predicted, the people said, 'God forbid' (ver. 16). These are all secondary variations. On the other hand Matthew and Luke have probably preserved a few primary details. The words 'for a long time' in Luke xx. 9 may be purely editorial, but a long time is certainly involved in the parable. We therefore accept these words. The conclusion of the parable in the first and third gospels must also be admitted into the text (Matt. xxi. 44; Luke xx. 18). Mark has omitted this saying, but the evidence in its favour is decisive. (1) Matthew and Luke are independent, and their agreement proves that the saying was contained in the apostolic source. (2) The saying is required by the parallelism. The rejected Stone is parallel to the killing of the heir in the parable, and the destructive Stone is parallel to the punishment of the husbandmen. (3) Mark has already abbreviated the original, and therefore might omit the conclusion. His addition to the quotation from Psalm cxviii. is probably an editorial substitute (ver. 11). The question remains, What did Jesus mean when He announced the alienation of the vineyard? Matthew supplies an interpretation. 'The kingdom of God shall be taken away from you, and shall be given to a nation bringing forth the fruits thereof' (ver. 43). He believes that Jesus intended to predict the rejection of the Jews and the ingathering of the Gentiles. Luke also has apparently the same idea, for according to him the parable was addressed to the people, and when the alienation of the vineyard was predicted they at once exclaimed, 'God forbid.' The people, however, were not addressed, and Matthew's explanation can scarcely be accepted as primary. (1) It interrupts the parallelism. (2) Luke's private opinion agrees with Matthew's, and therefore if he found the interpretation in his source, he would not be likely to omit it. (3) According to Matthew, who follows Mark, the parable was addressed to the chief priests and elders and Scribes; but according to his interpretation the kingdom would be transferred from one nation to another. He identifies the rulers with the Jewish nation; but that is scarcely legitimate. The statement in the parable simply is that the husbandmen will be destroyed, and the vineyard will be given unto others. (4) The fault of the husbandmen did not consist in bad management or in failure to bring forth the fruits of the vineyard. Their fault rather was that they wanted to keep the fruits to themselves, and for this end committed crimes, throwing off their allegiance, and even killing the heir. The exegesis of Matthew and Luke is an illustration of the allegorical method, and represents ecclesiastical opinion, not the thought of Jesus. The 'others' are not the Gentiles: they are simply other keepers of the vineyard. The rejection of the Jews is not predicted, but simply the rejection of the rulers.

d.—Matthew adds that the people took Jesus for a prophet (ver. 46).

§ 30.—*The Tradition of the Elders*

We are now approaching one of the longer discourses which will gather up the fragments we have left on our way; but a preliminary narrative demands our attention. The denunciation of the Pharisees in Luke xi. 42-52 is preceded by a fragment regarding which two statements may be confidently made. The first is that it represents the historical event which suggested the address on the Pharisees; and the second is that Luke has somehow modified the original to serve an editorial purpose. An historical motive and occasion must be found for the fierce prophetic denunciation. We may be very sure that the invective was not delivered like a bolt from the blue. Now Luke has supplied what is necessary; for he tells us that a question had arisen regarding the traditions of the elders, and that Jesus pronounced judgment on this subject. He even enables us to determine with accuracy the position of the incident in the series; for the two fragments which follow the incident in the synagogue have been taken from the address on the Pharisees (Luke xiv. 7–14), and the denunciation in Luke xi. 42–52, with its preliminary fragment (vv. 37–41), follows a demand for a sign. Considering these facts in relation to the evidence which has already been noticed, we infer that in the apostolic source the sequence was—the raising of the Sabbath question in a synagogue, the purging of the Temple, the challenge of Christ's authority and the demand for a sign, the incident concerning the traditions of the elders, and the address on the subject of the Pharisees. But if, in arguing thus, we are led by clear probability, the inference is not less surely involved that the fragment beside which we stand has been modified by editorial motive. That Jesus denounced the whole order so fiercely when He was the guest of a Pharisee is altogether incredible, and this objection is almost equally valid against the contents of the fragment (vv. 39–41). How, then, can we hope to reconstruct the original with any degree of success? Must not our method be purely conjectural? I invite the attention of the reader to a few significant facts. (1) The second gospel contains a narrative which resembles the fragment before us (Mark vii. 1–23). The outline is unquestionably similar. The disciples of Jesus eat their bread without first washing their hands. The Pharisees censure this breach of propriety; and Jesus strips off the veil of obligation which conceals the true nature of the Pharisaic traditions. (2) The context of Mark's narrative is editorial. A conflict with the Pharisees succeeded, as we have seen, the voyage across the sea; but this was on the subject of a demoniac, and not of the Pharisaic traditions. Two sources are here combined by Mark. One ends at ch. vi. 55. The other begins at ch. vii. 24; and the conflict concerning ablutions has been substituted by Mark for the original conflict, partly to avoid repetition, since the discourse on the demoniac has already been introduced (Mark iii. 22-30), and partly to prepare for the incident of the Syrophœnician woman who was as a Gentile unclean (Mark vii. 24-30). (3) The parallel narrative in the first gospel has not been reproduced from Mark (Matt. xv. 1-20). Matthew is following Mark as his standard, but when he comes to this particular narrative he adopts another version. The situation is Mark's, but the substance as clearly is not Mark's; and since, as far as we have gone, we have found not the slightest reason to believe that Matthew used more than two sources, the inference is inevitable that the conflict on the subject of ablutions has been taken by Matthew from the apostolic source. We arrive, therefore, at the following result. Three narratives have been preserved on the same subject, one in the second gospel, another in the first, and a third in the digression of Luke. Matthew's narrative represents the apostolic source in substance, but not in situation. Luke's narrative represents the apostolic source in situation, but less clearly in substance. On the supposition that the substance in the first gospel is original, can we account for the variations of Luke? Nothing can be done with less difficulty. Luke is writing for the Gentiles. He is not himself greatly interested in the Pharisaic traditions, and his desire for the edification of his readers induces him to abbreviate the original. He cannot altogether exclude the narrative; for he wishes to reproduce the important judgment which was afterwards delivered on the Pharisees, and this to be intelligible requires an historical situation. The incident is accordingly retained, but only in an editorial version. Luke's method is perfectly transparent. (1) The disciples had been eating with unwashed hands, and he infers that this happened in the house of a Pharisee, and that the judgment was delivered in the house. A similar adaptation of the original has already been detected in ch. xiv. 1. (2) The severity of the denunciation inclines him to believe that Jesus Himself had been directly censured (Luke xi. 38). (3) He omits the teaching in Matt. xv. 3-20 partly on account of the subject, which is not conducive to the edification of the Gentiles, but chiefly for the sake of transition to the denunciation which follows. Luke infers that the Pharisees were directly denounced. He must therefore exclude the address to the multitude (Matt. xv. 10, 11), and the subsequent explanation to the disciples (vv. 12-20), which interrupt the continuity of the discourse; but as obviously a substitute must somehow be found. The denunciation in ver. 42 would be simply impossible immediately after ver. 38. What, then, are the substituted sayings? They are an abstract, as we shall see, from the discourse on the Pharisees, that is, from the original sequel. They will soon be identified in their historical setting. The whole context is so clearly editorial, and the method of the evangelist is so apparent, that there is really no excuse for hesitation. Probability requires us to conclude that Matthew has preserved the original narrative and Luke the original situation.

a.—The statement that the Pharisees and Scribes came from Jerusalem (Matt. xv. 1) has been borrowed from Mark vii. 1, and is a relic of the original context. The explanation in Mark vii. 3, 4 is probably an editorial interpolation. When the tradition was first committed to writing, explanation would not be necessary. Mark has slightly altered his text for the sake of placing at the beginning of the reply the impressive quotation from Isaiah. Ver. 8 is an application of the quotation; ver. 9 is a return to the original beginning (Matt. xv. 3). The repetition of ver. 8 in ver. 9 is awkward and manifestly secondary. Mark's addition in ver. 13, ' And many such like things ye do,' is an evidence that the quotation was originally situated here.

c.—The house in Mark vii. 17 is probably an editorial inference, as in Matt. xiii. 36 (cf. Mark iii. 20). Mark simply gives the interpretation of the parable. The sayings in Matt. xv. 12-14 authenticate themselves. They are certainly here in their original context. The Pharisaic traditions are described as weeds, just as in an earlier passage they are a piece of undressed cloth with which the old garment is patched, not at all to the advantage of the garment. Luke places the parable of the Blind Guides in his version of the Sermon on the Mount as an introduction to the parable of the Mote and the Beam (Luke vi. 39). It has therefore been taken from the apostolic source. After Matt. xv. 17, Mark adds, 'This he said, making all meats clean' (ver. 19). The editorial parenthesis states well the significance of the teaching. The list of the things which proceed out of the heart and defile the man has been slightly enlarged by Mark (vv. 22, 23).

§ 31.—*The Righteousness of the Pharisees*

The indignation excited by the Pharisees, who made the law void by their traditions, and the respect, or at least wholesome fear, which the disciples still manifested towards the popular representatives of Judaism, induced Jesus to define with clearness and detail the righteousness of the kingdom of God in relation to the Pharisaic ideal and practice. The discourse was addressed privately to the disciples. He began by recognising the authority which the Scribes and Pharisees possessed, in so far as they expounded the law. He then criticised their conduct. They made the law heavy and grievous to be borne, and evaded their own regulations. They did all their works to be seen of men. They were pompous, artificial, self-centred, lovers of empty dignity. Their life was a pose and a profession. The speaker next defined the true worship and service of God. The righteousness of the kingdom of God must be visible, but must not consist in self-display. The sons of the Father are as lights in the world. They cannot be hid, but they display the glory of God. They do not give alms to be seen of men. They do not stand praying in public to gain a reputation for piety. They do not disfigure their faces when they fast, that men may admire their austerity. They take the lowest place. They give without seeking a recompense. They receive from the Father beatitude and a recompense in the resurrection of the just. Returning in conclusion to the Pharisees, Jesus predicted their destiny. No blessing for the showmen of religion, no recompense in the kingdom of God. Woe unto you, Scribes and Pharisees, hypocrites, ye sons of Gehenna, ye fools and blind! The measure has almost been filled, the set time almost consummated. Ye serpents, ye offspring of vipers, how shall ye escape the judgment of hell?

A more rounded and seasonable discourse can scarcely be conceived than the one thus sketched in outline. The adaptation to the history is so perfect that if the discourse was not delivered precisely in the form and at the time alleged, the student feels tempted to exclaim that it ought to have been so delivered. The judicious and prudent theologian may be ready, however, to reply that the rounded and luminous discourse exists only in the critic's imagination. Let us see. After the questioning in Jerusalem a brief warning against the Pharisees is recorded in the second gospel (Mark xii. 38-40). Luke simply reproduces this statement (Luke xx. 45-47). He is following Mark as his standard, and is not an independent authority. Matthew adopts a different method. He has already substituted for Mark's version of the conflict with the Pharisees on the subject of ablutions a version which he found in the apostolic source; and now when he reaches the brief warning, which is simply an extract from Christ's teaching (Mark xii. 38), he follows his own precedent. He rejects the extract, and substitutes a much longer address, which has evidently been taken from another source (Matt. xxiii. 1-39). That this address was delivered precisely as Matthew records it cannot be dogmatically maintained, for there are other two possibilities which are at least equally probable. One is that the original has been enlarged by sayings derived from another context; and the other is that the original has been abridged to avoid the repetition of sayings which have already been introduced. Three facts are here apparent. (1) The substitution by Matthew of a longer address for the one recorded by Mark is not in itself an evidence that the context of the source has been preserved. The situation is not Matthew's, but Mark's. The substance is different; but in placing the address after the questioning in Jerusalem, Matthew simply follows the example of the earlier evangelist. (2) The substance of Matthew's address has been taken from the apostolic source.

The context is Mark's, but the substance is Matthew's, and is not peculiar to himself; for Luke, in his second digression, has recorded parallel teaching. But Matthew and Luke possess only two sources in common. One of these is the second gospel, and the other is the apostolic source. We must therefore conclude that Matthew's address, whether an enlargement or an abridgment of the original, represents apostolic material. (3) The internal evidence, while not excluding the supposition of enlargement, is distinctly in favour of the conclusion that the address has been considerably abridged. Jesus begins by recognising the authority of the Scribes and Pharisees as the representatives of Moses (Matt. xxiii. 2, 3). He then criticises their practice (vv. 3-7), and proceeds to prescribe to His disciples conduct which is diametrically opposed to the practice of these Scribes and Pharisees (vv. 8-10); but the contrast is manifestly incomplete. On the one hand we have a detailed account of the conduct which distinguished the Pharisees. On the other hand we find simply the precept not to be called Rabbi or master, and not to call any man father on the earth (vv. 8-10). This precept is followed indeed by the general statement that the true measure of greatness is ministry, and that the proud will be humbled while the lowly will be exalted (vv. 11, 12); but that is scarcely what one would expect who is acquainted with the method of Jesus. Since the parallel method has been begun, we expect it to be continued to the end. The defects of Matthew's discourse become perfectly evident when the contents are arranged in tabular form. One table is complete: it contains an enumeration of the characteristics of Pharisaic righteousness. But the parallels in the other table have mysteriously disappeared. Matthew has preserved only one; and he fills up the vacant space by introducing a general precept which belongs properly, as we shall see, to a different context. The woes indeed remain to be taken into account (vv. 13-36), but these obviously cannot be substituted for the vanished parallels. They rather constitute an addition to the table which is already complete, and accordingly they make more apparent the unequal distribution of the teaching. How are these facts to be explained? Does it not seem probable that Matthew has abridged his original to avoid editorial repetition? The solitary precept in the table at the right to decline the title of Rabbi or master, and to call no man father on the earth, is otherwise simply inexplicable. The suggestion may be made that this precept is an editorial interpolation, like the general statement which follows; but greater difficulties are thus raised, for the detailed denunciations which conclude the discourse could not originally follow the list of characteristics at the beginning. The woes alone are impossible. The list alone is impossible. The combination of the two is impossible. And the only alternative is that ver. 8 originally followed ver. 7, of which it is the necessary sequel, and that Matthew has omitted the rest of the original between ver. 10 and the woes to avoid editorial repetition.

The question now arises, Have we any sayings at our disposal which continue the parallelism and make the discourse complete? The reader will remember that in our discussion of the Sermon on the Mount we rejected a number of sayings which are found in Matthew's version. These are waiting to receive their historical setting. The Sermon on the Mount was not a discourse on righteousness. As such it is historically unintelligible; but now the large subject of righteousness has obviously been suggested by an incident, and a discourse on this subject to the disciples, who have been censured by the Pharisees, and for whose instruction Jesus has distinguished the commandments of God from the precepts of men, is thus furnished with an historical motive. What, then, are the sayings which fit into the later context, and have we additional evidence that this was their original position?

(1) A few verses first present themselves in which the disciples are described as the light of the world. Their righteousness must be visible, not, however, that men may praise and honour them, but rather that the Father may be glorified (Matt. v. 14-16). Now these verses are obviously appropriate as a continuation of the discourse in Matt. xxiii. 1-10. They are parallel to the statement that the righteousness of the Pharisees is made visible for the sake of self-display; and they are otherwise appropriate. The city set on a hill is Jerusalem, in which the disciples are assembled. The lamp, which

could not be on the mountain in Galilee, is probably on the table at which the discourse is delivered.

(2) In a later section of the Sermon on the Mount the practice of the Pharisees is directly condemned, and the parallelism is further developed. A principle of conduct is stated —the righteousness of the disciples must not be done before men to be seen of them (Matt. vi. 1); and this principle is applied to almsgiving (vv. 2–4), prayer (vv. 5, 6), and fasting (vv. 16–18). The passage from ver. 7 to ver. 15 is obviously here an interpolation : it does not belong to the sequence which is represented by the three works of righteousness. This is proved (a) by the fact that ver. 6 is the conclusion of a paragraph like ver. 4 and ver. 18 ; (b) by the absence of all relation in vv. 7–15 to the principle stated in ver. 1 ; (c) by the fact that Luke enables us to place the interpolation in its original context, which is different, as we shall afterwards see. The objection may perhaps be made that, if the parallelism was defective before, it now errs quite as much on the other side; for among the characteristics of the Pharisees enumerated in Matt. xxiii. 1–7 we do not find any allusion to their almsgiving, prayer, and fasting; but in the section now taken from the Sermon on the Mount the parallelism is distinctly continued, for the teaching of Jesus on these subjects is compared with the practice of the hy ocrites. We have, therefore, something to add to each of our parallel tables. The evidence, as far as it goes, is distinctly in favour of our argument; for, as we have seen already, the two sections in question are out of place in the Sermon on the Mount, and, as we now see, they are quite as obviously appropriate in the later discourse. We may even proceed farther and declare that the later discourse demands them. Cuvier, it is said, could construct the skeleton of an extinct animal from a single scale. Our task is not so difficult. We have before us the beginning of an address which possesses an historical foundation, and the structure is so far complete that we can confidently recognise the original design. We have even found at some distance a number of loose stones left by a keeper of the building; and these stones, which fit into one another, bring the design nearer to completion. How can we avoid the conclusion that they formed part of the

original building? The inspector of critical works, that is, the conservative theologian, may demand, before granting the conclusion, that the original building should be completed. We are fortunately able to supply his demand. We have hitherto been confining our attention to the first of the three synoptists. The second affords no assistance. His version of the discourse on the Pharisees is certainly an editorial fragment: it professes to be nothing more. The parable of the Lamp occurs indeed in Mark iv. 21, and was intended, according to Wendt, to supplement the parable of the Sower; but the parable of the Sower was addressed to people who did not possess lamps, although no doubt they had bushels and beds. They were merely hearers of the word, and the lamp is an illustration for disciples. We must, therefore, reject Wendt's conjecture, which is otherwise quite untenable. The section in Mark iv. 21-25 is distinctly editorial and of no use in our present discussion. The third evangelist, however, is, as usual, when his method is clearly perceived, an invaluable source of information. The following facts should be noted:

(1) The denunciation of the Pharisees in Luke xi. 42-52 agrees almost verbally with the parallel texts in Matt. xxiii. 23, 6, 7, 27, 4, 29-36, 13.

(2) One of the sayings which Luke has substituted for the original defence of the disciples (Luke xi. 39, 40) occurs also in Matthew's parallel context (Matt. xxiii. 25, 26). The other saying (ver. 41) is not to be found in the first gospel, but may be adequately explained as an editorial abstract from Matt. vi. 2-4 and from the teaching on the subject of ablutions (Matt. xv. 1-20).

(3) The parable of the Lamp, which according to our argument originally followed Matt. xxiii. 7, is not far off in the third gospel (Luke xi. 33).

(4) Two fragments which complete the parallelism of Matthew's discourse on the Pharisees follow the incident in the synagogue (Luke xiv. 7-14); and the conclusion of the first (ver. 11) agrees verbally with Matt. xxiii. 12.

Now what do these facts mean? If the source which is represented by the digressions was a chronological gospel, the original arrangement of which was necessarily upset by the purpose of the evangelist to combine this source with Mark and to adopt the second gospel as his standard, the facts are perfectly intelligible in relation to the evidence already gained from Matthew. An address to the disciples on the Pharisees originally followed the conflict on the subject of ablutions. Luke has preserved a few fragments of this address in a relatively original position (Luke xi. 33, 39, 40, 42-52). The rest has in the meantime been omitted. He has afterwards occasion to return to the earlier period in his source. The healing of the palsy and the parables of the Mustard Seed and Leaven represent this earlier period (Luke xiii. 10-21). He reaches the incident in the synagogue (Luke xiv. 1-6); and passing through his source from this narrative, omitting what cannot be introduced for editorial reasons, he comes again to the discourse on the Pharisees. He selects the two fragments before omitted and inserts them here, adapting the incident to its sequel (Luke xiv. 1). His method is perfectly clear. There is absolutely no difficulty which remains to be overcome. The omissions both of Matthew and of Luke will be accounted for in the notes on the different paragraphs. The evidence is complete and decisive. The discourse in the first gospel is fragmentary. Its original design can be detected. The design is brought nearer to completion by sayings which are free for this purpose; and finally Luke completes the parallelism, rounds off the discourse, and reveals its original situation. One question may be asked in conclusion. If all this is true, why has the truth never yet been recognised? The answer is that the critics have made the fundamental mistake of taking for granted, as the result of an imperfect induction, that the apostolic source was a fragmentary collection of logia, either unrelated to the second gospel, or related as a small constituent. They have not kept their eyes open.

a.—The recognition of the authority of the Scribes and Pharisees as the representatives of Moses is quite in the manner of Jesus. He corrects a possible misconception. He again distinguishes the commandments of God from the traditions of men. Wendt takes for granted that the teaching in this paragraph had originally no connection with the denunciation of the Pharisees. His criticism is therefore arbitrary and mistaken. He omits the allusion to the Pharisees in ver. 2 and rejects altogether ver. 4 and vv. 6, 7ᵃ.[1] According to Weiss, the passage from ver. 8 to ver. 12 is ' undoubtedly extraneous.'[2] He is right as far as ver. 11 is concerned, but otherwise he is far astray. Wendt omits ' which is in heaven ' (ver. 9) and ' even the Christ ' (ver. 10). He is sometimes hypercritical. Luke has preserved parallel sayings in ch. xi. 46, 43. The rest of the paragraph is of less value to his readers.

b.—The aim of Jesus is to show that righteousness excludes self-display, but He begins as usual by making a distinction. The righteousness of His disciples must be visible. Wendt puts the city into an appendix.[3] According to Weiss the saying was derived from oral tradition.[4] The description of the eye as the lamp of the body in Luke xi. 34–36 will afterwards be found in its proper context. Wendt keeps this passage as an introduction to the denunciation of the Pharisees,[5] a subject to which it bears no relation.

c.—Wendt retains Matt. vi. 1–6, 16–18 in the Sermon on the Mount; but, as has already been shown, this section is historically unintelligible in the earlier period of the ministry, and completes the thought that the righteousness of the disciples must be visible. According to J. Estlin Carpenter, ' in the regulations for pious observance, for alms and prayer and fasting, as a kind of religious duty or sacred service, we hear the voice of later ecclesiastical usage.'[6] We hear many strange voices when we listen to the negative critic, whose standard of judgment is subjective. Luke has omitted the regulations, but certainly not because he hears in them the voice of later ecclesiastical usage. He cannot conveniently introduce them, and they do not seem conducive to edification. The Pharisees are not in vogue among the Gentiles.

d.—The introduction to the fragments in Luke xiv. 7–14 (ver. 7 and ver. 12) is in each case clearly editorial. The incident in the synagogue has been adapted to the fragments, and the

[1] *Die Lehre Jesu,* Erster Theil, S. 185.
[2] *Introduction to the New Testament,* vol. ii. p. 267.
[3] *Die Lehre Jesu,* Erster Theil, S. 174.
[4] *Introduction to the New Testament,* vol. ii. p. 274.
[5] *Die Lehre Jesu,* Erster Theil, S. 104.
[6] *The First Three Gospels,* p. 96.

fragments have received an editorial heading to adapt them to the earlier incident. If the teaching presupposes a feast, a marriage feast is demanded (ver. 8); but the truth is that these fragments were delivered, not at a feast of any kind, but in a private address to the disciples. They form a contrast to the practice of the Pharisees, who loved the chief places at feasts, and were not benevolent at their dinners. The conclusion of the first has been preserved by Matthew in ch. xxiii. 12. He omits the fragments themselves, because one of his characteristics is the adaptation of Christ's teaching to the supposed requirements of secular life.

e.—The disciples have been assured of a recompense from the Father, if not in this life, at least in the resurrection of the just; and now the destiny of the Pharisees is predicted. They have their reward in this life, but the Judgment Day is at hand. The parallelism is still continued. Matthew's order is distinctly preferable to Luke's. Luke has broken up his original, and the result is some confusion. Luke xi. 52 e.g. is an impossible climax, but, on the other hand, makes the transition easy from the last fragment (Luke xiv. 14) to the rest of the woes. Matt. v. 33–37 probably followed in the original Matt. xxiii. 22. The following passages have been omitted by Luke on account of his Gentile readers: Matt. xxiii. 15, 16–22; v. 34–37. Matt. xxiii. 24 is similar to a text already introduced (Luke vi. 39). Matthew's version contains probably a few secondary variations. (1) An editorial enlargement may be detected in ver. 29 (cf. Luke xi. 47). The allusion to the righteous is an anticipation of ver. 35. (2) A quotation has been turned into a direct and personal announcement in ver. 34. Luke has certainly preserved the original, but has substituted 'apostles' for 'wise men and scribes' (Luke xi. 49). (3) Zachariah has been identified with the son of Barachiah, who perished at the conquest of Gamala in the war which destroyed Jerusalem. (4) 'The righteous blood' (ver. 35) has been substituted for 'the blood of all the prophets' (Luke xi. 50), because Abel the righteous is not supposed to be a prophet. Finally, Matthew has detached the lament over Jerusalem (vv. 37–39) from its original context, as we shall afterwards see; and Mark has recorded a mere extract from the discourse. He is much less interested in the logia than in the incidents, and at the period which he has reached he is hastening to the history of the Passion.

§ 32.—*A Series of Catch-Questions*

Since the arrival of Jesus in Jerusalem, He has excited the antagonism of the classes, and now they manifest their antipathy. They endeavour to catch Him in His talk. The Herodians come with the Pharisees and artfully inquire, 'Is it lawful to pay tribute to Cæsar or not?' They hope to gain their end, whatever the answer may be. The Sadducees next come, with much conceit of superior wisdom. They expect to confound the enthusiast. They go away disappointed, with a subject for private reflection. The last inquirer is a Scribe. He wants Jesus to define the preparation which is necessary for the coming kingdom of God. The traditions of the elders have already been peremptorily set aside, but will Jesus recognise the law and the Jewish privilege? A cunning question may provoke an unsuspecting and imprudent reply. The Scribe, like the others, is baffled. The crafty wisdom of the schools is no match for the intuition of the Prophet. The questions are subtle; the answers are supreme. If the Pharisees and Sadducees and Herodians were emissaries of the chief priests and rulers, the report might well be handed in, 'Never man spake like this man' (John vii. 46).

We have now to show that these narratives were contained in the apostolic source, and that the context we have fixed upon is correct. Their claim to be regarded as constituents of the source is established by the following evidence. (1) The significance of the statement in Luke xi. 53, 54 cannot be mistaken by any student of the gospels whose attention is directed to the subject. If this statement was contained in the source, the sequel was a series of catch-questions. If the statement is purely editorial, the inference still remains. (2) One narrative of the series is in the second digression. The account of the lawyer who asked the question, 'What shall I do to inherit eternal life?' has certainly been taken from the apostolic source, and is not in its original position (Luke x.

25–37). It is parallel to a narrative which Mark includes in the series (Mark xii. 28–34). The two cases are in some respects different; but Luke indirectly identifies them, for in ch. xx. 19–40, when he is following Mark, he deliberately omits the case of the Scribe. He avoids editorial repetition. (3) The three narratives of the series are inseparable. If one was contained in the source, the others may be confidently inferred. A series is presupposed by Luke's statement, and Mark guarantees the succession. (4) The selection of one narrative and the omission of the others can be explained without any difficulty. The lawyer is one of the wise and understanding (Luke x. 21). He is therefore selected as an illustration. The other two narratives are omitted, because they are not useful as illustrations, and because Luke intends to return to Mark. The omission is merely provisional. What, then, we proceed to inquire, was the original context? If our reconstruction of the source is reliable, the question is merely one of precedence. Luke's statement follows the denunciation of the Pharisees; in the second gospel this order is reversed. Which represents the original? The evidence seems at first sight in favour of Mark, who accounts for the warning against the Pharisees by the attempts to catch Jesus in His talk—a much more probable view of the history than that which is involved in the statement of Luke, who apparently assumes that the attempts were provoked by the denunciation. It is scarcely conceivable that the Pharisees, after listening to the terrible invective, should proceed to ask such questions; and, on the other hand, if the questions were provoked by the earlier incidents, as Mark explicitly declares (Mark xii. 12, 13), the subsequent warning is intelligible. In favour of Luke's sequence, however, the following facts should be noticed. (1) The warning in the second gospel is simply an extract from Christ's teaching, and is not related to the questions. Jesus does not warn His disciples against the malice and cunning of the Pharisees, but against their ostentation and hypocrisy. (2) The denunciation, as we have decided, was not delivered at a feast in presence of the Scribes and Pharisees, but formed part of a private instruction, suggested by the conflict concerning the traditions of the elders. (3) On the supposition that

Luke's sequence is primary, Mark's divergence from the source can be explained. He has already in ch. vii. 1–23 recorded the conflict with the Pharisees, and now, when he reaches its original context, he carries forward the private instruction, partly to preserve the historical connection between the questioning and the earlier incidents, and partly to illustrate by contrast the piety and self-sacrifice of the poor widow (Mark xii. 41–44). Considering all the facts, we cannot hesitate to conclude that Luke is the more reliable authority; and in such a case the statement in Luke xi. 53, 54 is to be explained, not by the woes, of which the Pharisees were ignorant, but rather, as in the second gospel, by the earlier incidents, and especially by the rejection of the Pharisaic traditions.

b.—The prelude to the first question, though hypocritical, is noticeable as a compliment to Christ's fearlessness. Luke avoids the ambiguous acknowledgment, 'Thou carest not for any one' (Mark xii. 14). He substitutes an interpretation, 'Thou acceptest not the person of any' (Luke xx. 21). A good example of the free fidelity with which Matthew and Luke reproduce the narratives of Mark, is afforded by their account of this incident. Each uses a different word to indicate the character of the questioners. According to Mark, Jesus knew their 'hypocrisy' (ὑπόκρισις, ver. 15), according to Luke their 'craftiness' (πανουργία, Luke xx. 23), according to Matthew their 'wickedness' (πονηρία, Matt. xxii. 18). A hasty reader might conclude that the three evangelists have independently recorded a common tradition. The tradition-hypothesis has still, through the influence of Dr. Westcott, a number of English adherents. But Matthew and Luke show clearly that they found the word 'hypocrisy' in their source; for, according to Matthew, when Jesus perceived their wickedness, He said, 'Why tempt ye me, ye hypocrites?' (ver. 18) ; and Luke states at the beginning of the narrative that the questioners were spies, who feigned themselves to be righteous (ver. 20). Luke has no knowledge of the first gospel, and Matthew has no knowledge of the third, but the second is their common standard.

c.—The variations of Matthew and Luke are here again purely editorial. Matthew adds that the new incident happened 'on that day' (ver. 23), and that when the multitudes heard Christ's reply they were astonished at His teaching (ver. 33). He substitutes 'Moses said' for 'Moses wrote unto us' (ver. 24), and 'in the resurrection' for 'when they shall rise from the dead' (ver. 28). He omits 'In the book of Moses in the place concerning the bush,' and the last words, 'Ye do greatly err.' Luke's variations are more significant, but not less clearly editorial. (1) He avoids the possible misconception that all will attain to the resurrection from the dead and will be like the angels (Luke xx. 35). (2) He enlarges the allusion to the angels. To be like angels means, according to him, not merely to be free from marriage relationships, but also to die no more, and to be sons of God (ver. 36). (3) He defines the sons of God as sons of the resurrection (ver. 36). This does not necessarily exclude the sonship of believers on earth, but is rather parallel to Rom. viii. 19-23. The ethical relationship, however, is not prominent. (4) He adds to Mark xii. 27, 'for all live unto him'—an addition which is quite foreign to the subject.

d.—Matthew's version of the third incident is different in some respects from Mark's; and as our argument requires us to define clearly the relation of the one to the other, we must examine the details. The question is, Has Matthew taken his version from the apostolic source or from Mark? The variations seem at first sight so great as to exclude the latter alternative. The lawyer in Matthew's version is a different sort of man from Mark's Scribe. The Scribe assented to Christ's summary of the law: he answered discreetly, and was not far from the kingdom of God (Mark xii. 34); but the awyer was not commended. He received a curt reply, and went away baffled like the cunning Sadducees and Herodians. If Matthew is following Mark as his standard, what reason can he have for so freely revising the original? If all questions were as easily answered, there would be few enigmas. The reason is to be found in the context. The other questioners were malicious men, and they were sent to Jesus as the result of a conference among the Pharisees (Matt. xxii. 15); but according to Mark, if the Scribe had a bad motive at first, he restrained his tongue from evil and his lips from speaking guile. He was disarmed by the great answers of Jesus. This seems to Matthew to be inconsistent. He does not believe that the lawyer abandoned his mischievous purpose. On the contrary, he considers him to be a serpent, one of the offspring of vipers; and therefore he omits the extenuating circumstances. It is simply a case of omission. As far as the difference of character is concerned, there is no reason whatever to assume that Matthew takes his narrative from the apostolic source. And the rest of the variations are insignificant. Matthew explicitly declares that the lawyer represented the conspiracy (vv. 34, 35). He omits the introduction to the two commandments, 'Hear, O Israel, the Lord our God, the Lord is one' (Mark xii. 29). He omits 'with all thy strength' (Mark xii. 30), because strength is not co-ordinate with the heart and soul and mind. He substitutes 'On these two commandments hangeth the whole law and the prophets' for 'There is none other commandment greater than these.' We conclude that the variations are purely editorial.

A more difficult question now arises for discussion. Can Luke's lawyer be identified with Mark's Scribe? I submit the following facts. (1) The similarity of the narratives is so obvious that, if the differences in detail can be accounted for, the two men must be regarded as identical. The lawyer, like the Scribe, whatever his ultimate condition may have been, had at first a mischievous purpose. As Luke says, he tempted Jesus (Luke x. 25). In each narrative the two commandments are quoted; and the lawyer, like the Scribe, is commended because he answered discreetly (ver. 28). (2) A few of the details in Mark's narrative are scarcely compatible with the context. If the Scribe, as the context requires, approached Jesus not merely with a bad purpose, but also with a sense of previous defeat, he seems to be too much commended. The commendation, no doubt, is a feature which is common to Mark and Luke; but Mark enlarges it with the statement that the Scribe was not far from the kingdom of God, and there is little if anything in his version to indicate the truth that the man was really a hypocrite. He is introduced like a wolf, and goes away like a lamb. Matthew has observed this fact, and has made a necessary correction. We have, therefore, good reason to believe that Mark's version of the incident is secondary. (3) The version which Luke has preserved is authenticated by the parable of the Good Samaritan. Wendt, indeed, is of quite a different opinion. He accepts the parable, but rejects its historical setting, which, he says, has been borrowed from Mark.[1] His argument may be briefly stated as follows. The parable was intended to secure the concession that an Israelite may have a Samaritan for his neighbour; but this sense of the parable is obscured by its setting, for in ver. 29 the question is, 'Who is the neighbour whom one is to love?' and the answer should be, 'He who fell among the robbers' (cf. vv. 36, 37). Again, the parable was originally an example of the conduct by which one becomes neighbour to another; and the setting makes it an example of the fulfilment of duty towards one who is already a neighbour. These, Wendt declares, are obvious incongruities. The parable has been taken from the apostolic source, and therefore the setting is editorial: it has been borrowed from Mark. In arguing thus, Wendt is deceived by the requirements of his theory that the apostolic source was a collection of logia, entirely unrelated to the second gospel. He finds coincidences of expression and incident, and these seem to be incompatible with the theory; but Luke was unquestionably acquainted with the second gospel, which indeed he uses as his standard, and so the coincidences may be explained as reminiscences of Mark, combined with apostolic material. Since the theory is not to be abandoned, the explanation must be correct. Unfortunately, however, for Wendt's reasoning, the theory is quite untenable, as this volume has already abundantly proved; and in the case before us the explanation is by no means convincing. The fragment which remains when the setting is rejected, is like a body without the head. Wendt passes immediately from the first clause of ver. 25 to the second clause of ver. 29, and includes the whole of the parable. According to the supposition a certain lawyer stood up and tempted Jesus, saying, 'Who is my neighbour?' But surely this is unintelligible.

[1] *Die Lehre Jesu*, Erster Theil, S. 93-96.

The question is a very peculiar one, and must have been suggested by something that either Jesus or the lawyer had already said. The setting which is rejected by Wendt affords an explanation of the mystery. Luke leaves the key in the door; and instead of throwing away the key, as Wendt has done for the sake of a theory, we ought rather to accept it and be thankful. Again, the discovery that the parable is incompatible with its setting, is due to a misapprehension. Wendt seems to forget that the lawyer came tempting Jesus. When he asked the question, 'Who is my neighbour?' he was not anxious to love anybody. He was precisely in the position presupposed by the parable; for he did not believe that the Gentiles and Samaritans could be heirs of the kingdom of God, and his purpose was to provoke an imprudent reply. Jesus did not merely answer a question; He answered the question of this particular Scribe, who was a mischievous man. He detected the thought of the Scribe, and in His reply—a word most fitly spoken—He defeated the man's cunning, and administered a scathing rebuke. Wendt's criticism is almost pedantic. He exaggerates a verbal incongruity, and overlooks the inner unity of the narrative. We must therefore maintain that Luke's version is authenticated by the parable. The statement that the man was going down from Jerusalem to Jericho (ver. 30) confirms the conclusion that Jesus was at the time in Jerusalem. (4) Luke's version of the incident is much more than Mark's in agreement with the historical situation. We have already noticed the defects of Mark's account. Luke's version is entirely appropriate. The lawyer is not commended for his moral disposition, but simply for an accurate quotation. The disposition which is presupposed by his question, is exposed and rebuked in the parable; and the question itself takes its place in the hostile succession. The lawyer's aim is to bring forward the subject of the law in relation to the kingdom of God; and when his first question fails, he propounds immediately another, suggested by the failure of the first—a question which is more direct and thus throws light on its predecessor, but one which, being more direct, exhibits the defects of its qualities. The aim of the man is perfectly apparent, and does not escape the keen eye of Jesus, who replies with consummate wisdom. (5) When Luke in the later period reaches Mark's series of narratives, he omits the case of the Scribe, and simply records the statement which is made by Mark in conclusion (Luke xx. 40, cf. Mark xii. 34). This statement proves clearly that Luke has the second gospel before him, and intentionally omits the case of the Scribe. For what reason? Since Matthew has revised the original on account of its apparent incompatibility with the context, Luke may for the same reason have omitted the original; but he does not hesitate to revise Mark's narratives, and the account of the Scribe, as Matthew has shown, lends itself readily to revision. The true reason probably is, that he identifies the lawyer with the Scribe and avoids editorial repetition. In view of these facts we may claim the conclusion that the two narratives are historically identical, that Luke's version represents the original, and that Mark for the sake of edification has omitted the invidious parable.

§ 33.—*The Son of David*

We have no direct evidence that the three brief narratives now to be considered were contained in the apostolic source. We accept them on the authority of Mark. If the reader insists upon direct and decisive evidence, he is at liberty to exclude these narratives: they are not at all necessary for our argument; but if he suspects, as he has certainly reason to suspect, that the second gospel is a combination of versions, he will probably be willing to grant that the indirect evidence is sufficient.

At present we are concerned only with the first of the three. The interest of this narrative is out of proportion to its dimensions. We cannot infer from the teaching that Jesus had publicly announced his Messianic mission; but this at least is involved, that He thought of Himself as Messiah, that He pondered the Old Testament prophecies, and that although the Christ He was not the Son of David. The question has a personal significance. The reasoning is not merely an exercise of exegetical ingenuity. The purpose of the Speaker plainly is to persuade His hearers that Messiah need not be descended from David; and if He Himself was David's Son, the narrative is altogether unintelligible. The fact is worthy of notice that, according to the testimony of the fourth gospel, when Jesus was in Jerusalem at the feast of Tabernacles, His personality was discussed (John vii. 25-29). Matthew and Luke have reproduced this fragment from the second gospel. Their variations are purely editorial. Matthew omits the clause, 'As he taught in the temple.' According to him the question was addressed to the Pharisees. For 'the common people heard him gladly' he substitutes the statement, taken from Mark xii. 34, that 'no one was able to answer him a word, neither durst any man from that day ask him any more questions' (Matt. xxii. 46). The motive is here quite obvious. Matthew infers that Christ's question was addressed to the questioners immediately after their defeat. Luke substitutes 'they' for 'the Scribes,' because the case of the Scribe has been omitted by him, and 'in the book of Psalms' for 'in the Holy Spirit' to make the allusion more definite, and perhaps because he believes that the Holy Spirit is the special gift of Christ. The concluding statement, which he omits, was certainly in his source; for according to him the warning against the Scribes was delivered in the hearing of all the people (Luke xx. 45).

§ 34.—*The Widow's Mites*

Little can be said about the poor widow. The fragment has become isolated in the history. Wendt suggests that it was originally used as an example by Jesus in connection with the statement regarding the Pharisees that they devour widows' houses [1] (Mark xii. 40); but since Mark xii. 38-40 is a mere extract from Christ's teaching, and has been removed from its original position, apparently to illustrate by contrast the case of the widow, and since Matthew and Luke in their larger presentation of the discourse make no allusion to the devouring of widows' houses, the conjecture can scarcely be adopted

---

[1] *Die Lehre Jesu*, Erster Theil, S. 41, cf. *The Teaching of Jesus*, vol. i. p. 113.

with any degree of assurance. The allusion in Mark xii. 40 may quite as well be an editorial anticipation of the example. Matthew has omitted the fragment. He adapts Christ's teaching to the supposed requirements of secular and ecclesiastical life, and the piety of the poor widow who cast all her living into the treasury might seem to him more worthy of imitation than her liberality.

§ 35.—*The Temple made without Hands*

In the second gospel the reply of Jesus is reported as a prediction that the Temple would be destroyed : ' Seest thou these great buildings ? there shall not be left here one stone upon another, which shall not be thrown down ' (Mark xiii. 2). I venture to suggest that this is an editorial interpretation. The attention of the reader is invited to the following facts. (1) Matthew and Luke agree with Mark, but they are not independent authorities. They are following the second gospel as their standard, and simply reproduce Mark's report (Matt. xxiv. 1, 2 ; Luke xxi. 5, 6). (2) The connection of this fragment with the apocalyptic discourse in Mark xiii. 3–37 is purely editorial; for the subject of the discourse, as Matthew indirectly declares (Matt. xxiv. 3), and as our analysis will prove, was the coming of the kingdom of God, and the destruction of Jerusalem was not even mentioned as an episode. (3) When Jesus was before the chief priests and the council, some of the witnesses testified that they had heard Him say, ' I will destroy this temple that is made with hands, and in three days I will build another made without hands ' (Mark xiv. 58 ; Matt. xxvi. 61). This evidence could scarcely be fictitious. It is described by the evangelist as false witness, but to suppose that the accusers were guilty of perjury is an extreme and unnecessary hypothesis. It was simply a case of misunderstanding. The quotation authenticates itself. Now obviously the exclamation of the disciples when they passed out of the Temple with Jesus might suggest as a reply the saying which was afterwards quoted as an accusation, and quite as obviously the report which Mark gives of the reply may be a paraphrase or interpretation. The question is, Have we any reason to believe that Mark has thus modified the original? If the apostolic source contained an account of the trial, the saying which was quoted against Jesus would probably be also recorded in its historical context; and if, on the other hand, as the critics believe, the source contained no account of the Passion, the probability still remains, for a saying so pregnant would not be likely to be excluded from any collection of the logia. In the fourth gospel indeed we are told distinctly that when the Jews demanded a sign after the purging of the Temple, Jesus said, 'Destroy this temple, and in three days I will raise it up' (John ii. 19). This is unmistakably the later accusation, and so far our argument is confirmed; but the context of the saying in the fourth gospel is different from that of the prediction in Mark, and the explicit testimony of the fourth evangelist seems therefore to forbid the conjecture that the prediction was originally the saying. The context of the saying in the fourth gospel has, however, already been recognised as editorial. When the Jews demanded a sign Jesus did not say in reply, 'Destroy this temple, and in three days I will raise it up.' He did not grant any sort of sign. On the contrary, as we have seen, He reproached the Jews for their lack of intellectual and moral perception, and sternly rebuked the demand. But if the context in the fourth gospel is editorial, and if the saying was recorded in the source before the quotation at the trial, we have really some reason to believe that Mark has modified the original; for the only other context available is that of the prediction in the second gospel. Mark's sequel moreover is editorial. The apocalyptic discourse did not originally follow the exclamation of the disciples as they passed with their Master out of the Temple. The connection is not historical. A motive is therefore apparent for the change which according to the supposition has been effected. Mark wishes to pass to the discourse. He believes that when Jesus said, 'Destroy this temple that is made with hands, and in three days I will build another made without hands,' He predicted the destruction of Jerusalem; and so for the sake of transition he adopts a less mysterious reading. He substitutes an interpretation for the text.

The history of this text in our gospels is interesting and

worthy of notice. Two interpretations have been preserved, one of them prosaic and the other allegorical. Mark finds in the text a prediction of the destruction of the Temple; and according to the fourth evangelist Jesus 'spake of the temple of his body.' Theologians may accept one of these explanations if they please, or both if the two can be combined; but the critic whose aim is historical truth must remind theologians of the fact that the text is not a prediction, but simply a statement of the thought that the Temple, although God's house —a house of prayer for all the nations—is not essential to religion, that ceremonial is insignificant in comparison with the weightier matters of the law, that God is Spirit, and that they who worship Him must worship in spirit and truth.

§ 36.—*A Prediction of Judgment*

In our analysis of Luke's second digression and reconstruction of the source which it represents we have reached ch. xii. 2, and are entering now a dark labyrinth which has never been successfully explored. Luke almost seems to be conscious of the difficulty which the students of a distant critical age would find in his editorial method; for on the entrance gate he has inscribed these words, 'There is nothing covered up, that shall not be revealed: and hid, that shall not be known.' The assurance seems almost specially designed for the consolation and encouragement of the critic. The failure of scholars to pass through the windings of the labyrinth has hitherto been due to the fact that they have not perceived Luke's method. His digressions represent the apostolic source, a gospel complete in itself, and not a mere collection of logia. He preserves as far as possible the sequence of this source, but finds rearrangement necessary. For, in the first place, the source contains many narratives which have already been taken from the second gospel, and repetition must always be avoided; and secondly, he intends to return to Mark as his standard, and to reproduce Mark's account of the last events in Jerusalem. But the apostolic source contains also an account of the later period with additional incidents and logia, and this additional material must either be combined with Mark's narratives seriatim, or carried back to the earlier digressions and arranged for the sake of edification. Without altogether rejecting the first of these methods, Luke finds the second more convenient. His digressions accordingly exhibit the characteristics which have already been noted. They preserve an historical sequence and outline, allowance being made for omissions, but contain also many interpolations derived for the most part from the later period of the ministry. This statement has already been verified in the course of our critical investigation. We know, therefore, what to expect in advancing to the section before us. We have the clue in our hands, and may reasonably hope that the evangelist's promise will be fulfilled. I submit the following facts:

(1) From the beginning of the section to Luke xii. 59, the succession is editorial and not apostolic. A number of loose fragments have here been artificially combined. Luke xii. 10 has already been placed in its original context, and the subject of the rest of the discourse from ver. 2 to ver. 12 is obviously not hypocrisy. These verses could not originally follow ver. 1; the connection is simply verbal. Again, from ver. 13 to ver. 34 the subject is Christ's doctrine of riches, and from ver. 35 to ver. 48 the subject is the coming of the kingdom. That these discourses were addressed to the disciples one after the other without any interval, and in the case of the second without an historical suggestion, is in itself exceedingly improbable. The discourse on riches is introduced by an incident, and is therefore less clearly an editorial interpolation, but the incident is merely an introduction, retained for the sake of the discourse. The three subjects are distinct. The connection is too remote to be historical. A motive is apparent for the combination, since Luke wishes to preserve the teaching set free by his editorial method. We thus reach the conclusion that the evangelist has strung the jewels together with a charge to the twelve as his thread. Finally, the fragments from ver. 49 to ver. 53 are extracts from a later context; the fragment on spiritual meteorology (vv. 54–57) has already been placed in its historical setting, and the conclusion on the subject of

forgiveness is, notwithstanding Wendt, an unmistakably alien addition (vv. 58, 59). When the original situation of each fragment is discovered, the argument will be complete and decisive. In the meantime, provisionally, our statement may be claimed as a fact.

(2) In the section which follows from ch. xiii. 1 to ch. xiv. 35 a significant sequence is observable. In this section, as in the last, we can detect a number of interpolations. The following passages have already been located in the history: the healing of the daughter of Abraham (Luke xiii. 10-17), the parables of the Mustard Seed and Leaven (vv. 18-21), the raising of the Sabbath question in the synagogue (xiv. 1-6), the two fragments from the discourse on the Pharisees (vv. 7-14). The parable of the Fig Tree has been introduced by the evangelist to illustrate the necessity of repentance (Luke xiii. 6-9). The parable of the Great Feast (Luke xiv. 15-24) is another interpolation suggested by the preceding fragment. The historical situation of these passages will soon be discovered. In the meantime they may be provisionally set aside. What, then, are the incidents which remain? An account is first given of a few doctrinaires who believed, like Job's comforters, that calamities are providential dispensations, intended for the punishment of sin. They came to Jesus with their comfortable piety, and received an unexpected electric shock; for He emphatically replied, 'Except ye repent, ye shall all likewise perish.' The question is next asked and answered, 'Lord, are they few that be saved?' (Luke xiii. 23-30). According to the evangelist, Jesus is on His way through cities and villages, teaching, and journeying to Jerusalem (ver. 22); but the journey to Jerusalem after the delivery of the parables at the seaside has already received its place in the history, and the heading in ver. 22 is merely an indication that two sources are being combined. Luke does not expressly say that he is combining the apostolic source with Mark, but this heading is a clear intimation of the fact; for the journey is a reminiscence of the second gospel to which the evangelist intends to return, and is run through the apostolic material to make the whole work more compact. Jesus is at present in Jerusalem. He

has publicly declared that repentance is the only means of escape from impending judgment; and now one asks, apparently for the sake of obtaining more information concerning this judgment which according to Jesus will soon be inflicted, 'Lord, are they few that be saved?' A motive is provided for the question when the two narratives are thus brought together; and since the intervening material is editorial, there is nothing to keep them apart. The next narrative in the series is an account of a warning which Jesus received from the Pharisees (Luke xiii. 31–33), and to this is added a brief address to Jerusalem (vv. 34, 35). Now obviously the first of these fragments presupposes that Jesus is not in Jerusalem; for the jurisdiction of Herod extended only to Peræa and Galilee, and according to the explicit declaration of Jesus, He was safe at the time of the warning, as it could not be that a prophet should perish out of Jerusalem. And quite as obviously the brief invocation which follows is impossible as an historical sequel; for the reception anticipated in ver. 35 is different from the reception to which He looked forward when He delivered the saying in ver. 33. The truth is, as we shall afterwards see, that the address to Jerusalem belongs properly to a later context, and is here an editorial addition. We therefore find as the result of our analysis that Jesus has left Jerusalem and is either in Peræa or Galilee; and now we have reached the end of the series. Great multitudes are going with Jesus, and He warns them to count the cost of discipleship (Luke xiv. 25–35). In the fourth gospel a similar discourse is recorded after the last entry into Jerusalem (John xii. 20–32). The thought is identical, and the agreement is in a few details verbal. The apostolic source has already been found to coincide in its general outline with the history presented in the fourth gospel. The full extent of this coincidence is not yet apparent, and cannot be shown in this volume; but the agreement is already sufficiently obvious to justify the provisional conclusion that the teaching in Luke xiv. 25–35 was associated in the apostolic source with the last entry into Jerusalem. A sequence has therefore been discovered which has every appearance of being historical. Jesus is at first in Jerusalem, then He leaves the city, and goes into Peræa or Galilee, and finally He returns to be present at the last feast of the Passover.

(3) We now turn to a narrative which Matthew alone has preserved. In ch. xvii. 24-27 he gives an account of an incident which happened in Capernaum before the last Passover in Jerusalem. This incident has been taken from the apostolic source, and has been inserted in the outline of the second gospel. The context is not Matthew's, but Mark's. A reason must, however, be found for the insertion of the incident in this particular position; and the only possible reason is that in the apostolic source, from which the narrative has been taken, it was connected with a journey to Galilee made before the last Passover. But according to our analysis of Luke's digression Jesus left Jerusalem after the feast of Tabernacles, and went into Peræa or Galilee. Apparently, therefore, the original context has been found. If the Capernaum incident in the first gospel has been taken from the apostolic source, and if Matthew has preserved the original position in recording the narrative before the last visit to Jerusalem—two inferences which can scarcely be disputed— the incident takes its place as one of the apostolic series discovered in Luke's digression.

(4) Returning to the digression, we now note another incident, detached by Luke from its original context. In Luke x. 38-42 an account is given of a visit to Bethany. The context is unmistakably editorial; for after the return of the twelve, instead of going to Bethany, Jesus went with His disciples to the villages of Cæsarea Philippi, and Mary is one of the babes to whom the Father reveals Himself (ver. 21). Now the visit to Bethany could scarcely be earlier than the last journey to Jerusalem. No earlier context is available; and the narrative itself, with its emphatic announcement of the one thing needful, and its warning against anxiety, is thoroughly in harmony, not merely with the later discourses, but also with the tone and substance of thought which one would expect to find in Jesus, when the end was drawing near. We may therefore reasonably conclude that this visit was made to Bethany after the journey into Galilee and before the last Passover in Jerusalem.

(5) Our inductive argument is confirmed throughout by the testimony of the fourth evangelist. The coincidence of the discourse delivered at the entrance into Jerusalem has already been noted ; and now we have also to observe (a) that the residence in Jerusalem was prolonged for a considerable time after the feast of Tabernacles (John vii. 10, 37 ; x. 22) ; (b) that when Jesus left Jerusalem 'He went away beyond Jordan into the place where John was at the first baptising, and there He abode' (John x. 40) ; (c) that He subsequently paid a visit to Bethany, the village of Martha and Mary, and that Martha served at the supper while Mary sat at His feet (John xii. 1–3) ; (d) that He went from Bethany to Jerusalem and remained in the city until the end (John xii. 12). Combining all these details, and attaching due weight to the Johannine confirmation of the argument, we gain a new series of incidents and logia, consisting of a prediction of judgment, a discourse in reply to the question, 'Are they few that be saved?' a journey to Peræa and a warning against Herod the fox, a visit to Capernaum in the days when the Temple tax was gathered, a visit to Bethany the village of Martha and Mary, and a discourse on the cost of discipleship at the last entrance into Jerusalem. These incidents and logia require to be examined more minutely, but we cannot hesitate to conclude that a distinct advance has been made, and indeed that by keeping the clue in our hands we have passed through the labyrinth into the light of day.

The claim of the prediction of judgment to be regarded as the first narrative in the new series may perhaps be disputed by the reader. If the section consists in so many cases of fragments combined by the evangelist, how can we be sure that this narrative is an historical exception? May it not quite as well be a similar fragment inserted here to illustrate the punishment of the unforgiving? (Luke xii. 58, 59). Or, again, may it not belong properly to the historical sequence, which is represented by the healing of the daughter of Abraham and the parables of the Mustard Seed and Leaven? (Luke xiii. 10–21). I reply (1) that the other fragments which have been provisionally set aside as editorial interpolations will be afterwards placed in their original context, whereas no other context can be found for the prediction of judgment; (2) that the earlier sequence represented by the narratives above mentioned, if not altogether excluded by the reconstruction already accomplished, is definitely discredited by the question, 'Are they few that be saved?'—a question which presupposes the prediction and must be viewed as the historical sequel. The omission of the narrative by Matthew and Mark is not a serious difficulty. In the case of Mark such omissions are not exceptional; and Matthew, having otherwise disposed of the teaching in reply to the question, 'Are they few that be saved?' must omit the introductory incident.

§ 37.—*The Narrow Gate*

a.—The answer to the question in the third gospel coincides with a fragment which Matthew has inserted in the Sermon on the Mount (Matt. vii. 13, 14). Matthew has reduced the difficulty, 'Enter ye in by the narrow gate.' Luke's word 'strive' (ἀγωνίζεσθε) is demanded by the context; for the necessity of repentance has been proclaimed, and repentance according to Jesus is not merely turning and walking, but is rather an athletic exercise, the endeavour of a man of violence. Luke has abridged the original, which undoubtedly contained a contrast between the two gates and two ways. He omits the contrast, and mentions only the narrow door for the sake of transition to the fragment in vv. 25-30, which was not, as we shall see, the original sequel. The gate has been turned into a door on account of ver. 25.

b.—The sequel in our reconstruction is obviously a continuation of the thought which Jesus has already expressed. The question is, 'Are they few that be saved?' The answer has been an affirmative, and the difficulty of repentance has been given as a reason. In the parable of the Great Supper the supplementary thought is conveyed that the difficulty does not consist in any want of attraction, but is due to the worldly attachments of men. The call to repentance is a call to escape from impending judgment; but that is not the whole of the truth, for salvation is a positive as well as a negative. A certain man made a great supper, and bade many, and they all with one consent began to make excuse. The narrowness is defined by the excuses. The gate and the way are so narrow that no one can enter with his fields or oxen or wife. He must choose between the world and the kingdom of God. The great supper is evidently intended to represent the heavenly kingdom, for it is a positive of which the negative is judgment; and according to the parable the heavenly consummation is so near that the invitations have already been issued, and there seems to be some likelihood of a lack of guests. The worldly will not accept the invitation. All this is undoubtedly appropriate; but the question is, What are the facts? So the reader may exclaim with commendable dislike of exegetical or critical assumptions. I reply by enumerating the facts.

(1) The parable of the Great Supper in Luke xiv. 15-24 is the parable of the Marriage Feast in Matt. xxii. 1-10. This is not a conjecture, but a fact. It is antecedently improbable that two parables which are so coincident in aim and outline and details should be historically distinct; and the differences can easily be accounted for. The following is a list of Matthew's variations. (a) He omits the excuses. He does not wish to represent farming and commerce and marriage as preoccupations which keep men out of the kingdom. He adapts the teaching of Jesus to the supposed requirements of secular life. (b) He omits the charge to go into the streets and lanes, and to bring in the poor and maimed and blind and lame. He believes in respectability. A king's guests, he thinks, should be more select. He adds, however, with an awkward fidelity to his original, that the servants went out into the highways and gathered together as many as they found, both good and bad (ver. 10). The presence of the bad at the feast is an editorial addition suggested by the guests in the original, and intended to prepare the way for the parable of the Wedding Garment (vv. 11-14). (c) He interpolates the statement that the servants were killed by the people who made light of the invitation, and that the king sent his armies, and destroyed the murderers, and burned their city (ver. 7). This is unmistakably an editorial allusion to the destruction of Jerusalem. The servants are killed in

P

ver. 6, and restored to activity in ver. 8. (*d*) He combines the parable of the Wedding Garment with the parable of the Great Supper. That these were originally distinct is proved by the editorial transition in ver. 10, by the absence of allusion to the necessity of a wedding garment in the earlier parable, and by the fact that the conclusion involved in the second parable is not the conclusion of the first. The lesson conveyed by the first parable is that all who do not accept the invitation will be excluded from the kingdom of God. According to Matthew, however, the murderers have already been destroyed, and their city has been burned. The sentence of exclusion cannot therefore be pronounced, though required by the original parable. Matthew omits the conclusion, and substitutes the parable of the Wedding Garment, which conveys the supplementary but different lesson that moral fitness is necessary, and not merely the acceptance of an invitation, if men would enter into the kingdom. (*e*) In combining the two parables Matthew has been compelled to make another alteration. The second is a parable of a marriage feast; the first is an account of a great supper. The second cannot be adapted to the first, and therefore the first has been adapted to the second. The great supper has been converted into a marriage feast, made by a king for his son. These variations are all manifestly secondary. Matthew's parable is the same as Luke's, and Luke has preserved the original.

(2) Each evangelist has placed the parable in a different context. According to Matthew, it was addressed to the people after the purging of the Temple; according to Luke, on the other hand, it was delivered in a Pharisee's house. Both contexts cannot be original; and the truth is that each is secondary. The section in the third gospel from ch. xiv. 1 to ver. 14 has already been analysed in detail. The house, as we have seen, was really a synagogue. The instruction from ver. 7 to ver. 14 was given neither in a Pharisee's house nor in a synagogue, but in a private discourse to the disciples. The introduction to the parable of the Great Supper is therefore clearly editorial (Luke xiv. 15), and the context is not historical. Again, the parable of the Vineyard was not, as Matthew appears to believe, intended to teach that the

kingdom of God would be taken from the Jews, and given to a nation bringing forth the fruits thereof. What Jesus taught was simply this, that the Pharisees on account of their perverseness and occupation with purely personal aims could no longer be the keepers of the vineyard. But the parable of the Marriage Feast or Great Supper is obviously an alien addition to the thought thus emphatically conveyed by the other. The two have really nothing in common but an insignificant verbal coincidence. The connection depends altogether on the interpretation of the parables; but Matthew's interpretation is ecclesiastical, and the conclusion inevitably follows that the connection is purely editorial.

(3) The adaptation of the parable of the Great Supper to the situation adopted in our reconstruction has not yet been sufficiently observed. We have noticed that the parable carries forward the thought expressed in the preceding verses; but that is not the whole of the truth, for the sequel is quite as appropriate. The parable concludes with a sentence of exclusion, 'I say unto you, that none of those men which were bidden shall taste of my supper;' and Luke proceeds to describe the vain and bitter regret of those men, when the master of the house is risen up and hath shut the door, and repentance is too late (Luke xiii. 25–30). These are the facts, and the reader may be left to draw the conclusion.

c.—The transition from Luke xiii. 24 to ver. 25 is so abrupt that we must take for granted either interpolation or omission. Wendt adopts the first of these alternatives. He passes from ver. 24 to ver. 26, rejecting ver. 25, which is, as he says, a reminiscence of the parable of the Ten Virgins [1] (Matt. xxv. 10–12). Wendt usually attempts to get rid of his difficulties by invoking the theory of reminiscence, but unfortunately he seldom succeeds. In the present case the interpolation is unnecessary, and Luke's motive for introducing a reminiscence is not by any means obvious. He gains nothing: on the contrary, as Wendt admits, he makes the text precipitous. The truth rather is that the parable of the Great Supper was originally situated between ver. 24 and ver. 25. Ver. 25 is a rock which stands in the way of the

[1] *Die Lehre Jesu*, Erster Theil, S. 131.

critic. Wendt proposes to use dynamite; but such a method is destructive and dangerous to the critic himself, and the difficulty may surely be otherwise avoided. Wendt perceives that the parable of the Great Supper was originally a part of this context, for he places it after Luke xiii. 30. This situation, however, is remarkable for nothing but awkwardness. The end is placed at the beginning, and the beginning is placed at the end. The natural order is inverted. By carrying the parable back to the difficulty, two notable ends are gained. We are able to scale the rock, which indeed is seen to be necessary; and the continuity of the discourse is preserved. If the question is asked why Luke has omitted the parable, the answer is perfectly evident and equally satisfactory. He does not omit the parable: he simply reserves it to illustrate by example the blessedness of inviting to a dinner or supper the poor, the maimed, the lame, and the blind (Luke xiv. 13). A few facts still require to be noted. (1) Luke xiii. 25-27 has been partly preserved by Matthew in ch. vii. 22, 23. Matthew's text is secondary. He adapts the original to the warning against the false prophets (Matt. vii. 15). The call to enter in by the narrow gate and to walk on the narrow way is introduced almost immediately before (Matt. vii. 13, 14). (2) Matthew has also preserved Luke xiii. 28, 29. He has inserted this fragment in the narrative of the centurion's son, and has modified both the narrative and the fragment in adapting the one to the other (Matt. viii. 11, 12). According to the original narrative, as we have seen, the centurion sent elders of the Jews to Jesus. This detail has been omitted by Matthew on account of the fragment, which is, as he believes, a prophetic intimation of the rejection of the Jews and the ingathering of the Gentiles. And, on the other hand, the text has been modified to convey more clearly the interpretation; for the Jews are described as 'the sons of the kingdom' who shall be cast forth into the outer darkness (ver. 12). The meaning, however, simply is, that although the excuses of the impenitent may become earnest pleas for admission, the pleas will be unavailing when the door has been shut by the master of the house. The ingathering of the Gentiles is certainly permitted by the text, but the rejection of the Jews is foreign to the thought. The rejected ones are the impenitent, those who received the invitation and began with one consent to make excuse. Matthew substitutes 'Many shall come' (ver. 11) for 'They shall come' (Luke xiii. 29). The reader should also notice that Luke xiii. 30 presupposes in the preceding context some such passage as Luke xiv. 21-23. The last in this world are the poor and maimed and blind and lame, and the vagrants of the highways and hedges; but some of these will be among the first in the kingdom. The true inequality will be revealed when the world is judged by God.

d.—The parable of the Wedding Garment appropriately concludes the discourse. Its lesson is obviously the climax; for men are not admitted into the heavenly kingdom merely because they accept an invitation. They must sincerely repent. Many are called, but few are chosen. The choice rests ultimately with God, and is determined by moral fitness. Luke has omitted this fragment to avoid repetition. The final sentence is already involved in Luke xiii. 28. The parable besides is so short as to seem comparatively unimportant. A reason need not be given for the omission of these discourses by Mark. He omits the logia systematically. He is interested chiefly in the incidents and in the development of the Messianic mission.

§ 38.—*The Morrow of Messiah and Afterwards*

We have now to consider in detail a series of three brief narratives contained in the apostolic source between the teaching on repentance and the last entrance into Jerusalem. After a residence in Jerusalem, prolonged, according to the fourth gospel, beyond the feast of Dedication (John x. 22), Jesus left the city. He went away beyond Jordan into the place where John was at the first baptising, and there He abode (ver. 40). He was warned by the Pharisees that Herod desired to kill Him (Luke xiii. 31-33). He went to Capernaum and paid the Temple tax (Matt. xvii. 24-27). And in returning to Jerusalem to be present at the feast of the Passover, He visited Bethany, the village of Martha and Mary (Luke x.

38-42; John xii. 1). These are the facts with which we are at present concerned.

The incident reported in Luke xiii. 31-33 has been adopted as the first of the series for the following reasons. (1) An interval of a few months is presupposed between the feast of Dedication and the visit of Jesus to Capernaum; for the feast was observed in December, and the Temple tax was levied in March. We possess no record of this interval, and that is somewhat surprising; but if Jesus was in danger of being seized by Herod, the silence of the history is accounted for. (2) According to the testimony of the fourth gospel, Jesus went away beyond Jordan, and abode there after the feast of Dedication; in other words, He went into Peræa, a district which was included in the tetrarchy of Herod Antipas. (3) The Capernaum incident has been interpolated by Matthew in Mark's narrative immediately after the announcement that the Son of Man would be delivered up into the hands of men and killed, and on the third day raised up (Matt. xvii. 22, 23; Mark ix. 31, 32). This announcement may not be historically the same as the statement made in reply to the Pharisees (Luke xiii. 32). That is a matter which can only be determined by a careful analysis of the second gospel; but at least the resemblance is sufficient to justify the inference that in the apostolic source, from which Matthew has taken the interpolated fragment, the reply to the Pharisees preceded the Capernaum incident. We may now proceed to examine the details. The statement that the Pharisees delivered their warning 'in that very hour' (ver. 31) is too indefinite to be historical, and too precise to be inadvertent. If the hour is supposed to be that of the discourse on repentance, the inference is involved that the whole discourse, with the doctrinaire incident which suggested it (Luke xiii. 1-5), was delivered in Peræa or Galilee; but Luke has broken up the discourse, for the parable of the Great Supper is carried beyond 'that very hour' (Luke xiv. 16-24), and the time is still indefinite. A similar statement is made in Luke xiii. 1. We are there told that the doctrinaires came to Jesus 'at that very season;' but the season is not otherwise indicated. The section which immediately

precedes the statement is a combination of fragments derived
for the most part from a later period. No reliance can be
placed on Luke's digression chronology. His precision must
be due to editorial motive. What, then, has induced the
evangelist to connect so closely the warning against Herod
with the discourse on the subject of repentance? Jesus has
said, 'There are last which shall be first, and there are first
which shall be last' (ver. 30). This is a prediction, and its
fulfilment is illustrated in the sequel. 'In that very hour
there came certain Pharisees, saying to him, Get thee out,
and go hence: for Herod would fain kill thee' (ver. 31). Herod
is one of the first, and Jesus is one of the last; but the
Fugitive in danger of man's judgment has still a present and
a future—to-day and to-morrow—and on the third day He
will be perfected (ver. 32). The last will become the first.
The allusion here is not to the physical resurrection. The
meaning simply is that Jesus will be perfected as Messiah.
By being faithful to the Spirit of the kingdom, by humbling
Himself even unto death, He will vindicate His mission and
attain the end of His calling. The Bridegroom will be taken
away from His friends, and they will fast in those days; but
the separation will be the consummation of His hopes. He
will pass through the narrow gate and along the narrow way
into the promise of God. Continuity of life is certainly
expected; but the resurrection from the dead on the third
day is an idea which is foreign to the text. The third day is
defined by the morrow. The morrow means a future on
earth—a short future, no doubt, but longer than the interval
which is measured by the rising and the setting of the sun;
and the third day means an afterwards beyond the future on
earth, when Messiah, through the suffering of death, will be
crowned with glory and honour.

§ 39.—*The Temple Tax*

Wendt suggests that the fish miracle is an editorial
addition to the original narrative.[1] He is probably not far
wrong. The miracle is unnecessary and exceptional, and may

[1] *Die Lehre Jesu*, Erster Theil, S. 181.

well be a traditional accretion suggested by the two principles of freedom and expediency. Freedom requires that the legal exactions should be denied, expediency that no one should be caused to stumble. The money is paid; but it comes from the sea, not from the apostolic bag.

§ 40.—*Martha and Mary*

The fourth evangelist has preserved a reminiscence of this incident. He relates that before the Passover, Jesus went to Bethany, and they made Him a supper, and Martha served, while Mary anointed His feet (John xii. 1-3). Two narratives have here been combined, and one of them is obviously the account of the sisters contained in the apostolic source. The historical situation which is thus confirmed increases the significance of the incident. Jesus is going up to the feast of the Passover. In Galilee Herod is His enemy; in Jerusalem the Pharisees are implacable. He still has a morrow, but the time is far spent, and the after-day is at hand. This accounts for the concentration of His mind. ' One thing is needful, and Mary hath chosen the good part which shall not be taken away from her.'

The picture is exquisitely beautiful—Jesus with the shadow on His face, Mary with her tender solicitude, the housewife with her zeal and anxieties. Martha, Martha, thou art careful and troubled about many things, but these things are not needful. The one necessity is to know the truth and keep it, waiting for the kingdom of God.

§ 41.—*The Entrance into Jerusalem*

The coincidence of the two discourses in Luke xiv. 25-35 and John xii. 20-32, when considered in relation to the cumulative evidence which has already been brought forward, is sufficient in itself to justify the inference that the discourse in Luke's digression represents the entrance into Jerusalem. John's version of the apostolic tradition is probably different from Luke's, and he makes a free use of his material, restating the thought, and even adding to it for the sake of presenting to his readers a more mature and dogmatic conception of the Person of Christ; but the original identity of the incidents and logia has never been altogether obscured, and in the case of the discourse before us it may be recognised at a glance. The question, however, may be asked, What has become of the narrative in which the discourse was originally set? Does the critic not seem to resemble the companions of Saul who stood speechless on the road to Damascus, hearing a voice but beholding no man? I invite the attention of the reader to the following facts. (1) The details of time and place and incident have necessarily been omitted by Luke. He is combining the apostolic source with the second gospel, and intends to return to Mark for the history of the Passion. He is introducing the apostolic material as a series of episodes in the last journey. The Capernaum incident recorded by Matthew has therefore already been omitted, and Bethany has simply been described as 'a certain village' (Luke x. 38). In a journey from Galilee to Jerusalem an account of the entrance into the city would obviously be out of place, and Luke does what his method requires him to do. He puts into his digression the discourse which Mark has, for editorial reasons, detached from its historical setting; and afterwards, when he returns to the second gospel, he reproduces the narrative of the earlier evangelist. (2) In reproducing Mark's narrative of the entrance into the city Luke records additional details which can only be accounted for as fragments of the apostolic source. The colt incident has been taken from Mark (Mark xi. 1-8; Luke xix. 29-36), but the passage which immediately follows represents the apostolic source (vv. 37-44). Now what does this passage contain? Jesus with His disciples is approaching the city. He has reached the descent of the Mount of Olives. The disciples who believe that their Master at last is entering into His kingdom advance with demonstrations of joy. They are neither rebuked nor corrected; but when the city stands clearly in view Jesus bursts into tears, foreseeing with prophetic compassion the sad and terrible end. This addition proves quite conclusively that the apostolic source contained an account of the entrance into the city; and by combining the details thus gained with the discourse put into the digression, we are able with approximate completeness to reconstruct the original.

a.—Matthew has interpolated in Mark's account of the purging of the Temple an apostolic fragment which is here available for comparison (Matt. xxi. 14–16). He relates (1) that a number of blind and lame people were healed; (2) that there were children in the Temple who cried, 'Hosanna to the Son of David;' (3) that when the chief priests and Scribes saw the miracles, and heard the crying of the children, they were indignant and addressed a complaint to Jesus, who replied, 'Yea: did ye never read, Out of the mouth of babes and sucklings thou hast perfected praise?' This passage is a curious combination of apostolic with editorial material. The situation is clearly editorial, for the conjunction of events is far too deliberate to be historical; but the entrance into Jerusalem is described immediately before, and Matthew, as Luke shows, has simply carried forward an incident which happened at the entrance into the city (cf. Mark xi. 9, 10). The healing of the blind and lame is an editorial inference intended to account for the praise of the children, and suggested by the allusion to Christ's mighty works in Luke xix. 37. The children have been projected into the Temple by Matthew from the text concerning the babes and sucklings. Luke shows that these details are secondary, and that the babes and sucklings were really the disciples, who gave expression to their joy, not in the Temple, but on the way to Jerusalem. Finally, the allusion to the stones (Luke xix. 40) has been omitted by Matthew because the incident, according to his report, happened in the Temple; the description of the disciples as 'a great multitude' (Luke xix. 37) was probably suggested by Mark's account of the triumphal progress; and Luke has omitted the quotation because it seems scarcely appropriate.

b.—When Jesus wept over the city, He predicted, according to Luke, its destruction (Luke xix. 43, 44). The following facts should be noted. (1) A similar prediction in Mark xiii. 2 has already been recognised as editorial. (2) The apocalyptic discourse in the second gospel contains an unmistakable allusion to the days of the Jewish war (Mark xiii. 14–20), and Luke has added a more definite statement which presupposes the destruction of the city (Luke xxi. 24); but the statement in the third gospel is editorial, and, as we shall see, the subject of the original discourse was the coming of the kingdom of God, and the events which afterwards happened were not at all foreseen. (3) In our analysis of the second digression we have already found a fragment which Luke has detached from its original context and has added to the statement that a prophet is safe anywhere out of Jerusalem (Luke xiii. 34, 35). This fragment, if originally situated in the position now occupied by the prediction, would necessarily be omitted by Luke to avoid repetition; and since the rest of the original in Luke xix. 41, 42 is obviously incomplete, demanding some sort of sequel, a few words would require to be substituted. Now the fragment in Luke xiii. 34, 35 would probably suggest the prediction, which is indeed simply an interpretation of the saying, 'Behold, your house is left unto you' (ver. 35). If the R.V. text can be trusted, Matthew considers this saying to be a prediction of the destruction of Jerusalem, for he says that the house would be left desolate (Matt. xxiii. 38); and whether this word 'desolate' was originally in Matthew's text or not, it is unquestionably an ancient interpretation. The explanation proposed is therefore simply this, that Luke to avoid repetition has substituted an interpretation for the text. (4) The fragment in question agrees much better with the context than the prediction put into its place; for the prediction is a catalogue of calamities in which no emotion is perceptible, and the fragment is wet with tears. The things which belong unto peace are not the things which belong unto freedom from war. The contrast is not between war and peace, but rather between impenitence and the things which belong unto peace with God. The truth of the kingdom has been hid from Jerusalem. The city will not repent. The destroyer of the prophets will rise against Messiah Himself and will remain impenitent, until, when the kingdom comes and Messiah appears in the glory of God, repentance will be too late; and the cry, 'Blessed is he that cometh in the name of the Lord,' will then be as vain as the urgent entreaties of the men in the parable who rejected the invitation to the supper and were themselves rejected though they pleaded for admission with tears. This is the sort of sequel which is demanded by the beginning of the lamentation. The details of a military siege are utterly alien to the thought. The prediction is Luke's, and not Christ's. The words, 'Ye shall not see me henceforth until ye shall say, Blessed is he that cometh in the name of the Lord,' were evidently regarded by the early Christians as a prediction which was fulfilled when Jesus entered Jerusalem (Mark xi. 9, 10; Matt. xxi. 9; Luke xix. 38; John xii. 13). The truth is that the prediction was made at the entrance into the city. The blessed coming is the second one. The saying, 'Your house is left unto you,' obviously does not mean, 'Your house is left unto you desolate,' as Matthew seems to believe (Matt. xxiii. 28); nor does it simply mean, as Wendt suggests, 'I leave you and trouble you no further.'[1] The meaning is, 'You have rejected the kingdom of God. You have preferred an earthly inheritance, a house that is made with hands, to the eternal tabernacles unto which you have been called. Behold your house is left unto you. Your choice will not be disputed. Verily you have your reward— until the kingdom comes.' Matthew has attached the lament as a pendant to the discourse on the Pharisees (Matt. xxiii. 37-39). This context is unmistakably editorial.

c.—The original situation of the discourse in Luke xiv. 25-35 has now become perfectly evident. Jesus has alluded to the choice of Jerusalem. When the kingdom is proclaimed a choice must be made; for no one can enter into life through the narrow gate with the things of this world in his hands. Jerusalem has chosen the poorer part. Jesus has said, 'Behold, your house is left unto you.' And now He turns to the disciples and warns them to count the cost of discipleship. They apparently need the warning. They have not yet counted the cost. They may not have much to renounce, but at least they have their earthly hopes—those hopes so triumphantly expressed when they shouted for joy on the way to Jerusalem. They are willing to follow their Master, but the cross is hid from their eyes. They anticipate a different

[1] *The Teaching of Jesus*, vol. ii. p. 278.

'perfecting.' The salt is in danger of losing its savour. This discourse is manifestly the sequel. Nothing more appropriate can be conceived.

Since the discourse is addressed to disciples, to men who, like salt, have a savour to lose, 'the great multitudes' are clearly editorial (ver. 25). The precept, 'Hate your friends' (ver. 26), is similar to the earlier precept, 'Love your enemies.' The hatred is defined by the love, and the love is defined by the hatred. Jesus does not expect from His disciples moral impossibilities. The enemy is to be loved as oneself, and the friend is to be hated as oneself; and the meaning clearly is that there is a higher love which is and must be supreme. Matthew tones down the original, which he puts into the charge to the twelve (Matt. x. 37-39). Mark records similar sayings after the confession of Peter (Mark viii. 33, cf. Luke xix. 42; Mark viii. 34, cf. Luke xiv. 26, 27; Mark ix. 1, cf. Luke xiii. 35). The arrangement in this section of the second gospel is utterly unhistorical. Wendt believes that Matt. x. 39 originally followed Luke xiv. 27;[1] but a motive for the omission is not obvious, and as the saying, 'He that loveth his life shall lose it, and he that loseth his life shall find it,' will afterwards be discovered in a context more probably original, we must rather conclude that this saying was suggested both to Matthew and to Mark (Mark viii. 35) by the original words which Luke alone has preserved, 'yea, and his own life also' (Luke xiv. 26). The comparison of the disciples to salt which is in danger of losing its savour has been placed by Matthew in the Sermon on the Mount (Matt. v. 13), and by Mark in a context as clearly secondary (Mark ix. 50). Luke has slightly modified the original. Mark adds the awkward conclusion, adapting the comparison to its setting, 'Have salt in yourselves, and be at peace one with another' (ver. 50). The only detail which remains to be accounted for is the omission of Mark xi. 1-8 from our reconstruction. Luke gives an account of the triumphal progress (Luke xix. 29-36); but his narrative is a reproduction of Mark's, and the mere fact that Luke has reproduced Mark's account is no guarantee that the narrative

[1] *Die Lehre Jesu*, Erster Theil, S. 124.

was contained in the apostolic source. That Matthew's version is a reproduction of Mark's with variations which are purely editorial is also indisputable. The testimony of the fourth gospel is independent, and may perhaps be considered to afford sufficient evidence that the narrative was contained in the source; but what is the testimony of the fourth gospel? According to Mark two of the disciples were sent into a village for the colt (Mark xi. 1-6), but John has no knowledge of this mission. The shouting of the people in John xii. 13 is a secondary combination of the original texts in Luke xix. 37; xiii. 35; and therefore when subjected to analysis the narrative becomes reduced to two statements, the first that a great multitude went out of the city to meet Jesus with branches of palm trees in their hands, and the second that having found a young ass He sat thereon. If these statements are supposed to be sufficiently attested by the fourth gospel, the reader is at liberty to insert them as an introduction to the text reconstructed; but in the first place he may fairly be asked to explain the following words, 'These things understood not the disciples at the first; but when Jesus was glorified, then remembered they that these things were written of him, and that they had done these things unto him' (John xii. 16). The evangelist seems almost to make an apology for the introduction of a narrative which was not contained in his source and did not form part of the original apostolic tradition.

§ 42.—*The Story of a Penitent Woman*

The introduction to the parables of the Lost in Luke's second digression is almost as useful to the critic as a note written by the evangelist on his own method. The statement is made that 'both the Pharisees and the Scribes murmured, saying, This man receiveth sinners, and eateth with them' (Luke xv. 2); and in the preceding verse we are simply told that the publicans and sinners were drawing near to hear Him. But the mere fact that the publicans and sinners were drawing near to hear Him, could not provoke the murmuring. A dinner or a supper is obviously presupposed, and therefore the original has been abbreviated. Again, just because the original has been abbreviated, the order of the source has been preserved. The complaint of the Pharisees and the parables of the Lost bear no relation to the preceding discourse. The connection betrays no editorial motive. The parables of the Lost might be detached from their original context and introduced here as an illustration of the complaint, or, if the parables originally followed the entrance into Jerusalem, the complaint might be introduced to account for them; but in either case a narrative is demanded on Christ's relation to the sinners, and the peculiar abbreviation of the heading in Luke xv. 1, 2 is altogether inexplicable, unless on the supposition that such a narrative was contained in the source after the entrance into Jerusalem, and has here been omitted by Luke to avoid editorial repetition. Now in Luke's digressions there are only two narratives which are at all appropriate to the situation. One of these is the story of the publican who received Jesus into his house (Luke xix. 1-10), and the other is the story of the penitent woman (Luke vii. 36-50). But according to the explicit testimony of Luke, confirmed, as we have seen, by the second gospel, the first of these incidents happened in Jericho, when Jesus was going up to Jerusalem. The second, therefore, alone remains. A narrative like the story of the penitent woman is imperatively demanded by the heading in Luke xv. 1, 2. No other narrative is available. This narrative is waiting to be restored to its original context; for Luke has introduced it in an earlier section to illustrate the saying, 'The Son of Man is come eating and drinking, a friend of publicans and sinners' (ver. 34). In view of these facts, the conclusion is surely inevitable that the heading in Luke xv. 1, 2 has been substituted for the story of the penitent woman. But the evidence has not yet been exhausted; for the significant fact still remains to be noticed that the second and fourth evangelists both give an account of the anointing of Jesus by a woman, and that these narratives occupy a position which is almost, if not altogether, identical with the position just found for Luke's narrative. Mark's narrative occurs in ch. xiv. 3-9, and the entrance into Jerusalem is recorded in ch. xi. 1-10; but the most of the intervening material, as we have learned in our reconstruction of the apostolic source, belongs properly to the earlier residence at the time of the feast of Tabernacles. Mark's arrangement is editorial. A motive, moreover, is perceptible for his choice of the later position; for he betrays by his addition in ver. 9 that he intends the narrative to serve as an introduction to the history of the Passion. The fourth evangelist, again, instead of recording the incident after the entrance into Jerusalem, places it immediately before (John xii. 1–8), but a motive for the transference is perfectly obvious, as the woman has been identified with Mary of Bethany, and the narrative has been combined with the account of the sisters which Luke has preserved, and which, as we have seen, preceded in the apostolic source the entrance into the city. Matthew's version of the anointing need not be separately considered, as it is simply a reproduction of Mark's (Matt. xxvi. 6–13). The other three versions are independent. They are almost identical in position, and the difference can in each case be accounted for on the supposition that the narrative was originally situated immediately after the discourse on counting the cost of discipleship. But the reader may object that we are taking for granted the historical identity of the incidents. No one will dispute the identity of the second and fourth gospel narratives. They obviously coincide, and are admitted to be independent versions of one event; but they differ in several details, and in one of these the fourth gospel coincides with Luke's narrative. This is a fact of some importance. According to Mark, the ointment was poured on the head of Jesus: according to the other two evangelists, the woman anointed His feet and wiped them with her hair. John differs from Mark and agrees with Luke; but the event recorded by John is the same as that recorded by Mark. The three are therefore linked together. The differences in other details are undoubtedly sufficient to constitute a difficulty. If the three represent the same event, one must be primary, and the others derivative, or each must be partly editorial; and we ought to be able to account for the origin of the secondary details. How, then, did the variations arise? The following facts should be noted. (1) Luke's version illustrates Christ's compassion for the sinful, and the devotion which He excited in those who, submitting to His influence, were restored to themselves and to God; and that is a characteristic not merely of this particular narrative, but also of the apostolic source. (2) The parable of the Two Debtors is admirably appropriate to the occasion, and cannot be detached from its setting without destroying the unity of the narrative. This parable authenticates itself. (3) In the versions of Mark and John some of the details are unmistakably secondary. The introduction of Martha and Mary in the fourth gospel narrative is due to the combination which has already been noted. The statement made by Mark that the ointment was poured over Christ's head is at variance with the other two narratives, and has an official significance; and the saying with which Mark concludes, 'Wheresoever the gospel shall be preached throughout the whole world, that also which this woman hath done shall be spoken of for a memorial of her' (Mark xiv. 9), must be regarded as a later addition unknown to John, who would otherwise not have failed to insert a prediction so congruous with his own belief in the ultimate triumph of the Cross. (4) On the supposition that the distinctive features of Luke's version are primary, the omission of these features by Mark and John can be satisfactorily accounted for. In the original tradition the woman was represented as a sinner; but if she anointed Jesus for the burying, how could she be an unknown sinner? The question would be asked and inferences would be made. Mark simply omits the element of sin. John proceeds farther and identifies the woman with Mary of Bethany. John's inference is certainly conjectural; but the tendency which is unmistakable in John's version is also apparent in Mark's, and if in the one case it is a departure from the original, in the other case it is presumably the same. (5) Luke's version also may be confidently recognised as in some respects secondary, and his variations are equally intelligible. His aim is to illustrate the accusation of the Pharisees, and the friendship of Jesus for the sinners. He therefore makes Simon a Pharisee, and he omits both the murmuring against the wastefulness of the woman and the allusion to the burying of Jesus. The commendation of the woman's prodigality does not suit his purpose, and cannot indeed be preserved for the simple reason that the narrative has been transferred to an early period of the ministry. Since the Passion in Jerusalem is still far off, an anointing for the burial would be here out of place; but the commendation of the woman and the murmuring of the guests against her are inseparable from the allusion to the burying. The whole passage would therefore be omitted. The difficulty which is at first sight presented by the variations, thus vanishes when the narratives are carefully studied in relation to their position in the history; and our conclusion is, that the three incidents are historically identical, that one feature of the original has been preserved by Luke, and another by Mark and John, and that by combining the versions and excluding the secondary details the original can be approximately restored. Returning now to our starting point, we have finally to notice what Luke has done. He cannot insert the story of the woman, since that has already been introduced; and the story of Zacchæus is not available for his purpose, since the visit to Jericho would be premature. He therefore writes first an editorial heading suggested by these two incidents, and then he removes the parables of the Lost from the publican narrative with which they were originally connected, and inserts them as a justification of Christ's conduct in receiving and eating with the sinners (Luke xv. 1-32). The parables are demanded by Luke xix. 10; and an additional confirmation of our argument is provided by the fact that the sinner was a woman in the city, that is, a woman of Jerusalem (ver. 37). Luke vii. 49 is probably an editorial parenthesis. It interrupts the connection between ver. 48 and ver. 50.

§ 43.—*The Doctrine of Riches*

In the interpretation of Christ's teaching on the subject of riches, as well as in the reconstruction of the text, there is much diversity of opinion. Starting from the presupposition that the apostolic source was a mere collection of logia, containing no doubt a few incidents, but not arranged in chronological order, and not a complete account of the ministry, the critics have gained little success. A few of the mistakes which they have made in their admirable and most stimulating attempts to reconstruct the original will be noticed when we proceed to details. At present the question is, Can the original text of the doctrine of riches be reconstructed with greater assurance when the truth is recognised that the apostolic source, instead of being a mere collection of logia, was a chronological narrative, the arrangement of which has been obscured by combination with our second gospel? I venture to reply in the affirmative; and in accordance with the method adopted in this volume, for the sake of clearness and brevity, I enumerate the following facts:

1. The parable of the Steward, which we have reached in our analysis of the digression (Luke xvi. 1–12), bears obviously no relation to the murmuring of the Pharisees on account of Christ's friendship for the sinners. A new incident is demanded by the new parable. Its subject is the use of wealth, and Jesus would certainly not begin to instruct anyone on such a subject without an historical suggestion. The teaching is invariably suggested by an incident, and in this case would not be exceptional. Now in Luke's digressions there is only one incident which could bring forward the subject. In Luke xii. 13 we are told that a young man, who had a financial dispute with his brother, desired Jesus to exercise His authority as a prophet, that he might secure what he considered to be his rights. 'Master, bid my brother divide the inheritance with me.' It is antecedently probable that Jesus would take advantage of this incident to instruct the man and His own disciples on the subject of riches, and as a fact the instruction was given (Luke xii. 15–34).

2. The dismemberment of a discourse on any subject by either Luke or Matthew is not a phenomenon which should excite surprise, for the evangelists have certainly rearranged their apostolic material; and since in the case of Luke the discourses of the last period in Jerusalem have been carried back into the digression, because the second gospel has been accepted as the standard of history, we can see the necessity of rearrangement. The question, however, arises, When did the incident happen? Does the instruction in ch. xii. or the parable of the Steward in ch. xvi. represent the original

situation? At first sight one is disposed to decide in favour of the earlier context, for the incident is there reported, and the parable of the Steward who wasted his master's goods might conceivably be carried forward to supplement the parable of the Prodigal who wasted his substance with riotous living (Luke xv. 13); but the following considerations are decisive in favour of the other alternative. (*a*) The whole context in ch. xii. is editorial. Luke has, as we have seen, grouped together a number of fragments, which bear no inner relation to one another, but are strung on the thread of a charge to the twelve. The fragments in Luke xii. 2-9, 11, 12, 35-53, 58, 59, have been taken from the last period of the ministry; and the teaching from ver. 13 to ver. 34 has not been interpolated on account of the incident. The incident has rather been recorded to make the teaching more intelligible; and both have been detached from their original connection. (*b*) The resemblance of the steward who wasted the property of his master to the prodigal who wasted his substance with riotous living has no doubt been observed by the evangelist, for the word is in each case the same; but the inference does not follow that the parable of the Steward has been introduced to supplement the parable of the Prodigal. It is quite as conceivable that the parable of the Prodigal is itself an editorial interpolation; and indeed, as we have seen, there is really no room for doubt, for the three parables of the Lost were originally associated with the call of Zacchæus the publican, and have here been substituted by Luke for the story of the penitent woman. If a choice must be made between the two situations, we must therefore choose the second. The first is excluded by the nature of the context, and the second is less clearly editorial.

3. The parable of the Steward is supplementary to, and is even demanded by, the parable of the man who pulled down his barns to build greater. An examination of the thought will make this plain. Jesus has warned His hearers against covetousness, which He describes as an appetite for what cannot be assimilated. 'A man's life consisteth not in the abundance of the things which he possesseth.' He then teaches by a parable the folly of laying up treasure on earth

for the sake of personal enjoyment, without security of tenure. An abundant provision has been made for a long and pleasant future; but when at last the man is about to spend the hoard of years, and says to his life, 'Take thine ease, eat, drink, and be merry,' he is roused from his dream by a summons to give in his account. 'Thou foolish one, this night is thy life required of thee, and the things which thou hast prepared, whose shall they be?' The answer is, They will not be yours. So far the teaching is intelligible, but certainly it is not complete. The definition of life e.g. is purely negative. Life does not consist in the abundance of the things which a man possesseth; but the disciples would expect to be told wherein life does consist, and since Jesus was not a negative moralist He would not leave them uninstructed. Again, the parable, like the definition, is negative. It is simply an illustration of folly, and the question arises, Wherein does wisdom consist? In other words, What use is a man to make of the things which he possesses, but which do not constitute his life? Now Jesus as a fact continued the subject beyond the parable of the Rich Fool; for, as we have seen, the thread which connects the fragments in ch. xii. is a charge addressed to the disciples, and in the case of the doctrine of riches the charge begins at ver. 22. The section from ver. 13 to ver. 21 is considered by Luke to be introductory. The discourse from ver. 22 to ver. 34 is certainly a continuation of the instruction suggested by the demand of the young man; but as certainly the transition from ver. 21 to ver. 22 is far too precipitous to be practicable. No man can pass from the one to the other, not even the most agile of critics. What, then, are we bound to conclude? That a part of the original has been lost irrecoverably? By no means; for the parable of the Steward is a bridge. It does not enlarge the definition of life, but it supplements the earlier parable. It introduces, in the first place, the idea of stewardship. The rich dreamer was not a steward. He was a man in an independent position; and yet, according to the parable, he was responsible for his life. This thought of responsibility is carried forward and developed in the later parable. Secondly, after the summons to give in his account, the rich dreamer had no opportunity to make a better use of his hoard; but the steward was able to do something. He received a preliminary warning. He said within himself, What shall I do? Thirdly, the question, as we have seen, remains to be answered, What is a man to do with his treasure? And now the answer is given. The steward is not a wise man: on the contrary, he is decidedly foolish, as foolish as the dreamer, as foolish as the prodigal. He wasted his master's goods; and no wise steward would be guilty of conduct so stupid. A wise steward might embezzle the property of his master; but he would not send it to open waste like the foolish man in the parable. When the guilt of the steward was detected, and he said within himself, 'What shall I do?' he could only see three alternatives. One was to dig; another was to beg; and the third was to ingratiate himself with the debtors at his master's expense. He could neither dig nor beg. He had not strength enough to dig; he was ashamed to beg. His strength and wisdom were just sufficient to execute the other fine scheme, which would be sure to be discovered, and would probably fail to secure his end. Surely a foolish steward, the very prince of stupidity, the prodigal advanced without repentance from the feeding of swine to a position of responsibility and authority. It is astonishing and almost inconceivable that this man should have gained among scholars a high reputation for wisdom. The fact, however, is indisputable. His morality is generally suspected; but theologians and interpreters and critics unite in extolling the man's sagacity. They have curiously failed to perceive that the central fact in the parable is just the steward's folly. He was indeed commended by his master, and commended because he had done wisely; but his was the wisdom of a foolish man, and just for that reason it was worthy of some recognition. The sons of this world, according to the statement of Jesus, are for their own generation wiser than the sons of the light; that is, even the most foolish of the sons of this world learn wisdom when reduced to extremity, and yet the sons of the light, who know that this world is passing away, and that the kingdom of God is at hand, may be foolish enough to cling to their earthly possessions. Learn wisdom, Jesus says, from the foolish steward. Do not imitate his dishonesty; but expend your treasure wisely. Make to yourselves friends by means of the mammon of unrighteousness, that when it shall fail they may receive you into the eternal tabernacles. The parable of the Steward is thus supplementary to the parable of the Rich Dreamer. The men are both foolish. They are both like the foolish young man who approached Jesus with his financial difficulty. The parables were suggested by the incident, and the second was suggested by the first.

4. The attention of the reader is now invited to a parable which Matthew alone has preserved. In ch. xix. he is reproducing the narrative of the second gospel. He borrows from Mark the story of the rich young man (Matt. xix. 16-22), and the instruction addressed afterwards to the disciples (vv. 23-30); but he makes a few additions. He interpolates ver. 28, a fragment which will soon be found in its original context; and then, at the end of the whole passage, he adds the parable of the Labourers (Matt. xx. 1-16). This parable has certainly been taken from the apostolic source, and as certainly its original situation has been approximately preserved. The narrative in the second gospel concludes with the saying, 'Many that are first shall be last, and the last first' (Mark x. 31; Matt. xix. 30); and Matthew has repeated this saying at the end of the parable (Matt. xx. 16), thus distinctly suggesting an interpretation. But the parable is not an illustration of the text, for the last labourers were not put first. There is no inequality in the parable. On the contrary, the labourers receive the same wages; and the moral is that, instead of murmuring and being envious, the labourers in the vineyard should be pleased because the Master is good. The parable is a rebuke of the desire to gain an extra reward. Now the following facts should be observed: (*a*) The parable could only be addressed to the disciples, since the men are all labourers in the vineyard; and it clearly presupposes a manifestation of the spirit which is rebuked. (*b*) It could not originally follow Matt. xix. 30, for the truth there stated is not the subject of the parable. (*c*) The question in ver. 27 affords obviously an occasion for the parable. Peter says, 'Lo, we have left all and followed thee; what then shall we have?' This is precisely the spirit which is afterwards

rebuked; for Peter in the name of the twelve claims a special reward. (*d*) In the third gospel the question or exclamation is rendered a little differently. Peter says, 'Lo, we have left our own and followed thee' (Luke xviii. 28). (*e*) The transition from Luke xvi. 12 to ver. 13 is impossible; and as a fact the saying about the two masters in ver. 13 is preceded in the first gospel by a passage which Luke has omitted (Matt. vi. 19-23). The omission will be proved in the sequel. (*f*) The question in Luke xvi. 12 is connected almost verbally through Luke xviii. 28 with the parable of the Vineyard Labourers. Jesus asks, 'If ye have not been faithful in that which is another's, who will give you that which is your own?' (τὸ ὑμέτερον τίς δώσει ὑμῖν; Luke xvi. 12). Peter exclaims, 'Lo, we have left our own and followed thee' (ἀφέντες τὰ ἴδια, Luke xviii. 28). And the parable of the Labourers is delivered by Jesus in rebuke of the covetous spirit. (*g*) The parable is preceded in the second gospel by an assurance of ultimate reward (Mark x. 29, 30; Matt. xix. 29; Luke xviii. 29, 30). This assurance was probably contained in the source. It exemplifies the method of Jesus. He does not merely rebuke His disciples. He recognises in the first place that their expectation is to some extent legitimate. He distinguishes the good from the bad. He approves their self-sacrifice before He corrects their mistake. (*h*) If Matthew has wrongly inferred that the parable of the Labourers is an illustration of the text, 'Many that are first shall be last, and the last first,' Mark, on the other hand, has substituted the text for the parable. He reduces the logia systematically; and the text, as Luke shows, was originally situated in an earlier discourse (Luke xiii. 30). Matthew adopts Mark's conclusion and repeats it at the end of the parable. These facts are interesting, but what is their significance? Do you really intend to identify the rich young man in the second gospel with the man in the apostolic source, who wanted the inheritance to be divided? The question may be asked with some degree of asperity. I reply without hesitation that I even venture to make so great a demand upon the credulity of the reader. Perhaps, after all, some reason may be found for the identification. Let us put the matter to the test. (1) The lesson taught by the two narratives is identical, and they exhibit the same general features. The two men were each seeking an inheritance, and they agreed in their conception of life. (2) The differences can be satisfactorily explained on the supposition that Mark's version is secondary. (*a*) The question of the man in the second gospel was, according to the apostolic source, asked by another man on an earlier occasion. A certain lawyer stood up and said, Master, what shall I do to inherit eternal life? and Jesus referred him to the law, just as in the case of young Dives (Luke x. 25-28; Mark xii. 28-34). (*b*) The final answer to the rich young man was more definite than the first. Jesus said, 'Go, sell whatsoever thou hast, and give to the poor, and thou shalt have treasure in heaven; and come, follow me.' These words were not addressed to the lawyer, but they occur in Luke's digression; for, after warning the people against covetousness, Jesus delivered the parable of the Rich Fool, the conclusion of which is 'So is he that layeth up treasure for himself, and is not rich toward God' (Luke xii. 21), and afterwards He said to His disciples, 'Sell that ye have and give alms; make to yourselves purses which wax not old, a treasure in the heavens that faileth not, where no thief draweth near, neither moth destroyeth; for where your treasure is, there will your heart be also' (Luke xii. 33, 34). The critics are disposed to believe that Luke has detached this saying from the narrative of the rich young man for the sake of giving a general application to a precept intended for a particular case; but the contrary supposition is quite as conceivable, and indeed, when the nature of the second gospel as a secondary compilation is taken into account, is by far the more probable of the two. (3) Matthew and Luke have each reproduced the story of young Dives from the second gospel (Matt. xix. 16-22; Luke xviii. 18-23). Their variations are purely editorial, and consequently afford no evidence that the narrative was contained in the apostolic source. The second gospel does not contain Luke's narrative, and the apostolic source, as far as we can judge, did not contain Mark's narrative. The parable of the Labourers has been taken from the apostolic source, and is added by Matthew to Mark's story of the rich young man, and this may be urged as an evidence that Mark's story was contained in the apostolic source; but the conclusion is too large for the premises. Since no other context is available for the parable of the Labourers, and since this parable authenticates itself as Christ's reply to the question, 'What then shall we have?' we must certainly conclude that Mark x. 23-30 was contained in the apostolic source; but the question still remains whether the incident in Mark x. 17-22 is not a secondary version of the incident in Luke's digression. The evidence is in favour of identification, and the objection above noticed simply requires that Mark x. 23-30 should be included in our reconstruction of the narrative. The parable of the Labourers, instead of guaranteeing Mark's version, must rather be regarded as an evidence that Matthew recognises the resemblance and virtually identifies the two incidents. (4) A decisive fact still remains to be considered. We have already found in the apostolic source, associated with the feast of Tabernacles, a series of incidents which Mark has carried forward beyond the last entrance into Jerusalem (Mark xi. 15-18; 27-xiii. 2); and now we observe that a new series of incidents, contained in the apostolic source after the last entrance into Jerusalem, has been carried back by Mark to the journey from Galilee to the city. Mark records among the episodes of the journey the ambitious request of the sons of Zebedee (Mark x. 35-45), the blessing by Jesus of little children (vv. 13-16), and a discourse on the subject of marriage and divorce (vv. 2-12); but these were not episodes of the journey to Jerusalem. They were episodes of the last residence in the city before the feast of the Passover, as we shall afterwards see; and the comparison of the disciples to salt which is in danger of losing its savour (Mark ix. 50)—a comparison which, as we have already observed, was made at the entrance into Jerusalem—represents the beginning of the series. But the story of the rich young man is recorded by Mark as a member of the series, and the similar narrative in the apostolic source is a member of a similar series. The coincidences are thus multiplied exceedingly, and the only conclusion is that the similarity is an indication of historical identity. What, then, have we gained as the result of the discussion? We have gained a sequel to the parable of the Steward. Jesus turned to the disciples and said, 'How hardly shall they that have riches enter into the kingdom of God.' He subsequently explained this exclamation. Peter asked what reward the twelve disciples would have in return for their renunciation of the world; and in reply to this question Jesus first announced the certainty of reward, and then in the parable of the Labourers He rebuked the covetous spirit (Mark x. 23–28; Matt. xx. 1–15).

5. We now proceed to complete the reconstruction of the original. We have advanced beyond the parable of the Steward, but our bridge has not yet taken us to the other side, represented by Luke xvi. 13. The saying concerning the two masters is, however, reported by Matthew, who may help us to pass safely across. In the Sermon on the Mount, a context which is unmistakably editorial, Matthew brings together a few passages which have been separated by Luke. Matt. vi. 19–21 is parallel to Luke xii. 33, 34, Matt. vi. 22, 23 to Luke xi. 34–36, and Matt. vi. 24 to Luke xvi. 13. In the case of Luke xi. 34–36 the third gospel context is certainly editorial, as we have already decided; and the question is, Has Matthew preserved the original connection of these fragments? I reply that he has obviously a reason for making a slight rearrangement. He begins a new section at ch. vi. 19, and if the fragment in vv. 22, 23, which Luke has placed earlier in the digression, was really the first of the series, it would inevitably be carried some distance forward. The clear and peremptory precept, 'Lay not up for yourselves treasures upon the earth,' is an appropriate introduction to the section, whereas vv. 22, 23 would be impossible as a beginning. Now let us return to our bridge. The parable of the Labourers concludes with the question, ' Is it not lawful for me to do what I will with mine own? or is thine eye evil because I am good?' (Matt. xx. 15). The fragment in Matt. vi. 22, 23, Luke xi. 34–36, is obviously an appropriate sequel, with both an inner and a verbal connection. Jesus proceeds to say, ' The lamp of thy body is thine eye:

when thine eye is single, thy whole body also is full of light; but when it is evil, thy body also is full of darkness.' Matthew's version of the saying is a little different from Luke's, but the two are admitted to be identical. The question whether Matthew or Luke has preserved the original text may be conveniently reserved. In the meantime we simply notice the transition of thought from the parable of the Labourers to the fragment on the lamp of the body. The fragment evidently means that a divided life is dangerous. When the eye is single and good, the whole body is full of light; when the eye is evil, the whole body is full of darkness; that is, a man's life is determined by his affections. And, on the other hand, when the whole body is full of light, that is, when the life is good, luminous with the goodness of the kingdom of God, the affections are necessarily good, and no desire for the wealth of the world can be cherished. Now after such teaching the precept appropriately follows, ' Sell that ye have and give alms; make for yourselves purses which wax not old, a treasure in the heavens that faileth not, where no thief draweth near, neither moth destroyeth. For where your treasure is, there will your heart be also' (Luke xii. 33, 34; Matt. vi. 19–21). And this again is completed by the saying concerning the two masters, the meaning of which is that a divided life is not only dangerous but becomes sooner or later impossible. The sequence surely authenticates itself; and the reader will observe that our reconstruction is not at all arbitrary, for the order in which Matthew has preserved the fragments has here been adopted and reproduced, with the single readjustment made necessary by his transference of the second fragment to the beginning. We have therefore succeeded in crossing the chasm which Luke's method has left in our way.

6. The rest of the section which Matthew has inserted in the Sermon on the Mount consists of an exhortation to dismiss all anxious thoughts (Matt. vi. 25–34). This is what we find on the other side. We find it not merely in the first gospel, but also in the digression of Luke; for after the parable of the Rich Fool he records a parallel exhortation (Luke xii.

22-31). The transition is here perfectly easy. 'No man can serve two masters; you are the servants of one. You have chosen the good part which shall never be taken away from you. Be not anxious for your life, what ye shall eat or what ye shall drink, nor yet for your body, what ye shall put on. Your life consists in its relation to God, and not in the abundance or scarcity of the things you may possess. Seek ye the kingdom of God, and these things shall be added unto you. Be not anxious for the morrow: the morrow will be anxious for itself.' The only question which remains to be considered is, whether Matthew or Luke has preserved the original text. To this we now proceed.

a.—The parable of the Rich Dreamer has been omitted by Matthew and Mark. In the case of Mark such omissions are not exceptional, and scarcely require to be explained. Matthew systematically avoids the depreciation of secular interests.

b.—The parable of the Steward, as Strauss has said, is 'notoriously the *crux interpretum.*' It raises questions to which many different answers have been given. The following is a list of the difficulties: (1) The disciples had given up all to follow Jesus, and yet apparently they are counselled in the parable to make friends by means of the mammon of unrighteousness. (2) The friends thus made are supposed to be able to receive them into the eternal tabernacles. (3) The steward is commended by his master because he acted wisely; and yet through the steward's wisdom the master lost fifty measures of oil and twenty measures of wheat in addition to the previous wasting of his goods. The commendation seems rather surprising. (4) The selection of a dishonest man to serve as an example of wisdom is even more surprising, and certainly requires to be accounted for. Wise men are usually honest. Why, then, does Jesus teach wisdom at the risk of encouraging dishonesty?

The finest specimen of uncritical interpretation which the present writer has seen is contained in a book entitled 'Pastor Pastorum.' The author of this book makes the first of these difficulties his starting point; and although 'far from positive about the interpretation of a parable which has caused such an infinitude of comment,'[1] he succeeds in exhibiting some positive qualities. His method is allegorical. 'As the disciples,' he says, 'had no worldly goods at all, it cannot be the main drift of the parable, as has been sometimes maintained, to inculcate Christian prudence in the use of these. The drift of the parable is indeed to teach a kind of prudence, but not one in which money is concerned. The administration of property is only the vehicle in which the lesson is conveyed. What I take to be inculcated here is true Christian wisdom as to the exercise of authority, spiritual authority above all. The moral that I discern is this : that the apostles and their successors may do more good by showing a little indulgence—by conceding something to weak human nature, not enforcing Jewish formalities, and not insisting too inflexibly upon every point which they think may touch the honour or the privileges of Christ's Church—than by adhering to the strictest regard for observances and imposing rules for sanctity of thought and conduct with which only a chosen few would be able to comply.'[2] The reader will probably, like the author of 'Pastor Pastorum,' be 'far from positive' that this interpretation is correct. If Jesus intended to convey such ideas, He possessed a great talent for concealing His thought; and if the disciples perceived what He meant, they were more ingenious than the Rabbis. They might even have written 'Pastor Pastorum.' The opinion which 'has sometimes been maintained' that prudence in the use of worldly goods is the lesson conveyed by the parable will probably continue to be 'sometimes' maintained, notwithstanding the allegorical interpreters. The difficulties are not insuperable. The disciples were not wealthy men. They were even distinctly poor, for Peter could say to his Master, 'Lo, we have left all, and have followed thee ; ' but the fact should not be forgotten that they were poor disciples. They had not divorced their wives, and yet Jesus said, 'Every one that putteth away his wife and marrieth another, committeth adultery' (Luke xvi. 18). They were interested as disciples in the subject of marriage, and similarly as disciples they were

[1] *Pastor Pastorum*, by the Rev. Henry Latham, M.A., p. 398.
[2] *Ibid.* pp. 886–898.

interested in the subject of riches. The assumption that because they had no worldly goods at all, the parable of the Steward could not be intended to inculcate prudence in the use of these, requires the interpreter also to assume that because they had not divorced their wives the teaching on divorce could not be intended to inculcate the preservation of the marriage relationship. Impossibilities soon multiply when men reason thus, but the truth is not likely to be gained. Again, Mr. Latham assumes, like all the interpreters, that the parable was addressed specially to the disciples; but this assumption is not justified by the evidence. Luke indeed distinctly states that the parable was addressed to the disciples (Luke xvi. 1); but Luke has removed the parable from its original context, and the heading is purely editorial. In the sequel Jesus instructed the twelve. He looked round about and said unto His disciples, 'How hardly shall they that have riches enter into the kingdom of God' (Mark x. 23); and then He proceeded to explain and enlarge the lessons already conveyed. But the earlier teaching was immediately suggested by the request of the rich young man, and was addressed to the applicant and the people. This is proved not merely by the testimony of the second gospel, but also by the internal evidence afforded by the parable of the Steward; for the disciples did not need to make friends who would receive them into the eternal tabernacles. They were already heirs of the kingdom. The teaching involved in the parable is inexplicable on the assumption that it was specially addressed to the twelve; and, on the other hand, when the truth is perceived that the teaching was addressed to a general audience, and specially to the rich young man, the whole subject becomes perfectly clear. The young man possessed the mammon of unrighteousness. He did not possess friends to receive him into the eternal tabernacles. And finally the precept in the second gospel, 'Go, sell whatsoever thou hast, and give to the poor' (ver. 21), though transferred from the private instruction which followed, is simply an equivalent for the lesson conveyed by the parable of the Steward.

The difficulties which have puzzled interpreters and critics have arisen out of two mistakes. (1) Being wise men themselves, they are able to appreciate wisdom, and they give the steward credit for this excellence. 'The moral quality of his proceedings,' as J. Estlin Carpenter says, 'does not come into view: he simply serves as an illustration of worldly wisdom.'[1] 'The honesty or dishonesty of the steward,' according to the author of 'Pastor Pastorum,' 'is not the central point on which the moral turns. It is his tact in remitting part of his claims with a long-sighted view.'[2] 'Being represented as a dishonest spendthrift and lazy fellow, it is evident,' to Wendt, 'that in his forethought alone lay the ground of his future well-being.'[3] Whatever the man's moral eccentricities may have been, he is thus recognised by interpreters, who have little else in common, as a person of considerable sagacity. Reputations are sometimes easily gained. The truth is that the man is a fool. In the days of his prosperity he was scarcely wise. He wasted his master's goods, scattering them abroad like the prodigal (διασκορπίζων). Adversity sharpened his wits, but his wisdom was never remarkable. It was remarkable for him, but not remarkable as wisdom. He wasted his master's goods again, scattering fifty measures of oil and twenty measures of wheat with invincible prodigality. The fine scheme by which he hoped to provide for his future well-being was in itself superlatively foolish. He was not paid by a poundage on the net receipts or by some similar method, as the author of 'Pastor Pastorum' suggests, so that his interest and his master's would generally speaking coincide. He was supremely indifferent to his master's interests; and his wisdom simply consists in this, that he had once been indifferent to his own. When summoned to give in his account he at last asked, 'What shall I do?' He became deliberately foolish in the hope of providing for the future. The moral of the parable is, If a foolish man learns wisdom for his own generation when reduced to extremity, how much more should the sons of the light, who are not foolish, prepare themselves wisely for the age to come! (2) The original connection of the parable has hitherto never been perceived.

[1] *The First Three Gospels*, p. 324. [2] *Pastor Pastorum*, p. 392.
[3] *The Teaching of Jesus*, vol. i. p. 138.

According to the critics who believe, like Renan, that Luke 'hates riches and regards the simple attachment to property as an evil,'[1] there was no original context. J. Estlin Carpenter e.g. says, 'In its present form the story seems plainly to belong to that section of the Church which viewed wealth as unrighteous and found merit in poverty. This is closely connected with the conception that the suffering are entitled to compensation, which is seen in the story of the rich man and Lazarus.'[2] To J. Estlin Carpenter the parable of the Steward seems plainly to have originated, as far at least as its present form is concerned, in a certain section of the Church, and not in the mind of Jesus. To critics less devoted to a negative theory the semblance is plainly different. Wendt e.g. accepts the parable of the Steward as a genuine fragment of Christ's teaching, and attempts to reconstruct the original context. He argues with Holtzmann and Weiss that the parables of the Steward and of the Faithful and Unfaithful Servants (Matt. xxv. 14; Luke xix. 12) were originally connected as a pair, the first commending 'the wisdom of providing by means of present goods for future welfare, and the second enjoining faithfulness in the management of goods entrusted to us, as the right means of attaining the end thus wisely aimed at.'[3] Holtzmann places the second parable after Luke xvi. 12, Wendt after Luke xvi. 9, with the reservation that ver. 9 may be editorial. Wendt's whole reconstruction consists of the following passages: Luke xvi. 1–9; Matt. xxv. 14–29; Luke xvi. 10–12; Luke xii. 47, 48; Luke xvi. 13. The parable of the Faithful and Unfaithful Servants cannot at present be discussed; it will soon be found in its proper place, and will then be considered in relation to its context. In the meantime I simply point out the facts: (a) that Matthew and Luke agree in placing this parable in the discourse on the coming of the kingdom; (b) that the fragment in Luke xii. 47, 48 has been placed by Luke in a section taken from the same discourse (vv. 35–48); (c) that both in the parable and in the fragment the second coming of Messiah

---

[1] *The Gospels*, p. 143. [2] *The First Three Gospels*, p. 324.
[3] *The Teaching of Jesus*, vol. i. p. 128, cf. *Die Lehre Jesu*, Erster Theil, S. 146.

is the prominent thought, whereas this thought is not at all present in the parable of the Steward. These facts are sufficient to discredit the conjecture of Wendt and Holtzmann and Weiss; and, on the other hand, as we have seen, the parable of the Steward is demanded as a sequel by the earlier parable of the Rich Dreamer. The evidence need not be repeated. The point to be noticed at present is that in failing to perceive the original context of the parable of the Steward and in giving the man credit for sagacity, the critics leave the difficulties unremoved. They cannot account for the mysterious precept to make friends by means of the mammon of unrighteousness, that when it would fail a place might be secured in the eternal tabernacles. They cannot satisfactorily explain the master's commendation of the man, and still less the selection of such a man to serve as an example of wisdom. If the steward was really sagacious, he was no doubt worthy of commendation, but the master after his heavy losses would scarcely be disposed to admire him. And although it is true, as Wendt points out, that 'the value of wise forethought is most strongly accentuated by its being exhibited as isolated from other virtues,' the accentuation is greater, and the dishonesty of the man is made more intelligible in relation to the aim of the parable, when he is seen to be a fool, to whom dishonesty is natural, and forethought is not natural. The most foolish of men becomes wise, as far as his capacity permits, when he is reduced to extremity and is in danger of starvation. The most foolish of men is not likely to be scrupulously honest. His dishonesty is explained by his folly; and when the folly is recognised he is not likely to be imitated. The most foolish of men who has hitherto been indifferent to his own interests, as well as to those of his master, might well be commended for attending to his own interests at last, even in his own foolish way. And if a man like the steward could have his wits thus sharpened, and be stimulated to take thought for the morrow, the folly of the sons of light, who do not make provision for the future, is exhibited in the clearest way possible. They are more foolish than the most foolish of men.

c.—Mark's story of the rich young man has been reproduced by Matthew and Luke. The variations are purely editorial. We have therefore no reason to believe that this narrative was contained in the apostolic source. The sequel, however, as we have seen, is authenticated by the parable of the Labourers, which presupposes Peter's question (Mark x. 28). Here the variations are significant. (1) Matthew and Luke omit the explanation, 'Children, how hard is it for them that trust in riches to enter into the kingdom of God' (ver. 24). They have the second gospel before them, and deliberately omit these words. The reason probably is that the explanation was not contained in the source. The amazement of the disciples in ver. 24 is an editorial anticipation of the astonishment in ver. 26, and ver. 24 is an interpolation. (2) Matthew adds to Mark x. 28 the question, 'What then shall we have?' This addition, though perhaps editorial, expresses more clearly the desire which Peter intended to convey, and may therefore be placed in the text. (3) Luke substitutes 'our own' (τὰ ἴδια) for 'all.' Since the substituted word agrees better than Mark's with the question at the end of the parable of the Steward (Luke xvi. 12), Luke has here probably reproduced the original. (4) The assurance of reward is rendered differently by the three evangelists. 'Verily I say unto you, There is no man that hath left house, or brethren, or sisters, or mother, or father, or children, or lands, for my sake, and for the gospel's sake, but he shall receive a hundredfold now in this time, houses, and brethren, and sisters, and mothers, and children, and lands, with persecutions; and in the world to come eternal life' (Mark x. 29, 30). 'Every one that hath left houses, or brethren, or sisters, or father, or mother, or children, or lands, for my name's sake, shall receive a hundredfold, and shall inherit eternal life' (Matt. xix. 29). 'Verily I say unto you, There is no man that hath left house, or wife, or brethren, or parents, or children, for the kingdom of God's sake, who shall not receive manifold more in this time, and in the world to come eternal life' (Luke xviii. 29, 30). In each of these versions there are probably secondary details. 'For my name's sake' in the first gospel is certainly editorial. 'Manifold more' is Luke's equivalent for a hundredfold. The more definite word is primary. 'For the kingdom of God's sake' is simply an editorial combination of the two expressions 'for my sake and for the gospel's sake.' So far we have no reason whatever to believe that Matthew and Luke have derived their versions from the apostolic source. Again, the omission by the later evangelists of the assurance that the reward would be in 'houses, and brethren, and sisters, and mothers, and children, and lands, with persecutions,' is also perfectly intelligible; for, in the first place, the persecutions might be considered to be scarcely compatible with the promise, and secondly, reflection might suggest that the promise had been seldom fulfilled. On the other hand, Mark's version is in some respects secondary. (1) The words, 'For the gospel's sake,' have probably been added by the evangelist. These words occur also in Mark viii. 35, and there, as we shall see, they are editorial (cf. Luke xvii. 33). (2) The authenticity of the assurance that the disciples would receive a hundredfold in this time, houses, and brethren, and sisters, and mothers, and children, and lands, with persecutions, is at least exceedingly doubtful. The context contains nothing to authenticate such a recompense. The saying is unique, and is indeed foreign to the teaching of Jesus. He taught His disciples to expect persecution; but He did not on any other occasion assure them that their reward would be great in this life. On the contrary, He directed their thoughts to the kingdom of God, to a recompense in the resurrection of the just. 'Blessed are ye, when men shall hate you, and when they shall separate you from their company, and reproach you, and cast out your name as evil, for the Son of Man's sake. Rejoice in that day, and leap for joy: for behold, your reward is great in heaven' (Luke vi. 22, 23). This is the consistent teaching of Jesus. The unique text reported by Mark must therefore be rejected, if we can account for its origin. The last words in Mark's narrative, 'But many that are first shall be last; and the last first,' have been borrowed, as we have seen, from an earlier discourse (Luke xiii. 30), and substituted for the parable of the Labourers; and the fact is worthy of notice that Mark does not record the parable of the Great Supper, which originally preceded this text. The earlier discourse was suggested by the question, 'Lord, are they few that be saved?' And after the question, 'Then who can be saved?' (Mark x. 26) Mark reports that the man, who instead of excusing himself on account of fields, or oxen, or wife, leaves house, or land, or friends, for the sake of Christ, will inherit eternal life. The hundredfold more with persecutions may be an application of the original to the circumstances of the early Church, and the whole passage from ver. 26 to ver. 30 may be an abstract from the earlier context. So one might argue with some degree of plausibility. The passage in question, however, is certainly not altogether editorial; for, in the first place, ver. 28 is presupposed by the parable of the Labourers, and secondly the rebuke which is involved in the parable of the Labourers does not sufficiently distinguish the good from the bad in Peter's desire. We may even infer, from the agreement in the parable for a penny a day, that the disciples had received some assurance of reward. How, then, is the difficulty to be avoided? The assurance in the apostolic source consisted of the following words: 'Verily I say unto you, There is no man that hath left house, or brethren, or sisters, or mother, or father, or children, or lands, for my sake, but he shall receive a hundredfold, and shall inherit eternal life.' Mark has inferred that the increase would be similar to the renunciation, and that persecutions would accompany the reward. Matthew and Luke are combining the apostolic source with Mark. They omit Mark's additions, and reproduce the original with approximate fidelity. Wendt has failed to perceive that the parable of the Labourers is Christ's reply to the exclamation of Peter, 'Lo, we have left all, and have followed thee.' He puts the parable into an appendix,[1] and remarks, with a singular lapse from his usual acuteness, that the context which Matthew gives to it is due to the agreement of Matt. xx. 16 with the conclusion of the whole passage in Mark x. 31. The truth is that the parable of the Labourers is not an illustration of the text, and that Matt. xx. 16 is an editorial addition repeated from Mark x. 31.

d.—Matthew has omitted Luke xi. 36 because the saying seems scarcely intelligible. It really, however, completes the thought expressed in Matt. vi. 22, 23, Luke xi. 34, 35; for the

[1] *Die Lehre Jesu*, Erster Theil, S. 183, cf. *The Teaching of Jesus*, vol. ii. p. 53.

eye represents affection or desire, and the body represents the whole nature, and what Jesus says is (1) that when one is free from private passion his nature is free from evil; (2) that when his nature is good, the lamp with its bright shining gives him light, and does not occasion distraction. The meaning of the fragment is obscure, but when placed in its proper context there is no difficulty whatever. The meaning is, keep the eye pure for the sake of the body, and keep the body pure for the sake of the eye. Luke xii. 32 is an interpolated fragment, which will soon be found in its original context. The precept in ver. 33 is parallel to Matt. vi. 19-21, and the parallel text in the second gospel (Mark x. 21) is a clear proof that Matthew's version of the saying is secondary. Weiss believes that the demand of Jesus in the single instance of young Dives has been made absolute by Luke,[1] and Wendt agrees with Weiss;[2] but the saying in Matt. vi. 19 is also absolute, although slightly different in form from that in Luke xii. 33, 34, and the story of young Dives is a secondary compilation. Matthew's precept forbids the laying up of treasure on the earth, but the context requires something more than that; for the question is, What is one to do with the treasure which he happens to possess? The answer is, Sell that ye have, and give alms. Be wise, like the foolish steward. Make friends, that they may receive you into the eternal tabernacles when the mammon of unrighteousness fails. If this is Ebionism, the teaching of Jesus was Ebionitic; but the truth is that He did not proclaim the blessedness of the poor just because they are poor. Wealth is the mammon of unrighteousness. It is morally a negative, and only becomes positively evil when it keeps a man out of the kingdom. The direct and absolute precept, 'Sell that ye have, and give alms,' is explained by the fact that, according to the teaching of Jesus, the things of this world would be utterly worthless in the day of account which was at hand. He anticipated the speedy coming of the heavenly kingdom. He did not anticipate a long historical development and the formation of a church on the earth.

[1] *Introduction to the New Testament*, vol. ii. p. 309.
[2] *Die Lehre Jesu*, Erster Theil, S. 118.

e.—Matthew's text agrees here almost verbally with Luke's. The following details should be noticed. (1) The more definite word 'ravens' in Luke xii. 24 is preferable to 'the birds of the heaven' in Matt. vi. 26. The word 'birds' occurred originally at the end of the verse, and Matthew has substituted it for 'ravens' at the beginning. (2) Luke has substituted 'God' (Luke xii. 24) for 'your heavenly Father' (Matt. vi. 26). The words 'your Father' in Luke xii. 30 show that Luke's reading in the earlier connection is probably secondary. He seems to avoid the explicit identification of the God of nature with the God of grace. (3) Luke has changed 'the Gentiles' (τὰ ἔθνη, Matt. vi. 32) into 'the nations of the world' (τὰ ἔθνη τοῦ κόσμου, Luke xii. 30), thus avoiding the special significance of the word ἔθνη. (4) To the original text, 'Seek ye the kingdom of God' (Luke xii. 31), Matthew has added 'and his righteousness' (Matt. vi. 33), thus spiritualising the original idea, and avoiding the inference that the heavenly kingdom was expected soon. (5) Matthew interpolates the word 'first'—'Seek ye first the kingdom of God.' He thinks that other things may be sought second. He avoids the depreciation of secular interests, whereas according to the teaching of Jesus these interests were all insignificant on account of the approaching end. (6) Luke omits Matt. vi. 34. He substitutes a fragment taken from another context (Luke xii. 32), and then returns to the precept, 'Sell that ye have, and give alms' (ver. 33). He carries forward this text to the end as the practical conclusion of the whole instruction.

§ 44.—*The Pharisees and Dives allied and condemned*

The discourse on the subject of riches was suggested, as we have seen, by an incident, and was delivered in public. The disciples were astonished at the teaching. They expressed their astonishment openly; and at the end of the discourse, as Luke reports, the Pharisees, who had also been listening to Jesus and were lovers of money, scoffed at Him (Luke xvi. 14). This statement represents the apostolic source, and Christ's reply to the scoffers authenticates itself. He said unto them, 'Ye are they that justify yourselves in the sight of men; but

God knoweth your hearts: for that which is exalted among men is an abomination in the sight of God' (ver. 15). So far the connection is plain. The sequel, however, introduces a difficulty, for the transition from ver. 15 to ver. 16 is abrupt and unexpected. After rebuking the Pharisees, Jesus could not at once proceed to the new subject of the relation of the law to the gospel of the kingdom of God. The Pharisees scoffed at Christ's doctrine of riches, and according to the sequence in Luke's digression He proceeded to state His doctrine of marriage (ver. 18); but obviously the connection is editorial. The new subject demands a new incident, which has for some reason been omitted. How, then, are we to make an advance? (1) In ch. xviii. 9–14 at the end of the second digression Luke records the parable of the Pharisee and the Publican, who went up into the Temple to pray. This parable bears no inner relation to the discourse on the second coming, to which it is attached as a pendant. The later context is unmistakably editorial. (2) The lesson conveyed by the parable is precisely the thought expressed in Christ's reply to the Pharisees, 'Ye are they that justify yourselves in the sight of men; but God knoweth your hearts' (Luke xvi. 15). The situation in which Luke places the parable is editorial. The original context requires to be found. The context now reached leaves nothing to be desired; and as a fact no other is available. (3) The parable of Dives and Lazarus (Luke xvi. 19–31) is obviously an enlargement and illustration of the saying, 'That which is exalted among men is an abomination in the sight of God' (ver. 15); and as clearly it is supplementary to, and even demanded by, the parable of the Pharisee and the Publican. The Pharisee justifies himself in the sight of men. He prays and fasts and gives tithes. His religion is ostentatious, and he is sent home condemned. So far the reply to the scoffers is illustrated; but the Pharisee is merely one among many who are exalted among men and an abomination in the sight of God. The rich man who is indifferent to human misery is another representative of the type; and a distinction must be made between the formal ostentatious self-righteousness of the Pharisee and the law which is his pride and hope. The

Pharisee brings discredit on the law, but the law itself is holy, just, and good. These thoughts occur to the reader who remembers the teaching of Jesus; and the fact to be noticed is that they are just the thoughts conveyed by the parable of Dives and Lazarus. Wendt perceives the connection between the two parables. He brings them together in his reconstruction, which consists of the following passages: Luke xviii. 9; xvi. 15^a; xviii. 10-14; xvi. 15^b, 19-31;[1] but according to Wendt the parable of Dives and Lazarus is simply an illustration of the saying, 'That which is exalted among men is an abomination in the sight of God,' and thus obviously a difficulty remains. Dives remembers his five brethren on the earth, and desires that Lazarus should be sent to save them from the torments of Hades. He believes in the evidential value of miracles. Abraham believes in the law and the prophets. 'If they hear not Moses and the prophets, neither will they be persuaded if one rise from the dead' (ver. 31). Wendt leaves this dialogue unexplained. It clearly does not illustrate the text in ver. 15, and yet is essential to the parable. The truth is that the parable is not merely, as Wendt supposes, an illustration of the earlier text. It is supplementary to the parable of the Pharisee and the Publican. It conveys the additional and necessary thought that the law, which is represented by the Pharisee, is not in itself such as to lead men to conduct like his. The Pharisee by his traditions makes void the law, which leads rather to the penitent cry of the publican, who would not lift up so much as his eyes unto heaven, but smote his breast, saying, 'God be merciful to me a sinner.' Through Moses and the prophets even those who are exalted among men, and an abomination in the sight of God, may escape from the torments of Hades. The condition of safety is repentance; and the law summons men to repent. Wendt's reconstruction is thus open to serious objections. He fails to perceive the whole of the truth, and the consequence is that he makes mistakes. A half-truth is little better than an error. He breaks up Luke xvi. 15 into two clauses, the first of which he places before the parable of the Pharisee and the Publican, and the second of

[1] *Die Lehre Jesu*, Erster Theil, S. 150-153.

which he reserves as an introduction to the parable of Dives and Lazarus; but the parable of Dives and Lazarus illustrates more than the half-text, and the parable of the Pharisee and the Publican is an illustration of more than the other half. The whole text is an introduction to the parables, which constitute a pair, requiring no mediation. The second has been carried forward by Luke to illustrate the saying, 'It is easier for heaven and earth to pass than for one tittle of the law to fall' (ver. 17), and the first has thus been set free to be afterwards inserted at the end of the digression. Luke xviii. 9 is an editorial heading bstracted from the story which follows.

§ 45.—*The Doctrine of Marriage*

The fragment which Luke inserts between the condemnation of the Pharisees and the parable of Dives and Lazarus has baffled the penetration of the critics (Luke xvi. 16–18). J. Estlin Carpenter e.g. finds a 'perplexing neighbourship' in the two verses (16 and 17) which now stand side by side.[1] His opinion is that they did not originally stand side by side. He is even disposed to believe that they represent two different sources, in one of which Jesus enforces 'the strictest perpetuity of the law like a rabbi of the austerest type.' Wendt is less easily puzzled. He agrees with Holtzmann, Weizsäcker and Weiss that the whole fragment is an editorial interpolation;[2] but he is not perplexed by 'the opposite principles' which are apparently laid down. He knows precisely what Luke has done. The first principle (ver. 16) was stated by Jesus in His reply to the messengers of John (Matt. xi. 12, 13). The second was delivered in the Sermon on the Mount (Matt. v. 17, 18, 32). Matthew, therefore, has preserved in each case the original context, and Luke has interpolated the two fragments between the condemnation of the Pharisees and the parable of Dives and Lazarus to prepare the way for the dialogue (vv. 27–31). The difficulty is thus satisfactorily overcome. The hypothesis of two sources is unnecessary, and the apparently opposite principles

[1] *The First Three Gospels*, p. 327.
[2] *Die Lehre Jesu*, Erster Theil, S. 151.

need not be sent off to an appendix. Unfortunately, however, there are still a few difficulties to disturb the critic's mind. His satisfaction is a little premature. (1) The law of marriage, if stated in the Sermon on the Mount (Matt. v. 32), was also according to Mark delivered on a later occasion (Mark x. 11, 12); and since the subject was then introduced by an incident Mark's context is much more likely to be original than the Sermon on the Mount, which, as Wendt admits, Matthew has considerably enlarged. (2) The appropriateness of the principles in the contexts which Matthew has given to them is not at all self-evident. If the Sermon on the Mount was a discourse on righteousness, and especially on the relation between the old and the new, the principle in Matt. v. 17, 18 forms undoubtedly an appropriate beginning; but the Sermon on the Mount was not a discourse on righteousness—as such it is historically unintelligible—and therefore the propriety disappears. Wendt's argument depends upon an assumption which is altogether untenable, and has already been discredited. He assumes again that the principle in Luke xvi. 16 was originally delivered in the reply to the messengers of John (Matt. xi. 12, 13), and this context he considers to be most appropriate; but he adapts the context to the principle, rejecting one verse which is guaranteed by Luke (ver. 10, cf. Luke vii. 27), and readjusting another which is inconvenient (Matt. xi. 11, 13, 14, 12, 15), and after these feats of criticism he invites the reader to admire a sequence which is purely fictitious. (3) If the one principle was originally situated in the Sermon on the Mount, and the other in the reply to the messengers of John, Luke has intentionally transferred them from these early contexts to serve as an introduction to the parable of Dives and Lazarus. But that in itself is scarcely credible, for one of the principles bears no inner relation to the parable, and the other would not be likely to be set aside for such a long-sighted purpose; and the law of marriage in ver. 18 still obviously requires to be explained. If Luke's aim was to interpolate one of the fragments as an introduction to the parable, he would surely not obscure this aim by interpolating also the others which bear no relation to the parable, unless all the fragments were originally together. But if they were originally together, Wendt's argument is absolutely futile; and instead of going back to the earlier contexts we must rather assume that a discourse on the subject of marriage originally followed the condemnation of the Pharisees, and that Luke has carried forward the parable of Dives and Lazarus to serve as a pendant to the fragments. The question is, Have we any reason to believe that such a discourse was really delivered at this particular time, and can we reconstruct the original? I reply by enumerating the following facts:

1. The reduction of a discourse to a few fragments is not an exceptional phenomenon in Luke's digressions. He repeatedly omits material contained in the apostolic source for the sake of avoiding editorial repetition, of returning at last to Mark, and of ministering to the edification of his Gentile readers.

2. The law of marriage (Luke xvi. 18) is connected in the second gospel with an incident. Certain Pharisees came and asked Jesus, 'Is it lawful for a man to put away his wife?' tempting Him. He answered this question, and subsequently explained the matter to His disciples in private (Mark x. 2–12). The explanation, however, is scarcely sufficient. If the disciples had really a difficulty, as their desire for an explanation presupposes, they would not be likely to be satisfied with the mere statement of a law, however direct and peremptory it might be; and Jesus was not accustomed to instruct them with such forbidding brevity. He reserved his curt replies for the tempters. Mark's narrative has probably been abbreviated.

3. Matthew reproduces Mark's narrative (Matt. xix. 3–9), but enlarges the explanation to the disciples (vv. 10–12). According to Weiss this enlargement has been derived from oral tradition.[1] The theory of an independent oral tradition is no doubt convenient when a critic gets into a difficulty; but it is simply a sort of balloon in which both the critic and the difficulty float away through the air. Wendt prefers to have solid ground under his feet. He is sometimes erratic, but is never disposed to turn aëronaut. He is puzzled by Matthew's

[1] *Introduction to the New Testament*, vol. ii. p. 274.

enlargement. He thinks that the exclamation of the disciples, 'If the case of the man is so with his wife, it is not expedient to marry' (ver. 10), would be much more likely to be suggested by the saying, 'If any man cometh unto me, and hateth not his wife, he cannot be my disciple' (Luke xiv. 26), than by the law of marriage which Mark has reported and Matthew reproduced;[1] but he does not adopt the context suggested, and so, being wisely persuaded that the enlargement has been taken from the apostolic source, he puts it into an appendix—which is quite as convenient, and on the whole much safer than the alternative balloon. If a man must hate his wife, marriage is clearly inexpedient—so clearly inexpedient that no one would think of disputing the fact; but the exclamation of the disciples is not an emphatic and decisive conclusion. It is rather an expression of surprise, a doubtful request for further instruction. It betrays the recognition of a risk rather than of the inevitable misery which the hatred of a wife would involve; and the law of marriage which was stated by Jesus, if adopted and acted upon, would involve precisely such a risk as the disciples appear to have anticipated, for the teaching is that the marriage relationship should never be dissolved. The wife may be unfaithful, or the husband may be unfaithful; but the two, being one, can never become two. They are one, until death parts them, or until the kingdom comes. The risk is surely sufficiently apparent, and the exclamation is not surprising. We must therefore conclude that the teaching which Matthew has enlarged had previously been abridged by Mark; but Matthew's enlargement represents the apostolic source, and so we gain the additional conclusion that the whole of the teaching, with the incident which suggested it, was contained in the apostolic source.

4. Returning to the Sermon on the Mount, we observe the fact that the law of marriage is there preceded by a contrast between the old and the new law of purity (Matt. v. 27-30). Since the Sermon on the Mount was not a discourse on righteousness, but an instruction adapted to the historical situation, this contrast is waiting to be restored to its original

[1] *Die Lehre Jesu*, Erster Theil, S. 183.

context; and the question arises whether Matthew has preserved the original sequence in placing the two fragments side by side. Since the subject is the same and no other context is available, the probability is that they were originally together; but, as far as we have gone in our reconstruction, no room has been found for the law of purity. It could not originally precede the law of marriage in Mark x. 12; for the matter regarding which the disciples questioned Jesus was not moral purity, but divorce. How, then, are we to account for Matthew's combination? If the law of purity originally followed Matt. xix. 12, the difficulty entirely disappears. In the first place the transition is easy. The disciples have inferred from the teaching of Jesus that marriage is not expedient. They are surprised and desire further instruction; and in reply He partly confirms and partly corrects their inference. The question of expediency, He says, depends upon the individual concerned; but the man who is waiting for the kingdom of God, and whose heart is 'surely fixed where true joys are to be found,' will keep free from earthly bonds. 'He that is able to receive it, let him receive it.' So far the inference is confirmed; but a mistake still requires to be corrected, for the evil does not consist in marriage alone. It rather consists in the evil motions of the heart, which induce men to contract such earthly alliances, and against which, whether married or single, every man must violently contend. The law of purity is here obviously a continuation of the thought, and indeed is even demanded by the teaching on the subject of expediency. And, secondly, a motive is perfectly apparent for Matthew's transpositions and omissions. In the Sermon on the Mount he can introduce neither the incident nor the subsequent exclamation of the disciples, and so the apostolic material is free for rearrangement; and since in ch. v. 21 he has already quoted the sixth commandment, with the new teaching of Jesus on the subject involved, he begins the new section in ver. 27 by quoting the seventh commandment, with the teaching of Jesus on purity. The law of marriage was originally situated before the law of purity; but, for the sake of systematic arrangement, Matthew transposes the original order. He first reports the teaching on purity, which is parallel to the seventh commandment, and then on account of the community of subject he detaches the law of marriage from its historical setting, and appends it to the law of purity. The method of the evangelist is transparent, and his motive is equally perceptible. We therefore conclude, reserving the details of the text, that the original consisted of the following passages: Mark x. 2-12; Matt. xix. 10-12; v. 27-30.

5. The principles which stand side by side, in a 'neighbourship' so 'perplexing' to J. Estlin Carpenter, assume now their place in the sequence of thought. The connection is so plain as to constitute a confirmation of our argument. The necessity of subduing, at any cost, the evil motions of the heart has been emphatically stated. 'If thy right eye causeth thee to stumble,' Jesus has said, 'pluck it out and cast it from thee; for it is profitable for thee that one of thy members perish, and not thy whole body be cast into Gehenna' (Matt. v. 29); and this teaching has been distinctly contrasted with one of the ancient commandments, and with the permission of divorce on account of man's hardness of heart. The contrast is now repeated in a brief but comprehensive saying, which explains the necessity of repression and conquest. 'The law and the prophets were until John: from that time the kingdom of God suffereth violence, and men of violence take it by force.' The necessity is explained by the urgency of the times. The kingdom of God has now come nigh, and the relationships of the world have assumed quite a different aspect. Marriage is not sinful in itself, but evil passion requires to be subdued; and since the ties which bind a man to the world are apt to loosen his hold on eternal life, he must be severe and inflexible, a man of violence taking the kingdom by force. He will not enter by compromise and feebleness. 'Strive to enter in by the narrow gate: for wide is the gate and broad is the way that leadeth to destruction, and many be they that enter in thereby. For narrow is the gate and straitened the way that leadeth unto life, and few be they that find it.' What, then, are the disciples to infer? Has the law been finally superseded and annulled? The kingdom of God is not related to the kingdoms of the world. The age

to come is not an historical continuation of the ages lying behind. A new epoch has been introduced since the days of John ; and now men may hope, by exercising violence, to enter the kingdom of God—by exercising violence, not by accommodation to the world ; for the kingdom of God is in heaven, and in heaven they neither marry nor are given in marriage. The inference seems to be involved that the old law is also subjected to violence, but that is not really the case. The old law was a preparation for the new law. It was a gift of God ; but it was also essentially an accommodation to the world, a mundane legislation intended to restrain and thus to shut up men unto the faith which should afterwards be revealed. ' For your hardness of heart Moses wrote his commandments.' Moses and the prophets adapted their teaching to the necessities of the times ; and similarly the teaching of Jesus is adapted to the necessities of the new times. The difference between the old and the new is merely a difference of method. The old represents compromise. The new represents violence ; and violence is imperatively demanded, because the kingdom of God is at hand. ' Think not that I came to destroy the law or the prophets : I came not to destroy, but to fulfil ; for verily I say unto you, Till heaven and earth pass away, one jot or one tittle shall in no wise pass from the law, till all things be accomplished.' The principles are not opposed to one another. The first demands the second, and both are demanded by the contrast in the earlier teaching.

6. The statement of the second principle is continued, and the whole discourse is rounded by Matthew's sequel in the Sermon on the Mount (Matt. v. 19, 20). The Pharisees who asked the question, ' Is it lawful for a man to put away his wife ? ' were distinguished for their ostentatious devotion to the law ; and the disciples, who were prophets of the kingdom of God, might conceivably infer that they ought no longer to insist upon obedience to the ancient commandments. This inference has already been corrected, and now in conclusion the disciples are directly addressed as teachers. Do not, on account of your devotion to the kingdom of God, teach men to set the law at nought ; and do not, on the other hand, follow the example of the Pharisees by teaching men to observe

the law without yourselves obeying its precepts. Be teachers of the law and examples of obedience to the law; and you will be great in the kingdom of God.

7. The combination of the fragments in Luke xvi. 16-18, as has already been observed, is an indication not merely that they originally formed part of one connected discourse, but also that this discourse followed the condemnation of the Pharisees (Luke xvi. 14, 15; xviii. 10-14; xvi. 19-31). The arrangement of the section cannot otherwise be satisfactorily explained. In reconstructing the contents, we have therefore also discovered the original situation of the whole; but the situation of Mark's fragment does not quite agree with the result of our criticism (Mark x. 2-12), and the question arises, Can Mark's arrangement be explained? A detailed analysis of the second gospel must be reserved for another occasion, but at present a few facts may be noticed. (*a*) The question of the Pharisees in Mark x. 2 is one of a series of incidents which did not happen on the road to Jerusalem, but during the last residence in the city. This has already been shown in the case of young Dives, and now we have another example before us. The whole of Mark's second period from the confession of Peter to the entrance into Jerusalem is an editorial combination. (*b*) The necessity of exercising violence to enter into the kingdom of God has been quoted by Mark in ch. ix. 43-49. The context is certainly editorial; but since a fragment of the original discourse has been here introduced, the introduction of the incident and another fragment immediately afterwards in ch. x. 2-12 is intelligible. The original sequence has not been preserved in ch. ix. 43-49, and therefore we are at liberty to believe that the incident and fragment in ch. x. 2-12 have been detached from their original setting. (*c*) The teaching on the subject of the law in the discourse on marriage and divorce would be sufficient in itself to suggest to an editor the transposition of the incidents. The teaching indeed has been partly omitted by Mark, but the necessity of observing the law has been transferred to the story of young Dives; for the quotation of the commandments in Mark x. 19, as we have seen, was not an original feature of the narrative. The two narratives have been to some extent combined, and the

source has been placed before the stream. The evidence above mentioned is sufficient to confirm the conclusion, which we have independently gained, that the whole discourse reconstructed was originally situated after the condemnation of the Pharisees. We now proceed to details.

a.—Dr. Abbott finds in the difference between Mark x. 3–5 and Matt. xix. 7, 8 a confirmation of his telegram theory.[1] His theory is that the memoirs of the apostles consisted of notes put together without connection very much as one writes a telegram, and that the three synoptic evangelists have independently translated this earlier gospel into coherent narratives. He denies the dependence of Matthew and Luke upon Mark. The theory need not be examined in detail. At present we have only to notice the fact that, instead of confirming Dr. Abbott's hypothesis, the variations of Matthew in the passage before us are all distinctly editorial. (1) The statement in Mark x. 1 was not contained in the apostolic source before the teaching on marriage; but Matthew reproduces this statement, merely substituting, 'He healed them there' for 'He taught them again' (Matt. xix. 2; Mark x. 1). (2) He adds 'for every cause' to the question of the Pharisees (ver. 3). (3) He places the old law of marriage before the command regarding divorce (vv. 4–8), not because he is independently translating a telegram gospel, but simply because the statement of a law ought logically to precede the exceptions. (4) Having already in ver. 4 quoted Mark x. 6, 'from the beginning of the creation, male and female made he them,' in returning to Mark x. 6 he writes for the sake of avoiding repetition, 'from the beginning it hath not been so' (ver. 8). This is a clear proof that Matthew's report is an editorial version of Mark's. The telegram theory is inadequate to account for the facts. (5) He represents the new law as addressed to the Pharisees, and not to the disciples in the house (ver. 9). (6) He adapts the new law to the supposed requirements of secular life (ver. 9). As this last variation is important we must enter into details, and compare the different versions. Luke's version is, 'Every one that putteth away his wife, and marrieth another, committeth adultery; and he that marrieth

[1] *The Common Tradition of the Synoptic Gospels*, p. xxix.

one that is put away from a husband committeth adultery' (Luke xvi. 18). This agrees with the teaching of the discourse as a whole, for Jesus certainly made an absolute statement, which astonished and perplexed His disciples. Their exclamation is otherwise inexplicable. Mark's version is slightly different, but he preserves the absoluteness of the law. No exceptions are recognised. 'Whosoever shall put away his wife, and marry another, committeth adultery against her; and if she herself shall put away her husband, and marry another, she committeth adultery' (Mark x. 11, 12). The only notable difference here is in the second clause. The case of a woman divorcing her husband is recognised and provided for by Mark; but the initiative of the woman was not contemplated by the Pharisees when they asked their question, 'Is it lawful for a man to put away his wife?' and the discourse from beginning to end is only concerned with the man. We must therefore conclude that the second clause in Mark's version is editorial, and has been intended to provide for a case which was permitted in the Gentile world. Matthew has preserved two versions, one in the Sermon on the Mount, and the other in the context borrowed from Mark; and each of these versions exhibits a characteristic variation. In the Sermon on the Mount the law is quoted thus: 'Every one that putteth away his wife, saving for the cause of fornication, maketh her an adulteress: and whosoever shall marry her when she is put away committeth adultery' (Matt. v. 32). Two facts are here worthy of notice: the first, that an exception has been put into the text; and the second, that the man has been spared at the expense of the woman. The other version is, 'Whosoever shall put away his wife except for fornication, and shall marry another, committeth adultery; and he that marrieth her when she is put away committeth adultery' (Matt. xix. 9). The man is not here spared—a confession that in the original he was not spared; but the exception is still in the text. Is this original or secondary? Unquestionably secondary; for after Matthew's version the exclamation of the disciples is inconsequent. If a man may divorce an unfaithful wife he does not run much risk. The expediency of remaining unmarried could scarcely in such a case occur to anybody; and the commendation of celibacy, as well as the earlier teaching, and the searching exhortation to beware of the passions in the heart, is not altogether intelligible. Matthew has deliberately sided with the Pharisees on account of the hardness of his heart. For the sake of accommodating Christ's teaching to the requirements of a later time when the heavenly kingdom was no longer urgently expected, he has reduced the absoluteness of the law.

b.—The precept to subdue evil passion at the cost even of an eye or a hand has been recorded twice by Matthew: first, in the Sermon on the Mount (Matt. v. 29, 30), and again in ch. xviii. 8, 9. The later quotation, however, has simply been taken from the second gospel (Mark ix. 43–48). Mark's context is certainly editorial; for in ver. 42 the subject is 'the little ones,' and the only connection is the stumbling. The saying in ver. 49, 'For every one shall be salted with fire,' might belong, as far as its present situation is concerned, either to the teaching on purity or to the discourse delivered at the entrance into Jerusalem (ver. 50); but the second of these contexts is excluded by the fact that the disciples were themselves then compared to salt, whereas in ver. 49 the statement is that every one shall be salted. The saying does not mean that everyone in Gehenna shall be salted; for Gehenna represents the punishment of the corrupt, and salt is intended to preserve from corruption. The meaning, therefore, is that if one would escape from Gehenna at last, he must burn out evil passion; and so the saying takes its place in the discourse on moral purity. Since ver. 48 obscures the significance of ver. 49, the words, 'Where their worm dieth not, and the fire is not quenched,' must be regarded as an editorial enlargement. The tendency to introduce such descriptions into the text is illustrated by the fact that ver. 44 and ver. 46 are omitted by the best ancient authorities and by the R.V. translators.

c.—The two clauses of Luke xvi. 16 have been transposed by Matthew for the sake of adapting the saying to its editorial context (Matt. xi. 12, 13). Wendt here makes two mistakes. In the first place he admits the transposition but leaves it unintelligible, failing altogether to perceive that

Matthew's context is editorial, and that the transposition is an evidence of the fact. In the reply to the messengers of John, the first of Luke's principles is an interpolation suggested by ver. 11. And secondly, he accepts Matthew's version of the second clause, but reduces it in his interpretation to Luke's. According to Luke's version the kingdom of God is a present reality into which men violently enter, that is, with eager and impetuous haste, or by the exercise of force; and Wendt similarly interprets the original. 'When Jesus contrasts the prophetic period of promise and expectation ending with John the Baptist with the present realisation of the kingdom of God, He uses this strong figurative expression of violence and seizure, which in their peculiar meaning were applied to the unjust forcible appropriation of others' goods, not, of course, because He finds the point of analogy in the injustice and violence, as if men could appropriate a share in the kingdom of God in opposition to the Divine Will, but because He sought to lay stress upon the necessity of urgent energetic laying hold of a good to which they can make no claim.'[1] This exegesis is ingenious, but is open to a few serious objections. (1) The contrast alleged between the prophetic period of promise and expectation, and the realisation of the kingdom of God, is purely subjective; for the point in the second clause is not the realisation of the kingdom of God, but rather a method of appropriation. If men require to seize the highest good like a robber, the kingdom of God can scarcely be said to be realised. The necessity presupposes the opposite. The contrast is not between expectation and fulfilment: it is simply between the law and the prophets, and a certain method of appropriation; and the inference is that the law and the prophets represent an earlier method. Wendt takes for granted that the realisation of the kingdom was explicitly taught by Jesus when He said, 'Among them that are born of women there hath not arisen a greater than John the Baptist: yet he that is but little in the kingdom of God is greater than he' (Matt. xi. 11); but the assumption is not one to be taken for granted, and is besides irrelevant, since the contrast in vv. 12, 13 did not

[1] *The Teaching of Jesus* vol. ii. pp. 48, 49.

originally follow. It is 'evident' to Wendt that by 'those born of women' Jesus means all men up to that time, that is, up to the advent of the kingdom of God;[1] but in such a case Jesus does not say what He means. Those born of women are deliberately contrasted in the text with those who are not born of women, that is, with those who are supposed to be in the heavenly kingdom, into which men do not enter as they enter into the world; and the meaning is that he who is comparatively little among the great ones in heaven is greater than the greatest on earth. The present realisation of the kingdom of God was not taught by Jesus in His reply to the messengers of John; and the interpolated saying (vv. 12, 13) does not in itself convey the idea which Wendt so confidently assumes. (2) The necessity of the urgent energetic laying hold of a good to which men can make no claim is a thought which is foreign to Matthew's context. There is nothing whatever in the context to suggest either the idea of grace or the necessity of violence. (3) In the discourse on marriage and purity the saying becomes intelligible; for Jesus has already taught His disciples to pluck out an eye and to cut off a hand, rather than to stumble and fall into Gehenna, and now He adds that since the days of John the kingdom of God suffereth violence, and men of violence take it by force. The kingdom is the opposite of Gehenna: it is therefore the heavenly kingdom. The violence is defined by the plucking out of an eye and the amputation of a hand. The contrast is not between expectation and fulfilment, but rather between compromise and violence; and the new method taught since the days of John is made necessary by the urgency of the times.

d.—The meaning of the famous words, 'Think not that I came to destroy the law or the prophets: I came not to destroy, but to fulfil,' has been discussed into deep obscurity. J. Estlin Carpenter believes that Jesus here 'enforces the strictest perpetuity of the law, like a Rabbi of the austerest type.'[2] He even declares that Jesus 'enforces the observance of the vast mass of traditional ordinances connected

[1] *The Teaching of Jesus*, vol. ii. p. 29.
[2] *The First Three Gospels*, p. 327.

with the law by the diligence of the Rabbis'[1] (Matt. v. 17, 18; xxiii. 2, 3); and he evidently agrees with Baur in supposing that the original utterance received a Judaistic bias in passing through the medium of the early Church. Professor Bruce suggests an evasion. 'It seems,' he says, 'as if it were not a question of mere destroying, but rather of the right way of doing it.'[2] In other words, although Jesus 'came not in the spirit of a destroyer, full of headlong zeal against rude imperfect statutes and antiquated customs,' He was conscious that the law would be destroyed 'in the way of necessary effect.' The convenient distinction between aim and effect does not seem to have occurred to Wendt; but, assuming that the text was contained in the apostolic source, he attempts, like Professor Bruce, to evade the difficulty.[3] The following is a brief statement of his argument. As far as the idea of fulfilment is concerned, Jesus might mean that He came to realise practically the Old Testament hopes and promises, to which the law and the prophets bear witness; but the connection in the Sermon on the Mount tells decidedly against this interpretation, for the fulfilment of the Old Testament promises is not treated in the rest of the discourse. Again, as far as the idea of fulfilment is concerned, the meaning might be, as Weiss maintains, that Jesus came to fulfil the Old Testament revelation of law through the complete practical performance of the revealed will of God; but this interpretation is excluded by the verses which immediately follow, for Jesus proceeds to enforce the strictest perpetuity of the law (vv. 18, 19); and since He could not intend to teach and command the indefeasible authority and strictest observance of the Old Testament law, in its historically existing elements, we must either assume that vv. 17-19 were not spoken by the historical Jesus, or that Jesus 'understood by law something other and higher than the simple historically delivered form of the Old Testament revelation of the will of God.' The first of these alternatives is rejected by Wendt, and ultimately, after an elaborate discussion, which rolls heavily through his pages like the waves of the German Sea, he

---

[1] *The First Three Gospels*, p. 372.   [2] *The Kingdom of God*, p. 65.
[3] *The Teaching of Jesus*, vol. ii. pp. 7-29.

persuades himself that the second is the truth. 'Jesus,' he says, 'judged the law and the prophets, not according to the standard of an idea derived from themselves, but according to the standard of an ideal, of which He had the certainty that it was the right leading idea of that true revelation of the will of God.'[1] All this is interesting and ingenious; but the question is, Does the context permit such evasions? Wendt is perfectly sure that the text was originally delivered in the Sermon on the Mount; and the writers from whom he differs do not disturb this confidence, for no other context has been suggested. But obviously, if the statement was not made in the Sermon on the Mount, if, on the contrary, we can prove that Matthew's context is editorial, the exegetical ingenuity of the critics is misdirected energy. 'No man rendeth a piece from a new garment, and putteth it upon an old garment: else he will rend the new, and also the piece from the new will not agree with the old.' But this is precisely what Matthew has done; and the perplexity of modern interpreters is simply an evidence that the predicted result has followed. The much-discussed text was not delivered in the Sermon on the Mount. Jesus did not speak 'as if He were conscious that an opposite rôle would be expected of Him, and desired as early as possible to correct the misapprehension.'[2] The suggestion that at the beginning of the ministry He was expected to be antagonistic to the law and the prophets shows some lack of historical perception. The misapprehension is not hypothetical. It was corrected as early as possible after the statement which provoked it; but this statement was made near the end of the ministry in a discourse on the subject of marriage, and the text is explained by its context. The fulfilment which Jesus anticipated was not merely a fulfilment of the ancient revelation of law—that no doubt is in some way involved; but, as Wendt points out, 'the practical performance of the precepts of the law is by no means the exact logical opposite of the abrogation of the law,'[3] and the meaning rather is that by faithfully observing the Mosaic commandments, the promise would at last be fulfilled, and all

[1] *The Teaching of Jesus*, vol. ii. p. 15. [2] *The Kingdom of God*, pp. 63.
[3] *The Teaching of Jesus*, vol. ii. pp. 11, 12.

things would be accomplished which the law and the prophets foretold. The statement that Jesus announced the practical realisation of the kingdom of God is therefore entirely a mistake. The kingdom of God, as preached by Him, was not a spiritual kingdom on earth: it was the kingdom of His Father in heaven; and all things, He said, would only be accomplished in accordance with the terms of the covenant.

The scholars whose opinions have been quoted above agree in taking for granted that Jesus did not as a fact enforce the perpetuity of the ancient law. They differ only in their method of escaping from the text. Baur, followed by J. Estlin Carpenter, transfers it from Jesus to a section of the Church. Professor Bruce reduces its significance by a copious admixture of pure Loch Katrine water. By a private process of evaporation Wendt makes the law an ideal. But these methods are all equally illegitimate. The text was contained in the apostolic source, and must therefore be regarded as a genuine utterance of the historical Jesus. The emphatic clearness of the words forbids the distinction between aim and effect. The law of marriage was not an ideal: it was a literary and legislative reality. What, then, is the meaning of the text? Are we to believe with J. Estlin Carpenter that Jesus enforces 'the strictest perpetuity of the law, like a Rabbi of the austerest type'? By no means; for, in the first place, the word 'perpetuity' suggests quite a wrong idea. 'Till heaven and earth pass away' does not mean beyond the nineteenth century. It simply means 'till all things be accomplished,' that is, till the promise is fulfilled in the heavenly kingdom of God; and Jesus expected fulfilment soon. He did not anticipate a long historical development, and the establishment of the law among the Gentiles. He did not exclude the Gentiles from the kingdom of God, but as certainly He did not foresee the mission of Paul. His message was, 'Repent ye, for the kingdom of God is at hand.' And secondly, the ceremonial legislation of the Old Testament is distinctly excluded by the context; for the subject of the discourse was not the Old Testament legislation as a whole, but simply the moral code represented by the seventh commandment and by the statute of divorce. Again, instead of enforcing the traditions of the elders, like a Rabbi of the austerest type, Jesus deliberately and emphatically rejected these traditions as evasions and transgressions of the covenant. He instructed His disciples to pay proper respect to the Scribes and the Pharisees in their official capacity and to observe their precepts, but only in so far as these precepts were in accordance with the Mosaic legislation, which was a commandment of God. And finally He advanced even beyond the law, as the Rabbis did not attempt to do, by expounding its inner significance, and by teaching a method of morality demanded by the urgency of the times. The contrast in the text is not between a period of expectation and one of accomplished desire, but is rather a contrast between different degrees of expectation, and therefore a contrast of method. For the near approach of the consummation, in fulfilment of the law and the prophets, required not merely that these should be still faithfully observed, but also that men, instead of using the ancient legislation as a means of accommodation to the world, should henceforth live for that kingdom of God in relation to which, as He taught, all worldly things are insignificant, and the heavens and the earth are provisional. When the text is placed in its historical setting, the meaning is unmistakable, and evasions are both futile and unnecessary.

The omissions of the evangelists must now in conclusion be accounted for. Matthew has preserved the whole discourse with the exception of Mark ix. 49, a fragment which seems obscure and superfluous. Mark has much abbreviated the original. He is interested chiefly in the incident. Luke has deliberately omitted the incident and has reduced the discourse to three fragments. He avoids, like Mark, the commendation of celibacy. He omits, like Matthew, Mark ix. 49. He spiritualises the announcement of the kingdom (Luke xvi. 16), an end which is also gained, whether intentionally or not, by the redistribution of the fragments in the first and second gospels. He omits the severe teaching on the subject of purity and the allusion to the righteousness of the Scribes and the Pharisees. And all this has been done, partly for the sake of edification, and partly to preserve an editorial connection between ver. 17 and the parable of Dives and Lazarus.

§ 46.—*The Kingdom and the Child*

We have now to investigate an apostolic fragment which is situated in Luke's digression after the parable of Dives and Lazarus. Jesus said unto His disciples, 'It is impossible but that occasions of stumbling should come: but woe unto him through whom they come! It were well for him if a millstone were hanged about his neck, and he were thrown into the sea, rather than that he should cause one of these little ones to stumble' (Luke xvii. 1, 2). The attention of the reader is invited to the following facts:

1. The connection between the fragment and the parable is clearly not editorial. We may therefore provisionally conclude that the fragment was originally situated after the doctrine of marriage.

2. The allusion to 'the little ones' is unintelligible unless on the supposition that Luke has omitted an incident. An incident is clearly presupposed, and its nature is defined by the allusion. Wendt expresses the opinion that 'the little ones' in Luke's digression are not little children, but 'outwardly insignificant members of the kingdom.'[1] In this brief statement, however, there are two mistakes; for, in the first place, since the kingdom of God was in heaven, the believers on the earth were not members but heirs; and, secondly, we have no reason whatever to suppose that when Jesus spoke of 'the little ones' He did not mean little children. Wendt's criticism of the text is a failure, and his exegesis is not a success.

3. After the statement of Christ's doctrine of marriage, Mark records a brief narrative on the subject of little children (Mark x. 13–16). This is precisely the sort of incident which is demanded by the fragment in the third gospel; and since the parable of Dives and Lazarus originally preceded the doctrine of marriage, it is obvious that, as far as situation is concerned, the fragment coincides with the narrative.

4. Luke's fragment occurs also in the second gospel (Mark ix. 42). The section from Mark ix. 38 to ver. 50 is certainly an editorial mosaic. It consists of fragments which have

[1] *Die Lehre Jesu*, Erster Theil, S. 155, cf. *The Teaching of Jesus*, vol. i. p. 344.

been detached from their original contexts—vv. 38–40 from the early demoniac narrative, vv. 43–49 from the discourse on marriage and purity, and ver. 50 from the address to the disciples at the entrance into Jerusalem. The fragments which remain (vv. 41, 42) are therefore not in their original setting, and so far they are free to be transferred to the incident in Mark x. 13–16. But here the context presents a difficulty; for, when the exclamation of John (vv. 38–40) is recognised as an editorial interpolation, the fragments in question immediately follow ver. 37, and two facts are perfectly obvious. The first is that Mark has adapted the fragments to the interpolation, substituting the disciples for 'the little ones' in ver. 41 (cf. Matt. x. 42), and again in ver. 42 identifying the little ones with the disciples (cf. Luke xvii. 2); and the second is that the fragments, when thus corrected, constitute an appropriate continuation of the instruction in ver. 37. Apparently, therefore, in looking for one incident we have really found two, each of which has some claim to be accepted; for the first in Mark ix. 33–37 has a part of Luke's fragment for its sequel, and the second in Mark x. 13–16 coincides in situation with Luke's fragment. How, then, are we to reconstruct the apostolic original with any degree of assurance? If one incident is accepted, the other still requires to be accounted for; and as far as we have gone we have only found room for one. A closer examination of the first may suggest a way out of the difficulty. Four facts are worthy of notice. (a) The contentious rivalry of the disciples (ver. 34) is an effective contrast to the self-sacrifice of the Son of Man, who, according to the announcement reported immediately before, would be delivered up into the hands of men and killed (ver. 31). Since Mark is certainly a writer who makes a free use of his material, an editorial motive may be confidently recognised in this contrast. (b) The report that the saying regarding the little ones was delivered in Capernaum (ver. 33) is clearly incompatible with the situation of Luke's fragment. When the instruction was given, Jesus was in Jerusalem. (c) The text in ver. 35 was not delivered in Capernaum, but at the Supper in Jerusalem. This statement will be verified when we reach the later context. Mark is not a writer of reminiscences : he is an editor who has documents before him. The supposition that the text was delivered on two or more occasions is therefore scarcely probable. (*d*) The presence of the child in the house is not in any way explained. He is merely introduced as an illustration; and since the whole narrative is a mosaic, like the combination of fragments in the sequel, the illustration may be purely editorial. The house was not in Capernaum. That is forbidden by the apostolic source; and the more definite incident in Mark x. 13–16 is in favour of the conclusion that the child was not in the house. In other words, the whole narrative is an editorial combination, and the child has been borrowed from the later incident for the sake of teaching a lesson suggested by the self-sacrifice of Jesus. Reserving the discussion of the second gospel, we may therefore provisionally conclude that the incident which originally introduced Luke's fragment has been preserved by Mark in ch. x. 13–16.

5. Matthew in following Mark introduces two additional verses which enable us to reconstruct the original. Matt. xvii. 24–xviii. 14 is parallel to Mark ix. 33–50. The Temple tax incident has been taken from the apostolic source and interpolated after the allusion to Capernaum (Mark ix. 33). The parable of the Lost Sheep has been taken, as we have seen, from the context of Zacchæus the publican. These fragments represent the apostolic source; and at first sight one is disposed to believe that the incident in Matt. xviii. 1–5 has also been taken from the apostolic source, and substituted for the version of Mark (Mark ix. 33–37). But the truth is that Matthew's narrative is simply an editorial version of Mark's. (*a*) He avoids the statement that the disciples disputed who was the greatest, but the reply of Jesus (ver. 3) proves clearly that their question was personal and not abstract. (*b*) He identifies the last of all and the servant of all (Mark ix. 35) with the child (Matt. xviii. 3, 4), but the return to Mark in ver. 5 shows that this is an editorial enlargement. (*c*) He omits the exclamation of John and passes at once to the fragment on occasions of stumbling; and for the sake of transition he omits also the words, ' And whosoever receiveth

me, receiveth not me, but him that sent me' (Mark ix. 37). These variations are certainly not such as to demand documentary authority. They are purely editorial, and therefore we cannot infer from Matthew's version that the incident was contained in the apostolic source. Again, Matt. xviii. 14 is simply an editorial application of the parable of the Lost Sheep. Wendt's supposition that the parable is here in its original context is peremptorily forbidden by the fact that the subject is little children, who could not be described as lost sheep. Excluding these interpolations, two verses remain to be accounted for. Matt. xviii. 7 is authenticated as an apostolic fragment by Luke xvii. 1; and Matt. xviii. 10 is also unmistakably apostolic. The question is, How can we reconstruct the original from the data thus provided by the three evangelists? The incident in Mark x. 13-16 clearly constitutes the introduction, but how are the loose fragments to be rearranged and put into their original position? Matt. xviii. 10 has been omitted by Luke, and might therefore be originally situated before Luke xvii. 1; but Luke xvii. 1 is parallel to Matt. xviii. 7, and so this arrangement appears to be forbidden. A reason, however, can be given for Matthew's transference of ver. 10 to a later position, on the supposition that it was originally situated before ver. 7; for ver. 10 is obviously intended to serve as an introduction to the parable of the Lost Sheep. And the sequence authenticates itself when the rearrangement suggested is adopted. Some people have been rebuked by the disciples for bringing little children to the Master. He has rebuked the disciples. He has told them that, if one would enter the kingdom of God, he must receive it as a little child, without hesitation, with simple faith, and without entanglements; and now as usual He continues to instruct the disciples. The little ones, he says, have guardian angels who behold the face of the Father in heaven. See that ye despise them not. They are not despised by God. They may be prevented from entering the kingdom, for occasions of stumbling must come; but woe to that man through whom they come. It were well for him if a great millstone were hanged about his neck, and he were sunk in the depth of the sea, rather than that he should cause one of these little ones to stumble.

6. The discourse thus partially reconstructed is made complete and rounded by a fragment which Matthew has inserted in the charge to the twelve (Matt. x. 41, 42). The allusion to the little ones in this fragment proves conclusively that it could not be addressed to the twelve before they went out on their mission; and Mark in ch. ix. 41, a verse which Matthew has omitted to avoid repetition, has clearly preserved the original context. But the text in Mark's version is secondary; for ver. 41 has been adapted to the interpolation in vv. 38–40, and ver. 37, which is scarcely appropriate to the occasion, is perfectly intelligible as an editorial version of Matt. x. 41. And finally, since the whole of Mark's narrative is a mosaic, the fragments of which have been editorially arranged, the position of ver. 37 and ver. 41 at the beginning of the instruction cannot be regarded as original, if the sequence of thought demands a later situation. What, then, is the thought-connection? Jesus has warned His disciples not to despise the little ones who have guardian angels in heaven, and will enter the kingdom of God if not prevented by men. He has distinctly said, 'Of such is the kingdom of God.' But how are the children to be treated? Do they really represent, as Mark suggests (ch. ix. 35) and Matthew seems also to imply (ch. xviii. 4), the last who will become first, the servants of the servants of God? Not so: in the teaching of Jesus there is no exaggeration of sentiment. The child is the least of all, but is not on that account the greatest in the sight of the heavenly Father, and must not be honoured as the greatest by the heirs of the kingdom on earth. The child is an unproved disciple at the stage of receptivity and inexperience. He is not greater than the righteous man who has gained stability of character. He ranks far below the prophet who is righteous and inspired by the Father. 'He that receiveth a prophet in the name of a prophet shall receive a prophet's reward; and he that receiveth a righteous man in the name of a righteous man shall receive a righteous man's reward. And whosoever shall give to drink unto one of these little ones a cup of cold water only, in the name of a

disciple, verily I say unto you, he shall in no wise lose his reward.' These words are demanded as the original conclusion by the antecedent instruction.

a.—Matthew and Luke have each borrowed the incident from Mark (Matt. xix. 13–15; Luke xviii. 15–17). The variations are certainly editorial. (1) Matthew omits the statement that Jesus took the children in His arms and blessed them; but according to his version the people wished Jesus to pray (ver. 13). This wish is a translation of the blessing. (2) Luke also omits the blessing of the children. He seems to have no fondness for the little ones. (3) Matthew and Luke both spare the disciples by omitting the statement that Jesus was moved with indignation. (4) To avoid repetition Matthew omits Mark x. 15 (cf. Matt. xviii. 3, 4).

b.—Luke has toned down the severity of the original. He substitutes 'a millstone' (λίθος μυλικός) for 'a great millstone,' i.e. one turned by an ass (μύλος ὀνικός), and 'thrown into the sea' for 'sunk in the depth of the sea.'

c.—The conclusion has been entirely omitted by Luke—perhaps on account of the description of the child as one to be received in the name of a disciple. Mark also has avoided this description (Mark ix. 37).

§ 47.—*The Doctrine of Prayer*

In the first and third gospels the duty of forgiveness is inculcated immediately after the teaching regarding the little ones (Matt. xviii. 15; Luke xvii. 3); and Wendt, assuming that the original sequence has been preserved, boldly combines the two subjects. His reconstruction consists of the following passages: Luke xvii. 1, 2; Matt. xviii. 10, 12–16, 21–35.[1] The discourse thus formed is open to a few serious objections. In the first place it is scarcely articulate. It begins with an allusion to the love of the Father for the little ones, and to His desire that they should not perish; but the connection between this and the duty of brotherly forgiveness is not by any means obvious. The love of the Father might

[1] *Die Lehre Jesu*, Erster Theil, S. 154–157.

certainly be mentioned as a reason why men should love one another; but the specific application to the duty of forgiveness is still unexpected and obscure. If the parable of the Lost Sheep was originally a part of the discourse, the sequel ought rather to be the duty of seeking and saving the lost. Wendt gives the discourse an introduction which might be conveniently omitted. It is both inadequate and misleading. Again, when the discourse is thus reconstructed, 'the little ones' necessarily mean outwardly insignificant disciples, the least of the brethren of Jesus; but this is strained exegesis which is not very creditable to the critic. If the apostolic source was a mere collection of logia, entirely unrelated to the second gospel, the incident in Mark ix. 33-37 and Mark x. 13-16 must be excluded from the reconstruction, and thus the little ones are not explicitly identified with the children; but the conclusion does not follow that they are insignificant disciples. The theory is rather discredited by the greater probability that they are precisely the children who were fondled and blessed by Jesus. How hardly shall they that have theories enter into the kingdom of fact! The Sermon which Wendt has submitted as the result of his critical investigation is remarkable, not only for an introduction which does not really introduce, but also, and thirdly, for the absence of a text which is indispensable. The teaching of Jesus was invariably suggested by an incident; and the writer of the apostolic source, even although he intended to make merely a collection of logia, would not be likely to leave unrecorded the events which explain the teaching. As a fact he is not accustomed to omit the text. The exception proves the rule, but the rule does not prove the exception. A new subject demands a new incident, unless the exception can be proved. The subject of the little ones is certainly distinct from the subject of marriage and purity, and therefore it is antecedently probable that a narrative regarding the little ones has been omitted by Luke; and similarly, since the subject of forgiveness is distinct from the subject of the little ones, an incident suggesting the duty of freely forgiving a brother has also been probably omitted. Here, however, we are confronted by an obvious difficulty. When the truth is recognised that the apostolic

T

source was not a mere collection of logia, unrelated to the second gospel, an historical suggestion is apparent for the teaching regarding the little ones; but how are we to find an incident to introduce the subject of forgiveness? The agreement of Matthew and Luke, in divergence from Mark, appears to prove conclusively that an exceptional case has been discovered. An omission by Luke is intelligible, and an omission by Matthew is intelligible; but when the two independent evangelists agree in recording the duty of forgiveness immediately after the instruction suggested by the children, we seem to be forced to the conclusion that in the apostolic source there was no intermediate event. I do not see the necessity. I decline to be forced by bad logic. If Matthew and Luke have both for editorial reasons already inserted the incident, their agreement in avoiding repetition is surely not a wonderful coincidence. The critics do not contemplate the possibility of such a sensible proceeding; but even the most observant of men are occasionally blinded by their theories. I submit the following facts:

1. An appropriate incident has been recorded by Luke in ch. xi. 1. Jesus had been praying in a certain place, and when He ceased, a disciple said, 'Lord, teach us to pray, as John also taught his disciples.' In response to this request, a brief but comprehensive prayer was recited and commended by Jesus; and one of the petitions, 'Forgive us our debts, as we also have forgiven our debtors,' introduces the subject of forgiveness. The context in the third gospel has already been analysed in detail, and has been found to be secondary. The lawyer did not ask his tempting question after the return of the twelve from their mission. The visit to Bethany was paid at a much later time; and the instruction on the subject of prayer has been placed by Luke in the series, partly to illustrate the spirit of the babes who receive a revelation from the Father (Luke x. 21), and partly to define the good part which Mary had chosen and Martha was in danger of losing (ver. 42). The good gift of God is the Holy Spirit, received through sitting at the feet and hearing the word of the Lord (Luke xi. 13). The context is unmistakably editorial, and the incident with its sequel is accordingly free to be transferred to the later occasion.

2. Matthew enables us to determine the original sequence of thought. He inserts the Lord's Prayer in the Sermon on the Mount (Matt. vi. 7–15). The context here is as clearly editorial as in the case of the third gospel; for the warning against doing one's righteousness to be seen of men, with the illustrative examples of almsgiving, prayer and fasting, was delivered, as we have seen, in a discourse on the righteousness of the Pharisees (Matt. vi. 1–6, 16–18), and the prayer which Jesus taught His disciples is foreign to this discourse, as well as to the Sermon on the Mount. It is an interpolation within an interpolation. The fact to be specially noted at present is that according to Matthew's version Jesus proceeded to instruct His disciples on the subject of the petition for forgiveness. He said, 'For if ye forgive men their trespasses, your heavenly Father will also forgive you. But if ye forgive not men their trespasses, neither will your Father forgive your trespasses' (vv. 14, 15). These words pass over ver. 13, and connect themselves immediately with ver. 12. The transition from ver. 13 to ver. 14 is abrupt, and at once suggests the possibility that Matthew has omitted a fragment, which seemed to him to be unnecessary on account of the proximity of ver. 12. Now the precept which Luke has preserved in ch. xvii. 3, 4 fulfils obviously the requirements of the case. It introduces an instruction on the subject of forgiveness, and makes the reason intelligible, which Matthew, omitting the precept, has abruptly added to the petitions. We may therefore provisionally conclude that Luke xvii. 3, 4 originally preceded Matt. vi. 14, 15.

3. In an earlier section of the Sermon on the Mount Matthew has preserved a few fragments which continue the subject of forgiveness and carry forward the exposition of the prayer. The passage which begins with the quotation of the sixth commandment will reward the attention of the student (ch. v. 21–26). This passage owes its position to the quotation. Matt. v. 17–20 has been inserted in the Sermon as an introduction to the editorial subject, and the interpolations which follow exhibit Christ's relation to the law and the prophets in the order of the Mosaic commandments. The sixth is represented by ch. v. 21–26, the seventh by ch. v.

27-32, the ninth by ch. v. 33-37, the tenth by ch. vi. 19-34. As far as the Sermon on the Mount is concerned, ch. v. 21-26 might therefore originally follow ch. vi. 15. But a slight readjustment of the fragments in ch. v. 21-26 is necessary to make the combination coherent; for vv. 23, 24 could scarcely follow vv. 21, 22 in the original discourse. In vv. 23, 24 the lesson is to make amends to an injured brother before asking forgiveness from God. In vv. 25, 26, a secondary version of Luke xii. 58, 59, the complementary lesson is conveyed to forgive a private wrong, even on the road to the magistrate, lest the Judge who is in heaven should with equal or greater severity punish the implacable spirit. Now the statement in ver. 22 that everyone who is angry with his brother shall be in danger of the judgment is unrelated to the first of these cases; for the man in the first case is not supposed to be angry with his brother. He has not been in any way injured: he has himself been the aggressor. But the man in the second case is angry. He is indeed so indignant, and exhibits so much animosity, that he is taking his brother to the magistrate for the sake of obtaining justice or vengeance. The statement that everyone who is angry with his brother shall be in danger of the judgment is inappropriate before ver. 23, and is demanded as the sequel to ver. 26. And such a readjustment is permitted by the context; for the evangelist is recording Christ's teaching in the order of the Mosaic commandments, and obviously he has an editorial reason for transferring the fragment which contains the quotation of the sixth from the end to the beginning of the passage. We have therefore gained two results. We have seen in the first place that ch. v. 21-26 might originally follow ch. vi. 15; and secondly the inner relation of the fragments in ch. v. 21-26 has required us to conclude that ver. 26 had originally for its sequel vv. 21, 22. But in reaching this conclusion we have also converted the possibility that the fragments in question originally followed ch. vi. 15 into a decisive probability; for the sequence authenticates itself. Jesus instructs His disciples to forgive a brother who repents. He tells them that, unless they forgive, they will not be forgiven by the Father. He then supposes two cases which illustrate the precept. The first is the case of a man who has somehow offended a brother, and is seeking forgiveness from God. Jesus says, Be reconciled to your brother. Confess your fault to him, and then go and offer your gift. The second is the case of a man who has himself been wronged. He has apprehended the wrongdoer as a criminal, and is about to demand justice from the magistrate. Jesus says, On the way give diligence to be quit of him. Forgive the wrong if you wish to be forgiven. You owe your brother forgiveness, and unless the human debt is paid a greater penalty will soon be exacted by God. Do not assert your legal rights. ' Ye have heard that it was said to them of old time, Thou shalt not kill; and whosoever shall kill shall be in danger of the judgment : but I say unto you, that every one who is angry with his brother shall be in danger of the judgment ; and whosoever shall say to his brother, Raca, shall be in danger of the council; and whosoever shall say, Thou fool, shall be in danger of the Gehenna of fire.' The precept which follows the prayer would not be likely to be delivered by Jesus without being explained and enforced in relation to particular cases. The fragments in Matt. v. 21-26 are certainly foreign to the Sermon on the Mount. They are waiting to be restored to their original context. The only available context is the one which we are at present reconstructing ; and the sequence of thought is so clear and inevitable that the argument is verified by the result. As far as we have gone, the original discourse consists, therefore, of the following passages: Luke xi. 1-4; xvii. 3, 4 ; Matt. vi. 14, 15 ; v. 23, 24; Luke xii. 58, 59 ; Matt. v. 21, 22.

4. The words Raca and Moreh in Matt. v. 22 carry us another stage forward. These words have been abruptly introduced, and as they are merely representative they would not be likely to be left by Jesus without an explanation in the sequel. The man who says Raca or Moreh in anger is in danger of the Gehenna of fire. So Jesus has affirmed to the disciples ; but the words Raca and Moreh are not more opprobrious than others, and the statement is scarcely complete as it stands. The nail requires some hammering. In ch. xii. 25-37 Matthew reports the reply of Jesus to certain Pharisees who had accused Him of casting out devils by Beelzebub, the

prince of the devils. The reply concludes thus, 'And I say unto you, that every idle word that men shall speak, they shall give account thereof in the day of judgment. For by thy words thou shalt be justified, and by thy words thou shalt be condemned' (vv. 36, 37). This narrative has already been analysed, and the conclusion of Matthew's version has been recognised as an editorial addition. It is therefore free to be restored to its original context; and obviously it continues and completes the statement regarding the words Raca and Moreh; for these are idle words, not specially culpable in themselves, but representative of a class, which serves no useful purpose and exposes the speaker to condemnation on account of the anger betrayed. Matthew has hammered the wrong nail.

5. The instruction which Matthew records after the discourse on the little ones affords a confirmation of our argument, and enables us to make another advance. In Luke xvii. 3, 4 the disciples are instructed to forgive every wrong as often as the wrongdoer repents. In Matt. xviii. 15–17 forgiveness is reduced to a system. A remonstrance is in the first place to be privately addressed to the offender, and then, if he does not repent, the proceeding is to be repeated in the presence of two or three witnesses. If these measures fail, complaint is to be made to the church; and if the offender remains still impenitent, refusing even to hear the voice of the church, he is to be treated as the Gentile and the publican. The question is, Has this teaching been taken from the apostolic source? Wendt accepts vv. 15, 16, but rejects ver. 17; and in the passage which immediately follows he rejects ver. 18, but accepts vv. 19, 20, placing these verses in an appendix.[1] The injunction that an impenitent brother, who will not hear the church, is to be treated as the Gentile and the publican, is certainly of doubtful authenticity; for the text presupposes that the disciples are members of a church which is strictly confined within the limits of Jewish nationality. But if Jesus did not anticipate a long historical development, He did not contemplate the formation of a church; and in any case the classification of impenitent offenders with

[1] *Die Lehre Jesu*, Erster Theil, S. 155, 182.

the Gentile and the publican is incompatible with the teaching of the Friend of publicans and sinners. The claim of ver. 17 to be regarded as a genuine fragment of the apostolic source must therefore be absolutely rejected; but Wendt is scarcely justified in separating this verse from its context. The remonstrance with the offender in the presence of two or three witnesses is a semi-judicial proceeding, which is only intelligible as the preliminary of a more serious and public investigation. Why should the witnesses be present to establish every word, if the complaint can proceed no farther? The truth is that ver. 16 demands ver. 17 as its sequel, just as clearly as ver. 16 is demanded by ver. 15. The whole passage is therefore unapostolic; and the only question is, How are we to account for its interpolation in the teaching of Jesus? The discourse on prayer and forgiveness, which we are at present reconstructing, was originally situated in the position now occupied by the interpolated fragment, that is, after the blessing of the children. But Matthew has already inserted in his gospel the prayer which Jesus taught His disciples, the two cases which define the duty of forgiveness, and the warning against anger and idle words. These fragments cannot be repeated; but Peter's question in ver. 21 obviously requires some sort of introduction. What, then, has Matthew done? He has certainly substituted an ecclesiastical regulation; but how did this originate, and how could the evangelist justify his conduct in ascribing it so boldly to Jesus? I venture to make the suggestion that the whole passage before us (Matt. xviii. 15-17) is an ecclesiastical abstract and adaptation of the teaching which Matthew has omitted for the sake of avoiding repetition. Ver. 15 is parallel to Luke xvii. 3. Ver. 16 represents the precept to agree quickly on the road to the magistrate (Matt. v. 25; Luke xii. 58); and the complaint before the church in ver. 17 is parallel to the legal prosecution which according to the original was to be avoided (cf. Matt. v. 22). A civil action has thus been transferred to the ecclesiastical court. The prohibition of legal proceedings has been supposed to involve the institution of ecclesiastical proceedings; and the interpolated fragment is simply an editorial version of the instruction which was addressed to the disciples. The rest of Matthew's fragment (vv. 18–20) has been transferred from a later context for the sake of completing the allusion to the church by a statement of its judicial authority. These verses will be afterwards considered. In the meantime we may carry them forward, and proceed to the rest of the discourse. We have now reached Peter's question (ver. 21). The conclusion has already been provisionally gained that Luke xvii. 3, 4 originally preceded Matt. vi. 14, 15, and now we are able to verify the fact; for Luke xvii. 3, 4 is presupposed by Peter's question. The idea that according to the teaching of Jesus an offending brother should be forgiven until seven times obviously requires explanation. How could Peter imagine that his Master had set such a limit? The answer is that Jesus had said, 'If he sin against thee seven times in the day, and seven times turn again to thee, saying, I repent, thou shalt forgive him' (Luke xvii. 4). The question presupposes the statement regarding which Peter was doubtful; and the reply of Jesus, 'I say not unto thee, Until seven times; but, Until seventy times seven,' that is, without any calculation, is clearly an allusion to the earlier precept which Peter had misapprehended. The fragment which Luke has preserved is therefore authenticated by Matthew. Our argument is so far confirmed, and we gain in addition a question and reply, including the parable of the Unmerciful Servant (Matt. xviii. 21–35).

6. The parable of the Fig Tree, which a certain man planted in his vineyard, has been placed by Luke in an editorial context (Luke xiii. 6–9). This parable could scarcely be addressed to the people who reported the slaughter of the Galileans by Herod; for these people were not disciples. They were summoned by Jesus to repent; and the fig tree represents the case of men who have entered the fellowship of faith, and from whom not merely repentance is expected, but also a certain character and fruit. The context has already been analysed, and the parable of the Fig Tree has been recognised as an editorial interpolation; but Luke xii. 58, 59 is a fragment from the discourse on forgiveness, and the discovery soon afterwards of another fragment is not to be considered surprising. The discourse on forgiveness was

addressed to the disciples, and the parable of the Fig Tree was addressed to disciples. After Luke xii. 58, 59, Peter asked his question, and was charged in reply to forgive without calculation, not merely until seven times, but even until seventy times seven. The parable of the Unmerciful Servant was then delivered to illustrate the mercy of God, and the punishment of those who, having been forgiven, do not forgive from the heart. So far we are following Matthew; and now, turning to Luke, we find the parable of the Fig Tree, which did not originally follow the call to repentance in Luke xiii. 1-5, but might, as far as position is concerned, be a fragment from the discourse on forgiveness represented by Luke xii. 58, 59. The question is, Do the streams as a fact unite? Does the parable of the Fig Tree exhibit any inner relation to the teaching reported by Matthew? Two lessons are conveyed by this parable. The first is that a certain type of conduct is expected from disciples, just as a fig tree is expected to bear figs; and the second is that God is long-suffering and patient, willing to listen to the intercession of the merciful, and slow to execute judgment on those who are not irreclaimably bad. Now obviously the first of these lessons is also taught in the discourse on forgiveness, and quite as obviously the second supplements, and is even demanded by, the parable of the Unmerciful Servant; for God is not like the king in the parable who delivered his servant to the tormentors without leaving room for repentance. His judgment is not immediate. He does not punish a sinner as soon as the sin is committed. He grants delay, and thus manifests the merciful spirit which He requires from men. The two parables were originally associated as a pair. The second corrects and completes the first. Matt. xviii. 35 was therefore followed in the apostolic source by Luke xiii. 6-9.

7. Immediately after the prayer which Jesus taught His disciples, Luke reports a passage to which we are now able to return (Luke xi. 5-13, cf. Matt. vii. 7-11). Three facts are here worthy of notice. (*a*) The disciples requested to be taught to pray, and therefore it is antecedently improbable that, after reciting the Lord's Prayer, Jesus merely inculcated the duty of forgiving one another. (*b*) The omissions of

Luke can be accounted for on the supposition that the teaching on forgiveness originally followed the prayer, and was followed by Luke xi. 5-13; for the aim of the evangelist is to define the one thing needful, the good part which Mary had chosen, and which would not be taken away from her (Luke x. 41, 42). He deliberately identifies the one thing needful with the Holy Spirit, which the Father will give to those that ask Him (Luke xi. 13), and omits the teaching on forgiveness because it does not at present serve, but would rather obscure, his purpose. (c) The encouragement to be importunate in prayer is related inwardly to the parable of the Fig Tree. The vine-dresser intercedes for the tree, and the petition is supposed to be granted; but we are not told that the tree is spared. The parable ends abruptly. It is not incomplete as a parable, but is scarcely able to stand alone. The parable of the Fig Tree supplements the parable of the Unmerciful Servant, but requires itself to be supplemented; for Jesus here returns to the larger subject of prayer, and the efficacy of intercession is suggested. But no definite assurance is conveyed that the Father will answer prayer, and the case is merely one of intercession. A sequel is imperatively demanded: and the teaching reported by Luke immediately after the Lord's Prayer is precisely the addition which is needed; for here the disciples are told that importunity is successful, and that the heavenly Father, much more than the fathers of the earth, will give good things to His children. The sequence verifies our reconstruction.

8. We have now reached the last stage of the argument. The only passage which remains to be discussed is Luke xvii. 5-10. In one of his interesting volumes Tolstoi attempts to explain ver. 5 in relation to the charge to forgive a penitent brother. 'A drowning man calls for aid'—these are his words —' a rope is thrown to him, and he says, Strengthen my belief that this rope will save me. I believe that the rope will save me, but help my unbelief. What is the meaning of this?' I still quote the words of the popular writer. 'If a man will not seize upon his only means of safety, it is plain that he does not understand his position.'[1] This, we must grant, is plain

[1] *My Religion*, p. 160.

enough; but it might be well to inquire, in the first place, whether Tolstoi understands the text. His description of the charge in Luke xvii. 3, 4 as a rope which is thrown to a drowning man, is in itself sufficiently erratic; but his paraphrase of the petition, 'Increase our faith,' is perhaps the most wonderful example of undisciplined interpretation which has recently been presented to the credulous public. He convicts the apostles of absurdity for the sake of connecting their petition with the charge, and of enforcing his private opinion that the centre of Christ's teaching, His one great message to the world, is the law of non-resistance; but the absurdity, which is certainly involved, need not be attributed to the apostles. It may quite as well, and on the whole with greater reason, be attributed to the popular mystic who assumes without any question that the petition, 'Increase our faith,' was suggested by the charge to forgive a penitent brother. Tolstoi is an imaginative writer: he is not a New Testament critic. His intense moral earnestness is worthy of all admiration, but his knowledge of the gospels is less remarkable. No man, not even a man of genius, can leap from ver. 4 to ver. 5 in the seventeenth chapter of Luke without dislocating his exegetical faculty. The attempt is entirely unnecessary, since Matthew and Luke provide, for the convenience of the student, a safe and movable bridge. The precept in Luke xvii. 4 represents a connected discourse, which consisted of the following fragments: Luke xi. 1–4; xvii. 3, 4; Matt. vi. 14, 15; v. 23, 24; Luke xii. 58, 59; Matt. v. 21, 22; xii. 36, 37; xviii. 21–35; Luke xiii. 6–9; xi. 5–13. The pieces of the bridge have already been combined and placed in their proper position, and what remains to be done is simply to walk across without any fear or trembling. The disciples have been assured that God is not like an earthly friend who is only moved by importunity. He is the heavenly Father who knows how to give good things. This almost seems too good to be true. But with God the better the truer: with Him the best is the truth. 'Ask, and it shall be given you: seek, and ye shall find: knock, and it shall be opened unto you. For every one that asketh receiveth, and he that seeketh findeth, and to him that knocketh it shall be opened.' The apostles say, 'Increase our faith.' They wish to believe in the heavenly Father, and to trust Him with all their heart; but they are conscious of an obstacle within them. They do not need to be saved by a rope. They have been saved through faith in God; but their faith is still immature, and their petition involves a mistake. Faith is not increased from without. It is not like a house or a snowball, but is rather a manifestation of life. It grows: it does not accumulate. No one by being anxious can add a cubit to his stature, and no one can do so by praying that it may be done. We find accordingly in the sequel that Jesus first commends the apostles by assuring them that all things are possible to the man who truly believes in the Father, and then corrects their mistake by warning them in a parable to take heed to themselves. 'Who is there of you, having a servant plowing or keeping sheep, that will say unto him, when he is come in from the field, Come straightway and sit down to meat; and will not rather say unto him, Make ready wherewith I may sup, and gird thyself, and serve me, till I have eaten and drunken; and afterward thou shalt eat and drink? Doth he thank the servant because he did the things that were commanded? Even so ye also, when ye shall have done all the things that are commanded you, say, We are unprofitable servants; we have done that which it was our duty to do.' The apostles appear to have expected their Master to invite them to come straightway and sit down to meat. They said, 'Increase our faith.' Jesus said, Increase your service. Do not desire God to wait upon you. If you wish to eat and drink, you must in the first place wait upon Him; and you must not imagine that in doing so you are performing extra service, which entitles you to receive an extra reward. The parable corrects the petition in relation to the promise that the Father would give good things, as well as in relation to the duty to forgive until seventy times seven. The teaching therefore takes its place as the conclusion of the connected discourse.

a.—The request of the disciples (Luke xi. 1) has been omitted by Matthew, because he places the Lord's Prayer in the Sermon on the Mount. Luke, on the other hand, has omitted the introduction (Matt. vi. 7, 8) on account of the disparagement of the Gentiles. The simpler text in the third gospel is certainly to be preferred to Matthew's. The prayer might well be enlarged for ecclesiastical purposes, but would not be likely to be reduced. The pronoun 'our' and the words 'which art in heaven' (Matt. vi. 9) are involved in Luke's simpler version. The petition, 'Thy will be done, as in heaven, so on earth' (Matt. vi. 10), defines 'Thy kingdom come;' but, according to the teaching of Jesus, when the kingdom would come, the doing of God's will would be transferred from earth to heaven. The definition is therefore ecclesiastical. The last petition, 'Deliver us from the evil one' (Matt. vi. 13), defines the earlier words, 'Lead us not into temptation;' but temptation or trial does not necessarily proceed from the evil one, and if the suppliants require to be delivered from the devil, they have been led into temptation. These additions are secondary. In Luke's version, on the other hand, the petition, 'Forgive us our sins ($\tau\grave{a}s$ $\dot{a}\mu a\rho\tau\acute{\iota}as$ $\dot{\eta}\mu\hat{\omega}\nu$), for we ourselves also forgive every one that is indebted to us,' is unmistakably editorial (Luke xi. 4). The second clause proves that the word in the first clause was originally 'debts' ($\tau\grave{a}$ $\dot{o}\phi\epsilon\iota\lambda\acute{\eta}\mu a\tau a$ $\dot{\eta}\mu\hat{\omega}\nu$, Matt. vi. 12). Luke distinguishes the sins which God forgives from the debts which are forgiven by man, and he avoids the inference that the measure of man's forgiveness is equal to the measure of God's.

b.—Wendt's criticism of the fragments in this section is exceedingly unsatisfactory. (1) He rejects Matt. vi. 14, 15 as an editorial addition borrowed from Mark xi. 25,[1] whereas the truth is that Mark xi. 25 has been borrowed from the apostolic source. The words, 'Whensoever ye stand praying,' prove that the precept which follows was originally delivered in a discourse on the subject of prayer, and not after the cursing of the fig tree. (2) He rejects Luke xvii. 3, 4, and substitutes in his reconstruction Matt. xviii. 15, 16,[2] whereas Luke xvii. 3, 4 is demanded by Matt. vi. 14, 15; xviii. 21; and Matt. xviii. 15, 16 is inseparable from ver. 17. If ver. 17 is secondary, as Wendt believes, the whole passage is ecclesiastical from ver. 15 to ver. 17. (3) He leaves Matt. v. 21-24 in

---

[1] *Die Lehre Jesu*, Erster Theil, S. 98.   [2] *Ibid.* S. 155, 156.

the Sermon on the Mount, and does not even observe the fact that vv. 21, 22 have been placed at the beginning to serve an editorial purpose.[1] (4) He separates Matt. v. 25, 26 from its context in the Sermon on the Mount, and places it in a fictitious discourse consisting of Luke xiii. 1-9; xii. 54-59,[2] whereas the truth is that Luke xii. 58, 59 (Matt. v. 25, 26) has been taken by the evangelist from the discourse on prayer and forgiveness, and added to ver. 57 on account of the verbal connection between τὸ δίκαιον, 'what is right,' and ὁ ἀντίδικος the adversary. The adversary means primarily the plaintiff in a suit at law; but two suits are presupposed by the illustration, one before a magistrate on the earth, and the other before the heavenly Judge; and the ἀντίδικος is both plaintiff and defendant. He is defendant or debtor, inasmuch as his brother is taking him before the magistrate to be judged; and he is plaintiff or creditor, inasmuch as the implacable spirit of the other reverses the relation in God's sight. The magistrate in Luke's version is clearly distinguished from the judge, and this shows that the interpretation here given is correct. Matthew has obscured the significance of the original by representing the ἀντίδικος as one who is simply the plaintiff. The precept thus means, 'When your adversary is taking you to the court of justice, agree with him quickly. Make amends for your fault, if you wish to escape the penalty.' This is no doubt excellent advice, but the wisdom of the precept is not remarkable. Jesus really said, When your brother has committed a fault, or incurred a debt, and you are taking him to be judged by the magistrate, abandon your revenge. Repress the implacable spirit; for, if your brother is cast into prison on earth, he will condemn you before God. Wendt fails to perceive the meaning of the fragment, and he places it in a context which is purely fictitious. (5) He leaves Matt. xii. 36, 37 in the reply of Jesus to the Pharisees, who accused Him of casting out devils by Beelzebub, the prince of the devils.[3] This is a black list of blunders.

c.—The parable of the Unmerciful Servant has been omitted by Luke, and the parable of the Fig Tree by Matthew.

[1] *Die Lehre Jesu*, Erster Theil, S. 58, 59. [2] *Ibid.* S. 125-127.
[3] *Ibid.* S. 102.

How can these omissions be explained? The parable of the Fig Tree was originally followed by the encouragement to be importunate in prayer (Luke xi. 5–8), and both have probably been omitted by Matthew for the same editorial reason—partly to avoid the mistake of the Gentiles who thought they would be heard for their much speaking (Matt. vi. 7), and partly to prevent the possibility of misapprehending the mercy of God. Luke, on the other hand, has deliberately distinguished the grace of God from the mercy which is manifested by man. He has modified the fourth petition in the Lord's Prayer to serve this purpose. For the same reason he has omitted Matt. vi. 14, 15; v. 23, 24. The aim of the evangelist evidently is to avoid the mistake of supposing that God's forgiveness is merited. Jesus distinctly told His disciples that, if they did not forgive, they would not be forgiven; and the parable of the Unmerciful Servant was delivered to enforce this lesson. Luke avoids the lesson, and therefore omits the parable.

d.—Luke has substituted 'the Holy Spirit' (Luke xi. 13) for the 'good things' which the Father will give (Matt. vi. 11). He wishes to define the one thing needful (Luke x. 41, 42). The promise requires definition; but the good things are defined by the Lord's Prayer, and not by the Holy Spirit.

e.—The reply of Jesus to the petition, 'Increase our faith,' seems very mysterious to Wendt. He is disposed to omit the petition altogether, and he separates Luke xvii. 7–10 from ver. 6. He substitutes 'in yonder place' (Matt. xvii. 21) for 'in the sea' (Luke xvii. 6), and declares that without doubt Luke has modified the original on account of his recollection of the second gospel (Mark xi. 23).[1] Wendt is not usually distressed by doubt, but he distresses his readers by the want of it. His reasoning is magnificently imperfect. The theory that when the apostolic source appears to coincide with the second gospel, the coincidence is always to be explained by a recollection of the second gospel, on the part of Matthew or Luke, can scarcely be maintained without doubt. It is exceedingly doubtful. Matthew's variation in ch. xvii. 21 is much more probably editorial; and instead of confirming the

[1] *Die Lehre Jesu*, Erster Theil, S. 157, 158.

assumption that the apostolic source was entirely unrelated to the second gospel, the evidence afforded by the cursing of the fig tree and its sequel (Mark xi. 12–14, 20–25) tends rather to the conclusion that Mark's narrative is a compilation from the apostolic source. The miracle is parallel to the parable. The encouragement to be importunate in prayer is represented by Mark xi. 24, and the charge to forgive a penitent brother is represented by ver. 25. Mark xi. 23 coincides with Luke xvii. 6, and Mark's variations are secondary. The casting of a mountain into the sea is not so great a wonder as the planting of a tree in the sea. It is an illustration more liable to be mistaken, and therefore less likely to be original; and Mark as a fact has almost encouraged misapprehension, for faith according to him is belief in the efficacy of prayer, and its potency is enlarged to omnipotence, whereas in the discourse on prayer and forgiveness faith is belief in the heavenly Father and is limited by the goodness of God. Matthew has omitted the parable of Extra Service because Luke xvii. 6 has already been inserted in Mark's narrative of the demoniac boy (Matt. xvii. 21), and because the parable when detached from its context could not be conveniently introduced. The unprofitableness of doing one's duty might also constitute a difficulty.

§ 48.—*The Coming of the Kingdom*

The discourse on the coming of the kingdom, with which Luke's digression ends, represents perhaps the most complicated problem which arises for solution in reconstructing the apostolic gospel. A few preliminary facts demand the attention of the student. (1) As far as situation is concerned, Luke xvii. 20–xviii. 8 coincides with the apocalyptic discourse in Mark xiii. 1–37; Matt. xxiv. 1–xxv. 46; Luke xxi. 5–36. The coincidence is sufficiently obscure to escape the casual or theoretic observer, for in the first case the context is fragmentary, and Luke returns to Mark at ch. xviii. 15; but, in following Mark from ch. xviii. 15 to the end of the gospel, he introduces additional material which has been taken from the apostolic source. Part of this material has already been accounted for (Luke xix. 1-10, 37-44), and the fragments recorded next in the sequel are the parable of the Pounds (Luke xix. 11-27), and an addition to Mark's narrative of the Supper (Luke xxii. 15-38); but the parable of the Pounds was delivered, according to Matthew, in the apocalyptic discourse which has for its sequel the Supper (Matt. xxv. 14-30), and the fragments in Luke's digression before the discourse on the coming of the kingdom represent a series of instructions addressed to the disciples after the last entrance into Jerusalem. The coincidence is therefore incontestable, a manifest and significant fact. (2) Matthew has considerably enlarged Mark's version of the apocalyptic discourse, and a few of these enlargements obviously coincide with the instruction in Luke's digression—Matt. xxiv. 26, 27 with Luke xvii. 23, 24, Matt. xxiv. 28 with Luke xvii. 37, and Matt. xxiv. 37-41 with Luke xvii. 26, 27, 34, 35. It is possible that Matthew has combined a number of fragments which were originally distinct; but, since the two discourses coincide in situation and agree in subject, the probability is that Mark has for editorial reasons abridged the common original. (3) The differences between the version with which Luke concludes his digression and the versions of Matthew and Mark are perfectly compatible with the inference that each represents a common original; for, in the first place, Luke intends to return to Mark, and therefore has a reason for provisionally omitting the material which Mark has reported; and, secondly, a few of Matthew's enlargements have already been placed by Luke in an earlier editorial context—Matt. xxiv. 43, 44 coinciding with Luke xii. 39, 40, and Matt. xxiv. 45-51 with Luke xii. 41-46. Assuming that the apostolic source was a mere collection of logia, entirely unrelated to the second gospel, or only slightly related, the critics distinguish the two discourses, not even contemplating the possibility that they were originally identical; but the assumption of the critics has already been sufficiently disproved, and the facts above mentioned afford presumptive evidence that the instruction in Luke xvii. 20-xviii. 8 is an editorial version of the apocalyptic discourse, which Mark has abridged, and which, by the addition of apostolic material, Matthew has imperfectly restored. How, then, can we reconstruct the original? As clearness is of the utmost importance in the discussion of a subject so complicated, I submit the facts numerically.

1. The incident which Luke has recorded constitutes the text of the Sermon. Jesus was asked by the Pharisees when the kingdom of God would come, and He said in reply, 'The kingdom of God cometh not with observation; neither shall they say, Lo here! or There! for lo, the kingdom of God is in the midst of you' (Luke xvii. 20, 21). Wendt separates this incident from the instruction afterwards addressed to the disciples;[1] and he says in exposition of the text, 'Certainly the closing words of this saying could not mean that the kingdom of God has not external forms of expression, but has its seat within men; for Jesus assuredly did not imply that the kingdom of God was realised within these Pharisees to whom He spoke. The meaning of those concluding words can only be that the kingdom of God was no longer a thing of the future merely, but was already being realised in the very midst of those who asked the question; realised, that is, in Jesus and His disciples.'[2] If Wendt has correctly expounded the text, its historical relation to the Sermon is certainly open to question; but has the text been correctly expounded? Jesus did not intend to say that the kingdom of God had been realised within the Pharisees—that is perfectly evident; but did He say that the kingdom of God had been anywhere realised? The question was, when the kingdom would come. The Pharisees did not believe in its realisation; and Jesus so far agreed with them, for He began His reply by declaring that the kingdom of God would come. It would not come with observation; that is, it would not be gradually and visibly introduced in such a way that men could exclaim, Lo here! or There! When it came it would be everywhere. The concluding words, ἰδοὺ γὰρ ἡ βασιλεία τοῦ Θεοῦ ἐντὸς ὑμῶν ἐστίν, are parallel to ἰδοὺ ὧδε ἡ ἐκεῖ, and are therefore dramatic in form; and they simply mean that, when the kingdom would come, it would be instantaneously in the midst of men. This is by far the most

[1] *Die Lehre Jesu*, Erster Theil, S. 159, 160.
[2] *The Teaching of Jesus*, vol. i. p. 366.

probable interpretation, and indeed is the only permissible one; for in the subsequent address to His disciples Jesus expounded His reply to the Pharisees. He is His own interpreter. 'They shall say to you, Lo there! lo here! go not away nor follow after them; for as the lightning when it lighteneth out of the one part under the heaven, shineth unto the other part under heaven, so shall the Son of Man be in his day' (Luke xvii. 23, 24). These words are parallel to the text. They express more clearly the same thought; and yet according to Wendt the meaning can 'only be that the kingdom of God was no longer a thing of the future merely, but was already being realised in the very midst of those who asked the question.' Wendt's exegesis has evidently been determined by the presupposition that Jesus repeatedly taught the realisation of the kingdom of God; but such an idea is foreign to the apostolic logia, and in the case before us is quite as much 'perverted' as the idea which Wendt attributes to the Pharisees, who, as he says, believed 'that the expected kingdom was one of external might and glory, and would be inaugurated in visibly striking circumstances, and would be constituted with forms and boundaries, which could be externally marked out like other earthly kingdoms.' Presumably Jesus knew what He meant much better than the German critics, better even than all the theologians. He predicted His second coming, and the coming of the kingdom of heaven, as an instantaneous universal event. The attempt to separate the reply to the Pharisees from the subsequent address to the disciples has been dictated by the requirements of a theory. The incident suggested the private instruction, and makes it historically intelligible. Here, however, we encounter a difficulty; for the apocalyptic discourse in the second gospel is introduced by a different incident (Mark xiii. 1, 2). If the two discourses are editorial versions of a common original, how could this difference arise? Is the identification not forbidden? By no means; for one of the incidents may be editorial. Matthew and Luke agree with Mark, but they are not independent authorities. They are simply reproducing the second gospel (Matt. xxiv. 1, 2; Luke xxi. 5, 6). The incidents and logia in the second gospel before the apocalyptic discourse belong, as we have seen, to a series which has been taken from an earlier period. Mark's history is not chronological. His arrangement is decidedly secondary. The announcement regarding the Temple in Mark xiii. 1, 2 belongs to the earlier series, and has been adapted by Mark to the apocalyptic discourse which follows. This conclusion has already been gained. If the subject of the discourse was the coming of the kingdom of God, the incident recorded in Luke's digression is much more appropriate as an introduction than the announcement regarding the Temple. If the original discourse contained an allusion to the destruction of Jerusalem, the announcement in the second gospel is not inappropriate; but in such a case the destruction of Jerusalem is one of the signs of the end, and yet, according to the apostolic source, the kingdom would not come with observation, that is, its coming would not be preceded by any signs, in heaven or on the earth. It would come like a lightning flash, unexpected, instantaneous, incalculable. The version of Mark will afterwards be analysed in detail, and we shall then see clearly that the section regarding the destruction of Jerusalem is incompatible with the rest of the discourse. In the meantime the evidence is sufficient to prove that Mark's introduction is unreliable, and that Luke's is apostolic.

2. If the discourse was originally preceded by the incident which Luke has preserved, the position of the section from ver. 22 to ver. 37 is authenticated; for vv. 22–24 constitute an exposition of the reply to the Pharisees, and the rest of the section from ver. 26 to the end is bound to the beginning by necessary sequence of thought. Jesus has already announced to His disciples that He is about to leave them. His death will be His perfecting, the consummation of His hope; but when the bridegroom at last is taken away, the sons of the bridechamber will fast. They will desire to see one of the days of the Son of Man, and will not see it. The coming of the kingdom is now distinctly identified with His own second coming as Messiah. He will come like a lightning flash, like the flood in the days of Noah, like the fire which burned Sodom in the days of Lot. Do not, Jesus says, take thought for your worldly goods. Wherever you may be, remain where you are. Do not seek to save your life by

fleeing from the coming destruction. You will be safe if you do not try to escape; for in that day or night one will be taken and another will be left, according to the election of God. One will be taken to the heavenly kingdom, and another will be left like carrion for the birds of prey. The position of this section at the beginning of the discourse is not merely required by the reply to the Pharisees and by the consecutive thought, but is also confirmed by Matthew's disposition of the fragments; for the first of Matthew's additions to the version of Mark (Matt. xxiv. 26, 27) is parallel to Luke xvii. 22–24, and the second (Matt. xxiv. 37–41) to Luke xvii. 26–35. The context of Matt. xxiv. 28 is certainly editorial. In Luke xvii. 37 the saying is intelligible, but in Matthew's context the meaning is exceedingly obscure. The first evangelist has transposed the text to an earlier part of the discourse for the sake of concluding a section, and has omitted the question of the disciples to preserve the continuity of the instruction. Luke, on the other hand, has probably substituted an editorial saying for the original text in Luke xvii. 25. Three facts are here worthy of notice. (*a*) Matt. xxiv. 37 coincides with Luke xvii. 26, and therefore ver. 36 in Matthew's version is parallel to ver. 25 in Luke's. Matt. xxiv. 36 may simply be a reproduction of Mark xiii. 32; but Mark xiii. 32 has itself been probably taken from the apostolic source, and in such a case Matthew has simply restored the sequel which Mark has greatly abridged. (*b*) Luke xvii. 25 is much less appropriate to the context than Matt. xxiv. 36; for Matthew's text continues the thought and prepares the way for the sequel, whereas Luke's is a superfluous parenthesis. The rejection by the people of that generation is not a new idea. On the contrary, it is presupposed by the whole discourse, and Jesus would not be likely to interrupt the continuity of His thought by repeating an announcement which would divert the attention of His hearers to a necessity which they did not understand. (*c*) When Luke is reproducing Mark's version of the apocalyptic discourse, he deliberately omits the words, 'But of that day or that hour knoweth no one, not even the angels in heaven, neither the Son, but the Father' (Mark xiii. 32); and the omission is perfectly intelligible, for Luke has a conception of the person of Christ which forbids the ignorance avowed. But the text which was afterwards deliberately omitted would certainly be avoided in the digression. The probability is therefore established that Mark xiii. 32 (Matt. xxiv. 36) originally followed Luke xvii. 24, and that Luke has substituted the editorial parenthesis, 'But first must he suffer many things and be rejected of this generation' (ver. 25).

3. In reconstructing the original from Luke xvii. 37 onwards, a number of facts may be conveniently grouped together. (a) The parable of the Unjust Judge (Luke xviii. 1–8), while obviously related to the preceding instruction, is somewhat abruptly introduced, and the heading in ver. 1 reduces the significance of the lesson. Jesus certainly intended to teach His disciples that they ought to be importunate in prayer like the widow who wearied the judge; but the widow was importunate for justice, and the lesson explicitly taught at the end of the parable is, not merely that the disciples should pray without fainting, but also, and more specifically, that they should persistently plead for the coming of that great Day of Judgment which would vindicate the elect and overwhelm the ungodly. Now Luke has added to Mark's version of the apocalyptic discourse an apostolic fragment which is available for comparison with the heading in ch. xviii. 1 (Luke xxi. 34–36). The probability has already been suggested that Mark xiii. 32 was contained in the apostolic source, and was followed by Luke xvii. 26–37. But Luke xxi. 33 is a reproduction of Mark xiii. 31, and therefore at this point Luke would have before him, not only Mark xiii. 32–37, but also the original sequel of Mark xiii. 32, that is, Luke xvii. 26–37. What, then, has the evangelist done? He has omitted Mark xiii. 32 to avoid the confession of ignorance, and Mark xiii. 33–37 because a similar passage has already been introduced in Luke xii. 35–40. To avoid repetition he has also omitted Luke xvii. 26–37. We therefore find that Luke xxi. 34–36 is parallel to Luke xviii. 1. As far as situation is concerned, Luke xxi. 34–36 might originally precede the parable of the Unjust Judge. But the heading in Luke xviii. 1 is not an adequate introduction to the parable, and the later passage, which is much more

appropriate as an introduction, connects the parable more closely with the earlier context in ch. xvii. Again, the parable of the Pharisee and the Publican (Luke xviii. 9–14) originally followed Luke xvi. 15, and the heading in ver. 9 has been substituted for Luke xvi. 14, 15 to avoid editorial repetition. The supposed substitution of Luke xviii. 1 for Luke xxi. 34–36 is therefore not exceptional. The two cases are precisely parallel; and since in the one case the substitution is a fact, in the other it may confidently be inferred. The only question is, What motive could Luke have for omitting ch. xxi. 34–36 before the parable of the Unjust Judge, and for substituting the heading in ch. xviii. 1 ? A motive is perfectly evident. The purpose of the evangelist is transparent. He wishes to connect the two parables, and gives prominence in the case of the first to the general lesson that prayer should be importunate, for the sake of transition to the second, one lesson of which is that prayer should be humble and contrite. Luke xviii. 1 is therefore probably editorial, and has been substituted for Luke xxi. 34–36. (b) The parable of the Unjust Judge, although complete in itself, could scarcely be the end of a discourse, for it concludes with the question, 'When the Son of Man cometh, shall he find faith on the earth?' (ver. 8). A sequel is imperatively demanded, and clearly it must answer the question. How, then, are we to make an advance? Since Luke no longer assists us, we turn to the first evangelist. An analysis of Matthew's version from the point at which he leaves Mark may take us out of the difficulty. Matt. xxiv. 26, 27 and ver. 28 have already been identified as interpolations derived from the apostolic source. The confession of ignorance in ver. 36 is a meeting place of Matthew's two sources. Mark has reported this text (Mark xiii. 32), but has omitted the original sequel. Matthew restores the original by consulting his apostolic authority. Matt. xxiv. 37–41 coincides with Luke xvii. 26, 27, 34, 35. Luke xvii. 37 has been omitted by Matthew to avoid editorial repetition (cf. ver. 28). So far the disposition of the fragments in the first gospel is perfectly transparent. But according to our reconstruction the parable of the Unjust Judge, with its introductory warning (Luke xxi. 34–36), originally followed

Luke xvii. 37, and Matthew's sequel is different (Matt. xxiv. 42-51). Does this not constitute an objection sufficiently serious to invalidate the whole of the argument? By no means; for the arrangement in the first gospel is still explicable. The parable of the Fig Tree (Luke xiii. 6-9), and the encouragement to be importunate in prayer (Luke xi. 5-8), have already been deliberately omitted by Matthew to avoid an erroneous conception of God, and obviously for the same reason he would omit the parable of the Unjust Judge. But when in a connected discourse any part is omitted, the transition to the sequel is abrupt, and rearrangement becomes sometimes expedient. It is therefore antecedently probable that Matt. xxiv. 42-51 has been substituted for the parable of the Unjust Judge. As a fact ver. 42 coincides with Luke xxi. 34-36, and is simply an adaptation of the original to the editorial interpolation which follows (cf. Mark xiii. 33); and this interpolation from ver. 43 to ver. 51 will soon be claimed by a later context. We thus reach the parable of the Ten Virgins (Matt. xxv. 1-13). But this parable is an answer to the question, 'When the Son of Man cometh, shall he find faith on the earth?' (Luke xviii. 8), for the bridegroom represents the Son of Man, who is expected to return, and the answer is that faith will be found on the earth, but foolish virgins as well, that is, believers who not being ready will be excluded from the kingdom of God. The parable of the Ten Virgins thus authenticates itself as a sequel to the parable of the Unjust Judge, and when Matthew's editorial method is perceived the thought-connection is confirmed by the situation of each in the source. (c) The coincidence of the parable of the Ten Virgins with a fragment which Luke has interpolated in an earlier context has been observed by the critics (Luke xii. 35 36). Two explanations have been suggested. Weiss finds in the fragment a reminiscence of the parable, which is therefore accepted by him as a genuine utterance of Jesus.[1] J. Estlin Carpenter, on the other hand, expresses the opinion that 'a case of the working up of earlier material into new forms is probably to be found in the parable of the Virgins, the germ of which lies in the thought expressed in

[1] *Introduction to the New Testament*, vol. ii. p. 267.

Luke xii. 35, 36.'[1] The probabilities of J. Estlin Carpenter are as a rule entirely subjective: they are not based on documentary evidence. The parable of the Virgins is demanded by the parable of the Unjust Judge, and the supposition that these are both secondary compilations, for which we are indebted to the genius of the early Church, is unworthy of serious consideration. Are we, then, to conclude with Weiss that the fragment in Luke's digression is a reminiscence of the parable which Matthew alone has preserved? The theory of reminiscence is the most persistent delusion of the critics. They seem scarcely to contemplate the possibility that the apostolic source had been committed to writing before the days of Matthew and Luke; but the distinctly editorial character of the first and third gospels affords convincing evidence that the evangelists are working with documents and not with an oral tradition, and in the case before us the theory fails utterly to account for the facts. In the parable the bridegroom returns for, in the fragment from, the marriage feast. According to the supposition this indicates defective recollection on the part of the third evangelist; but Luke is much too familiar with the apostolic tradition to miss so completely the significance of the feast in the parable, and the sequel in vv. 37, 38 still obviously requires to be explained. These verses are not a reminiscence of the parable, and yet they are inseparably connected with vv. 35, 36. Again, ver. 38 is similar to Mark xiii. 35, and the parable of the Porter in Mark xiii. 34–36 is closely related in its inner significance to the whole passage in Luke xii. 35–38. When Luke is reproducing Mark's version of the apocalyptic discourse he deliberately omits the parable of the Porter, thus virtually identifying it with the fragment already inserted in ch. xii. 35–38. But the charge in ver. 35, 'Let your loins be girded about, and your lamps burning,' as well as the allusion in ver. 36 to the marriage feast, is certainly an abstract from the parable of the Virgins. The whole passage is therefore a combination of the two parables, and the bridegroom returns from the feast because the master returns from a foreign country (Mark xiii.

[1] *The First Three Gospels*, p. 358.

34). The combination, moreover, is unmistakably deliberate. It cannot be explained by inadvertence or by the theory of defective recollection, but only by something in the parable of the Virgins which Luke desires to avoid. Now the foolish virgins were excluded from the feast, not because they went to buy oil, but because they went too late; and the buying of oil might well seem to Luke to be incompatible with his doctrine of grace, according to which there is neither buying nor selling in relation to God, but only giving and receiving. The parables in Matt. xiii. 44–46 have already been omitted for this reason. A motive is therefore apparent for avoiding the mercantile details, and here, as elsewhere in the third gospel, we have evidence of deliberate editing. The fact, however, to be specially noted at present is that Luke's combination of the two parables is preceded in ch. xii. 32 by a fragment which still remains to be restored to its original context in the source. The words ' Fear not, little flock; for it is your Father's good pleasure to give you the kingdom,' do not belong to the instruction on the subject of riches (Luke xii. 13–31, 33, 34). They have already been recognised as an interpolation. But in such a case it is antecedently probable that they were originally situated in the discourse on the coming of the kingdom before the parable of the Virgins (ver. 35). Now the parable of the Virgins is demanded immediately by the parable of the Unjust Judge, and this again was preceded without intervention by Luke xxi. 34–36. If Luke xii. 32 has been taken from the discourse on the coming of the kingdom, we must therefore conclude that the original situation of the fragment was at the latest between Luke xvii. 37 and Luke xxi. 34–36. Two questions thus arise for investigation. The first is, Can we account for Luke's selection of the fragments in ch. xii. 32, 35–38 to follow the doctrine of riches, and for his omission of the teaching which, according to our argument, originally separated ver. 32 from the parable of the Virgins represented by ver. 35? In ver. 31 the charge is reported to seek only the kingdom of God, with the assurance that other things will be added, and in ver. 32 the disciples are assured that the kingdom of God will be given. The connection is clearly editorial; for although anxiety is presupposed in the earlier teaching, it is anxiety concerning the things of the world, whereas in ver. 32 the fear rather is that the heavenly good will be withheld. Again, the fragment in vv. 35-38 illustrates the necessity of seeking the kingdom of God in such a way that the disciples will always be ready for the great Divine event. The connection is evident, but is as certainly editorial; for the subject of the earlier teaching is right conduct in relation to the things of the world, and in vv. 35-38 the one thought is the proximity of the end and the duty of watchful anticipation. But in the parable of the Unjust Judge with its heading (Luke xxi. 34-36) the idea of judgment is prominent, and this is also the prominent idea in Luke xvii. 22-37. It is obvious, therefore, that these passages are unsuitable for the context in ch. xii., and that the selection which Luke has made, instead of invalidating, is really a confirmation of our argument. The second question is, Does the fragment in Luke xii. 32 fit into the later context in the discourse on the coming of the kingdom? Incontestably it does. It is indeed a necessary link of connection between Luke xvii. 37 and Luke xxi. 34-36; for Jesus has announced to the disciples that one will be taken to the heavenly kingdom and another will be left for destruction, according to the election of God, and the sequel may be paraphrased thus: 'Do not be afraid in anticipating the event. The choice must remain with God, but He is your heavenly Father. Do not be afraid of the coming destruction: it is your Father's good pleasure to give you the kingdom. But take heed to yourselves. Be vigilant at every season, and pray to God that you may prevail to escape. Be importunate in prayer that the heavenly kingdom may come; for the judgment will be a vindication of the elect; and if importunity succeeds with the unrighteous, how much more will your Father be disposed to grant your request?' Luke xii. 32 is thus demanded by both Luke xvii. 37 and Luke xxi. 34-36. It constitutes the original transition. The fear which is presupposed by Luke xii. 32 is explained by Luke xvii. 37, and the description of the disciples as a little flock takes its place as a continuation of the figure already employed in the allusion to the carcase and the eagles (Luke xvii. 37). We have now completed the argument.

The facts grouped together have enabled us to make a considerable advance. As far as we have gone, the original discourse consisted of the following passages: Luke xvii. 20–24; Mark xiii. 32; Luke xvii. 26–37; xii. 32; xxi. 34–36; xviii. 2–8; Matt. xxv. 1–13.

4. The two brief parables of the Porter and the Thief supplement the parable of the Ten Virgins, which Luke has combined with the first (Luke xii. 35–40). In answer to the question, 'When the Son of Man cometh, shall he find faith on the earth?' the disciples have been warned against the danger of losing their faith, and of being taken by surprise when the day comes suddenly as a snare. This thought is now further illustrated. The virgins in the parable are not under any obligation to be prepared for the bridegroom's coming. They are foolish because, being not prepared, they are excluded from the marriage feast, at which they wish to be present; but in the case of the disciples there is a mora obligation, and the penalty is not simply exclusion. The duty of servants is to work, and the duty of a porter is to watch. If these obligations are fulfilled, the reward given by the Master will be great. He will even serve His servants (Luke xii. 37). But if, on the other hand, the disciples are negligent, and forgetful of the danger to which they are exposed, they will be like the master of a house, who loses his goods when the thief breaks in unexpectedly. 'Be ye also ready, for in an hour that ye think not the Son of Man cometh.' The parable of the Porter can be reconstructed without any difficulty by comparing Mark's version with Luke's. We simply require to substitute Mark xiii. 34–36 for the abstract from the parable of the Virgins (Luke xii. 35, 36). Mark omits the parable of the Thief, in which the penalty of negligence is stated, and therefore he also omits the assurance of reward in Luke xii. 37, 38. Mark's version of the discourse is so obviously abbreviated in accordance with his habitual practice, that the omissions scarcely need to be explained. He is more concerned with the incidents than with the logia, and in the case before us is content to enforce as briefly as possible the duty of watchfulness and prayer. The question, however, arises whether Matthew's arrangement is compatible with the

supposition that the parable of the Virgins was originally followed by the parables of the Porter and the Thief. Matt. xxiv. 42 coincides, as we have seen, with Luke xxi. 34–36, and is explicable as an adaptation of the original to the interpolation which follows (vv. 43–51); but ver. 42 coincides almost verbally with the conclusion of the parable of the Virgins (Matt. xxv. 13), and its sequel is the parable of the Thief (Matt. xxiv. 43, 44). We must therefore conclude that ver. 42 represents not merely Luke xxi. 34–36, but also the parable of the Virgins, which thus takes its place before the parable of the Thief. So far our argument is confirmed; and the rest of the interpolation presents no difficulty whatever. Matthew has omitted the parable of the Porter, partly on account of the verbal connection between 'Ye know not' in ver. 42 and 'Know (or 'ye know') this' in ver. 43, and partly because he intends to add a somewhat similar parable (vv. 45–51). The 'servant' in Matthew's version is a 'steward' in Luke's (Luke xii. 42). Luke's word, as we shall see, is demanded by the original context, and Matthew's has obviously been suggested by the servants in the parable of the Porter (Mark xiii. 34). We have thus abundant evidence to confirm the thought-connection between the parable of the Virgins and the parables of the Porter and the Thief. Matthew's arrangement is perfectly intelligible; and the original sequence was Matt. xxv. 1–13; Mark. xiii. 34–36; Luke xii. 37–40.

5. The attention of the reader is now invited to a last induction of facts, which will enable us to complete the reconstruction. (a) We begin with a passage which Luke has recorded immediately after the parable of the Thief. Peter said, 'Speakest thou this parable unto us, or even unto all? He wished to know definitely who might expect the reward, and who were in danger of the penalty; or, in other words, he wished to be able to identify the servants, the porter, and the master of the house. The question is appropriate to the occasion, and is authenticated by Mark, who adds to the parable of the Porter, 'And what I say unto you, I say unto all, Watch' (Mark xiii. 37). These words betray an acquaintance with the question. What, then, is the answer of Jesus? He describes the twelve as stewards. They have a special

responsibility and special duties to discharge. It is not enough in their case merely to be watchful and expectant. They must give the servants their portion of food, and keep the household in order. Their reward will be greater than that of others; and if they are found unfaithful, their punishment will be proportionately severe. The servant who wilfully neglects his duty will be beaten with many stripes: the servant who fails through inadvertence will be beaten with few; but the unfaithful steward, to whom much is given and of whom the more is required, will be cut asunder with scourging (Luke xii. 41-48). The situation of this parable in the first gospel, as we have already seen, is editorial. It forms part of an interpolation which Matthew has substituted for the parable of the Unjust Judge, and has itself been substituted for the parable of the Watchful Porter (Matt. xxiv. 45-51). The situation in Luke's digression is unmistakably primary. (b) The parable of the Talents is the next fragment in Matthew's version of the discourse (Matt. xxv. 14-30). The relation of this parable to the parable of the Pounds in the third gospel has been much discussed (Luke xix. 11-27), and notwithstanding the obvious similarity of the two there are still some writers who contend that they were originally distinct. Professor Bruce e.g. has repeatedly distinguished the one from the other. 'Ability being equal, quantity determines relative value: such is the lesson of the parable of the Pounds; ability varying, then, not the quantity viewed absolutely, but its relation to ability, determines value: such is the truth taught in the parable of the Talents.'[1] Professor Bruce is well known as a sympathetic student of the synoptic logia, and his writings are justly esteemed; but they are marred by one serious defect. The value of his exegesis if determined by Luke's standard is great, but its critical quality is less notable. The difference to which he alludes in the case of the two parables before us is no doubt perfectly evident; but in the first place it has not been quite correctly stated, and secondly the question surely requires to be considered whether one of the evangelists has not modified the original to serve an editorial purpose. The word 'ability' in Professor

[1] *The Kingdom of God*, p. 324.

Bruce's interpretation is entirely misleading, for in the ordinary sense of the word the ability of the servants is not equal. The first is a man of exceptional ability: he multiplies his capital by ten. The second is less successful, because less accomplished as a trader. The third does not exhibit the little business faculty he possesses. The equality does not, properly speaking, consist in ability: it consists rather in the amount of capital originally given by the master; and Luke, who does not believe that there is any inequality in grace, has obviously an editorial reason for modifying the parable in such a way as to avoid the possibility of mistake. The internal evidence is distinctly in favour of the modification supposed; for ten servants are mentioned at the beginning of Luke's version, and of these only three give in their account. But according to Matthew's version there were only three at the beginning. The other seven are superfluous; they pass immediately out of sight, and have merely been introduced for the sake of effecting an equal division of the money. Again, the master in Luke's version is a nobleman who goes to a far country to receive for himself a kingdom, and to return, and in Matthew's version he is simply a private capitalist. This difference has exercised the ingenuity of the interpreters. Professor Bruce infers that the two parables were originally distinct. J. Estlin Carpenter asks, commenting on Matt. xxv. 30 and Luke xix. 27, 'What is the cause of this sudden leap in the story according to the third evangelist? It is in reality,' he says, 'the conclusion of another story, which Luke has combined with the parable of the Pounds—the story of the nobleman who went into a distant country to receive for himself a kingdom, and to return.'[1] Wendt also believes in 'the other story.' He is able indeed to inform his readers that it was originally delivered in a discourse which consisted of the following passages: Luke xvii. 22-30, 34, 35, 37; xxi. 34-36; xviii. 2-8; xix. 12, 14, 15^a, 27.[2] Unfortunately, however, for Wendt's critical judgment, the discourse thus constituted is fictitious; and the necessity of separating 'the other story' from the parable of the Pounds is not sufficiently

[1] *The First Three Gospels*, p. 309.
[2] *Die Lehre Jesu*, Erster Theil, S. 160-165.

obvious to justify such works of imagination. If Luke has modified the original to serve an editorial purpose—this is granted by Wendt—Matthew might presumably modify the original to serve a different purpose. The parable of the Virgins was originally followed, as we have seen, by the parable of the Porter; and the parable of the Porter begins thus: 'It is as when a man sojourning in another country, having left his house and given authority to his servants, to each one his work, commanded also the porter to watch' (Mark xiii. 34). But in Matthew's version of the discourse the parable of the Virgins is followed by the parable of the Talents, the beginning of which is, 'For it is as when a man going into another country called his own servants, and delivered to them his goods' (Matt. xxv. 14). The beginning of the two parables is verbally almost identical; and since Matthew has omitted the parable of the Porter, the coincidence at once suggests the possibility that the parable of the Talents has been modified to avoid the designation of the master as a nobleman who went to the far country for a kingdom. Now Matthew is careful to avoid misconception in relation to the nature of God. For this end he omits the parables of the Fig Tree and the Unjust Judge, and the encouragement to be importunate in prayer; and a writer so jealous of the attributes of God might well avoid the comparison of Jesus to one of the petty princes who derived their authority from Rome. The judgment moreover in Luke xix. 27 has already been anticipated by Matthew in an editorial addition to the parable of the Great Supper (Matt. xxii. 7). The omission of the details peculiar to Luke's version is therefore perfectly intelligible, and the version of Luke need not be regarded as a combination of two independent stories. The greater probability rather is that Matthew and Luke, for different reasons, and in a different way, have each modified the original parable. An objection to this argument may be confidently anticipated on the part of interpreters who suspect the critical method. Unaccustomed to balance probabilities, and naturally averse to the delicate and perilous mode of reasoning which is concerned with motives, they may be disposed to reject our argument as at the best conjectural. Have we, then, reached the end of the discussion? Are we bound to admit the propriety of the epithet? Perhaps before arriving at a definite conclusion, which might be a little premature, the upholders of exegetical traditions will consider two additional facts. The first is that the parable of the Talents coincides in situation with the parable of the Pounds. This statement is approximately correct, apart from the results already gained; for in Matthew's version of the apocalyptic discourse the parable of the Talents is one of two which constitute the conclusion, and Luke in reproducing Mark's narrative from Luke xviii. 15 onwards interpolates the parable of the Pounds soon after the instruction on the coming of the kingdom (Luke xvii. 20–xviii. 8), to which it is related by community of subject, and in which it takes its place at the end of all the fragments which have been dispersed in the third gospel. When the results already gained are taken into account, the coincidence is precise and indisputable. The heading in Luke xix. 11 is unmistakably editorial; for the parable could not be delivered because some people expected that Jesus would inaugurate the kingdom of God when He entered into Jerusalem. If He merely intended to correct such a mistake, the details of the parable are meaningless. The heading must therefore be rejected. But the instruction on the coming of the kingdom in Luke xvii. 20–xviii. 8 represents the beginning of the discourse, and the earlier interpolation in Luke xii. 35–48 originally followed Luke xviii. 8; and so the parable of the Pounds is Luke's sequel to the parable of the Steward (Luke xii. 41–48). In the first gospel, again, the interpolation Matt. xxiv. 43–51 originally followed the parable of the Virgins (Matt. xxv. 1–13); and thus the parable of the Talents coincides with the parable of the Pounds, each taking its place after the parable of the Steward (Matt. xxiv. 45–51). This fact is sufficient in itself to weigh down the balance of probability. The evidence, however, may still be regarded as defective; for, although the two parables are clearly identical, the constituent details have not yet been completely verified. How, then, are we to avoid the reproach of conjectural reconstruction? I reply by stating a second fact, which is, that Matthew's inequality of endowment is authenticated by the parable of the Steward, and that 'the other story' is demanded as an integral element by the question which Peter addressed to Jesus. The parable of the Steward was intended by Jesus to convey the truth that 'to whomsoever much is given, of him shall much be required : and to whom they commit much, of him will they ask the more' (Luke xii. 48). But the parable of the Talents is a development and illustration of this lesson, and is thus the necessary sequel. Again, Peter said, 'Lord, speakest thou this parable unto us, or even unto all?' (Luke xii. 41). In the parable of the Steward, Jesus spoke specially to the twelve. In the parable of the Talents, He enforced the duty of every disciple. But disciples and apostles are not 'all;' and since Peter wished to learn the relation of Jesus in the day of His power to all who would be judged, it is antecedently probable, and indeed is required by the context, that the teaching in reply should be extended beyond the limits of expectant faith. But in the parable of the Pounds the enemies are the unbelieving Jews, who disdainfully rejected Messiah and appealed against His supremacy. If therefore the inequality of the servants is demanded by the parable of the Steward, the details of 'the other story' are equally demanded by the request of Peter. The facts are not conjectural. The evidence is not inconclusive. The original may be and must be restored by combining the versions of Matthew and Luke. (c) The discourse appropriately concludes in Matthew's version with another representation of the judgment. 'When the Son of Man shall come in his glory, and all the angels with him, then shall he sit on the throne of his glory : and before him shall be gathered all the nations : and he shall separate them one from another as the shepherd separateth the sheep from the goats' (Matt. xxv. 31–46). The nations are here certainly the Gentiles; and whatever opinion may be held regarding the original situation of the parable, it was clearly intended to teach that the Gentiles would be judged by the Son of Man according to their treatment of His brethren, that is, of the believing Jews. This fact has been curiously urged by Wendt as a reason for concluding that the parable of the Sheep and the Goats was not delivered in the apocalyptic discourse. He does not know when it was delivered. He puts it in one of his appendices;

but he is certain that the context in the first gospel is editorial.[1] Wendt's certainties are sometimes insecure. Luke has omitted the parable of the Sheep and the Goats, but a writer who has always in view the edification of Gentile readers would inevitably avoid a parable in which the judgment of the Gentiles is determined by their relation to the Jews; and the reason which Wendt urges against the supposition that Matthew's context is original is almost incredibly perverse. The truth is, that after Peter's question Jesus delivered a series of parables which represent successively the judgment of all the different classes of men in any way concerned with His mission. The parable of the Steward represents the judgment of the twelve. In the parable of the Talents the larger circle of disciples and the unbelieving Jews are rewarded or punished according to their works and different degrees of responsibility. And finally the parable of the Sheep and the Goats represents the judgment of the Gentiles. The three pictures are thus closely related. The third completes the series. The Gentiles are not disciples, but the unbelieving Jews are not disciples; and the word 'all' is large enough to include both. Overlooking Peter's question, Wendt has missed the truth. By certainties such as his the problem of the gospels is not solved.

We have assumed in the preceding pages that Mark's version of the apocalyptic discourse has been reproduced by Matthew and Luke, who do not therefore authenticate its contents. We now proceed to substantiate this assumption and to determine the relation of Mark's version to the original discourse as reconstructed. The priority of the second gospel and its use as the standard of history by the later synoptists are established results of criticism. A few English scholars, however, resist stoutly the current of opinion. Dr. Abbott e.g. maintains that the three synoptic gospels are independent deposits of an earlier source; and he finds 'demonstrative evidence' in the apocalyptic discourse 'that Matthew has borrowed, not from Mark, but from some common tradition, probably Greek, from which Mark has also borrowed.'[2] That

[1] *Die Lehre Jesu,* Erster Theil, S. 186-188.
[2] *The Common Tradition of the Synoptic Gospels,* p. xxxii.

Matthew in ch. xxiv. 9, 14 and Mark in ch. xiii. 9, 10 have independently reproduced a common original, he regards as a probable conjecture; and after comparing Mark xiii. 9-11 with Matt. x. 17-19, he asks, 'Can any Greek scholar, or can even any ordinary English reader, retain a particle of doubt that the words—"for a testimony unto them and unto all the nations"—represent an original tradition variously interpreted by Mark and Matthew?'[1] 'Matthew,' he concludes, 'has two versions of the original tradition which he assigns to different periods in the life of Christ.' The evidence, he says, is 'demonstrative.' Dr. Abbott has a peculiar conception of demonstrative evidence. The Greek scholar and the ordinary English reader will admit without any doubt that the words above quoted represent a common original variously interpreted by Matthew and Mark; and the inference will even be granted that Matthew has two versions of the original, one in ch. x. 17-19 and the other in ch. xxiv. 9, 14. But, in the first place, this original was not necessarily an oral tradition, and secondly the conclusion that the two versions in Matt. xxiv. 9, 14 and Mark xiii. 9, 10 are independent is not contained in the premises. The conjecture is still merely a conjecture. The difference between Matt. xxiv. 9-14 and Mark xiii. 9-13 is no doubt such as to suggest to an ordinary English reader that the two passages are independent, but Dr. Abbott is not an ordinary English reader: he is an accomplished Greek scholar who possesses some faculty of observation and should not make ordinary mistakes. Since Matthew has already inserted in his gospel a passage which is parallel to Mark xiii. 9-13 (Matt. x. 17-22), it is surely perfectly obvious that he cannot reproduce Mark xiii. 9-13 in the apocalyptic discourse without editorial repetition. To avoid repetition he must either omit the later passage altogether or substitute a paraphrase for the text. But Matt. xxiv. 9-14 is as a fact related to Mark xiii. 9-13 as a free translation to the original. Dr. Abbott's probable conjecture is therefore scarcely probable. The truth is that the parallel passage in Matt. x. 17-22 represents the apostolic source, and therefore the original tradition, that Mark xiii. 9-13 is a secondary

[1] *The Common Tradition of the Synoptic Gospels*, p. xxxiii.

rendering of the original represented by Matt. x. 17–22, and that Matt. xxiv. 9–14 is an editorial paraphrase of Mark xiii. 9–13. The telegram theory is not confirmed by the facts; and the demonstrative evidence that in the apocalyptic discourse Matthew has borrowed, not from Mark, but from some common tradition, from which Mark has also borrowed, is utterly undemonstrative. The text will be analysed in detail when we reach the original context. At present we are simply concerned with Dr. Abbott's reasoning, which is singularly destitute of logical necessity.

The following is a list of Matthew's variations: (1) He substitutes 'the disciples' for Peter and James and John and Andrew (ch. xxiv. 3). (2) The disciples ask, 'What shall be the sign of thy coming and of the end of the world?' instead of, 'What shall be the sign when these things are all about to be accomplished?' (ver. 3). Mark's question has here been adapted to the contents of the apostolic discourse. (3) He paraphrases Mark xiii. 9–13 to avoid editorial repetition (vv. 9–14). (4) He adds, 'which was spoken of by Daniel the prophet,' and defines 'where he ought not' as 'in the holy place' (ver. 15). (5) He adds 'neither on a sabbath' (ver. 20). (6) He converts a parenthetical statement of fact into a prediction (ver. 22). Mark's text is an editorial comment added after the event. Matthew thinks that it belongs to the text. He does not observe the parenthesis, and so he makes it an announcement of a calamity which is still in the future. (7) He transposes an adjective for the sake of literary improvement, and adds, 'then shall appear the sign of the Son of Man in heaven, and then shall all the tribes of the earth mourn' (ver. 30). (8) He converts 'the angels' into 'his angels,' and adds 'with a great sound of a trumpet,' and substitutes 'from one end of heaven to the other' for 'from the uttermost part of the earth to the uttermost part of heaven' (ver. 31).

Luke's version, on the other hand, is distinguished from Mark's as follows: (1) He omits the allusion to the Mount of Olives and to the four disciples (Luke xxi. 7). He does this for the sake of connection. He infers that the discourse was delivered at the Temple. (2) He adds, 'And the time is at hand' (ver. 8). (3) He substitutes 'tumults' for 'rumours of wars,' and 'terrified' for 'troubled,' and 'not immediately' for 'not yet' (ver. 9). (4) He adds, 'pestilences and terrors and great signs from heaven' (ver. 11). (5) He omits 'Take ye heed to yourselves,' and paraphrases Mark xiii. 9 (ver. 12), and converts 'for a testimony unto them' into 'It shall turn unto you for a testimony' (ver. 13). (6) He omits 'The gospel must first be preached unto all the nations.' Why? Because he understands the discourse to be primarily a prediction of the destruction of Jerusalem, and because the gospel did not require to be preached unto all the nations before that event. (7) He paraphrases Mark xiii. 11, and avoids the negative 'It is not ye that speak.' According to Luke it is really the disciples who speak, but God gives them a mouth and wisdom (vv. 14, 15). (8) He avoids the direct statement that brother would deliver brother to death. The death follows, but not necessarily in the purpose of the brother (ver. 16). (9) He adds 'not a hair of your head shall perish' (ver. 18). This seems directly to contradict Mark, but the meaning is that although others would be betrayed the twelve would be preserved. The saying has been borrowed from a later context to which we are approaching (Matt. x. 30; Luke xii. 7). (10) 'In your patience ye shall win your souls' is his equivalent for 'He that endureth to the end, the same shall be saved' (ver. 19). (11) He avoids the allusion to the abomination of desolation on account of his Gentile readers (ver. 20). (12) He omits the allusion to the housetop and the cloke (ver. 21, cf. ch. xvii. 31), and introduces an editorial reason (ver. 22), and omits 'Pray that it be not in winter,' and reduces the unparalleled distress (ver. 23). (13) He interposes the times of the Gentiles between the destruction of Jerusalem and the coming of the Son of Man (ver. 24). (14) He omits the statement that the days had been shortened. Matthew gets out of this difficulty by converting the past tense into a future. (15) He avoids the repetition of the warning against false Christs. (16) He adds 'signs on the earth' to 'signs in the sun, moon, and stars' (vv. 25, 26). (17) He substitutes 'a cloud' for 'clouds,' and 'with power and great glory' for 'with great power and glory' (ver. 27, cf. Matt. xxiv. 30). (18) He omits the sending forth of the angels and the gathering together of the elect, and substitutes a few words of his own (ver. 28). (19) He adds 'and all the trees' (ver. 29). (20) He substitutes 'the kingdom of God is nigh' for 'he is nigh,' and therefore omits 'even at the doors' (ver. 31).

The reader who will seriously maintain that these variations in the first and third gospels imply independence of source and authenticate the contents of Mark's version as constituents of the original apostolic tradition is incapable of scientific induction. I do not say that they afford 'demonstrative' evidence of the dependence of Matthew and Luke upon Mark; but I say without hesitation that they do not prove the contrary. Being perfectly intelligible as editorial variations, they even confirm the probability, which is otherwise gained, and is indeed almost universally acknowledged by those who are qualified to judge, that the second gospel is the standard of the later synoptists. The versions of Matthew and Luke, in so far as coincident with Mark's, may therefore be left out of account, and we may now proceed to analyse the version of Mark for the sake of determining its relation to the apostolic source. The opinion is prevalent among the critics that Mark has combined two elements which were originally distinct, and one of which is later than the teaching of Jesus. Weiss does not accept this opinion. Comparative textual criticism, he says, teaches that the very section attributed to the later apocryphal element 'forms the proper nucleus of the authentic discourse on the Second Coming according to the oldest tradition.'[1] In his analysis of the second gospel Wendt gives a list of German scholars with whom he agrees in upholding the prevalent opinion—Colani, Weizsäcker, Pfleiderer, Weiffenbach.[2] Wendt's argument may be briefly stated thus. The original discourse consisted, he believes, of the following passages arranged in consecutive order: Mark xiii. 1-6, 21-23, 9, 11-13, 28, 29, 32-37; and the rest of Mark's version constitutes the apocryphal element, Mark xiii. 7, 8, 14-20, 24-27, 30, 31. He points out the indisputable fact that in the first of these elements the predicted trials proceed from the Jews, whereas in the other they are wars and

[1] *Introduction to the New Testament*, vol. ii. p. 237.
[2] *Die Lehre Jesu*, Erster Theil, S. 10.

physical calamities, which distress the whole land of Judæa. He endeavours also to prove that the internal evidence demands a readjustment of the fragments. He argues that 'these things' in ver. 29 cannot mean the things in vv. 24-27, because the Second Coming is there included. They can only mean the things in vv. 21-23. Again, vv. 30, 31 could not originally follow ver. 29, because 'these things' in ver. 30 include the Second Coming and are therefore the things in vv. 24-27. The final result of this reasoning is the readjustment presented above. If we are bound to choose between the opinions of Wendt and Weiss, we are in a serious predicament; for, in the first place, the two elements, as Wendt points out, are really scarcely compatible, and secondly, on the supposition that Wendt's analysis is correct, the element which he rejects as apocryphal may be, quite as well as the other, the nucleus of the authentic discourse. The introduction, indeed, seems to demand an announcement, not of trials which would proceed from the Jews, but of calamities which would distress Jerusalem (Mark xiii. 1-4). How, then, are we to get out of the difficulty? The critics have made a fundamental mistake. They have taken for granted that the second gospel was in its origin either wholly unrelated or very slightly related to the apostolic source. The truth, as we have seen, is very different. The introduction in the second gospel is editorial (Mark xiii. 1-3). The original discourse included a number of fragments, which have been added by Matthew, and which Luke has dispersed in his digression. The section at the end of Mark's version coincides with original fragments authenticated by Matthew and Luke (vv. 32-37). The earlier section vv. 9-13, which coincides with Matt. x. 17-22, Luke xii. 11, 12, and must therefore be regarded as apostolic, will be claimed by a later context. Excluding these sections the remainder consists of Mark xiii. 5-8, 14-31, a self-contained and coherent prediction. If the element which Wendt believes to be apocryphal is incompatible with the other element which he accepts as authentic, the remainder above indicated is much more incompatible with the original discourse as reconstructed in these pages. The two cannot possibly be combined; they

represent different orders of ideas. We must therefore
conclude that Weiss is mistaken in his opinion regarding
the nucleus of the discourse. Mark has not only abbreviated
the original; he has also introduced an interpolation, which
does not represent the teaching of Jesus, and the adoption of
which accounts for the abbreviation. But if the opinion of
Weiss must be rejected, Wendt, on the other hand, is equally
astray. His readjustment of the fragments is hypercritical,
his reconstruction not sufficiently critical. His generalisa-
tions are exceedingly defective; and the secret of his failure
is that, in company with Weiss and all the critics, he has
mistaken the nature of the apostolic source and its relation
to the second gospel.

a.—The question of the Pharisees was probably sarcastic.
They no doubt themselves expected 'a kingdom of external
might and glory, with forms and boundaries which could be
marked out like other earthly kingdoms;' but they did not
ask Jesus when the kingdom in their sense of the word would
come. Their question was an expression of scornful incredulity. They received, therefore, a curt reply.

b.—Luke's text is here in a few details secondary. He
has abbreviated the original in ch. xvii. 23 (cf. Matt. xxiv. 26).
The one part under the heaven and the other part under
heaven (ver. 24) are his equivalents for the east and the west
(Matt. xxiv. 27). In these verses the more definite words
are certainly primary. Again, ver. 25 has been substituted
for Mark xiii. 32 (Matt. xxiv. 36), and in ver. 37 the body
($\tau\grave{o}$ $\sigma\hat{\omega}\mu a$) for the carcase ($\tau\grave{o}$ $\pi\tau\hat{\omega}\mu a$, Matt. xxiv. 28).
Matthew, on the other hand, has omitted a few verses —
Luke xvii. 20–22 on account of Mark's introduction to the
discourse, vv. 28–30, 32 on account of the thought already
conveyed in the allusion to the days of Noah, ver. 31 to avoid
editorial repetition, and ver. 33 partly to avoid repetition and
partly because in the apocalyptic discourse the text conveys
a meaning which Matthew believes to be secondary.

Two questions here arise for discussion. The first is, What
was the original context of Luke xvii. 31? This text is parallel
to Mark xiii. 15, 16 (Matt. xxiv. 17, 18), and Wendt assumes
that Luke has interpolated in the midst of his apostolic

material a reminiscence of the second gospel;[1] but Mark xiii. 15, 16 may quite as well be a reminiscence of the apostolic text. Wendt does not contemplate the possibility. He invariably assumes that when the second gospel coincides with digression material, Luke has borrowed from Mark; but this assumption has already been disproved, and as a fact the apocryphal element in Mark's version of the discourse coincides at several points with Luke's apostolic material (Mark xiii. 5, 6, 21, 22, cf. Luke xvii. 21, 23, 24). The greater probability, therefore, is that the author of Mark's apocryphal element was acquainted with the apostolic original, and adapted a few of its details to the circumstances and expectations of a later time.

The second question is, What was the original context of the words, 'Whosoever shall seek to gain his life shall lose it; but whosoever shall lose his life shall preserve it'? This saying is to be found in three different situations: (1) in Mark viii. 35 (Matt. xvi. 25; Luke ix. 24); (2) in Matt. x. 39; (3) in Luke xvii. 33. The first of these situations depends entirely for its authority on the second gospel, since Matthew and Luke have simply reproduced Mark's text; and the context in the second gospel, as we have already seen, is editorial. The statement in ver. 34 was made by Jesus at the entrance into Jerusalem, and Mark viii. 38–ix. 1 was originally in a context which has not yet been reached. Mark's situation is, therefore, not historical. Again, Matt. x. 39 is one of a series of additions which Matthew has made to the charge addressed by Jesus to the twelve before they set out on their mission. Wendt contends that ver. 39 originally followed vv. 34–38, and he places the whole passage in one of his fictitious discourses — Luke xii. 49, 50; Matt. x. 34–36; Luke xiv. 26, 27; Matt. x. 39; Luke xiv. 28–35.[2] He is certainly right in identifying Matt. x. 37, 38 with Luke xiv. 26, 27; but the whole section Luke xiv. 25–35 represents, as we have seen, an instruction addressed to the disciples at the entrance into Jerusalem. The question thus comes to be, Was Matt. x. 39 originally situated in this instruction after Luke xiv. 27? The sequence in Mark viii. 34, 35 appears at first sight to warrant an

[1] *Die Lehre Jesu*, Erster Theil, S. 161.   [2] *Ibid.* S. 122-125.

affirmative reply, and the evidence of the fourth gospel may be supposed to settle the question (John xii. 25, 26). The concurrent testimony of Matthew, Mark, and John constitutes a threefold cord which is not quickly broken; and Luke's omission of the text is intelligible on the supposition that it was originally situated after Luke xiv. 27, for in ch. ix. 24 he has already reproduced the parallel text Mark viii. 35. The evidence seems to be decisive. On the other hand, however, two weighty facts should be noted. The first is, that Luke xvii. 33 is demanded by vv. 34, 35. The transition from vv. 28-32 to ver. 34 is mentally impracticable. In vv. 34, 35 the thought is that in the day of the kingdom the safety of men will be determined by the election of God; but this thought is not directly connected with the teaching in vv. 28-32. The day, Jesus says, will be unexpected. The judgment will come like the fire which burned Sodom in the days of Lot. Do not take thought for your goods when you see the lightning flash. Do not leave the housetop; do not leave the field. Remain wherever you may be. Remember Lot's wife, who looked back with longing eyes, and lost more than she wished to save. The subject here is the relation of the believer to his property, whereas in vv. 34, 35 the subject is his personal relation to the judgment and election of God. The allusion to Lot's wife no doubt introduces the idea of personal safety, but in such a way that an explanatory sequel is absolutely necessary; and as a fact ver. 33 continues the thought expressed in the preceding verses, and enables us to pass to ver. 34. Remember, Jesus says, Lot's wife, who lost more than she wished to save. Do not even seek to save your life when the great day comes at last. He who is concerned for his personal safety will lose what he seeks to save; but he who takes no thought for himself will be preserved by God. Self-preservation will be useless. In that night there shall be two men on one bed: the one shall be taken, and the other shall be left. There shall be two women grinding together: the one shall be taken, and the other shall be left. The continuity of thought authenticates ver. 33 as a constituent of the apocalyptic discourse. Again, in Luke's version of the charge to the disciples at the entrance into Jerusalem the words, 'and his own life also,' are included (Luke xiv. 26). These words may be an abbreviation of the text reported by the other evangelists (Matt. x. 39; Mark viii. 35; John xii. 25), but they may quite as well have suggested the text as an interpolation to each of the evangelists independently. The internal evidence is distinctly in favour of this supposition; for, notwithstanding Wendt and the critics, Luke xvii. 33 is not an appropriate sequel to Luke xiv. 26, 27. Jesus requires His disciples to hate father, and mother, and wife, and children, and brethren, and sisters, yea, and their own life also. The word is the strongest possible, and the statement appropriately follows, ' Whosoever doth not bear his own cross, and come after me, cannot be my disciple ' (ver. 27) ; but the losing of one's life is not an illustration of hatred to it, nor is life lost by bearing the cross. Hatred is active, and cross-bearing is active, but loss is a negative idea. Life may be lost when one is attempting to escape from an imminent danger, or without attempting to escape, but is never wilfully lost. The Greek word may mean 'to destroy,' but the idea of deliberate self-sacrifice is excluded by the antithesis in the text. The impropriety of the text is accordingly quite as evident in the earlier charge as its propriety in the later discourse ; and we must conclude that it was originally delivered in the apocalyptic discourse, that the additions ' for my sake ' in Matt. x. 39, xvi. 25, Luke ix. 24, and 'for my sake and the gospel's' in Mark viii. 35, are both editorial, and that the famous paradox was not intended by Jesus to teach Hegelian Christianity.

We are now able to complete the reconstruction by restoring a last fragment to its apostolic situation. Immediately after Mark viii. 35 the words are reported in the second gospel, ' For what doth it profit a man, to gain the whole world, and forfeit his life ? For what should a man give in exchange for his life ? ' These words could not originally follow Luke xvii. 33, but might follow ver. 32. They are, indeed, demanded by the allusion to Lot's wife, and make the transition easier from ver. 32 to ver. 33. Do not, Jesus says, like Lot's wife, take thought for the preservation of your property. A man's life is worth more than his possessions, more even to him than all the world. Do not sacrifice your ife to your property. A man's life, again, is worth little in comparison with the kingdom of God. Do not, therefore, sacrifice your hope of the kingdom to the hope of saving your life. Turn resolutely, like Lot, from the things and the life of the perishing world, and thus you will receive a greater compensation for any loss you may sustain. The fragment in Mark viii. 36, 37 forms evidently a connecting link between Luke xvii. 32 and ver. 33; and Mark has a reason for reversing the sequence, since he connects the whole passage with ch. viii. 34. Luke, again, has a reason for omitting Mark viii. 36, 37 after Luke xvii. 32. He has already reproduced Mark's fragment (Luke ix. 25), and wishes to avoid repetition. He repeats Mark viii. 35 in Luke xvii. 33; but Mark by removing this text from the apocalyptic discourse has given it a new application, and the verbal repetition in the third gospel is justified by the difference of meaning.

c.—The parable of the Unjust Judge is rejected by J. Estlin Carpenter. 'The obvious reference of this parable,' he says, ' to the delay in Messiah's coming withdraws it at once from the cycle of the original sayings of Jesus, and thus relieves his teaching about the Father from what many have felt to be a most disturbing comparison between God and the godless officer.'[1] Mr. Carpenter is too easily disturbed. The parable is explained by its context. The delay is not supposed to extend beyond the lifetime of the disciples. The comparison between God and the godless officer is parallel to an earlier comparison, which Mr. Carpenter presumably accepts, ' If ye, being evil, know how to give good gifts unto your children, how much more shall your Father give good things to them that ask him?' The point in the parable is that God is not like the godless officer, but is Himself willing to vindicate the elect. ' Fear not, little flock, it is your Father's good pleasure to give you the kingdom.' The precept, ' Watch and pray,' in the second gospel (Mark xiii. 33) shows that Mark was acquainted, if not with the parable of the Unjust Judge, at least with the admonition in Luke xxi. 34–36.

d.—The severity of the judgment on the steward has either

[1] *The First Three Gospels*, p. 323.

been reduced by Luke or increased by Matthew. In the third gospel he receives his portion with 'the unfaithful' (Luke xii. 46); but other servants who fail in their duty receive their portion with the unfaithful, and the point is that, since much has been committed to the steward, of him the more will be required. On the other hand, the allusion to the hypocrites is scarcely in agreement with the parable, and the severity of the scourging is sufficient to meet the requirements of the case. We adopt the version of Luke. Matthew has omitted Luke xii. 47, 48 because he interpolates the parable of the Virgins between the parable of the Steward and the parable of the Talents. The following details are worthy of notice in the parable of the Talents: (1) The heading in Luke xix. 11 is an editorial duplication of the question which was asked by the Pharisees (Luke xvii. 20). (2) Matthew has omitted the allusion to the citizens (Luke xix. 14), and has substituted an account of the servants (Matt. xxv. 16–18). This account is included in the report which was given to the nobleman when he returned, and is therefore probably editorial. It is intelligible as an amplification of the charge, 'Trade ye herewith till I come' (Luke xix. 13). (3) The words 'after a long time' in Matthew's version (ver. 19) are also probably editorial. They agree neither with the mission of the nobleman nor with the context of the parable. They have perhaps been borrowed from the parable of the Vineyard (Luke xx. 9). If the words are accepted as primary, the long time is defined by the context, and does not mean very long. (4) The words, 'Enter thou into the joy of thy lord,' in Matthew's version are significant (vv. 21, 23). They are not intelligible unless on the supposition that the master was a nobleman who went to the far country for a kingdom. The kingdom is the joy of the lord. The allusion to the cities (Luke xix. 17, 19) has been necessarily omitted by Matthew. (5) The hiding of the money in the earth (Matt. xxv. 18, 25) is probably a reminiscence of an earlier parable (Matt. xiii. 44). (6) The exclamation of those that stood by, in Luke's version, is a detail which authenticates itself (ver. 25) and accounts for the principle which follows (ver. 26). The people thought that the servant with the ten talents had enough, and that the man with the napkin should not be deprived of his capital; but the nobleman was a merchant as well as a king. He withdrew his money from a risky venture and increased his stake in a safe investment. The lesson therefore is, that servants will receive more capital in proportion to the interest which they give, and that the servant who does not give any interest will lose the whole of his capital. That is a good business principle. (7) Mark has detached the principle from the parable of the Talents, and has inserted it in ch. iv. 25. This context is manifestly editorial; for ver. 24 was originally situated in the Sermon on the Mount, and the earth bears fruit of itself. Growth is a spontaneous process, and the increase proceeds from within: it is not given from without. Matthew and Luke have reproduced Mark's text (Matt. xiii. 12; Luke viii. 18). Luke tries to make it more intelligible, and thus loses more completely the original meaning. He substitutes 'that which he thinketh he hath' for 'that which he hath.' (8) Matt. xxv. 30 has probably been substituted for the charge to slay the enemies (Luke xix. 27). 'The outer darkness' agrees with the allusion to 'the joy of the lord,' but not with the original text of the parable (cf. Matt. viii. 12; Luke xiii. 28).

Wendt pairs the parable of the Talents with the parable of the Wise Steward (Luke xvi. 1-12), and the parable of the Faithful and Wicked Servants (Matt. xxiv. 45-51) with the parable of the Wise and Foolish Virgins. These combinations need not be discussed in detail. They illustrate the helplessness of the critics.

§ 49.—*The Last Supper*

From ch. xviii. 15 onwards Luke borrows his material from the second gospel, but adds to Mark's more meagre history a few apostolic fragments. The apocalyptic discourse is represented by Luke xix. 11-27, xxi. 34-36, and the next fragment is unmistakably a report of the Supper (Luke xxii. 14-20, 24-30). Between the apocalyptic discourse and the Supper, Mark reports a visit of Jesus to Bethany; but the narrative of the anointing in Bethany coincides with the apostolic story of the penitent woman (Luke vii. 36-50). The coincidence has already been discussed, and need not be verified anew. At present we have only to observe the additional fact that the continuity of the history is broken by Mark xiv. 3-9, which has otherwise been recognised as an interpolation. Ver. 10 is so intimately related to vv. 1, 2 that, apart from the other convincing evidence, we have good reason to suspect that Mark is reproducing a document in which ver. 10 immediately followed ver. 2. But the whole passage Mark xiv. 1, 2, 10, 11 constitutes an introduction to the Supper. The two sources are therefore again coincident, and we are bound to conclude that the Supper originally followed the instruction on the coming of the kingdom. The only question is, How can we determine the details of the new narrative now before us? The fragmentary nature of Luke's additions has been recognised by the critics, but they are not able to suggest an explanation. Wendt e.g. consigns them to one of his appendices, and distinctly acknowledges that the thought-connection has been lost. He is not content, however, to leave the fragments as he finds them. He passes at a leap from Luke xxii. 17 to the words, 'He that is the greater among you, let him become as the younger' (ver. 26), rejecting the intermediate verses as editorial. He believes that vv. 18, 19^a, 21-23 have been borrowed from Mark xiv. 18-25, vv. 24-26^a from Mark ix. 34, x. 42, and vv. 33, 34 from Mark xiv. 30, 31. He believes also that vv. 19^b, 20, which are absent from a few manuscripts, were added at a later time to the third gospel from 1 Cor. xi. 24, 25 ; and the result of his criticism is a text consisting of the following passages: Luke xxii. 14-17, 26^b-32, 35-38.[1] Every honest attempt by a qualified scholar to remove inveterate difficulties is worthy of respectful acknowledgment, and Wendt's reconstruction, as far as it goes, unquestionably possesses this merit. He ranks not merely among the latest, but also among the most helpful, of the critics. He must not, however, expect to have his criticism of the Supper accepted. He has left undone the things which he ought to have done, and has done the things which he ought not to have done. Vv. 21-23 have probably been borrowed from the second gospel. They are perfectly intelligible as an editorial rendering of Mark xiv. 17-

[1] *Die Lehre Jesu*, Erster Theil, S. 171-174.

21, and, as we shall see, they are incompatible with the original context; but the supposition of borrowing in the other cases is forbidden by the textual evidence. Instead of being an editorial reproduction of the second gospel, vv. 18, 19ᵃ, 24-26ᵃ, 33, 34 represent rather the original text, in relation to which Mark's is secondary. The omission at a later time of the fragment extending from the words, 'which is given for you: this do in remembrance of me' (ver. 19) to the end of ver. 20 is quite as conceivable as its interpolation, and indeed is much more probable; for the text does not verbally agree with 1 Cor. xi. 24, 25, and a copyist would be more likely to omit the allusion to the cup on account of vv. 17, 18 than to interpolate a fragment from one of Paul's epistles. Wendt leaps from ver. 17 to ver. 26. His agility is indisputable, but the wisdom of excluding from the apostolic source Luke's account of the Supper is not at all so obvious. It is antecedently improbable that the source should contain a few fragments of instruction without the ever-memorable incident; and the allusion to the Passover and the cup in vv. 15-17, though not implying that the occasion was the feast of the Passover, is scarcely intelligible when separated from the verses which follow. Wendt's criticism is not convincing. Again, he has himself frankly acknowledged the incoherence of the fragments accepted; that is, he has confessed his own failure, the leaving undone of the things which he ought to have done. He has not looked for the missing links. If the silver is not in the house, no amount of sweeping will find it; but perhaps, after all, the discovery of dust and clean boards might justify the use of the broom, and the question is, Does the house not contain the silver? The possibility has never been contemplated by any of the critics, but is not on that account excluded. They might on the whole with advantage apply to their studies the parable of the Broom. The accumulated dust of unverified theories might thus be removed from the gospels. If Luke in combining his two sources has rearranged the apostolic material, the fragments may not be hopelessly lost: they may simply be in an earlier context. Let us put the matter to the test.

1. The beginning of Luke's additions unquestionably

represents the apostolic source (Luke xxii. 15-18). Wendt's dismemberment of this fragment is inadmissible. Ver. 18 is not a reproduction of Mark xiv. 25. On the contrary, Luke has preserved the primary form and connection of the text, and Mark in abbreviating his original has transferred ver. 25 to a later position, thus intentionally or unintentionally suggesting to his readers that at the Supper Jesus drank of the fruit of the vine. The integrity of Luke's fragment may be taken for granted; but the sequel presents an obvious difficulty. The transition from ver. 18 to ver. 19 is unexpected. There is nothing in the earlier verses to prepare the way for the memorable saying: 'This is my body, which is broken for you.' Wendt suggests that ver. 19 has been partly borrowed from Mark, and partly added as an interpolation by a copyist; but that is exceedingly improbable, and is quite a superfluous conjecture. The greater probability is that between ver. 18 and ver. 19 a passage was originally situated which Luke has omitted to avoid editorial repetition. In Luke xii. 49, 50 we find as a fact precisely such a passage as is needed. The context here is certainly editorial; for the parable of the Steward or of the Faithful and Unfaithful Servants (Luke xii. 41-48) was originally included in the apocalyptic discourse, and in this discourse no room has been found for vv. 49, 50. These verses indeed are foreign to the contents of the discourse. But the Supper originally followed the instruction on the coming of the kingdom, and the verses in question are appropriate to the later occasion. They enable us to pass from ver. 18 to ver. 19, and thus authenticate themselves as the link of connection. Jesus says: 'I will not drink from henceforth of the fruit of the vine, until the kingdom of God shall come' (ver. 18). This suggests the expression of His ardent desire that the kingdom should come speedily. 'I came to cast fire upon the earth, and how I wish (τi $\theta \acute{\epsilon} \lambda \omega$) it were already kindled!' (Luke xii. 49). A condition, however, must first be observed: 'I have a baptism to be baptised with; and how am I straitened till it be accomplished!' (ver. 50). The thought, again, of baptismal suffering and death is completed by the action and words which follow in Luke's account of the Supper (vv. 19, 20); for the sufferings and death of Messiah have not merely a personal significance;

they are not merely a baptism through which He Himself must enter the kingdom of God. They have also a significance in relation to those who are waiting for the fulfilment of the promise; and so we are told that Jesus 'took bread, and when he had given thanks, he brake it, and gave to them, saying, This is my body, which is given for you: this do in remembrance of me' (vv. 19, 20). The thought-connection is apparent. The narrative is made coherent by the restoration of the fragment which Luke has omitted to avoid repetition.

2. For the sake of convenience we now pass to the dispute which arose among the disciples (vv. 24–27), setting aside provisionally the fragment concerning the traitor (vv. 21–23). Wendt assumes that the incident and part of the teaching which follows have been borrowed by Luke from the second gospel; but if vv. 26, 27 have been taken from the apostolic source, as Wendt believes, vv. 24, 25 are probably also apostolic. They do not verbally agree with Mark's parallel verses, and are required by the sequel. We must therefore choose between two alternatives. We must either reject the whole passage (vv. 24–27) as an editorial interpolation borrowed from Mark x. 35–45, or accept the whole passage as a transcript from the apostolic source. The question thus arises, Have we any reason to believe that Mark x. 35–45 was originally situated in the account of the Supper, and that Mark's situation is secondary? I submit the following facts: (*a*) We have already concluded in these pages that the whole of Mark's second period is editorial. The instruction in Mark viii. 34–ix. 1 was not delivered immediately after the confession of Peter, and the series of incidents from Mark ix. 33 onwards to Mark x. 31 was originally situated, with the exception of Mark ix. 38–40, after the last entrance into Jerusalem. But the request of James and John is situated at the end of these incidents, and thus occupies a relative position which agrees with that of the Supper in the apostolic source. (*b*) The request of James and John is immediately preceded by the announcement that the Son of Man would be delivered unto the chief priests and Scribes, and condemned to death, and delivered to the Gentiles, who would mock Him, and spit upon Him, and scourge Him, and kill Him (Mark x. 33, 34); and this

announcement is intelligible as an amplification of the statement which was made at the Supper (Luke xii. 50, cf. Mark xiv. 1, 2). The details of the later history have been put into the earlier text. (c) According to the testimony of the fourth gospel, the disciples were taught at the Supper to follow the example of Christ's great humility (John xiii. 1–15). The dispute is not directly recorded, and there are differences in detail which will be afterwards considered. In the meantime, we simply observe the general coincidence of the fourth gospel with Luke xxii. 24–27. (d) Although Luke xxii. 25–27 obviously coincides with Mark x. 42–45, the incident which suggested the instruction has not been recorded by Luke. He omits both the incident and the instruction when reproducing Mark's second period, and at the Supper he simply records the instruction, with the introductory statement that 'there arose also a contention among the disciples, which of them is accounted to be greatest' (ver. 24). On the supposition that the two passages are identical, we must conclude either that Mark has enlarged or that Luke has abridged the original. But the abridgment of the original by Luke is much more probable than its enlargement by Mark; for Luke might wish to spare the apostles, and might intelligibly think that the details of such a contention would not be conducive to edification, whereas these details, on the other hand, would not be likely to be invented. They not only authenticate themselves, they also prove conclusively that the incident did not happen before the last entrance into Jerusalem, but was included in the account of the Supper. When James and John had presented their petition, Jesus said in reply, 'Ye know not what ye ask. Are ye able to drink the cup that I drink? or to be baptised with the baptism that I am baptised with?' (Mark x. 38, cf. ver. 39). In Mark's context, these words are abrupt and unexpected. The allusion to the cup and the baptism could scarcely be intelligible to the disciples on the road to Jerusalem from Galilee. There is certainly nothing in the context to account for the use of these particular words. But in Luke's situation the words are intelligible and appropriate, for the disciples had immediately before received another cup from which Jesus had not been drinking, and He had previously said, 'I have a baptism to be baptised with; and how am I straitened till it be accomplished' (Luke xii. 50). The evidence is sufficiently complete to establish the probability that Luke has abbreviated the incident, the original situation of which he has, on the other hand, preserved.

3. The request of James and John, thus authenticated as an episode at the Supper, enables us to continue the reconstruction of the narrative. The agreement of these disciples reminds us of a promise which Matthew alone has recorded: 'If two of you shall agree on earth as touching anything that they shall ask, it shall be done for them of my Father which is in heaven. For where two or three are gathered together in my name, there am I in the midst of them' (Matt. xviii. 19, 20). The context of these words is editorial. In reproducing the second gospel, Matthew has reached a few fragments which coincide with the apostolic instruction on the subject of prayer and forgiveness, and has enlarged Mark's meagre report by the addition of apostolic material. He has substituted chap. xviii. 15-17 for the original precepts in Luke xvii. 3, 4; Matt. v. 23, 24; Luke xii. 58, 59. The section from ver. 21 to ver. 35 has been verbally transcribed from the apostolic source, and vv. 18-20 constitute an editorial interpolation. No room has been found for these verses in our reconstruction of the Doctrine of Prayer. The connection is not original. We must, therefore, either assume that they are purely editorial, like vv. 15-17, and not authentic words of Jesus, or we must find another context for them. But the only available context is the one which we are at present reconstructing; and since the promise in vv. 19, 20 is obviously related to the agreement of James and John, we are justified in concluding that it suggested the petition. Again, Matthew has already introduced chap. xviii. 18 in an earlier context, in which the words are addressed to Peter, and are preceded by the famous text, 'And I also say unto thee, that thou art Peter, and upon this rock I will build my church and the gates of Hades shall not prevail against it. I will give unto thee the keys of the kingdom of heaven' (Matt. xvi. 18, 19). We are here in a region of interminable controversies. That Peter was not as a fact the primate of the early Church, and that the Roman interpreta-

tion is incompatible with other passages in the gospels, Protestant interpreters have been able to show; but, although they have exercised their ingenuity for many centuries, they have not been remarkably successful in attempting to escape from this particular text. Their exegesis is distinctly evasive. Professor Bruce e.g. maintains the genuineness of the saying, and accepts without question Matthew's context. The absence of the text from the other synoptical records provokes in his case reflection, but not the least particle of doubt. 'In the case of the third evangelist,' he says, 'the motive for omission may have been a consciousness that the words were being used already for party purposes, in which case their exclusion from his pages is a silent protest against a prelatic or hierarchical spirit manifesting itself in the bud. The omission in Mark, on the other hand,' he proceeds to say, 'may be due to the influence of Peter himself. We can imagine the apostle, no longer the forward, self-asserting man that he was as a disciple, passing over in silence the strong language addressed to himself by the Master at Cæsarea Philippi, from a feeling of modesty, and doing so the more readily because he was conscious that he did not thereby sacrifice any important truth or seriously mutilate his testimony.'[1] Was Peter, then, modest enough to conceal a peculiar honour and dignity, which raised him above the other apostles, and gave him a position of supremacy? Was he really appointed the primate of the Church, with exclusive power to bind and loose? By no means; for, according to this interpreter, we must distinguish between the form and the essence of the thought. The text 'says in a highly emotional and Hebrew manner what can be expressed in abstract didactic language, which eliminates Peter's personality as of no fundamental moment.'[2] Imagination is sometimes a fatal gift, and the translation of a text from the Hebrew idiom into abstract didactic language, which is more in accordance with the prepossessions and style of the translator, may be a *reductio ad absurdum*. The exegesis of Professor Bruce illustrates these tendencies. If the second gospel is a reminiscence of the preaching of Peter, the modesty of the apostle may no doubt

[1] *The Kingdom of God*, pp. 261, 262. [2] *Ibid.* p. 261.

be suggested as an explanation of many surprising facts; but, before indulging in such conjectures, it might on the whole be advisable to verify the hypothesis. This has not been done by Professor Bruce. When the form of the thought is distinguished from its essence the modesty seems a little superfluous, and the significance of the text is reduced in a manner which is much more abstract than convincing. The distinction of Peter from the rest of the apostles, who were at the moment ignored, the association of his name with the rock on which the Church would be built, the emphatic repetition of the personal pronoun, 'Thou art Peter.... I will give unto thee the keys of the kingdom of heaven. Whatsoever thou shalt bind on earth shall be bound in heaven, and whatsoever thou shalt loose on earth shall be loosed in heaven' —all this proves conclusively that the elimination of Peter's personality as of no fundamental moment is a flagrant exegetical evasion. How, then, is the difficulty to be removed? If Peter was not raised as a fact above the other apostles, and if according to Matthew he was thus exalted to a position of hierarchical supremacy, what is the necessary conclusion? J. Estlin Carpenter replies, with his usual negative freedom, that the text in the first gospel is not genuine. It arose, he believes, 'in the course of the second century when the growing pretensions of the Bishop of Rome sought sanction at the hands of the divine Lord of the Church.'[1] To this, however, there are serious objections; for, in the first place, Matthew is not accustomed to introduce apocryphal sayings into his gospel; and secondly, as Professor Bruce truly says, 'the saying is far too remarkable to have proceeded from anyone but Jesus.' Wendt's criticism of the text is characteristic. He avoids the two extremes. He rejects Matt. xvi. 19; xviii. 18;[2] and adopting a suggestion from the Commentary of Ephrem Syrus on Tatian's 'Diatessaron,' he reduces Matt. xvi. 18 to the following words, which he consigns to one of his appendices: 'Blessed art thou, Simon Bar-Jonah: thou art Peter, and the gates of Hades shall not prevail against thee.'[3] When Wendt is reduced to extremity, he finds his

---

[1] *The First Three Gospels*, p. 377.
[2] *Die Lehre Jesu*, Erster Thiel, S. 156. [3] *Ibid* S. 180.

appendices convenient; and since the words above quoted have been taken from Ephrem Syrus, a writer of the fourth century, who elsewhere abbreviates the words of Jesus, and can scarcely be regarded as a reliable guide to the original text of the first gospel, an appendix is on the whole the best place for them. The remarkable feature of Wendt's accomplishment is his rejection of the text which enables us to get out of the difficulty. He stands beside the locked door, and deliberately throws away the key. The power to bind and loose, which in Matt. xvi. 19 is committed to Peter, is afterwards in Matt. xviii. 18 extended to all the apostles. The repetition of this text is a guarantee of its genuineness, and the question arises whether Matthew has not applied specially to Peter a saying which was originally addressed to the twelve. The following facts should be observed: (a) According to the testimony of the second gospel, Simon received the name Peter at an earlier time (Mark iii. 16, cf. John i. 42). (b) Our analysis has already excluded the supposition that the words which Matthew has interpolated in his reproduction of Mark's narrative after the confession of Peter have been preserved in their original context. The confession, as we have seen, was followed by Luke x. 21-24, and not by Matt. xvi. 17-19. (c) The words, 'Blessed art thou, Simon Bar-Jonah: for flesh and blood hath not revealed it unto thee, but my Father which is in heaven' (ver. 17), are intelligible as an abstract from, and special application of, Luke x. 21. Since the confession was made by Peter, the inference is not surprising that Jesus in reply alluded specially to him. (d) Matthew has already inserted Luke x. 21-24 in ch. xi. 25-27, xiii. 16, 17, and must avoid repetition. (e) In ch. xviii. 15-20 to avoid repetition he substitutes for the original text a special and editorial application (vv. 15-17), and adds a passage derived from a later context (vv. 18-20). (f) The famous passage in Matt. xvi. 18, 19 is intelligible as an example of the same method. The original text, Luke x. 21-24, obviously cannot be repeated; but ver. 17 is an abstract from Luke x. 21, and vv. 18, 19, which are somewhat similar to the original, may very well have been substituted. (g) If Matt. xvi. 19 was originally addressed to the twelve, it is antecedently probable that ver. 18 was also in part addressed to the twelve, and originally preceded ver. 19. But the designation of Simon as Peter has been borrowed from an earlier context, and the allusion to the Church in Matt. xvi. 18 and ch. xviii. 17 is probably an inference from ch. xviii. 18–20; v. 23–26. Since the apostles received power to bind and loose, and since the assurance was given, ' Where two or three are gathered together in my name, there am I in the midst of them,' an early interpreter would inevitably infer that Jesus provided for the formation of a church. Excluding the word ' church ' and the designation of Simon as Peter, the text consists of two clauses, ' And the gates of Hades shall not prevail against it. I will give unto thee the keys of the kingdom of heaven.' But if these words were originally addressed to the twelve, and if Jesus did not explicitly speak of the Church, the evangelist in applying his text to Peter has obviously inverted the original; and we find as the result of our analysis the following words: 'I will give unto you the keys of the kingdom of heaven, and the gates of Hades shall not prevail against you.' (*h*) Transferring the whole passage thus reconstructed to the context already discovered, the connection is perfectly clear. Jesus has announced to the disciples that the end has almost come. Through baptismal suffering and death He must enter the kingdom of God. He has given them bread and wine to symbolise His body and blood, the body broken for them, the blood poured out for them. The ritual is both significant and mysterious. What can be the meaning of these strange and solemn words, ' This is my body : this is the new covenant in my blood ' ? He certainly intends to teach not merely that the new covenant will be fulfilled in His own experience when He drinks the cup and is baptised with the baptism of death, but also that His death will ratify the covenant, and that if the disciples are faithful to the obligations incumbent upon them, the promise will be in their case also fulfilled in the heavenly kingdom of God. If they remember Messiah, God will remember them. But what is the meaning of the eating and drinking ? ' How can this man give us his flesh to eat ? ' The significance of the Supper is explained in the sequel.

The apostles receive Messiah's power and authority. With the bread and the wine Jesus gives them the keys of the kingdom of God, and the gates of Hades will not prevail against them. Their decisions on the earth will be confirmed in heaven. Their prayer will be answered by God, if two of them agree as touching anything that they shall ask; and all this will be in accordance with the covenant, because they are His representatives. 'Where two or three are gathered together in my name, there am I in the midst of them.' The Supper does not merely signify a general communion of the believer with Jesus: it signifies in the case of the apostles that as the representatives of Messiah on the earth they will possess His power and privileges. The communion is precise and exclusive. It is antecedently improbable that the great words at the Supper would be left altogether unexplained. A sequel is needed not merely to fill up the gap between the allusion to the new covenant and the dispute which arose among the twelve, but also to define the new covenant and the relation of the apostles to their Master in receiving the bread and the wine. The sequel which we have found is unquestionably appropriate. It accounts for the request of James and John, and defines the significance of the Supper. And the fact that it has not been preserved by any of the evangelists in its original context does not constitute a difficulty; for the evangelists have in view the general edification of believers, and have therefore a reason for avoiding after the institution of the Supper the special application to the apostles. The fourth gospel indeed affords a verification of our argument; for in the discourse which, according to John, was delivered to the disciples at the Supper, the following words are reported: 'Verily, verily, I say unto you, He that believeth on me, the works that I do shall he do also; and greater works than these shall he do; because I go unto the Father. And whatsoever ye shall ask in my name, that will I do, that the Father may be glorified in the Son. If ye shall ask me anything in my name, that will I do' (John xiv. 12-14). The coincidence of these words with the passage now under discussion can scarcely be disputed by the reader. The thought in the fourth gospel is less precise;

but John simply expresses, as Professor Bruce would say, 'in abstract didactic language,' what the original text conveys 'in a highly emotional and Hebrew manner.' And this method of translation is not exceptional; for the gospel according to John exhibits a long series of correspondences which inevitably lead to the conclusion that the fourth evangelist has translated in detail the apostolic source, avoiding what he considers to be merely temporary and accidental, and adapting his original to illustrate and commend a higher conception of the Person of Christ. In the meantime we are simply concerned with one particular coincidence, which verifies the result of our investigation, and thus decides the probability that the much-discussed text in the first gospel, with its sequel (Matt. xviii. 18-20), was originally situated in the apostolic account of the Last Supper. Reserving the determination of details, we have accordingly so far gained a narrative consisting of the following passages: Luke xxii. 14-18; xii. 49, 50; xxii. 19, 20; Matt. xvi. 18^b, 19^a; xviii. 18-20; Mark x. 35-41; Luke xxii. 25-27.

4. The next fragment in the third gospel is a promise addressed to the twelve: 'Ye are they which have continued with me in my temptations; and I appoint unto you, even as my Father appointed unto me a kingdom, that ye may eat and drink at my table in my kingdom; and ye shall sit on thrones judging the twelve tribes of Israel' (vv. 28-30). Matthew has recorded this text in a context which we have recognised as editorial (Matt. xix. 28). If the promise, however, was addressed to the disciples at the Supper, the link of connection in the third gospel has somehow disappeared. A bridge is absolutely necessary if the reader is to pass from ver. 27 to ver. 28. Has Luke, then, already recorded the passage which originally intervened? No critic has ever asked the question, but it must both be asked and answered; and fortunately, notwithstanding the critics, we are able to reconstruct the original. The following facts should be noted: (a) In the fourth gospel immediately after the lesson in humility the text is quoted, 'Verily, verily, I say unto you, A servant is not greater than his lord; neither one that is sent greater than he that sent him' (John xiii. 16). (b) This text is reported by Matthew in the first charge addressed to

the disciples, and is followed by a number of verses which unmistakably continue the subject (Matt. x. 24-33). The whole section is certainly an interpolation; for the early charge has been greatly enlarged by Matthew, and the transition is impossible from ver. 23 to ver. 24, and from ver. 33 to ver. 34. (c) Luke has reported the same passage after the warning against the leaven of the Pharisees (Luke xii. 2-9). The connection is here also editorial; for in the first place the words which follow bear no real inner relation to the leaven of the Pharisees, and secondly Luke has adapted the original to agree with his inference that the leaven of the Pharisees was hypocrisy (Luke xii. 3, cf. Matt. x. 27). The saying which John has reported and which introduces the section in the first gospel has not been recorded here by Luke; but since according to him the subject is hypocrisy, the saying in question could not be reported without loss of the verbal connection, and besides it has already been inserted in Luke's version of the Sermon on the Mount (Luke vi. 40). (d) When the whole passage thus free for transportation is conveyed to the account of the Supper, and placed before the promise which Luke has preserved in an approximately original situation, the sequence of thought authenticates itself, and the chasm is effectually bridged between ver. 27 and ver. 28. The disciples have been disputing about precedence and rank, and Jesus has rebuked them by precept and example: 'I am in the midst of you as he that serveth' (ver. 27). He now proceeds to enforce the lesson, and to remind them that instead of being reputed to be great they must expect, as long as they remain on the earth, to be despised and persecuted like their Master. Do not allow persecution, He says, to interfere with your testimony. What I tell you in the darkness speak ye in the light, and what ye hear in the ear proclaim upon the housetops. Do not be afraid of men who are able only to kill the body, but rather fear God who is able to destroy both soul and body in Gehenna. Your Father, who preserves even the sparrows, has numbered the hairs of your head. So far the connection is perfectly plain; and now, in conclusion, Jesus passes in thought from earth to heaven, and in two consecutive sayings He promises, first a reward to those who will confess Him before men, and then a special reward to the twelve who have continued with Him in His temptations. 'I appoint unto you, even as my Father appointed unto me a kingdom, that ye may eat and drink at my table in my kingdom ; and ye shall sit on thrones judging the twelve tribes of Israel.' The evidence is so complete and decisive that there is really no room for doubt.

5. We are now at last able to bring the argument to an end. The discourse is continued in the third gospel (vv. 31–38) ; but the sequel belongs properly to the next narrative, as we shall afterwards see. This need not at present be discussed. Two subjects remain for consideration. A reason must be given for the exclusion of Mark's additions, and the historical relation of the Last Supper to the Passover must, if possible, be precisely determined. These subjects cannot altogether be distinguished, for the one involves the other ; but the recognition of Judas as a traitor is distinct from the question regarding the Passover, and with this we begin our investigation. At first sight the evidence seems convincing in favour of the supposition that this fragment was a constituent of the apostolic narrative. It is reported by all the evangelists (Mark xiv. 18–21 ; Matt. xxvi. 21–25 ; Luke xxii. 21–23 ; John xiii. 21–30). Matthew, however, has certainly borrowed the fragment from the second gospel ; and that Luke's version has also been borrowed from Mark is proved by the fact that it interrupts the sequence of thought. We have, therefore, simply to take into account the testimony of Mark and John. Since these, however, are independent evangelists— we have no reason whatever to believe the contrary—the evidence seems still quite convincing. It is not antecedently impossible that each has independently adopted an ecclesiastical tradition ; but the habitual use by each of the apostolic source appears to exclude the alternative. Was Jesus, then, aware of the fact that Judas had become a traitor ? Did He identify the traitor at the Supper, and declare, ' Good were it for that man if he had not been born ' ? If this question is answered in the affirmative, the promise addressed to the disciples must be acknowledged to be surprising, ' Ye shall sit on thrones judging the twelve tribes of Israel ' (Luke xxii.

30). Did Jesus mean that the eleven apostles would judge the twelve tribes? The use of the numeral is in such a case scarcely intelligible. The thought could surely be expressed without mentioning the number of the tribes, and if Judas was deliberately excluded from the reward, the number would surely be also excluded. The twelve tribes presuppose the twelve apostles. The parallelism is such that demonstrative evidence is necessary to set aside the obvious inference; but the evidence in favour of Mark's fragment is not by any means demonstrative. It is, on the contrary, distinctly unreliable; for, in the first place, the differences between Mark's version and John's are such in themselves as to favour the hypothesis of an oral tradition, and, secondly, the woe which, according to Mark's account, was pronounced by Jesus on the traitor is an abstract from an earlier narrative. When the mothers who brought their children to Jesus were rebuked by the zealous disciples, the disciples in turn were sternly rebuked, and Jesus said, 'Woe unto the world because of occasions of stumbling: for it must needs be that the occasions come, but woe unto him through whom they come. It were well for him if a great millstone were hanged about his neck and he were sunk in the depth of the sea, rather than that he should cause one of these little ones to stumble.' The two texts are evidently coincident, and so far the woe which was pronounced at the Supper on Judas, according to the testimony of Mark, might be derived from the earlier narrative. But a mere possibility is not sufficient: we require more convincing evidence. The attention of the reader is invited to the following facts: (a) In teaching humility at the Supper, Jesus used a word which connects the lesson then taught with the earlier instruction suggested by the children. He said to His disciples, 'He that is the greater among you, let him become as the younger' (Luke xxii. 26). (b) Mark as a fact in chap. ix. 33-37 combines the two incidents and the two lessons. The dispute in ver. 33 is the dispute which arose at the Supper after the prediction of Christ's sufferings and death (cf. Mark ix. 31). The text in ver. 35, 'If any man would be first, he shall be last of all, and minister of all,' coincides obviously with the text delivered at the Supper (Mark x. 43, 44; Luke xxii. 26); and the rest of the narrative, as we have seen, is an abstract from the apostolic section regarding the kingdom and the child. The two incidents have clearly been combined. (c) Since Mark has abstracted from the account of the Supper an incident which he combines with the earlier narrative, the two narratives are associated in his thought, and the transference of the woe from the earlier to the later, for the sake of applying it to Judas, who became a notorious stumbling-block, ceases to be merely conjectural. But if the woe is excluded from Mark's fragment, little or nothing is left, and the whole becomes unreliable. These facts reduce the weight of the evidence, which at first sight seems to be convincing; and finally the original discourse at the Supper, as reconstructed in these pages, sends down to the ground the negative scale. The articulation of the thought, and the close connection between thought and action, exclude as an alien unapostolic addition the fragment recorded by Mark and John.

The next question to be considered is the relation of the Supper to the Passover. Three alternatives have been conceived as possible : (a) that the Supper was the paschal meal, and that Jesus was crucified on the 15th Nisan ; (b) that the Supper was instituted on the 13th, and that Jesus was crucified on the 14th ; (c) that the Supper was instituted on the evening at the beginning of the 14th, that is, after sunset on the 13th, and that Jesus was crucified on the 14th. The third only differs from the second as an attempt to reconcile Mark's statements. The reader need not be wearied with a minute discussion of the painful and laborious subject. A few facts, however, must be noticed. (a) The apostolic material in the third gospel is incompatible with the supposition that the Supper was the paschal meal; for Jesus began by saying that He had earnestly desired to eat the Passover with His disciples, but would not eat it until it would be fulfilled in the kingdom of God (Luke xxii. 15, 16). The supposition that these words were spoken on the 14th Nisan, and that He deliberately sacrificed a desire so earnestly cherished, is simply an exegetical evasion. Jesus did not drink of the fruit of the vine when He handed the cup to His disciples (ver. 17); but the inference that because He did not drink, the meal was the

Passover, of which He would not eat, is altogether unwarrantable. What He meant was that His enemies would prevent Him from eating the Passover, and that before the Passover He would not drink of the fruit of the vine. (*b*) According to the testimony of Mark, reproduced by Matthew and Luke, the Supper was really the paschal meal; and if Mark is right the inference necessarily follows that Jesus was crucified on the 15th Nisan. The attempts which have been made to escape from this obvious fact are futile evasions dictated by a theory of Scripture. 'On the first day of unleavened bread, when they sacrificed the Passover,' the disciples said unto Jesus, 'Where wilt thou that we go and make ready that thou mayest eat the Passover?' (Mark xiv. 12). This means, according to Dr. Westcott, immediately after sunset on the 13th Nisan; but the words are misleading if intended by Mark to convey such a meaning, for 'the first day of unleavened bread, when they sacrificed the Passover,' was a sunset later than the 13th Nisan. Dr. Westcott's exegesis is incredible. (*c*) The statement in Mark xiv. 12 presupposes that the crucifixion was on the 15th; but according to the testimony of the fourth gospel (John xix. 14), and indeed of Mark himself (Mark xv. 42), Jesus was crucified on the 14th, and according to the apostolic source the Supper was not the paschal meal. And, as Dr. Westcott says, 'the notion that Jesus was crucified on the 15th—a Sabbath—is set aside by the whole narrative, which is crowded with incidents of work.' What, then, are we bound to conclude? Indubitably this— that the fragment which Mark has recorded, identifying the Supper with the paschal meal, is an addition to the original narrative (Mark xiv. 12–16), and that the testimony of the fourth gospel is correct. (*d*) When Mark's interpolations are excluded from the narrative, the evening in ver. 17 is obviously the evening of the day on which Judas made his bargain (vv. 10, 11), and this again is described as 'two days before the Passover' (ver. 1). The story of the anointing is an interpolation which belongs properly to an earlier period. The date of the Supper is thus precisely defined—two days before the Passover, that is, according to the Hebrew mode of reckoning, any time before sunset on the 13th. We have no direct evidence to prove that Mark's introduction to the Supper (vv. 1, 2, 10, 11) was contained in the apostolic source, for these verses have been borrowed from the second gospel by both Matthew and Luke; but, on the other hand, we have no reason to reject them as editorial, and since they not only agree with the testimony of the fourth gospel, and of Luke's apostolic material, but also directly exclude the editorial interpolations of Mark, the probability is that they constitute the original introduction. In determining the relation of the Last Supper to the Passover, we have therefore also completed our reconstruction of the source.

b.—The hour in Luke xxii. 14 is the hour of the paschal meal. The apostolic source begins at ver. 15. The original of ver. 14 has probably been preserved by Mark, 'And when it was evening, he cometh with the twelve' (Mark xiv. 17). When the kingdom of God would come, the history of the Passover would be repeated; the old story would receive a new fulfilment. The judgment is certainly involved, and the allusion is to the heavenly kingdom. In the identification of the bread and wine with the body and blood of Jesus, Mark and Matthew are both secondary. They put out of sight the original application to the twelve, and keep in view the edification of believers. Mark thus writes, 'This is my blood of the covenant, which is shed for many' (ver. 24); and Matthew adds, 'unto remission of sins' (Matt. xxvi. 28). The original words at the institution of the Supper convey two thoughts. The first is that the death of Jesus would be a sacrifice well pleasing to God, whereby the new covenant would be sealed; and the second is that, in eating the bread and drinking the wine in remembrance of Him, the apostles would indicate their assent to the covenant, and as the representatives of Messiah would be made partakers of His body and blood. In the sacrifice of the old covenant (Exodus xxiv.), as Wendt truly says, 'there is no question whatever of an expiation of sins: the sprinkling was designed to bring the assembled people into a manifest relation to the sacrifice, so that it would be evident that this was the community for whom the offering was to be presented, who virtually signified by this offering their consent to the covenant, and who now expected from God the beneficent results of the covenant sealed by the sacrifice.'[1] Two mistakes, however, have been made by Wendt. In the first place, he enlarges the significance of the Supper in such a way that according to him Jesus anticipated the formation of a church. 'The disciples of Jesus,' he says, 'were to partake of His body offered and His blood shed, for the covenant sacrifice, in order by this partaking to confess His sacrificial death and to acknowledge themselves as His Church for whom the new covenant was sealed.'[2] But the words were addressed to apostles, who could not acknowledge themselves as Christ's Church, and were simply required to remember Him as His representatives on the earth. Wendt has failed to perceive the precise historical significance of the Supper. And, secondly, he has altogether misapprehended the nature of the covenant to which Jesus referred. 'In declaring His own death to be the sacrifice of the new covenant,' Jesus, according to Wendt, 'regarded that death as a valuable and well-pleasing offering or service to God, whereby the new and perfect relation of fellowship and blessing between God and men, denoted in the conception of the kingdom of God, would be brought to an established condition.'[3] This means that the kingdom of God had already been partially realised, and that Jesus contemplated an earthly enlargement and establishment of the new and perfect relation among men; but the conception of the kingdom of God, which is involved in the institution of the Supper and conveyed in the whole teaching of Jesus, does not denote a relation of fellowship and blessing between God and men on the earth. Such a relation is rather the necessary preparation for the coming of the kingdom. The Passover could not be fulfilled in such a relation, but is explained by the apocalyptic discourse; and the covenant, like the Passover, would be fulfilled in the kingdom of heaven, when, after passing through the baptism of death, Messiah would return in His glory to accomplish the good pleasure of God. The conception of Wendt is not the conception of Jesus. Professor Bruce makes a similar mistake. He translates into 'abstract

---

[1] *The Teaching of Jesus*, vol. ii. p. 318.   [2] *Ibid.* vol. ii. pp. 319, 320.
[3] *Ibid.* vol. ii. p. 237.

and didactic language' the words which, as he believes, were addressed to Peter, 'in a highly emotional and Hebrew manner,' after the confession at Cæsarea Philippi, but which, as we have seen, were really delivered, in so far as they are genuine words of Jesus, after the institution of the Supper. He finds in these words an announcement of three great truths: 'first, that the church to be founded was to be Christian, or, to put it otherwise, that the person of the Founder was of fundamental importance; second, that as such it should be practically identical with the kingdom of God He had hitherto preached; third, that in this Church the righteousness of the kingdom should find its home.'[1] The original of which this abstract and didactic language is a translation consists of the following texts: first, 'Thou art Peter, and on this rock I will build my church;' second, 'I will give unto thee the keys of the kingdom of heaven;' third, 'Whatsoever thou shalt bind on earth shall be bound in heaven, and whatsoever thou shalt loose on earth shall be loosed in heaven.' If Jesus intended to teach the three great truths which Professor Bruce finds in these texts, He adopted a strange mode of expression—not merely emotional and Hebrew, but entirely unintelligible and misleading. The keys of the kingdom of heaven were intended to open the kingdom of heaven, and surely not to identify it with a Petrine church on the earth. Binding and loosing do not constitute righteousness. When translated into abstract language, the third text does not amount 'to a declaration that the moral judgment of the church about to be founded would be sound, wholesome, in all its actings in accordance with eternal truth.'[2] Professor Bruce himself assumes that the text was addressed to Peter and not to the Church; and as a fact it was addressed to neither the one nor the other, but to the twelve apostles, who, instead of building a church to be the home of righteousness, were instructed by their Master to be always in readiness for His second coming, and for their home in the eternal tabernacles. When interpreters are reduced to such abstract didactic and fanciful translations, they have reason to suspect their theory of the gospels.

[1] *The Kingdom of God,* p. 262. [2] *Ibid.* p. 266.

c.—Matthew has reproduced from the second gospel the request of James and John (Matt. xx. 20-28). He spares James and John at the expense of their mother (ver. 20). He adds that they came 'worshipping' (ver. 20). He substitutes 'in thy kingdom' for 'in thy glory' (ver. 21), and 'am about to drink' for 'drink' (ver. 22). He omits the allusion to the baptism (vv. 22, 23), and adds the words 'of my Father' (ver. 23). He substitutes 'your servant' for 'servant of all' (ver. 27). These variations are distinctly editorial. We have, therefore, simply to take into account three versions of the famous text which is embedded in the narrative. The first is, 'If any man would be first, he shall be last of all, and minister of all' (διάκονος, Mark ix. 35); the second, 'Whosoever would become great among you, shall be your minister (διάκονος): and whosoever would be first among you, shall be servant of all (δοῦλος); for verily the Son of Man came not to be ministered unto, but to minister (διακονῆσαι), and to give his life a ransom for many' (Mark x. 43-45); the third, 'He that is the greater among you, let him become as the younger; and he that is chief, as he that doth serve (ὁ διακονῶν). For whether is greater, he that sitteth at meat, or he that serveth? is not he that sitteth at meat? but I am in the midst of you as he that serveth' (ὁ διακονῶν, Luke xxii. 26, 27). These texts clearly coincide, and each of them cannot be original. The question is, Which represents with greatest fidelity the words which were spoken by Jesus? Certainly not the first, which is merely an abstract, and may therefore be summarily dismissed. In favour of Luke's version I submit the following facts: (1) It is authenticated by the context. At the Supper Jesus neither ate nor drank. He said, 'I will not drink of the fruit of the vine, until the kingdom of God shall come' (ver. 18). He gave the bread and wine to His disciples, and could therefore appropriately ask, 'Whether is greater, he that sitteth at meat, or he that serveth? is not he that sitteth at meat? but I am in the midst of you as he that serveth' (ver. 27). Mark's version is much less appropriate. (2) We must choose between two alternatives. Either Mark has enlarged, or Luke has reduced, the significance of the original text. The enlargement is antecedently much more probable than the reduction. (3) Luke's words, 'the younger,' are authenticated by Mark's association of the teaching at the Supper with the lesson suggested by the children (Mark ix. 33-37). (4) The distinction in Mark's version between the minister and the servant is intelligible as an abstract from the original context; for, according to our reconstruction, Jesus proceeded to say, 'The disciple is not above his master, nor the servant (δοῦλος) above his lord; but the disciple when he is perfected shall be as his master, and the servant as his lord' (Matt. x. 24, 25; Luke vi. 40). These words might well suggest the idea that the disciple who would make himself a servant would rank higher in the kingdom than the minister on account of his greater lowliness and more exacting obligations. Mark's text is therefore probably secondary—'Whosoever would become great among you, shall be your minister: and whosoever would be first among you, shall be servant of all.' (5) On the supposition that the whole narrative was originally situated in the account of the Supper, Luke xxii. 27 would inevitably be modified when transferred to an earlier context. On the road to Jerusalem, Jesus obviously could not be reported as saying, 'Whether is greater, he that sitteth at meat, or he that serveth? is not he that sitteth at meat? but I am in the midst of you as he that serveth.' The transference of the incident to the open road would make modification imperative. (6) The last clause in Mark's version, 'For verily the Son of Man came not to be ministered unto, but to minister, and to give his life a ransom for many,' is similar to the additions which Mark and Matthew have made to the statement regarding the cup. Mark writes, 'This is my blood of the covenant, which is shed for many,' and Matthew adds, 'unto remission of sins.' But these additions are editorial. The ransom-text is therefore probably editorial. (7) This text, like the earlier clause, is intelligible as an inference drawn from the sequel. The ransom is the price given for the emancipation of a slave. Whatever the precise theological significance of Mark's text may be, it certainly means that Jesus gave His life to redeem many from bondage, that they might no longer be servants. But according to our reconstruction, Jesus proceeded to say that the servant when perfected would be as his lord, and He called the disciples His friends. 'I say unto you my friends, Be not afraid of them which kill the body, and after that have no more that they can do' (Luke xii. 4). The two thoughts are parallel, and Mark has simply inferred that Christ's sacrifice is the price of emancipation—an inference which is perfectly intelligible, since, according to Mark, the blood of the new covenant would be shed for many, and would, according to Matthew, be shed 'unto remission of sins.' (8) Luke's text is authenticated by the fourth gospel; for in the first place the aim of John is to show that at the Supper Jesus was in the midst as one that serveth (John xiii. 1–17), and secondly he translates the original of the ransom-text in such a way as to prove that the ransom is an editorial addition. 'Greater love hath no man than this, that a man lay down his life for his friends. Ye are my friends, if ye do the things which I command you. No longer do I call you servants; for the servant knoweth not what his lord doeth: but I have called you friends; for all things that I heard from my Father I have made known unto you' (John xv. 13–15). Mark and John have each interpreted the original. In the new designation of the disciples as friends, John sees a manifestation of love; and the sacrifice of the new covenant is also to him a great ethical fact, a revelation of the Father in the Son. Mark, on the other hand, is more distinctly theological. But if the version of John is editorial, Mark's is equally editorial, and the text as reconstructed in these pages represents with greatest fidelity the words which were spoken by Jesus.

The ingenuity of interpreters has been much exercised by the famous ransom-text. Wendt e.g. compares the text with the gracious invitation in Matt. xi. 28–30, and according to him, when Jesus announced that He would give His life to free many from a state of servitude, 'He meant the inward deliverance from the pressure of sufferings, which He taught from the example of His own course of action.'[1] But the gracious invitation belongs to a much earlier context, and the idea which Mark intends to convey must certainly be defined by the words at the Supper—'This is the new covenant in my blood, even that which is poured out for you.' Mark

[1] *The Teaching of Jesus*, vol. ii. p. 231.

enlarges the significance of these words. In his version the blood of the new covenant is shed for many; and the meaning obviously is that the Son of Man came to give His life a ransom for many. The one text defines the other. The idea cannot therefore merely be subjective emancipation from servitude by the patient endurance of sufferings. The deliverance becomes inward on account of an outward redemption; that is, according to the theology of Mark, the subjective state of salvation is conditioned by the objective self-sacrifice, which was accomplished by Jesus when He shed His blood for many. The sacrifice of the new covenant does not merely convey the ethical truth that by patient endurance the pressure of suffering is reduced. It is an offering well pleasing to God, which insures to those who acknowledge the obligations of the covenant the ultimate fulfilment of the promise; and this thought of the objective value of Christ's sacrifice in relation to God cannot be excluded from the word 'ransom.' In attempting to distinguish the two ideas, Wendt is guilty of an exegetical evasion. Professor Bruce is equally ingenious, but in a different direction. He does not attempt to make the ransom purely subjective and ethical. He maintains the genuineness of Mark's text and its objective significance. ' The solitariness of the utterance,' he says, ' has been pressed into the service of a suspicious criticism; but the genuineness of the word "ransom" can hardly be doubted in view of the fact that it is recorded by both Matthew and Mark, though the absence of a text so Pauline in character from Luke's narrative is certainly surprising.'[1] The unsuspicious nature of Professor Bruce's criticism is even more surprising. Matthew's text is simply a reproduction of Mark's. The statement, therefore, that the genuineness of the word 'ransom' is guaranteed by the agreement of these two evangelists is altogether incompetent. The criticism which rejects the word as editorial is not necessarily merely suspicious, but is, on the contrary, supported by adequate evidence. Professor Bruce traces the genesis of the saying to the Temple-tax incident, ' which happened at Capernaum just before the final departure from Galilee;' and he paraphrases the words

[1] *The Kingdom of God*, p. 235.

as follows: 'Then they asked of me a small coin for their temple, which I had not to give; now they ask of me my life, which it is in my power freely to lay down. This life, though they know it not, is, like the half-shekel, their ransom money, and I gladly yield it up to save their souls from death.'[1] No criticism could very well be more subjective than this; for the suggestion is altogether conjectural, without one particle of textual evidence. The genesis of the saying need not be traced so far back. The text is explained by its original context. In this 'profound saying' Jesus has not 'bequeathed to His Church a theological problem.'[2] The theology is Mark's; and the problem, which is purely critical, can be solved with little difficulty.

The few details which remain to be noticed need not be minutely discussed. (1) The example of lowly service which is recorded in the fourth gospel and is unknown to the other evangelists—the washing of the disciples' feet—is an object lesson derived probably from Luke xii. 37, and suggested by Luke xxii. 27. The earlier text was included in the apocalyptic discourse which immediately preceded the Supper. (2) Matt. x. 25 is secondary in form. Jesus did not say, 'It is enough for the disciple that he be as his master, and the servant as his lord.' The thought required by the context is that, when the disciple is like his master or the servant like his lord, he is complete and perfect (Luke vi. 40). (3) The allusion to Beelzebub (Matt. x. 25) accounts for the context in which Luke places the passage, and this context accounts for the omission of the allusion. The Pharisees against whom Jesus warned His disciples (Luke xii. 1) had said, 'By Beelzebub the prince of the devils casteth he out devils' (Luke xi. 15). (4) Matt. x. 29–33 is probably primary in form. Luke has made the sparrows a little cheaper, and has avoided the inference that God's fatherly love is manifested in the preservation of sparrows (Luke xii. 6). He has also substituted 'the Son of Man' for the pronoun of the first person, and 'before the angels of God' for 'before my Father which is in heaven' (ver. 8). (5) Mark has reported Matt. x. 26, Luke xii. 2 after the parable of the Sower, in a context which is manifestly secondary (Mark iv. 22). (6) He has

[1] *The Kingdom of God*, p. 240.   [2] *Ibid.* p. 242.

also reported Matt. x. 33 in a secondary form and context (Mark viii. 38). (7) The words, 'that ye may eat and drink at my table in my kingdom,' authenticate Luke's version of the promise addressed to the twelve (Luke xxii. 28-30). Matthew has transferred the saying from its original context, and has therefore omitted the allusion to the table (Matt. xix. 28). (8) The statement that, when Jesus and His disciples sang a hymn, they went out unto the Mount of Olives, presupposes that the Supper was the paschal meal, and must therefore be rejected with the rest of Mark's editorial additions (Mark xiv. 26). John's words, 'Arise, let us go hence,' represent the movement of the company from the room to the road (John xiv. 31).

§ 50.—*A Discourse on the Road to the Garden*

It is antecedently improbable that a source which is complete as far as the Supper should leave unrecorded the last events in Jerusalem. Weiss concludes with the narrative of the anointing, which followed, as he believes, the discourse on the second coming. Wendt rejects the narrative of the anointing, but in one of his appendices he adds the apostolic material which Luke has inserted in ch. xxii. 15-38. He does not pass beyond the Supper. He agrees with Weiss in assuming that the apostolic source contained no account of the Passion. The evidence which leads to so improbable a conclusion may be supposed to be at least sufficient to discredit the contrary opinion; but the truth is, as will be shown, that the evidence carries us on from the upper room to the garden, from the garden to the trial, from the trial to the cross, from the cross to the empty tomb. At present we are only concerned with a discourse which may be reconstructed as follows:

1. After the promise of the twelve thrones, Luke records a brief dialogue between Jesus and Peter (Luke xxii. 31-34). The original connection has clearly been lost, for there is nothing in the preceding verses to account for the words, 'Simon, Simon, behold, Satan asked to have you, that he might sift you as wheat.' How can these words be explained? According to the second gospel, after Jesus and His disciples

had left the upper room to go to the Mount of Olives, He foretold that the Shepherd would be smitten and the sheep would be scattered abroad; and Peter declared that, although all might be offended, he would not (Mark xiv. 27-29). Three facts are here quite obvious. The first is that the verses which follow in the second gospel (vv. 30, 31) coincide with part of Luke's dialogue (Luke xxii. 33, 34). The second is that Luke has not borrowed these verses from Mark, but has taken them from the apostolic source; and the third is that the address to Simon which Luke has preserved is made intelligible by the prediction in the second gospel. Again, Luke has a reason for omitting the prediction. According to Mark, Jesus said, ' Howbeit, after I am raised up, I will go before you into Galilee' (ver. 28). This seems to be an announcement of the resurrection, and was certainly regarded by the evangelists as such; but Luke does not believe that after the resurrection Jesus appeared to the disciples in Galilee. He deliberately avoids Mark's announcement in Luke xxiv. 6, 7 (cf. Mark xvi. 7); and according to him the manifestations were all in Judæa (Luke xxiv. 13-53). Mark also has a reason for omitting Luke xxii. 31, 32. After the announcement, reported to have been made at Cæsarea Philippi, that the Son of Man must suffer many things, and be rejected by the elders and chief priests and Scribes, and be killed, and after three days rise again, he has already recorded a similar saying. ' Peter took him, and began to rebuke him. But he turning about, and seeing his disciples, rebuked Peter, and saith, Get thee behind me, Satan: for thou mindest not the things of God, but the things of men' (Mark viii. 31-33). Mark's account of the confession of Peter is an editorial mosaic. The announcement in ver. 31 coincides with the announcement in Mark xiv. 27, 28. The rebuke of Peter in ver. 33 coincides with Luke xxii. 31, 32; and the coincidence is made more complete by Matthew's report, in which the saying, 'Thou art a stumbling-block unto me' (Matt. xvi. 23), is an abstract from the original context (Mark xiv. 27-29). Mark, therefore, has already combined the rebuke of Peter on the road to the garden with the confession at Cæsarea Philippi, and when he reaches the later context he omits Luke xxii. 31, 32 to avoid editorial repetition. Finally, Luke has a reason for adding vv. 31, 32 immediately to the promise of the thrones. He omits the movement from the room to the road, partly because he omits the prediction (Mark xiv. 27-29), and partly to connect the rebuke of Peter with the contention which arose among the twelve (ver. 24). The method of each evangelist is apparent. The fragments which each has recorded are demanded by the fragments of the other. The omissions are perfectly intelligible; and so we gain as the apostolic sequel to the Supper a narrative consisting of the following passages: Luke xxii. 39; Mark xiv. 27-29; Luke xxii. 31-34.

2. The next fragment in the third gospel is a charge addressed by Jesus to the disciples (vv. 35-38). Wendt makes the remark that there is no inner relation between this fragment and the preceding verses;[1] but, in the first place, no close inner relation is required, for Jesus has left the upper room, and the discourse at the Supper has been finished; and secondly, when Jesus announced to His disciples that He would go before them into Galilee as a shepherd before his sheep, He certainly contemplated the beginning of a new period in their testimony. But this announcement was made immediately before the charge at which we have now arrived. A sufficient connection is therefore obvious: the charge is historically intelligible, and Wendt's difficulty entirely disappears. Unquestionably, however, there is still a difficulty which Wendt has failed to perceive; for the fragment concludes unexpectedly, 'And they said, Lord, here are two swords: and he said, It is enough' (ver. 38). This is clearly a parenthesis, and a sequel is imperatively demanded to continue the interrupted discourse. Luke's conclusion is like the trunk of a tree which has been cut by the woodman's axe. The cleft is unmistakable. How, then, are we to reconstruct the original? I submit the following facts. (a) In the early charge to the twelve, Matthew has inserted a few passages which have not yet been considered; and one of these begins with the words, 'Think not that I came to send peace on the earth: I came not to send peace, but a sword' (Matt. x. 34-36). (b) Luke has

[1] *Die Lehre Jesu*, Erster Theil, S. 174.

inserted this passage immediately after a saying which was delivered by Jesus at the Supper (Luke xii. 51–53). The context in each case is certainly editorial. The fragment is therefore free to be transferred to the later charge. (c) Luke's version is slightly different from Matthew's. It begins thus: 'Think ye that I am come to give peace in the earth? I tell you, Nay; but rather division' (ver. 51). The critics have generally assumed that Luke's word 'division' is secondary, and that Matthew's word 'sword' represents the original text; and certainly the more definite and concrete word is much to be preferred to the other. The word 'division' is more closely related to the sequel, for Jesus proceeded to say that from henceforth five in one house would be divided, three against two, and two against three (ver. 52); but just for this reason Luke has probably altered the original. In any case the result is the same; for if Matthew's word is primary, it attests the sequence proposed; and if Matthew's word is secondary, it has been derived from the original context. A finger post points out the truth, and the critics have taken the wrong road. (d) The supposition that Luke xxii. 35–38 was originally followed by Luke xii. 51–53 (Matt. x. 34–36) is verified by the thought-connection. The disciples have been instructed to go no more without purse or wallet or shoes. They have been charged to buy a sword, and if necessary to sell their cloke that they may make the purchase. This obviously requires explanation. Jesus accounts for the charge by predicting the injustice to which He will soon Himself be subjected. 'This,' He says, 'which is written must be fulfilled in me, And he was reckoned with transgressors; for that which concerneth me hath fulfilment.' Are the disciples, then, to defend their Master with the sword? Certainly not. He is preparing them for a new period in their testimony, and He alludes to His own impending sufferings that they may know what to expect in bearing witness to Him. Think not, He proceeds to say, that I came to send peace on the earth: I tell you, Nay; but rather a sword. It is written that Messiah must suffer and be reckoned with transgressors; but it is not written that you must be killed. You need not go voluntarily to the cross without attempting to escape from injustice. He that hath none, let him sell his cloke and buy a sword. Be prepared for the inevitable future. Do not be taken by surprise. Jesus thus gives a second reason for the strange and unexpected charge. A second is necessary, since the first is incomplete and misleading. The interrupted discourse is continued. The difficulty of the parenthesis is avoided; and a context is found for a fragment which would be otherwise unattached. (e) In Matthew's version of the early charge to the twelve, there is another passage which has not yet been considered. The words in ver. 16, 'Behold, I send you forth as sheep in the midst of wolves,' have been carried forward by Matthew from the situation represented by Luke x. 3 to be combined with the first of the additions (vv. 16^b–23). These verses have been abbreviated by Luke, and inserted after a passage which belongs to the discourse at the Supper (Luke xii. 11, 12). Luke thus suggests that the whole fragment which Matthew has preserved was originally situated after the Supper; and certainly this fragment is an editorial addition which Matthew has made to the early charge. The experience which Jesus here teaches His disciples to anticipate is unintelligible at the beginning of the ministry, and, on the other hand, it is obviously in perfect agreement with the charge which was delivered on the road to the garden. It is indeed demanded by the later discourse; for although the connection, as far as we have gone in our reconstruction, is clear and articulate, the thought is still incomplete. The household divisions account for the charge to buy a sword, but they are not parallel to the experience which Jesus anticipated for Himself when He said, 'This which is written must be fulfilled in me, And he was reckoned with transgressors.' The fragment which Matthew has inserted in the earlier discourse sets forth the result of the divisions, and makes the parallelism complete. 'They will deliver you up to councils, and in their synagogues they will scourge you: yea and before governors and kings shall ye be brought for my sake, for a testimony to them and to the Gentiles.' Again, the use which Jesus intended His disciples to make of the sword is still unquestionably obscure. Did He really intend to teach that they should resist unto blood, fighting with the weapons of the world? To this there are three serious objections. In the first place, the precept thus interpreted contradicts His own earlier teaching (cf. Matt. v. 38, 39) ; and secondly, Luke's parenthesis shows that when the disciples understood Him to inculcate the use of the sword they betrayed a lack of apprehension. ' They said, Lord, here are two swords. And He said, It is enough.' And thirdly, when one of the disciples cut off the ear of a man in the garden, Jesus said quickly and sternly, 'Put up again thy sword into its place : for all they that take the sword shall perish with the sword ' (Matt. xxvi. 52). What, then, is the meaning of the precept ? It is antecedently improbable that Jesus would leave so important a saying unexplained, for ambiguity in this case might lead to serious mistakes ; and when the sequence proposed is adopted the ambiguity entirely disappears. After predicting the household divisions Jesus proceeds to state a rule of conduct which defines the earlier precept, and prevents the possibility of misapprehension. 'Be ye therefore wise as serpents, and harmless as doves' (Matt. x. 16). Wendt takes for granted that this saying was delivered in the early charge to the twelve, and immediately followed the words, ' Behold, I send you forth as sheep in the midst of wolves.'[1] But Luke does not record the later comparison ; and although the wisdom of the serpent might be useful to the disciples in their mission near the beginning of the ministry, the necessity of such wisdom is much more apparent in relation to the later persecutions. The combination in the first gospel is also somewhat superfluous. 'Be wise as serpents' is intelligible ; but ' be harmless as doves ' is certainly not a precept which one would expect to be addressed to men who have already and in the same breath been described as ' sheep in the midst of wolves.' The sheep or the lamb is at least as harmless as the dove, and why should a new figure be employed ? The truth is that the precept now under discussion is altogether out of place in the early charge, and is, on the other hand, demanded by the charge on the road to the garden. In the earlier case the one thought is that the disciples are to make no provision for their journey, whereas in the later the thought is precisely the opposite, and therefore the serpent must now be combined with the dove.

[1] *Die Lehre Jesu*, Erster Theil, S. 85.

The wisdom of the serpent consists in taking purse and wallet and shoes, and in being prepared for emergencies, like men with sword in hand. The harmlessness of the dove consists in doing violence to no man, in fleeing to the next city when persecuted in this (Matt. x. 23), and in trusting to the sword of the Spirit before councils and governors and kings. 'When they deliver you up, be not anxious how or what ye shall speak: for it shall be given you in that hour what ye shall speak. For it is not ye that speak, but the Spirit of your Father that speaketh in you' (vv. 19, 20). (*f*) According to the testimony of the fourth gospel, Jesus delivered on the road to the garden a discourse which is unmistakably a paraphrase of the original above reconstructed. The parable of the Vine with its sequel (John xv. 1-16) is a combination of apostolic passages (e.g. Luke xiii. 6-9; Matt. x. 24, 25; Luke xii. 4), suggested by Mark xiv. 27-29; Luke xxii. 31-34. The prediction in John xvi. 32 coincides verbally with Mark xiv. 27; and the rest of the discourse in the fourth gospel (John xv. 17-xvi. 33) is a free translation in the Johannine manner of Luke xxii. 35-38; xii. 51-53; Matt. x. 16^b-23. The evidence is thus complete and decisive in favour of the reconstruction proposed.

a.—Two questions here arise for consideration, one of them textual and the other exegetical; but as the textual question—whether Mark or Luke has preserved the original prediction regarding Peter (Mark xiv. 30; Luke xxii. 34)—cannot properly be answered without anticipating a later narrative, we may provisionally assume that Luke's text is the more reliable. What, then, did Jesus mean when He said, 'After I am raised up, I will go before you into Galilee'? (Mark xiv. 28). The saying must certainly be interpreted in relation to the preceding words, 'It is written, I will smite the shepherd, and the sheep will be scattered abroad.' The thought, therefore, is that the dispersion would not be final, but that in some way after being smitten the Shepherd would gather together and go before His flock. The text has been paraphrased by the fourth evangelist, and this is clearly the idea which it conveyed to his mind. 'My sheep hear my voice, and I know them, and they follow me: and I give unto them eternal life;

and they shall never perish, and no one shall snatch them out of my hand. My Father, which hath given them unto me, is greater than all; and no one is able to snatch them out of the Father's hand' (John x. 27-29). So far the meaning is plain; but did Jesus intend to assure His disciples that His body would be raised from the dead, and would appear to them visibly? I reply in the negative for the following reasons: (1) The text does not necessarily involve a physical resurrection and a visible appearance, but is perfectly intelligible on the supposition that what Jesus anticipated was simply the recovery of His disciples from their temporary panic, when He Himself would be raised to the heavenly kingdom. 'I will go before you' does not necessarily mean 'I will go before you in the body,' but is rather to be explained by the earlier saying, 'Where two or three are gathered together in my name, there am I in the midst of them' (Matt. xviii. 20). (2) By substituting for the text the parable of the Vine—an editorial version of the parable of the Fig Tree (Luke xiii. 6-9)—John shows that the idea conveyed to his mind is that of abiding in Christ. 'Abide in me, and I in you. As the branch cannot bear fruit of itself, except it abide in the vine: so neither can ye, except ye abide in me' (John xv. 4, cf. xiv. 19). (3) The charge which was subsequently delivered to the disciples is incompatible with the supposition that Jesus taught them to expect a visible appearance in Galilee. He instructed Peter to stablish the brethren (Luke xxii. 32). He assured them that He would indeed return, but not till the coming of the kingdom. 'Verily I say unto you, Ye shall not have gone through the cities of Israel, till the Son of Man be come' (Matt. x. 23, cf. John xvi. 17). The whole discourse is unmistakably the last charge to the disciples on earth, and therefore forbids the assumption that a return from the tomb had been announced. (4) If the three synoptists agree in supposing that the text is a prediction which was afterwards fulfilled in the resurrection of Jesus on the third day, Luke, on the other hand, by deliberately omitting the prediction, and by confining the manifestations to Judæa, shows clearly that he did not believe in the alleged fulfilment. The facts cannot otherwise be satisfactorily explained; and since the fourth gospel—excluding the appendix (ch. xxi.), which is probably a later addition—agrees in this respect with Luke, the probability undoubtedly is that the alleged fulfilment arose out of a misconception of the text, and that a visible appearance to the disciples, in Galilee or Judæa or anywhere else, before the coming of the kingdom, was not predicted by Jesus.

b.—Matthew has omitted Luke xxii. 35-38 because this passage could obviously not be combined with the earlier charge to the twelve. Luke has substituted 'the Holy Spirit' for 'the Spirit of your Father' (Luke xii. 12, cf. Matt. x. 20), and has adapted the original to his editorial context, omitting a few verses for the sake of connection. Mark has dispersed the contents of this section. Mark ix. 1 is parallel to Matt. x. 23, and Mark xiii. 9-13 to Matt. x. 17-22. Mark has omitted Matt. x. 23 because this verse has already been inserted by him in ch. ix. 1. He has simply adapted the original to his context. The words, 'Yea and before governors and kings shall ye be brought for my sake, for a testimony to them and to the Gentiles' (Matt. x. 18), have been rendered by Mark a little differently—'Before governors and kings shall ye stand for my sake, for a testimony unto them. And the gospel must first be preached unto all the nations' (Mark xiii. 9, 10). Dr. Abbott finds in these texts 'demonstrative evidence' in favour of his theory of a common tradition, but he has been deceived by his theory. The truth is perfectly evident. Matthew has preserved the original text, which was written in the apostolic source; and Mark has inferred from the testimony to the Gentiles that before the coming of the kingdom the gospel would be preached unto all the nations. His inference is purely editorial. In ch. xxiv. 14 Matthew has reproduced Mark's text.

§ 51.—*The Agony and the Arrest in the Garden*

That the apostolic source contained an account of the agony and the arrest in the garden is established by the following facts: (1) The source contained an account of the journey to the garden. This has already been proved. But if Jesus and His disciples left the upper room to go to the Mount of Olives, a sequel is absolutely necessary. No writer would stop so suddenly. It is altogether incredible that a history should be concluded on the road. (2) In reproducing Mark's account of the arrest, Matthew has added a fragment derived from the apostolic source (Matt. xxvi. 52-54). The quick and stern rebuke of the zealous disciple, 'Put up again thy sword into its place: for all they that take the sword shall perish with the sword' (ver. 52), is certainly not editorial; and although the words which follow are less clearly authentic, they would not be likely to be introduced without documentary authority. Ver. 54 is probably the original which suggested Mark xiv. 49 (Matt. xxvi. 56); ver. 53 might be omitted by Luke on account of Luke xxii. 43, and ver. 52 on account of Luke xxii. 86. Luke betrays by the words, 'Suffer ye thus far,' that he has abbreviated the original text, and added the healing of the ear (Luke xxii. 51). Again, since the two reasons reported by Matthew are parallel to the instruction delivered on the road (Matt. x. 16; Luke xxii. 37), each seems to be demanded by the context. The rebuke is not weakened by the second, but is rather made more severe. The whole fragment is therefore apostolic, and an account of the arrest in the garden was contained in the apostolic source. (3) The independence of Luke's version is guaranteed by its greater simplicity, and by details which are manifestly primary. Mark distinguishes Peter and James and John from the rest of the apostles (ver. 33, cf. Mark v. 37; ix. 2; xiii. 3). He represents the temptation of Jesus as three times repeated (cf. Matt. iv. 1-11; Luke xxii. 44). He introduces a distinction between the spirit and the flesh, which is without parallel in the teaching of Jesus (ver. 38). The allusion to the hour in ver. 35 is an abstract from Luke xxii. 53. The words, 'But this is done that the scriptures might be fulfilled' (ver. 49), have probably been borrowed from Matt. xxvi. 54 and substituted for Luke xxii. 53—'This is your hour, and the power of darkness.' The panic of the disciples (vv. 50-52) is unknown to the fourth evangelist, and has been reproduced by Matthew from Mark, and is intelligible as an inference drawn from the prediction in Mark xiv. 27. Again, the whole narrative of the agony, in the second gospel, is connected by coincidence of expression with the earlier narrative of the Transfiguration (Mark xiv. 33, cf. ix. 2; xiv. 40, cf. ix. 6).

Mark's version has probably been elaborated; and, on the other hand, Luke's has not merely the primary characteristic of greater simplicity, but also contains authentic details omitted by Mark, and is more in accordance with the historical situation. In ver. 43 we are told that an angel from heaven appeared unto Jesus strengthening Him, and in ver. 44 that His sweat became as it were great drops of blood falling down upon the ground. These verses do not occur in some of the ancient manuscripts, and the question arises whether copyists interpolated or omitted them. The omission of ver. 43 is intelligible on account of Matt. xxvi. 53 (cf. Matt. iv. 11), and ver. 44 is more intelligible as the original which suggested the repetition of the prayer in Mark's version than as a later addition. The evidence against these verses is not by any means convincing, and, on the whole, we must conclude that they were contained in the original text, and omitted by certain copyists. Again, the version of Luke is authenticated by its closer relation to the preceding discourse. On the road to the garden Jesus had been predicting the persecutions and trials which would beset the disciples; and at the Mount of Olives He said unto them, 'Pray that ye enter not into temptation,' and went apart and prayed Himself, 'Father, if thou be willing, remove this cup from me: nevertheless, not my will, but thine, be done' (vv. 40, 41). The connection is here self-evident; but Mark, by emphasising the necessity of watchfulness (Mark xiv. 34, 37, 38), identifies the anticipated temptation with the approach of Judas and the band. In the apocalyptic discourse, delivered no doubt also at the Mount of Olives, the disciples had been instructed to watch, but after the charge on the road to the garden the chief necessity was prayer. 'Why sleep ye? rise and pray, that ye enter not into temptation' (Luke xxii. 46). Mark has substituted the word 'watch' for 'rise' (Mark xiv. 38), and has applied the general precept to a definite and later situation. Luke's version is altogether more reliable. Ver. 39 originally preceded vv. 31–38, and the sequel from ver. 40 to ver. 53 has been taken from the apostolic source.

§ 52.—*The Court of the High Priest*

The connection between the arrest and the narrative which follows in the third gospel is such, that if the first is apostolic the other is also apostolic. According to the testimony of Mark, Jesus was seized immediately after He received the kiss (Mark xiv. 46). According to Luke, when the disciples saw what would follow, that is, saw that He would be seized, they asked, 'Lord, shall we smite with the sword?' (Luke xxii. 49). But the attack on the servant of the high priest is scarcely intelligible if Jesus was already in the hands of the soldiers, and the sequel in the third gospel is an obvious continuation of the earlier narrative. It begins with the following words, 'And they seized him, and led him away, and brought him unto the high priest's house' (ver. 54, cf. Mark xiv. 53). The connection in itself is sufficient to authenticate the narrative which follows as apostolic; and two facts establish the conclusion: (1) In the first place Mark's arrangement is editorial. He reports that, when Jesus was taken to the high priest's house, all the chief priests and the elders and the Scribes came together (ver. 53). In other words, there was a meeting of the Sanhedrin; but in the morning there was another meeting of the Sanhedrin—'the chief priests with the elders and Scribes, and the whole council, had a consultation' (Mark xv. 1). The necessity of the two meetings is not quite obvious; and the first is not only in itself improbable, but is also at variance with the third and fourth gospels, according to which Jesus was simply taken to the high priest's house (Luke xxii. 54; John xviii. 13). Luke's narrative is much more reliable than Mark's. The internal evidence is decidedly in favour of the conclusion that Mark xiv. 55-65 is an interpolation transferred from ch. xv. 1, for ver. 66 is a return to ver. 54; and since in the third and fourth gospels ver. 66 immediately follows ver. 54, the internal evidence is confirmed (Luke xxii. 56; John xviii. 17). The truth, therefore, is that Jesus was taken to the high priest's house, and was examined before the Sanhedrin next morning. John has inferred, without documentary authority, that He was taken first to the house of

Annas (John xviii. 13), and sent by Annas to Caiaphas (ver. 24), and that the examination was conducted by Annas. (2) According to the testimony of Mark, Peter denied his Master thrice before the second crowing of the cock (Mark xiv. 66-72). Since Matthew, who reproduces Mark's narrative, records in agreement with Luke and John a fulfilment of the simpler prediction, 'Before the cock crow, thou shalt deny me thrice' (Matt. xxvi. 69-75; Luke xxii. 56-62; John xviii. 17, 18, 25-27), Mark's version is certainly secondary, and Luke's represents with greater fidelity the common apostolic original. The original, however, has probably been enlarged by each of the evangelists for the sake of securing a literal fulfilment of the prediction. The following facts should here be noticed: (*a*) The first denial is recorded alike by each of the four evangelists. The person who challenged Peter was 'one of the maids' (Mark), 'a maid' (Matthew), 'a certain maid' (Luke), 'the maid who kept the door' (John). (*b*) In reporting the later denials the evangelists differ. In the second case the challenger was 'the maid' (Mark), 'another maid' (Matthew), 'another' (Luke), while John uses the plural verb—'they said unto him, Art thou also one of his disciples?' (John xviii. 25). In the third case the challenge was delivered by 'the people that stood by' (Mark and Matthew), by 'a man' (Luke), by 'one of the servants of the high priest, a kinsman of the servant whose ear had been cut off in the garden' (John). Matthew reproduces Mark's narrative. The other three evangelists are independent; and their differences certainly suggest the possibility that in the first case a common documentary original has been followed, and in the others an indefinite tradition. (*c*) John separates the first denial from the others by the examination in the house of Annas (John xviii. 17, 18, 25-27), and thus confirms the supposition that the others are editorial additions. (*d*) Mark's version of the prediction is unintelligible unless on the supposition that in the written source there was only one denial. If Peter as a fact denied his Master once, and if Jesus had said, 'The cock shall not crow this day, until thou shalt thrice deny that thou knowest me' (Luke xxii. 34), the history could only be brought into verbal agreement with the prediction in one or other of two ways. The second and third cases might either be added to the first before the crowing of the cock—the method independently adopted, according to the supposition, by Matthew, Luke, and John; or the crowing of the cock after the first case might be retained, and a second crowing added after the third, and the prediction adapted to the fulfilment. This, according to the supposition, is what has been done by Mark. The facts cannot otherwise be explained. The differences in the report of the later denials confirm the explanation suggested, and the motive of the evangelists is apparent. The supposition that Peter heard the first crowing of the cock, without remembering the prediction, may be set aside as incredible. The supposition that he deliberately denied his Master thrice, without remembering the prediction, is almost equally improbable. The first inadvertent speech of his traitor lips would surely be sufficient to awaken remembrance and regret, and to send him out weeping bitterly. The cursing and the swearing in Mark's version is an exaggeration which is far from the truth (Mark xiv. 71). Jesus did not intend definitely to predict a thrice-repeated denial. The precise numerical succession is not to be interpreted literally, and insisted upon as essential to the thought. The thought simply is that there would be a succession, or an almost incredible apostasy. In this sense the prediction was fulfilled.

§ 53.—*The Meeting of the Council*

If the earlier narratives were contained in the source, the proceedings at the meeting of the Sanhedrin were also unquestionably recorded. In situation and in the response of Jesus to the demand, 'If thou art the Christ, tell us,' Luke's narrative is probably apostolic (Luke xxii. 67); but Mark has certainly preserved original details. The testimony of the witnesses e.g. has not been quoted in the third gospel; but the exclamation of the councillors, 'What further need have we of witness? for we ourselves have heard from his own mouth,' conclusively proves that the evidence was recorded in the source. Again, a few of the details in Luke's version are obviously secondary. (1) He has transferred the humiliation of Jesus from the end to the beginning of the narrative (vv. 63–65). Mark's order is certainly correct (Mark xiv. 65); for Jesus would not be mocked and beaten before He was tried and condemned. Luke has spared the members of the Sanhedrin at the expense of the high priest's servants. (2) The words, 'From henceforth shall the Son of Man be seated at the right hand of the power of God' (ver. 69), have been substituted for the original text, which has been preserved in the second gospel—'Ye shall see the Son of Man sitting at the right hand of power, and coming with the clouds of heaven' (Mark xiv. 62). Luke has avoided the statement that the members of the Sanhedrin would behold the second coming of Messiah. He knows that as a fact they did not witness the event, and therefore he modifies the prediction. (3) The text, as modified by Luke, seems scarcely sufficient to provoke the exclamation of the high priest, and the subsequent decision of the council. A direct and personal question has therefore been added, 'And they all said, Art thou then the Son of God? And he said unto them, Ye say that I am' (ver. 70). Since Mark ultimately derives his information from the apostolic source, he enables us to detect the editorial variations in the third gospel. The details which are peculiar to Matthew and John are clearly editorial. In reproducing Mark's narrative Matthew interpolates an account of the repentance of Judas (Matt. xxvii. 3–10). This fragment interrupts the continuity of the history, and is proved to be a late and indefinite tradition by the different account given of the same event in Acts i. 18, 19. John avoids both the testimony of the witnesses and the prediction regarding the second coming. John xviii. 20 has been derived from Luke xxii. 53, and ver. 22 from Luke xxii. 63–65.

§ 54.—*The Court of Pilate*

In his account of the examination before Pilate, as in the preceding narrative, Luke has combined editorial with apostolic material. The beginning of the new narrative is probably apostolic (Luke xxiii. 1–3); for the question of Pilate in the second gospel, 'Art thou the King of the Jews?' (Mark xv. 2), presupposes the accusation, which Luke alone has preserved— 'We found this man perverting our nation, and forbidding to give tribute to Cæsar, and saying that he himself is Christ a king' (ver. 2). Mark has abbreviated the original. On the other hand, the sequel in the third gospel from ver. 4 to ver. 12 can scarcely be claimed as apostolic. Luke wishes to present Pilate to his Gentile readers as favourably as possible. He therefore introduces here a judgment which was afterwards delivered. According to Luke, Pilate said to the chief priests and multitudes, 'I find no fault in this man' (ver. 4); but, according to Mark's more probable account, Pilate simply wondered at the silence of Jesus, and Luke xxiii. 4 is intelligible as an editorial anticipation of Mark xv. 14. Again, in reproducing the second gospel, Luke has already interpolated the remark that Herod sought to see Jesus (Luke ix. 9). The interview before the crucifixion (Luke xxiii. 8-12) is obviously associated in the evangelist's mind with this earlier statement; but the statement is certainly editorial, and since according to the apostolic source Herod had recently attempted to get Jesus into his hands that he might put Him to death (Luke xiii. 31), the interview is probably an apocryphal tradition. Luke says that Herod had for a long time been 'desirous to see Jesus, because he had heard concerning him, and he hoped to see some miracle done by him' (ver. 8); but this is incompatible with the apostolic testimony. Luke spares the Gentiles at the expense of the Jewish tetrarch. After the decision of Pilate, Jesus was shamefully treated in the Prætorium (Mark xv. 16-20), but according to Luke this happened in Herod's house (Luke xxiii. 11). The motive of the evangelist is evident, and his additions are perfectly transparent. We must, therefore, complete the original text by adding Mark xv. 4, 5 to Luke xxiii. 1-3. John has paraphrased the original in his usual style (John xviii. 28-38).

§ 55.—*Barabbas and Jesus*

The introduction of Herod into the history, and Luke's desire to be favourable to Pilate, have largely determined the narrative now before us in the third gospel. If Jesus was not sent by Pilate to Herod, the beginning is obviously editorial (vv. 13-16); and if Pilate's indifference has already been interpreted as a distinct justification of the Accused, the sequel exhibits the same tendency. According to Mark, when the people applied for the release of a prisoner, Pilate asked in succession three questions: (1) 'Will ye that I release unto you the King of the Jews?' (Mark xv. 9); (2) 'What then shall I do unto him whom ye call the King of the Jews?' (ver. 12); (3) 'Why, what evil hath he done?' (ver. 14). In the third gospel these questions appear in a different form. (1) Pilate reports that he has examined the accused, and finds no fault in Him—'Behold, nothing worthy of death has been done by him. I will therefore chastise him, and release him' (Luke xxiii. 14-16). (2) Pilate speaks to the people again, desiring to release Jesus (ver. 20). (3) He says to them the third time, 'Why, what evil hath this man done? I have found no cause of death in him: I will therefore chastise him and release him' (ver. 22). It is perfectly evident that Luke has again interpreted the text, and that Mark has preserved the original. Matthew in reproducing Mark's narrative has interpolated two fragments. He reports in the first place that, when Pilate was sitting on the judgment-seat, he received a message from his wife, who pleaded for the release of Jesus on account of a dream which had troubled her (Matt. xxvii. 19); and secondly he reports that Pilate was anxious to obey the message, and after unavailing efforts took water and washed his hands before the multitude, saying, 'I am innocent of the blood of this righteous man: see ye to it' (vv. 24, 25). Such conduct is in itself scarcely credible; and the possibility that these fragments are apostolic is excluded by the fact that Luke, notwithstanding his desire to excuse the Roman, does not insert them in his history. The inference is inevitable that they represent an apocryphal tradition, with which Luke was altogether unacquainted. Like Luke and Matthew, but in his own distinctive way, John has favoured the Gentile at the expense of the Jews. He wishes to emphasise Christ's innocence (John xviii. 38-xix. 16). The explanation given in Mark xv. 10 of Pilate's question—'For he perceived that for envy the chief priests had delivered him up'—is probably a comment, for which Mark is himself responsible ; but otherwise the text in the second gospel represents with greatest fidelity the apostolic original.

§ 56.—*The Crucifixion*

The details of the last events in Jerusalem have unfortunately not been recorded by the evangelists with the jealous fidelity with which they have preserved the logia. The teaching of Jesus can be precisely determined, and the earlier events in the ministry are not involved in obscurity ; but who can tell what happened at the cross and at the tomb ? If the second gospel was written by a companion of Peter, and the fourth by one of the apostles, the differences in the testimony of these writers are astonishing and not easily reconciled ; but at least, in their own surprising way, they establish certain facts. The second gospel, however, was not written by a companion of Peter, and the fourth was not written by John. The evidence set forth in these pages, although not specially intended to refute the old theories, has deprived them of all their plausibility ; and the consequence is, or seems to be, that the cloud which received the ascending Messiah has overspread the end of His earthly life. At present we are concerned only with the narrative of the crucifixion. The evangelists here differ so much from one another, that in attempting to disentangle the apostolic original we seem to be undertaking a hopeless task. A few facts may nevertheless be confidently recognised.

1. The narrative in the first gospel is intelligible as an editorial reproduction of Mark's. Matthew reports that a reed was placed in the right hand of Jesus, when He was mocked in the Prætorium (Matt. xxvii. 29), and this is probably a primary detail ; for without a sceptre the mock coronation would not be complete ; and afterwards, according to Mark, the head crowned with thorns was smitten with a reed (Mark xv. 19). Since a reed was used by the soldiers, it had probably been placed in the hand of Jesus ; but the conclusion by no means follows that Matthew has borrowed his additional detail from another documentary

authority. He has simply inferred the truth. Again, the additional taunt of the chief priests and Scribes, 'He trusteth on God; let him deliver him now, if he desireth him: for he said, I am the Son of God' (Matt. xxvii. 43), was probably suggested to the evangelist by Psalm xxii. 7, 8, and by the subsequent cry of the suffering taunted Messiah, 'My God, my God, why hast thou forsaken me?' (Mark xv. 34). And finally the statement made by Matthew that after the rending of the veil of the Temple 'the earth did quake, and the rocks were rent, and the tombs were opened, and many bodies of the saints that had fallen asleep were raised, and coming forth out of the tombs after his resurrection they entered into the holy city and appeared unto many,' is altogether incredible (Matt. xxvii. 51–53). I do not say that the miracle could not happen: I leave that to those who are acquainted with the possibilities of the tomb; but I certainly say without the slightest hesitation that if these details were contained in the apostolic source, Mark and Luke would not have failed to record them. They clearly represent an apocryphal tradition which is utterly unreliable. The rest of the variations in the first gospel are too insignificant to be mentioned. We accordingly conclude that Matthew's narrative is not independent, but is simply an editorial reproduction of Mark's.

2. It is scarcely probable that Luke has throughout reproduced an independent report. In the narratives from the Supper to the crucifixion, we have found no evidence that he is following Mark as his standard. These narratives in the third gospel are rather combinations of apostolic with editorial material; but Luke's version of the crucifixion has probably to a large extent been based upon the account given by Mark. He substitutes for Mark xv. 23 the following words: 'And Jesus said, Father, forgive them: for they know not what they do' (Luke xxiii. 34). He omits Mark xv. 25, 'And it was the third hour, and they crucified him;' but the allusion to the sixth hour and the ninth hour in Luke xxiii. 44 is sufficient to prove that the third hour was also mentioned in the source. Luke therefore has substituted for Mark xv. 25, 'And the people stood beholding' (ver. 35). His motive for this substitution is perfectly evident; for

immediately afterwards he records the taunts (vv. 35-37), transferring them from Mark xv. 29-32 for the sake of carrying forward Mark xv. 26, 27, to which he intends to make an addition which will appropriately conclude the paragraph (vv. 38-43). He omits the taunt of those that passed by, 'Ha! thou that destroyest the temple, and buildest it in three days, save thyself, and come down from the cross' (Mark xv. 29), and he has added the following words: 'And the soldiers also mocked him, coming to him, offering him vinegar, and saying, If thou art the King of the Jews, save thyself' (vv. 36, 37); but the allusion to the vinegar has certainly been transferred from a later part of the narrative (Mark xv. 36; John xix. 29), and Luke has already omitted the words of which the taunt is composed, for he has not recorded the accusation which was made by the witnesses before the Sanhedrin (Mark xiv. 58). He therefore intentionally avoids these words, and inserts his addition as a substitute. The reader should also note that the two allusions to the robbers in Mark xv. 27, 32 coincide in Luke xxiii. 39-43—a fact which confirms our analysis. Again, the rending of the veil of the Temple has been reported by Luke immediately after the report of the darkness (ver. 45). His motive for doing so is obvious, since he brings two signs together; but certainly the combination is editorial, for the rending of the veil of the Temple loses its symbolical significance when transferred from its position in Mark's version (ver. 38). It follows, and ought to follow, the death of Messiah. Luke, therefore, is clearly secondary. He has also omitted the cry, 'My God, my God, why hast thou forsaken me?' (Mark xv. 34), and has substituted the less disturbing words, 'Father, into thy hands I commend my spirit' (ver. 46). The two sayings coincide in situation, and Luke's is undoubtedly secondary. Finally, the names of the women have been omitted (Mark xv. 40, 41), and a few words have been substituted by Luke for the sake of avoiding editorial repetition (cf. Luke viii. 1-3). The variations in the third gospel are thus perfectly intelligible on the supposition that Luke is following Mark as his standard. He is certainly reproducing with editorial liberty either the report of Mark or an account precisely like Mark's; but since Mark's report, as we shall see, differs considerably from the fourth gospel narrative, it is scarcely probable that Mark's version represents with absolute fidelity the apostolic source. The supposition that Luke's version has been directly based on the apostolic original is therefore distinctly excluded, and the only alternative is that, like Matthew, he has adopted the second gospel as his standard. In such a case we must also infer that for some reason, and no doubt on account of its richer details, he has preferred the version of Mark.

3. Since Matthew and Luke have reproduced Mark's version, the existence of such a narrative in the apostolic source may perhaps be disputed and denied. The question at least arises, What is the evidence which permits the supposition to be maintained? I reply, in the first place, that the second and fourth gospels have each been based on the apostolic source, and that the report of the crucifixion in these gospels is itself an evidence that the narrative is ultimately apostolic. The only question is how far Mark and John have departed from their common original. And secondly, if more direct evidence is required, it is afforded by a fragment in the third gospel. This is the fact to be specially noted. The following words occur in Luke's version: 'And there followed him a great multitude of the people, and of women who bewailed and lamented him. But Jesus turning unto them said, Daughters of Jerusalem, weep not for me, but weep for yourselves, and for your children. For behold, the days are coming, in which they shall say, Blessed are the barren, and the wombs that never bare, and the breasts that never gave suck. Then shall they begin to say to the mountains, Fall on us; and to the hills, Cover us. For if they do these things in the green tree, what shall be done in the dry?' (Luke xxiii. 27–31). The genuineness of these words may perhaps be disputed. Four reasons are conceivable for rejecting them. (*a*) The language has been derived from the Old Testament (Isaiah liv. 1; Hosea x. 8; Ezekiel xvii. 24). This must be granted; but surely the conclusion does not follow that, because the words are scriptural, Jesus could not employ them. If one of the early Christians could compile a few Scripture texts, Jesus,

who was profoundly influenced by the Old Testament, and anticipated the fulfilment of the prophecies, might also adopt such a mode of expression. As a fact He frequently did so. (*b*) The address to the women may be supposed to be an anticipation of the destruction of Jerusalem ; and if the other passages on this subject are later additions, the prediction now before us must also be rejected. The reasoning here is good, but the exegesis is decidedly bad. If the words in question were really delivered by Jesus, they refer to the coming of the kingdom, and not to the destruction of Jerusalem. (*c*) The omission of the address by the other evangelists is a much more serious objection ; but the case of John presents no difficulty, as he invariably omits such sayings, or translates them into his higher thought and diction ; and Matthew, who is following Mark as his standard, does not consult the apostolic source, and does not deliberately omit anything. The difficulty is therefore reduced, and the question simply is, Can any reason be given for the omission of the fragment by Mark ? I reply that the omission of Christ's sayings by the author of the second gospel is too frequent to possess in any particular case a significance demanding explanation ; and secondly, I dispute the assumption that the passage has been altogether omitted. In Mark's version of the apocalyptic discourse the following words occur : 'Woe unto them that are with child, and to them that give suck in those days ' (Mark xiii. 17). This fragment coincides with Luke xxiii. 29 ; and since the apocryphal element in Mark's version of the discourse is undoubtedly an early Christian document which contains reminiscences of Christ's teaching (Mark xiii. 5, 6, 21, cf. Luke xvii. 20, 21 ; Mark xiii. 15, 16, cf. Luke xvii. 31 ; Mark xiii. 26, cf. Mark xiv. 62, Matt. xxv. 31 ; Mark xiii. 27, cf. Matt. xxv. 31, 32 ; Mark xiii. 30, cf. Matt. x. 23 ; Mark xiii. 31, cf. Matt. v. 18), the probability is that another example of this borrowing is to be found in the passage before us. But in such a case the genuineness of the address to the daughters of Jerusalem is confirmed, instead of being discredited, by the objection to which reference has been made. (*d*) The rest of Luke's additions to the narrative of the crucifixion have already been rejected as editorial—the story of the penitent thief (vv. 39-43), the words, 'Father, forgive them; for they know not what they do' (ver. 34), and the last cry of Jesus, 'Father, into thy hands I commend my spirit' (ver. 46). If these passages are rejected, how can the other addition be retained as a genuine apostolic fragment? Does the distinction not seem to be arbitrary? I reply, in the first place, that Christ's prayer for His enemies has been substituted by Luke for Mark xv. 23, and the last cry for Mark xv. 34, and that the story of the penitent thief is an enlargement of Mark xv. 27, 32,[b] two verses which coincide in Luke's report; and secondly, I maintain that the cases are far from being parallel. The fragments rejected are not only rendered doubtful by the textual evidence, but are also in accordance with Luke's personal characteristics, and with his desire for the edification of his readers: whereas, on the other hand, the address to the women of Jerusalem is one of those distinctive sayings which authenticate themselves, and for the editorial introduction of which no plausible motive can be suggested. The objections may therefore be dismissed. They are conceivable, but not convincing. They are feathers in the scale of probability; and the balance is distinctly in favour of the conclusion that the address to the women of Jerusalem has been taken by Luke from the apostolic source, which thus contained an account of the crucifixion.

The difficulty of reconstructing the original must, however, be frankly acknowledged. If Luke had continued as he began, the truth would not be obscure; but in preferring the second gospel to the apostolic source, he has left us a hard critical problem. We possess two independent reports, each based on the original narrative; but Mark and John are not mere copyists. Mark freely edits his material, omitting much, inserting some later details, and rearranging the whole; and John systematically paraphrases the text, avoiding what seems to him to be accidental, and refining the rest by exegetical enlargements for the sake of commending a more developed conception of the Person of Christ. The opinions of an early Christian writer are no doubt interesting and important, and his exegesis is exceedingly valuable; but as students of the gospels we are chiefly concerned to discover the precise historical truth. How, then, is this end to be gained? By what method may we hope to succeed? A few details are verified by the independent testimony of each evangelist. We may thus conclude with confidence that Jesus was taken to Golgotha, that He was crucified between two robbers, that an ironical superscription was attached to the cross, that the soldiers cast lots for His garments, that they offered Him vinegar to drink, that He uttered some words with His dying breath, and that all this happened on the day of the preparation of the Passover, i.e. on the 14th of Nisan. These facts constitute a reliable history, and they are not altogether insignificant; but the negative result of the method by which they are gained is certainly not decisive, for the evangelists seek to gain their ends by omission as well as by addition. The possibility that each has preserved authentic details, which have not been preserved by the other, must therefore be taken into account, before pronouncing definite judgment. The following is a list of the particulars in which the two narratives differ: (1) John reports that Jesus bore His own cross (John xix. 17); Mark, that Simon of Cyrene, a man coming from the country, was compelled to bear it (Mark xv. 21). Since the address to the women of Jerusalem has been taken by Luke from the apostolic source, and since the examination of Jesus by Pilate in the third gospel is a combination of apostolic with editorial material, Luke xxiii. 26 is probably apostolic; and in such a case the evidence is in favour of Mark. The saying of Jesus, 'Whosoever doth not bear his own cross, and come after me, cannot be my disciple' (Luke xiv. 27), might suggest the variation in the fourth gospel. Mark, on the other hand, in describing Simon as the father of Alexander and Rufus, betrays that he belongs to the post-apostolic generation, and writes at a time when the two sons of Simon had become widely known in the Church. (2) John reports that Mary the mother of Jesus was standing with other women near the cross, and was committed by the Sufferer to the protection of the disciple whom He loved (John xix. 25-27). If the fourth gospel is a version of the apostolic source, compiled under the influence of Johannine traditions, this may be an historical detail; but since the women, according to Mark, were beholding from afar, and were not standing near the cross, the evidence is scarcely sufficient (Mark xv. 40, 41, cf. iii. 34, 35). (3) John reports that after receiving the vinegar Jesus said, 'It is finished,' and bowed His head, and gave up His spirit (John xix. 30). This saying is certainly editorial, and has been substituted, like Luke xxiii. 46, for the cry which Mark has preserved, 'My God, my God, why hast thou forsaken me?' We are told indeed by Mark, that after the last articulate cry Jesus uttered a loud voice, and so gave up the spirit (ver. 37); but the saying in the fourth gospel is articulate, and, if likely to be uttered at all, would not be uttered loudly. (4) John reports that on account of the Preparation the bodies were taken away from the cross, that the legs of the robbers were broken, that one of the soldiers pierced Christ's side with a spear, and that straightway there came out blood and water (John xix. 31–37). Since these things, as John says, happened in fulfilment of prophecy, it is improbable that Mark would omit them. They were written perhaps in the Old Testament, but not in the apostolic source. (5) Mark, on the other hand, has fixed the hour of the crucifixion. Jesus was crucified at the third hour (Mark xv. 25); from the sixth to the ninth there was darkness over the whole land (ver. 33), and at the ninth hour Jesus died (vv. 34–37). These details are incompatible with the testimony of John, who possesses no knowledge of the darkness, and reports that about the sixth hour Jesus was still before Pilate's judgment-seat (John xix. 14). (6) Mark reports that after Christ's death the veil of the Temple was rent in twain from the top to the bottom (ver. 38). The deliberate omission of this by John is altogether incredible. We must therefore conclude that the statement is not apostolic. (7) According to Mark, when the centurion who stood over against the cross saw that Jesus so gave up the spirit, he exclaimed, 'Truly this man was the Son of God' (ver. 39). The exclamation has not been recorded by John; and since Mark begins his gospel by describing Jesus as the Christ, the Son of God, he betrays an editorial purpose in concluding with the centurion incident. (8) Mark also reports that Jesus was taunted by the people (vv. 29, 30), by the chief priests and Scribes

(vv. 31, 32), and by the robbers who were crucified with Him (ver. 32). Since John has elsewhere avoided details of the humiliation (Mark xiv. 65), this fragment may reasonably be accepted. The others are unreliable, and must be excluded from the text.

§ 57.—*The Burial*

In their account of the burial the four gospels again exhibit the characteristics which have been discovered in the narrative of the crucifixion. (1) Matthew is distinctly secondary. He follows Mark as his standard, and his variations do not in any case presuppose another documentary authority. He omits 'because it was the Preparation, that is, the day before the sabbath' (Mark xv. 42) ; but he describes the morrow as the day after the Preparation, and so agrees with Mark (Matt. xxvii. 62). He omits the word 'boldly' from Mark's account of Joseph (Mark xv. 43), and does not record the statement that Pilate called the centurion to ask whether Jesus had been any while dead (Mark xv. 44). Luke also omits these details, and probably for the same reason—that they were not contained in the apostolic source (cf. John xix. 38) ; but since Matthew reports that Joseph was a disciple (ver. 57)—a detail which, if known by Mark and Luke, would not have been omitted—we cannot infer that the narrative in the first gospel is apostolic. The tomb, according to Matthew, was Joseph's 'own' new tomb (ver. 60), and a 'great' stone was rolled to the door (ver. 60, cf. Mark xvi. 4). These are editorial enlargements. Mark reports that Mary Magdalene and Mary the mother of Joses beheld where Jesus was laid (ver. 47). Matthew substitutes an equivalent: according to him, they were sitting together 'over against the sepulchre' (ver. 61). The report that the chief priests and Pharisees sought and obtained permission to seal the tomb on the Sabbath, lest the body of Jesus should be stolen by the disciples, is obviously an apocryphal tradition (vv. 62–66). Its omission by the other evangelists cannot otherwise be explained. We must therefore conclude, as before, that the narrative in the first gospel is not independent, but is simply an editorial reproduction of Mark's. (2) Luke's version, on the other hand, exhibits characteristics which are scarcely intelligible, unless on the supposition that his narrative is directly apostolic. The following facts should here be noted: (*a*) Like Matthew he omits the word ' boldly ; ' but, unlike both Matthew and John, he does not infer that Joseph was one of the disciples (Luke xxiii. 50-52). Since John reports that Joseph went secretly to Pilate for fear of the Jews (John xix. 38), the word 'boldly' could not be in the original. (*b*) Mark, followed by Matthew, reports that a stone was rolled to the door of the sepulchre (Mark xv. 46). Like John, Luke omits this detail (Luke xxiii. 53; John xix. 41). (*c*) The allusion to the Preparation, with which Mark begins his version (ver. 42), follows in the third gospel the account of the burial (ver. 54). Here again Luke agrees with John, according to whose report the body was placed in the garden-tomb because of the Jews' Preparation, and because the tomb was nigh at hand (ver. 42). The burial seems to have been provisional. That at least is a possible inference, which Mark has altogether avoided. (*d*) Mark reports that the women bought spices when the Sabbath was past before the rising of the sun (Mark xvi. 1, 2). In itself this is scarcely probable, and the statement is directly contradicted by Luke and John, according to whom the spices were prepared before the Sabbath began (Luke xxiii. 56; John xix. 39, 40). These facts are surely significant. Luke and John repeatedly agree in divergence from Mark. Luke is not acquainted with the fourth gospel. John is not acquainted with the third. The two evangelists are independent: we have no reason whatever to suppose the contrary. But each is acquainted with the apostolic source, and uses it—John exclusively, Luke in combination with Mark. What, then, is the necessary conclusion? The probability certainly is that the details above mentioned, in which they agree, have been taken directly from the apostolic source. (3) A few details may be confidently recognised as editorial. In the second gospel we have already detected the following: the allusion to the Preparation at the beginning of the narrative (ver. 42), the boldness of Joseph in his application to Pilate (ver. 43), the interview of Pilate with the centurion (ver. 44), and the rolling of the stone against the door of the tomb (ver. 46). John, again, has reported that Joseph was a disciple (ver. 38), that he went secretly to Pilate for fear of the Jews (ver. 38), and that Nicodemus and he prepared spices and afterwards buried the body (vv. 39–42). If these details had been contained in the apostolic source, the other evangelists would not have omitted them. The account given of Joseph is inferential. Nicodemus is the ruler of whom we are told that he had an interview with Jesus by night (John iii. 1-12); but if, as is probable, this ruler was the Scribe who asked, 'What shall I do to inherit eternal life?' (Luke x. 25-37), his name was not mentioned in the apostolic source, and the account there given of the man is incompatible with the tradition that he assisted at the burial of Jesus. Nicodemus seems to have been introduced to learn the heavenly things which at first were beyond his comprehension (John iii. 12), and to prove himself neighbour unto Jesus who fell among the robbers (Luke x. 36). He resembles in the fourth gospel the centurion in the second. He serves an editorial purpose, and we know nothing more about him. Luke's version, with the exception of the parenthesis (v. 51), which is almost avowedly editorial, must therefore be accepted as the most direct and faithful reproduction of the apostolic narrative.

§ 58.—*The Empty Tomb*

If in the apostolic source the crucifixion and the burial were recorded, we may be sure that it also contained some account of that subsequent wonder which lit up the clouds with the glow of the setting sun. The faith of the early Christians in the continuity of their Master's mission and in His second coming turned mourning into gladness and doubt into triumphant zeal; and the supposition that a Christian document concluded the history of the Passion without any expression of this faith may be dismissed at once as incredible. The question is, Are we able to show by direct evidence that the last narrative in the second gospel is in whole or in part apostolic, and can we with any degree of assurance distinguish the original from the versions? A preliminary and apparently insuperable difficulty arrests the attention of the student. The conclusion of Mark's narrative (vv. 9-20) has been separated by the latest revisers from the preceding verses, and they have stated in the margin that 'the two oldest Greek manuscripts and some other authorities omit from ver. 9 to the end,' and that 'some other authorities have a different ending to the gospel.' The different ending to which they allude consists of the following words: 'And all that had been enjoined on them they reported briefly to the companions of Peter. And after these things Jesus himself, from the east even to the west, sent forth by them the holy and incorruptible preaching of eternal salvation.' It is exceedingly improbable that the second gospel originally concluded with the words in ver. 8: 'And they said nothing to any one; for they were afraid' (ἐφοβοῦντο γάρ); and yet the evidence of the manuscripts does not permit us to pass beyond the particle. The two additional endings are equally doubtful when tested by the external evidence, and the internal evidence is acknowledged to be decidedly against the longer appendix which has been retained in the Revised Version. Mr. Simcox e.g. says, 'It is certain that these verses have quite a different character of diction from the rest of the gospel—whether we account for the fact by supposing that they are not St. Mark's or that they are St. Mark's own words, while the rest is given in St. Peter's, or in some other way.'[1] The alternatives here suggested are worthy of being classified among the curiosities of New Testament criticism. The 'some other way' is charmingly indefinite. Mr. Simcox does not suggest on his own responsibility that the second gospel as a whole has been preserved in the words of St. Peter, and that Mark added the appendix in his own words from ver. 9 to ver. 20; but Dr. Salmon, the author of an 'Introduction to the New Testament,' seems seriously to maintain this opinion. He is 'disposed to believe that Mark's is at once the oldest and the youngest of the three synoptics: the oldest as giving most nearly the very words in which the apostolic traditions were delivered: the youngest as respects the date when the independent traditions were set in their

[1] *The Writers of the New Testament*, p. 13.

present framework;'[1] and the framework, he thinks, is represented by the first fifteen and the last twelve verses in the gospel. The appendix therefore, though not written in the words of Peter, and not a constituent of the triple or Petrine tradition, was written by Mark, and formed part of the gospel from the first. The theory of the Triple Tradition, on which Dr. Salmon's opinion is based, contains one element of truth, which is that the material common to the three synoptists has been preserved, as a rule, in its earliest form by Mark. Beyond this all is mistaken conjecture. The first three gospels are not independent deposits of an oral tradition, but Matthew and Luke are dependent on Mark. The supposition that the second gospel was written by Mark in the words of St. Peter, or 'in some other way,' is not in any degree probable; and the framework hypothesis, which is one of Dr. Salmon's originalities, is untenable, apart from the general theory, and is not even accepted by the advocates of an oral tradition. The longer appendix, like the shorter, must be set aside as unauthoritative. How, then, are we to get out of the difficulty? Has the original ending been hopelessly lost? I venture to suggest that this conclusion is a little premature. Since the second gospel has been largely reproduced by both Matthew and Luke, the possibility requires to be considered that one of these later evangelists has preserved the lost fragment for us. Let us put the matter to the test.

As in the case of the narratives already examined, Matthew's version is an editorial reproduction of Mark's. He excludes Salome from the list of the women who went with their spices to the sepulchre (Mark xvi. 1). He omits the questioning of the women at the tomb (Mark xvi. 3, 4), but has already mentioned that the stone rolled to the door was 'great' (Matt. xxvii. 60). He excludes Peter's name from the text, 'Go, tell his disciples and Peter,' because Peter was one of the disciples (Mark xvi. 7; Matt. xxviii. 7). He avoids the allusion to the spices (Mark xvi. 1), because he infers that the body has already been anointed (Matt. xxvii. 59, cf. xxvi. 12); the women, he says, simply went to see the sepulchre (Matt. xxviii. 1). He infers that 'the young man' was an angel (Mark xvi. 5; Matt. xxviii. 2-5).

[1] *Introduction to the New Testament*, p. 158.

He substitutes 'They departed quickly from the tomb, with fear and great joy, and ran to bring his disciples word' (ver. 8), for 'they went out, and fled from the tomb; for trembling and astonishment had come upon them; and they said nothing to any one; for they were afraid' (Mark xvi. 8)—thus avoiding the strangeness of the original, and correcting the possible inference that the women, on account of their fear, disobeyed the charge which had been addressed to them. And, finally, he accounts for the rolling away of the stone by a curious combination of events. 'There was,' he says, 'a great earthquake; for an angel of the Lord descended from heaven, and came and rolled away the stone, and sat upon it. His appearance was as lightning, and his raiment white as snow: and for fear of him the watchers did quake, and became as dead men' (vv. 2-4). These words have been substituted by Matthew for the questioning of the women at the tomb, and they are certainly apocryphal, like the additions in the earlier narratives. We have, therefore, no reason to believe that Matthew is an independent authority. His variations are intelligible on the supposition that here, as elsewhere, he is following the second gospel as his standard. What, then, is the nature of the sequel? Has Matthew preserved the lost fragment? He reports (1) that the women ran from the tomb to deliver the angel's message (ver. 8); (2) that Jesus met them on the way, and repeated the message in His own name (vv. 9, 10); (3) that some of the watchers who quaked and became as dead men when they saw the angel, went off to the chief priests, and were bribed to spread the report that while they slept the body had been stolen by the disciples (vv. 11-15); (4) that the eleven disciples went into Galilee, in accordance with the message delivered to them, and there at the mountain saw Jesus, and received a last commission (vv. 16-20). The third of these details has certainly not been borrowed from Mark; for he does not know anything about the guard. The second is excluded by Mark's statement that the women being afraid said nothing to anyone. Whatever these words may mean, they certainly indicate some period of reserve, extending beyond the return to their friends, and would not be likely to be followed by an interview with Jesus on the road. Again, the fourth detail is discredited by its absence from the third and fourth gospels, and by the fact that the commission is in each gospel so different as to be incompatible with the assumption of a common documentary original (Matt. xxviii. 18-20; Luke xxiv. 44-49; John xx. 21-23; Mark xvi. 14-18). We are thus reduced to the single addition that the women delivered their message—a statement which no doubt might be included in the fragment which has disappeared from the second gospel, but one which itself is fragmentary. The lost ending has, therefore, not been preserved by Matthew. Turning now to the parallel narrative in the third gospel, we find that Luke's version is mixed. It is partly apostolic, and has partly been borrowed from Mark. Like Matthew and John, Luke has omitted the questioning of the women at the tomb; but, unlike Matthew, he has not substituted a later tradition. He reports the appearance to the women of two men in dazzling apparel (Luke xxiv. 4), thus agreeing less with Mark than with John, according to whose version of the story when Mary entered the tomb she beheld two angels in white, one at the head and one at the feet, where the body of Jesus had lain (John xx. 12). These facts no doubt are inconclusive, for they simply prove that Mark's narrative has not been verbally reproduced; and if Matthew altered his text without documentary authority, Luke might presumably do the same. But in the case of the third gospel there is this important difference—that Luke has already in his account of the Passion introduced apostolic material; and the evidence has not yet been exhausted. The women in Mark's version are Mary Magdalene, Mary the mother of James, and Salome (Mark xvi. 1). In Luke's version they are Mary Magdalene, and Joanna, and Mary the mother of James (Luke xxiv. 10). Since Matthew has omitted Salome, Luke, it may be said, might substitute Joanna on the authority of an oral tradition; but, in the first place, Joanna is mentioned by name in Luke viii. 3 among the women who followed Jesus, and ministered to the disciples of their substance. The earlier passage is apostolic, and the later is, therefore, presumably apostolic. And, secondly, the names in Luke xxiv. 10 have not been recorded in their original position. They form clearly an editorial parenthesis, and are introduced to rectify an omission. Now Luke, in his account of the crucifixion, has reproduced with editorial variations the version of Mark. He has substituted Luke xxiii. 48, 49 for Mark xv. 40, 41 to avoid editorial repetition (cf. Luke viii. 1–8); but the names of the women could not be altogether omitted. The sequel demands that their personality should be made quite definite. What, then, has the evangelist done? When he sees that the names are, after all, necessary, he transfers them to ch. xxiv. 10 from their original position in ch. xxiii. 48, 49. But Luke's narrative of the crucifixion is directly apostolic at the beginning (Luke xxiii. 26–31). Since Joanna's name is not mentioned by Mark, but is mentioned in the apostolic passage Luke viii. 3, we accordingly conclude that Luke does not, like Matthew, merely follow an oral tradition. The probability is that he takes the names from the apostolic source. His account of the wonder which happened on the first day of the week is, therefore, in part apostolic. So far we have gained nothing in fulfilment of the hope that the lost fragment will be found in the third gospel. We have now, however, to observe the fact that here, as elsewhere, Luke's narrative is in part an editorial reproduction of Mark's. The parenthesis in ver. 10 will reward a closer examination. It consists of the following words: 'Now they were Mary Magdalene, and Joanna, and Mary the mother of James: and the other women with them told these things unto the apostles.' The text is a little ambiguous. Does Luke intend to report that all the women told these things to the apostles, or does he exclude the three whose names are specially mentioned? I venture to suggest that the ambiguity represents editorial perplexity. Mark states that the women 'said nothing to any one; for they were afraid.' With these words before him Luke first explains that the women were Mary Magdalene, and Joanna, and Mary the mother of James. These said nothing to any one, for they were afraid; but, according to oral tradition, and probably also according to both the apostolic source and Mark, a communication was made to the disciples, and so Luke adds that the other women with them told what they had seen and heard. He does not explicitly exclude the three; but, on the other hand, he does not explicitly include them among those who delivered the message. He leaves the matter doubtful. Matthew altogether avoids the concluding words in the second gospel. Luke tries to reconcile them in a parenthesis with his other information, derived not merely from oral tradition, but probably also from Mark himself, that is, from the fragment which has been lost. If the above explanation may be accepted—a better will be heartily welcomed, but will not be so easily found—we possess direct and convincing evidence that Luke's narrative is in part an editorial reproduction of Mark's. Again, the words of the young man in the second gospel are reported as follows: 'Be not amazed: ye seek Jesus, the Nazarene, which hath been crucified: he is risen; he is not here: behold, the place where they laid him! But go, tell his disciples and Peter, He goeth before you into Galilee: there shall ye see him, as he said unto you' (Mark xvi. 6, 7). The parallel passage in Luke's narrative is different—'Why seek ye the living among the dead? He is not here, but is risen: remember how he spake unto you when he was yet in Galilee, saying that the Son of Man must be delivered up into the hands of sinful men, and be crucified, and the third day rise again' (Luke xxiv. 5-7). It is exceedingly improbable that either of these passages was contained in the apostolic source; for, in the first place, Jesus did not say to His disciples when He was with them in Galilee that He would be delivered up, and crucified, and on the third day rise again. The prediction is not apostolic, but has been borrowed from the second gospel, and is there, as we have seen, editorial (Mark viii. 31; ix. 31; x. 33, 34; Luke ix. 44; xviii. 31-33). And, secondly, the apostolic text, 'All ye shall be offended: for it is written, I will smite the shepherd, and the sheep shall be scattered abroad. Howbeit, after I am raised up, I will go before you into Galilee' (Mark xiv. 27, 28), is not a prediction that Jesus would appear visibly to His disciples. The saying simply means that when they recovered from their panic, and gathered together like a flock, their Shepherd would again go before them—not visibly as of old, but none the less truly and effectively. 'Where two or three are gathered together in my name, there am I in the midst of them.' We must, therefore, conclude that the prediction in Mark xvi. 6, 7 is editorial. But if Mark's prediction is editorial, Luke's is much more editorial: it is a secondary reproduction of Mark's. Luke has already avoided the saying which was delivered on the road to the garden (Mark xiv. 27, 28); and now he deliberately omits the words, 'He goeth before you into Galilee: there shall ye see him, as he said unto you,' and substitutes a text which is obviously a reminiscence of Luke ix. 44; xviii. 31-33. He does not believe that Jesus appeared to the disciples in Galilee. He has other information which seems to him more reliable. Clearly, therefore, in the apostolic source no account was given of a Galilean manifestation; and, indeed, it is scarcely probable that the fulfilment of Mark's editorial prediction was recorded in the ending which has been lost. In any case we possess sufficient evidence to establish the fact that here, as elsewhere, Luke's narrative is in part an editorial reproduction of Mark's. So far we have simply been using the broom. Let us now look for the lost piece of silver. Excluding ver. 10, which is, as we have seen, a parenthesis, the passage which follows Mark xvi. 8 in the third gospel consists of the following words: 'And they told all these things to the eleven, and to all the rest. And these words appeared in their sight as idle talk; and they disbelieved them. But Peter arose, and ran unto the tomb; and stooping and looking in, he seeth the linen cloths by themselves; and he departed to his home, wondering at that which was come to pass' (Luke xxiv. 9, 11, 12). This looks like a piece of silver. It is rounded and sufficiently small; and perhaps, notwithstanding Time's effacing hand, the image and superscription may be perceived. We proceed to investigate details.

1. Mark's statement that the women 'said nothing to any one; for they were afraid,' does not necessarily mean that they held their peace even from good. They were instructed, according to Mark, to tell the disciples and Peter (ver. 7). Their fear would dispose them to deliver this message as quickly as possible, and would only prevent them from spreading the report among the unbelieving Jews. If they said nothing to

anyone, the inference seems incontestable that they did not say anything to the disciples; but absolute silence is a psychological improbability, and the united testimony of Matthew, Luke, and John is sufficient to justify the assumption that, whatever the sequel may have been, it did not end with fear and silence (Matt. xxviii. 8; Luke xxiv. 9; John xx. 2). The reader who insists that Mark means exactly what he says is, no doubt, perfectly reasonable; but the question is, What does Mark say? The leper was charged to say nothing to any man; but he was also instructed to go and show himself to the priest, who was presumably a man (Mark i. 44). When the daughter of Jairus was raised from the dead, according to Mark's report, the people in the house were charged much that no man should know this (Mark v. 43); but the people themselves were obviously excluded. They could not be prevented from receiving the testimony of their senses (cf. Mark vii. 36). In Mark vii. 24 the statement is made that Jesus entered into a house, and would have no man know it; but the disciples were with Him, and from them the fact could not be hid. And, finally, when Mark reports that Peter and James and John were instructed to tell no man what things they had seen at the transfiguration of their Master (Mark ix. 9), he does not intend to suggest that the secret was to be kept from the rest of the twelve (cf. Mark viii. 30; ix. 30). These parallel passages prove conclusively that the statement regarding the women is not incompatible with the supposition that they delivered their message to the disciples.

2. Although Matthew has not preserved the fragment which has somehow disappeared, he enables us to measure its dimensions. The whole passage from Matt. xxviii. 9 to the end of the first gospel consists of no more than twelve verses; and these, as we have seen, are probably all editorial. They have not been borrowed from Mark. The only detail which is likely to have been taken from the lost fragment is the report that the women ran to bring the disciples word (ver. 8). But Matthew is following Mark as his standard, and instead of reducing he usually enlarges his original. If Luke xxiv. 9^b, 11, 12 originally followed Mark xvi. 8, the rejection of these verses is intelligible; for Matthew substitutes what seems

to him to be a much more edifying tradition. But if the lost ending of the second gospel was longer and more edifying than the verses which Luke has preserved, its rejection by Matthew is unaccountable. We must, therefore, conclude that the lost ending was shorter than Matthew's.

3. The agreement of Luke and John affords presumptive evidence that they derive their common information from the apostolic source. The antecedent probability may certainly be outbalanced by evidence which possesses more weight; but if not thus excluded in any particular case it is sufficient and worthy of acceptation. Now Luke and John agree in reporting (a) that the disciples received intelligence concerning the wonder (Luke xxiv. 9, 10; John xx. 2); (b) that there was doubt in the apostolic circle (Luke xxiv. 11; John xx. 8, 9, 24–29); (c) that Peter ran to the tomb to verify the news, and found only the linen cloths (Luke xxiv. 12; John xx. 3–7); (d) that he returned at once to his own home (Luke xxiv. 12; John xx. 10). Mary Magdalene is the only woman who is mentioned in the fourth gospel narrative, and according to John, Peter was accompanied by the disciple whom Jesus loved. These are unreliable details. In so far as the two evangelists agree they represent the apostolic source; but Mark also derives his information from the apostolic source. He has indeed no other documentary authority. It is therefore exceedingly probable that the four apostolic details as recorded in Luke's simpler version were contained in the fragment which has been lost. We may even proceed farther and affirm that the dimensions of the fragment as determined by Matthew exclude the probability of a longer ending.

4. The passage which is thus suggested by the independent testimony of Luke and John fulfils the conditions which are fixed by the requirements of the second gospel. Four conditions are imposed by the earlier history. (a) Since the women were instructed, according to Mark's report, to tell the disciples and Peter, Peter was specially mentioned in the lost fragment. The speech of the young man, as we have seen, is probably editorial, and therefore we need not infer that Mark proceeded to record a manifestation to the disciples in Galilee. The fact that Luke records no such manifestation is scarcely

compatible with the supposition that the second gospel contained a fulfilment of the prediction. But the manner in which Mark distinguishes Peter from the rest of the disciples shows clearly that the sequel was concerned with this disciple —not with Peter and another whom Jesus loved, but with Peter alone. (b) The discovery by the women of the empty tomb and their subsequent return to the disciples demand that Peter should also in the sequel be somehow associated with the empty tomb. (c) The statement that Joseph wrapped the body in a linen cloth (Mark xv. 46) is a detail too insignificant to be mentioned, unless we assume that the linen cloth became important in the sequel. (d) The ending which gathers together these details and brings them to an appropriate issue must also be in itself final, and related to the whole gospel in such a way as to make the history complete. Now certainly the first three conditions are fulfilled in the passage which is at present being discussed; for Luke reports that when Peter received the news he ran to the tomb, and stooped and looked in, and found only the linen cloths. The question is, Does Luke's fragment fulfil the fourth condition? At first sight one is not disposed to reply in the affirmative; for although the conclusion has some appearance of finality—' He departed to his home, wondering at that which was come to pass '—the history scarcely seems to be brought to a satisfactory termination. The question, however, is not whether the Christian Church would ultimately be satisfied with such a conclusion, but whether as a fact the second gospel was thus closed; and I venture to affirm that the evidence is not only otherwise sufficient to establish a predominant probability, but also that the incompleteness, which may conceivably be urged as an objection, is altogether fictitious. The finality of the wonder is, in the first place, unquestionable. This feeling was presumably excited at the beginning, when fear prevented publicity, and thought was less influenced by scepticism, and Peter verified the report; and after nineteen centuries the world still wonders before the old empty tomb. So far Luke's fragment is appropriate. And secondly, the Christian faith in the continuity of Christ's mission, or, in other words, in His resurrection from the dead, is sufficiently conveyed by the discovery which Peter verified. The reasoning which argues from the later gospels to the contents of the earlier is destitute of logical necessity. In the later gospels a series of manifestations is recorded, but we are not justified in concluding that the second gospel contained such a series. The visible appearance of Jesus to His disciples would no doubt constitute a convincing evidence that He had indeed risen from the dead, and ultimately such appearances would be sure to find a place in the authoritative Christian records ; but the empty tomb in itself directly suggests, if it does not necessarily involve, the resurrection of the body from the dead, and so the contention that the second evangelist, who believed not merely in the resurrection but also in the visible appearance, could not conclude with Luke's fragment, is utterly unconvincing. The requirements of early Christian faith would probably be abundantly satisfied by a simple statement of the wonderful fact that the body of Jesus was not found. 'They have taken away the Lord out of the tomb, and we know not where they have laid him.' The ending proposed is, therefore, not inappropriate. It is not discredited by the contents of the gospel nor by the faith of the evangelist. On the contrary, we may even affirm that the appropriateness of the ending is a decisive evidence in its favour. For, thirdly, the fragment which Luke has preserved is related to the second gospel in such a way as to make the whole history complete. Mark begins by stating his faith that Jesus is the Christ, the Son of God. He then proceeds to give a brief account of the Baptist as an introduction to the narrative of the baptism of Jesus. 'Straightway coming up out of the water, he saw the heavens rent asunder, and the Spirit as a dove descending upon him : and a voice came out of the heavens, Thou art my beloved Son, in thee I am well pleased' (Mark i. 10, 11). Such is the beginning of the gospel; and the aim of the evangelist obviously is to show by a record of the ministry that Jesus is indeed the Christ, and that the approving voice is confirmed by the testimony of the life. Now already in the narrative of the crucifixion Mark has introduced the centurion, who says, 'Truly this man was the Son of God' (Mark xv. 39). The personal faith of the writer thus receives a final acknowledgment, and is indeed accepted by a representative of the Gentile world; and the centurion is not more clearly related to the initial expression of the evangelist's faith than is the empty tomb to the open heaven at the baptism. A more appropriate conclusion can scarcely be conceived. At the beginning the heavens are rent asunder, and the Spirit descends as a dove; at the end the bonds of death are broken, and Jesus ascends from the tomb, attesting His mission, and returning like the dove to His Father. This is the thought which the evangelist intends to convey. He has even completed the analogy by reporting a voice from the tomb—'He is risen; he is not here: behold the place where they laid him.' Additional details would obscure the retrospective significance of the resurrection, and would imperil the unity of the gospel. The narrative of the baptism is short, and the narrative of the resurrection is correspondingly short. The beginning is an anticipation of the end, and the end is a return to the beginning. The gospel thus exhibits a literary completeness without any loss to faith, and the fourth condition, like the others, is fulfilled by the ending proposed.

5. The question now arises, How can the disappearance of the original be explained? As long as this question remains indefinite, the answer must be purely conjectural. Accidents may happen even to the most highly prized manuscripts, and the best of copyists may make some mistake; but random explanations such as these are not of very much value. If the ending has entirely disappeared beyond the possibility of recovery, the whole subject is involved in a hopeless obscurity. If a definite ending, however, can be found, the question may receive a definite answer, and such an answer must be given. How, then, was the piece of silver lost? The second gospel concludes with the words, 'And they said nothing to any one; for they were afraid.' The first words in Luke's fragment are, 'And they told all these things to the eleven, and to all the rest' (ver. 9). We have seen that these statements are not mutually exclusive; for Mark simply means that the people of Jerusalem learned nothing from the women. But obviously there is a verbal contradiction; and since in comparison with the later traditions the sequel seems insignificant and unedi-

fying, we can readily understand that for the sake of avoiding discrepancy, the end might be deliberately cut off. At first the loss would not be serious, for in oral tradition, as well as in the other gospels, believers would find fuller information; but ultimately the mutilated ending would inevitably be considered insufficient, and attempts would be made to supply the demand. Our two oldest Greek manuscripts represent the earlier stage: the appendices represent the later. The difficulty thus disappears when the truth is recognised that Luke has preserved Mark's text in its original integrity.

6. An objection of some importance still remains to be considered. We have hitherto been taking for granted that the fragment in the third gospel is itself original, and was contained from the first in Luke's text; but according to the margin of the Revised Version, some ancient authorities omit ver. 12; and this verse is considered by some scholars to be of doubtful authenticity. Westcott and Hort e.g. describe it as 'a Western non-interpolation;'[1] in other words they maintain that in the Eastern manuscripts the text has been interpolated from John xx. 3-10, and that the Western have preserved the original. A writer who does not profess to be acquainted with the manuscripts may well hesitate to dispute the conclusion of scholars, who have mastered the subject, and are justly considered to be authorities; but if the verse in question may be an Eastern interpolation, it may surely quite as well be a Western omission. The textual evidence is indeed distinctly in favour of the latter alternative. Dr. Westcott has failed to perceive the significance of the correspondence between the third and fourth gospels. He does not contemplate the possibility that the agreement of Luke and John may be due to their use of a common original. He suggests that a copyist has interpolated ver. 12 from the fourth gospel; but in such a case, as he acknowledges, the fourth gospel text has been condensed and simplified, a few words have been added, and everything has been omitted that relates to the other disciple. Now these are significant facts. They may, no doubt, be explained by the hypothesis proposed; but the alternative is much more probable that Luke and John have used a common

[1] *Greek Testament*, vol. ii. Appendix, p. 71.

original—Luke, perhaps, in this case directly from Mark, but ultimately from the apostolic source—and that John has enlarged this original by the addition of oral traditions. The information which relates to the other disciple would thus be unapostolic, and the simpler text would be primary. The derivation of ver. 12 by a copyist from the fourth gospel is altogether conjectural, and the conjecture depends ultimately on a theory of the gospels which has been shown to be untenable. Again, a sufficient reason must be given for the alleged interpolation, but none has been given by Dr. Westcott. When we proceed to inquire what motive could induce a copyist to take such a liberty with his original, we wait in vain for an answer, and what we are asked to acknowledge is simply an unintelligible freak; whereas, on the other hand, if ver. 12 was originally in the text, we can account for its omission. The disbelief in ver. 11 is corrected and removed in the sequel; but ver. 12 intervenes, and might seem to a copyist to be scarcely worth recording, in comparison with the fuller information contained in the fourth gospel (John xx. 3-10). The discovery by Peter of the empty tomb confirms the report of the women in so far as they announced the same discovery; and since the prediction that Jesus would appear to His disciples in Galilee is an addition which Mark has made to the original narrative, the verification is perfectly complete; but Luke has adopted Mark's addition, modifying it however, in such a way as to make it merely an announcement of the resurrection, and the discovery made by Peter does not directly verify the prediction that Jesus would rise from the dead. The sequel affords the evidence which is needed; and if Jesus appeared visibly to His disciples, the emptiness of the tomb is involved. The statement in ver. 12 might therefore well seem to be both unnecessary and unedifying; and besides, if this verse was removed from the second gospel, it might surely be also removed from the third. Luke has not reproduced the verbal contradiction; but the early copyists would presumably be acquainted with the original ending of the second gospel, and knowing that for some reason it had been rejected, they might also exclude the parallel passage from the work of the later evangelist. The difficulty must for these reasons be sent back to the students of the manuscripts. They have probably made a mistake. The evidence afforded by comparative criticism is distinctly opposed to the assumption of Westcott and Hort; and without undervaluing in any degree the excellent work of these scholars in the department which they have made specially their own, we must on the whole give the preference to results which are less conjectural. If they cannot produce convincing evidence in favour of the contrary belief, we are bound to conclude, in view of all the facts, that ver. 12 was contained in the original text, and that Luke has preserved the lost ending of Mark. We have even gained larger results. In discussing the preliminary difficulty we have touched the circumference of the whole subject, and have almost reached the end of the argument; for, in the first place, we have seen that the lost ending of Mark, as preserved both by Luke and John, is authenticated by this agreement, and by the internal evidence as the ending of the apostolic source. We have perceived on the piece of silver the apostolic image and superscription; and, secondly, we have been able to distinguish the original text from the versions. Matthew's version is altogether, and Mark's is in some respects, secondary. The questioning of the women at the tomb and the message of the young man to the disciples are probably secondary details. The first is excluded by its absence from the other three gospels, and the second not merely by the ending, which does not verify the prediction that Jesus would appear to His disciples, but also by the fact that the apostolic text, 'Howbeit, after I am raised up, I will go before you into Galilee,' has been misinterpreted by Mark. The disturbing words at the end of our second gospel (ver. 8) are probably also editorial, in form, if not in substance; for the parallel passages prove that the phraseology is peculiar to the evangelist. Again, John's version of the narrative, though based on the apostolic source, has been enlarged, like Matthew's, by the addition of oral traditions, and the original has been, as usual, restated in the distinctive Johannine style. And, finally, the names of the women in Luke's version (ver. 10) have been transferred from their original position in the account of the crucifixion (Luke xxiii. 48, 49), and the message sent from the tomb to the disciples is an editorial reproduction of the parallel passage in the second gospel. Excluding these secondary details, the result is a text complete in itself, and in all respects congruous with the rest of the apostolic source, which began, like the second gospel, with the opening of the heavens and ended with the opening of the tomb.

To complete the argument we have only in conclusion to examine the later details contained in our four gospels. These may be divided into two groups. The first consists of the traditions according to which Jesus appeared to His disciples in Galilee. Matthew reports that an appointment had been made at the mountain, that Jesus was there seen by the eleven, that some of them doubted, and that He gave them a last commission (Matt. xxviii. 16-20). In the fourth gospel we are told that He appeared to seven disciples at the Sea of Tiberias in a manner which is minutely described (John xxi. 1-23). The second group consists of the traditions according to which the manifestations were in Jerusalem and its neighbourhood. Luke reports that Jesus appeared to two of His disciples on the road to Emmaus—one of them Cleopas, and the other perhaps Peter (ver. 34), that in Jerusalem He appeared to the eleven, showing them His hands and His feet, eating in their presence a piece of fish, and giving them a last commission, and that afterwards from Bethany He ascended into heaven (Luke xxiv. 13-53). John reports that He appeared first to Mary Magdalene, then to the disciples in Jerusalem, showing them His hands and His feet, and giving them a last commission, and that after eight days, when Thomas the doubter was present, He was manifested again in the midst of them (John xx. 11-29). Matthew agrees with John in reporting first an appearance to the women (Matt. xxviii. 9, 10) ; and finally, in the appendix which has been added to the second gospel, we are told that He appeared first to Mary Magdalene, then to two disciples as they walked on their way into the country, then to the eleven in Jerusalem, when He gave them the last commission, and that after He had spoken He was received up into heaven, and sat down at the right hand of God (Mark xvi. 9-20). If our gospels were written by apostles, or by the companions of apostles, these details must be acknowledged to be surprising. They are like the tinted clouds of the evening sky, fugitive, uncertain, illusory. Remembrance, no doubt, transfigures the past, shedding through it a golden glory, and allowance must be made for the subjective differences of men; but when facts are converted into fleeting visions, indeterminate both in substance and in colour, the theory of reminiscence is discredited. To this the reply may conceivably be made that according to the supposition the gospels were transmitted as an oral tradition, that the surprising nature of the details may be due to the minds through which they passed, and that the original may thus still be apostolic. When the original has been disentangled from the later variations, this account of the matter may possess some value. If the theologians will perform such a service they will gain for their reward the hearty appreciation of all reasonable men, who are lovers of religion and of historical truth; but since they have not made the attempt, we may fairly assume that the result would be disastrous to their theories. The assumption indeed may be verified. (1) Our gospels are ultimately apostolic, being based, directly or indirectly, on the apostolic source which is their common original; but in this source there was no account of the manifestations. In determining the text of the Passion and the burial, we have already concluded that the agreement of Luke and John in divergence from Mark is an evidence of apostolicity, and certainly, notwithstanding their differences, they agree also to some extent in their version of the later traditions; but the possibility that these were contained in the apostolic source is summarily excluded by their absence from the text of the second gospel. The fragment which Luke has preserved in ch. xxiv. 9, 11, 12 may not be identified as Mark's lost ending. The evidence may not be accepted by the reader: that is perfectly conceivable; but Matthew proves beyond question that the ending, whether found or not, was much shorter than the additions of Luke and John, and if Mark had found these traditions in the apostolic source he would certainly not have omitted them. I do not say that all details which are later than the source are necessarily unreliable, but this at least may be confidently affirmed—that they are comparatively insecure. (2) The evidence is distinctly in favour of the conclusion that the Galilean manifestations are unhistorical. They depend for their credibility on the testimony of Matthew and of the twenty-first chapter in the fourth gospel. If the author of the first gospel and of the last chapter in the fourth were apostles, their testimony may be supposed to be sufficient, notwithstanding their inexplicable differences; but the assumption is forbidden by well-attested facts: (a) The last commission, which, according to Matthew, was delivered at the mountain, was, according to the other evangelists, addressed to the disciples in Jerusalem (Matt. xxviii. 18-20; Luke xxiv. 45-49; John xx. 21-23; Mark xvi. 15-18). (b) The twenty-first chapter in the fourth gospel is an appendix, which, whether written by the author of the gospel or not, was certainly added at a later time when Peter and John were both dead (vv. 18, 19, 22, 23). The original ending is unmistakable (John xx. 30, 31). (c) In this appendix two incidents are included, which happened, according to other accounts, at an earlier period in the ministry, and which in both cases are vague oral traditions unknown to the author of the apostolic source. The miraculous draught of fishes (John xxi. 3-6) is connected by Luke with the call of the disciples (Luke v. 3-7); and Peter's adventure in the sea (John xxi. 7) is recorded by Matthew after the feeding of the five thousand (Matt. xiv. 28-31). These facts are incompatible with apostolicity. And the origin of the traditions is in no degree obscure; for the statement made to the disciples on the road to the garden was interpreted as a prediction that they would see their Master in Galilee (Mark xiv. 27, 28, cf. xvi. 7; Matt. xxviii. 7, 10), and faith would inevitably infer that the event had happened as foretold. (3) The other traditions exhibit characteristics which make them almost equally unreliable. They are certainly similar in outline. The parallelism is even more complete than most students of the gospels are disposed to acknowledge. At first sight a few gaps are observed in the different accounts. Luke e.g. does not record, like Matthew, John, and the later Mark, an appearance of Jesus to the women. John does not record, like the later Mark, and Luke, the manifestation on the road into the country, and the ascension into heaven; and the second appearance to the disciples in Jerusalem, when Thomas the doubter was present, is peculiar to the fourth gospel. But two of these omissions are much more apparent than real; for John's acquaintance with the tradition of the ascension is proved by the words addressed to Mary—'I am not yet ascended unto the Father: but go unto my brethren, and say to them, I ascend unto my Father and your Father, and my God and your God' (John xx. 17)—and the tradition regarding the two disciples has already been utilised by John in a manner which shows how uncertain the original was (John i. 35-40). Matthew and Luke have each inserted in the midst of the ministry an incident which is mentioned in the fourth gospel appendix, and John has recorded at the beginning of the ministry an incident which happened, according to Luke and the later Mark, after the resurrection from the dead. The variations may obscure, but they do not altogether conceal, the original identity of the narratives. This parallelism may perhaps be considered to be an evidence in favour of the incidents involved, and unquestionably it proves that the traditions sprang from a common source; but the versions are so different from one another that, without some definite standard of judgment, the determination of the original is in each case hopeless, and all alike may be shown to be unreliable. (a) In his first Epistle to the Corinthians, Paul gives a list of the manifestations. Jesus, he says, appeared to Peter, to the twelve, to above five hundred brethren at once, to James, to all the apostles, and lastly to the convert who had persecuted the Church of God (1 Cor. xv. 5-8). This passage may perhaps be claimed as a confirmation of the traditions; but unfortunately it proves too much, for if any additional evidence were needed to show that the facts are hopelessly uncertain, it is afforded by the testimony of Paul. When the theorists reconcile the different lists, they will deserve to receive some attention. (b) The new commission which was given to the disciples is not only different in each version, but is also in each unhistorical. Here we possess a sure standard of judgment in the familiar teaching of Jesus; and when the question is asked whether the author of the logia could address such a commission to His disciples, the answer is prompt and unequivocal. Luke reports that the eleven were charged to remain in the city until they received power from on high, that is, the gift of the Spirit, and afterwards to preach repentance and remission of sins to all the nations, beginning from Jerusalem (Luke xxiv. 47–49). In John's version the charge is similar; but the disciples receive at once the gift of the Spirit, and power to forgive and retain the sins of men (John xx. 21–23). Now this conception of the Spirit as a *donum superadditum* is altogether foreign to the teaching of Jesus. He told His disciples that, when the Jews would attack and persecute them, the Spirit of the Father would be their sword (Matt. x. 20); but they already possessed this sword of the Spirit in the wisdom of the serpent and the harmlessness of the dove, with filial faith and obedience. The saying in the fourth gospel, 'Whose soever sins ye forgive, they are forgiven unto them: whose soever sins ye retain, they are retained,' is simply a Johannine paraphrase of the text delivered at the Supper: 'What things soever ye shall bind on earth shall be bound in heaven: and what things soever ye shall loose on earth shall be loosed in heaven' (Matt. xviii. 18); and the charge to preach to all the nations was certainly not given by the Teacher who said, 'Ye shall not have gone through the cities of Israel, till the Son of Man be come' (Matt. x. 23). Again, in the versions of Matthew and the later Mark, the commission is as clearly fictitious. The later universalism of the Gentile Church is here again attributed to Jesus (Matt. xxviii. 19; Mark xvi. 15). The words 'All authority hath been given unto me in heaven and on earth' (Matt. xxviii. 18) have clearly been borrowed from the apostolic text, preserved in Matt. xi. 27; Luke x. 22. The baptismal formula, 'baptising them into the name of the Father and of the Son and of the Holy Spirit' (ver. 19), is an ecclesiastical combination, suggested perhaps by the same original. The assurance, 'I am with you alway, even unto the end of the world' (ver. 20), is an editorial version of the authentic saying, 'Where two or three are gathered together in my name, there am I in the midst of them' (Matt. xviii. 20). The signs which, according to the later Mark, would follow them that believe (Mark xvi. 17, 18) were suggested by Luke x. 19;

and finally, the ecclesiastical ultimatum, 'He that believeth and is baptised shall be saved; but he that disbelieveth shall be condemned' (Mark xvi. 16), perverts in repeating the preaching of repentance unto life (Luke xiii. 5). In maintaining that these commissions are genuine, theologians simply waste their words and provoke unqualified scepticism. They are needlessly concerned for the credibility of the gospels. The credibility of the later traditions regarding the manifestations of Jesus is certainly involved; but prudence demands the removing of the things which are shaken that the things which are not shaken may remain. (c) The origin of the traditions in question can be traced to the apostolic source. According to the original narrative the women first found the empty tomb, and Peter verified the incredible news. These are the primitive facts. They are scarcely sufficient to prove that Jesus rose from the dead, although they suggest the belief. He had seemed Himself to predict a clear and infallible test—'After I am raised up, I will go before you into Galilee;' and when at a later time, on account of the requirements of faith, the evidence began to accumulate and to take the form of manifestations, the details were determined by the well-known apostolic facts. The women had first discovered the empty tomb: they are now the first to see Jesus. Peter had verified the report of the women: to him the risen Master is next revealed. The disciples were incredulous when the women announced their discovery: the Master therefore appears to them. And when Thomas at last in his turn beholds the risen Christ, and is invited to apply his rigid test, the doubt of the apostolic band is finally and for ever displaced by the glad impulsive cry, 'My Lord and my God'— a cry which sums up Christology, transcending the confession of Peter, and anticipating the faith which was yet to be. Whatever may be the value of the narratives, they contain unhistorical details, and their form had been determined by the source before they joined, as tributary traditions, the broad and clear apostolic stream which flows through our four gospels.

www.ingramcontent.com/pod-product-compliance
Lightning Source LLC
Chambersburg PA
CBHW051246300426
44114CB00011B/912